Mother Teresa

Mother Teresa was one of the most prominent religious figures of the twentieth century. During her lifetime, as well as posthumously, the figure, work and legacy of Mother Teresa generated, and continue to generate, a huge level of interest and heated debate.

Gëzim Alpion explores the significance of Mother Teresa to the mass media, to celebrity culture, to the church and to various political and national groups. Drawing on new research into Mother Teresa's early years, he charts the rise to fame of this pioneering religious personality, investigating the celebrity discourse in which an exemplary nun was turned into a media and humanitarian icon. The book provides an in-depth cultural and critical analysis of Mother Teresa, and the way she and others created, promoted and censored her public image, in the context of the sociology of fame, media, religion and nationality. A fascinating section explores the ways different vested interests have sought to appropriate her after her death, and also examines Mother Teresa's own attitude to her childhood and to the Balkan conflicts in the 1980s and 1990s.

Mother Teresa: Saint or Celebrity? sheds a new light on this remarkable and influential woman, which will intrigue followers of Mother Teresa and those who study the vagaries of stardom and celebrity culture.

Gëzim Alpion is Lecturer in Sociology and Media Studies at the University of Birmingham, UK. He received a PhD from the University of Durham, UK, in 1997. Alpion is a versatile academic, writer, playwright, essayist and journalist. His works include *Vouchers* (2001), *Foreigner Complex* (2002), *If Only the Dead Could Listen* (2006) and *Encounters with Civilizations* (2007).

Mother Teresa
Saint or Celebrity?

Gëzim Alpion

Routledge
Taylor & Francis Group

LONDON AND NEW YORK

SPECIAL INDIAN REPRINT 2008

First published 2007
by Routledge
2 Park Square, Milton Park, Abingdon, Oxon OX14 4RN

Simultaneously published in the USA and Canada
by Routledge
270 Madison Avenue, New York, NY 10016

Routledge is an imprint of the Taylor & Francis Group, an informa business

© 2007 Gëzim Alpion

Typeset in Sabon by
Florence Production Ltd, Stoodleigh, Devon
Printed and bound in India by
Saurabh Printers Pvt. Ltd.

British Library Cataloguing in Publication Data
A catalogue record for this book is available from
the British Library

Library of Congress Cataloging in Publication Data
A catalog record for this book has been requested

ISBN 10: 0–415–39247–0 (pbk)
ISBN 13: 978–0–415–39247–1 (pbk)

FOR SALE IN SOUTH ASIA ONLY.

For my son Klendi, my daughter Geila and
my wife, friend and colleague Dashi

Contents

Acknowledgements

This book would not have been written without the support of many people in the United Kingdom, several countries in the West and the Balkans and, of course, India. The following list is by no means complete:

Dr Ross Abbinnett, Rashmee Ahmed, Professor Ismail Ahmedi, Dr Daniele Albertazzi, Professor Peter Alcock, Dr Bonita Aleaz, Ben Andoni, Chris Arnot, Ruben Avxhiu, Jakup Azemi, Dr Sali Bashota, Dr Ashish Kumar Basu, Dr Manish Basu, Smita Basu, Swapan Basu, Stephen Bates, Paul Bernard, Amar Bhattacharya, Louise Brown, Osman Caka, Helen Carr, Shpend Çocaj, Merita Çoçoli, Dr Aroup Chatterjee, Tony Collins, Ian Critchley, Majella Cullinane, Gaston Dayanand, Subhandra De, Subhromoni De, Anna J. Dingley, Gemma Dunn (Editorial Assistant, Routledge), Henry D'Souza (former Archbishop of Calcutta), Esat Dujaka, Professor Jayasri Dutta, Krishna Dutta, Dr Tapati Dutta, Chereece Ebanks, Sister M. Edward MC, Sami Fejzullahu (Adviser to the President of Macedonia), Ilir Fetahu, Dr Sadri Fetiu, Blerta Foniqi, Dr Vassilis Fouskas, Alexander Fyjis-Walker, Dr Father Lush Gjergji, Ruth Gledhill, Paul Groves, Isaac Hamza, Eve Hancock, Phil Hazlewood, Renee Henson, Radije Hoxha, Sami Islami, Yvonne Jacobs, Lorna James (Senior Marketing Executive, Routledge), Sister M. Joanne MC, Amanda Johnson, Thanas Jorgji-Pilafas, Eni Kaçi, Petrit Kuçana, Artan Kutra, Bajram Lani, Mr and Mrs Dominique Lapierre, Lesley Leyland, Dr José Lingna Nafafé, Anthea Lipsett, Maureen Lobo, Sister M. Lynn MC, Margaret Macleod-Basu, Debabrata Maitra, Dr John Maltby, Professor David Marsh, Geraldine Martin (Production Editor, Routledge), Father P. C. Mathew SJ, Professor Enver Mehmeti, S. N. Misra, Sister Moira IBVM (Archivist of the Loreto Provincialate, Calcutta), Jenny Money, Pranvera Munishi, Dr Arun Nag, Jeton Neziraj, Sister Nirmala MC (Head of the Missionaries of Charity), Debasish Pal, Father C. M. Paul SDB, Geo Paul, Professor Stevan K. Pavlowitch, Primrose Peacock, Xhemail Peci, Admirina Peçi, Bashkim Pitarka (former Ambassador of Albania to the United Nations and Canada and high official in MINURSO – UN Mission for the Referendum in Western Sahara), Armand Plaka, Vladimir Prela (Ambassador of Albania to the Republic of Macedonia), Roland Qafoku, Bashkim Rama (Head of the Albanian Diplomatic Mission in Kosova), Albert Ramaj, Apratim Ray, Daragh Reddin, Dr Nuhi Rexhepi, Professor Father Gaston Roberge SJ, Kastriot Robo (Albanian Ambassador to the Court of St James's), Shyamal Baran Roy, Professor Cillian Ryan, Jayanta Sarkar, Judhajit Sarkar, Dr Walter Sawatsky, Anne Sebba, Dr Chandak Sengoopta, Anton Sereqi, Blerim Shabani, Dr Brian Shoesmith, Nabanita Sircar, Sam Smith, Dr Adrian Stokes, Enkeleida Tahiraj, Fatmir Terziu, Suleiman Tomçini (Ambassador of Albania to the Kingdom of Saudi Arabia), Dorina Topallaj, Sylë Ukshini, Xhevat Ukshini, Muhamed Veliu, Marie Walsh, Professor Seadin Xhaferi.

Grateful acknowledgement is made to the students, colleagues, reporters and members of the public for their feedback on my lectures on Mother Teresa at the University of Birmingham, Kingston University in London, University College London, University of Prishtina in Kosova, St Xavier's College in Calcutta, India, and Tetova State University in Macedonia.

I also want to thank the sisters and novices of the order of the Missionaries of Charity for their questions and comments during my talk at 'Mother House' and the two lectures I gave in Calcutta.

I am particularly grateful to the friends, colleagues, admirers and critics of Mother Teresa, and several people from the fields of politics, diplomacy, religion and media who agreed to talk to and exchange emails with me on the understanding that they would remain anonymous.

For their constructive criticism I am indebted to all blind reviewers who read parts of my study or the complete manuscript on behalf of several peer-reviewed journals and publishers.

A special thank you to Ms Lesley Riddle, Publisher, Religion and Anthropology, Routledge (Taylor & Francis Group Plc) for her continued interest in and valuable advice on the book.

My greatest debt is to my two most devoted, demanding but always objective 'editors', my wife Dashi and my daughter Geila, for reading several drafts of the manuscript. As for my son Klendi, his patience when the three of us were engaged in lengthy debates was always remarkable.

Although I have had so much external help in writing this book, I alone am responsible for any deficiencies.

G. A.

Preface

There is no doubt that Mother Teresa was, and is, a media celebrity. Indeed, any Internet Search Engine will confirm that assertion. So, typing Mother Teresa into Lycos produces 1,245,000 hits, which almost pales into insignificance compared with the 4,470,000 hits produced by a Google search.[1] At the same time, there are many books, of varying types and lengths, by and on Mother Teresa. Here, a search on Amazon produces 40 books by Mother Teresa (mostly collections of her speeches/thoughts) and a staggering 519 books on her. As such, one might ask who needs another book.

There are two easy answers to this question. Firstly, Mother Teresa remains an important figure who clearly had an impact, if more often indirectly rather than directly, on the lives of many people. Whatever the Google search indicates, it surely shows that the life of an Albanian nun who worked with the poor in India had resonance across the world. This interest is reflected in the amount of attention this book has received prior to its publication. Indeed, the *Guardian*, *The Times*, the *Times Higher Education Supplement*, the *Times of India* and the *Hindustan Times* have all interviewed Dr Alpion and published articles on the book over the last three years. At the same time, he has already been interviewed by, or is booked to appear on, British, European, Balkan, American and Indian TV networks. Secondly, although Mother Teresa has received a great deal of attention, much of this attention amounts to little more than hagiography. Of course, as Dr Alpion makes clear, there are authors who are critical of Mother Teresa but they are in a tiny minority; so of the first 50 hits in Google, only three articles are critical and all are written by Christopher Hitchens. As such, the first claim this book has to make is that it presents a very informed, balanced account, avoiding

---

1   For comparison, on Google, typing in Princess Diana produces 4,250,000 hits, Adolf Hitler 4,090,000, Robert De Niro 4,790,000, David Beckham 5,150,000, Tony Blair 21,700,000, Michael Jordan 31,000,000, Jesus Christ 28,000,000, the Pope 37,400,000, Michael Jackson 56,300,000, George W. Bush 69,900,000 and God 168,000,000. Make of that what you will. Accessed 26/11/2005.

both hagiography and vitriol. However, its strengths go well beyond this and reflect both Dr Alpion's experiences and expertise.

Gëzim Alpion was born in Albania, which, of course, is one of the reasons he was drawn to a focus on Mother Teresa, who, despite the counter-claims advanced by Serbs, Croats and Macedonian Slavs and examined in the book, is generally acknowledged as an Albanian by birth. Certainly he uses his knowledge of Albania and the Balkans more generally to good effect particularly in Chapter 2. Subsequently, Dr Alpion was educated in Egypt and the UK and he has travelled widely. As such, he is a cosmopolitan scholar who serves as an informed guide through many of the complexities involved in Mother Teresa's life and, particularly, in her role as a media and cultural icon. It is also relevant here, that his Ph.D. was in English Studies and that he is a published playwright and essayist and a very frequent contributor to a broad range of media outlets. This not only ensures that he has a practical insight into how the media works, but also that he writes very well; so the reader should approach his prose with expectation, not with the trepidation often associated with academic monographs.

Three other facets of Dr Alpion's life also contribute to the quality of this book. Firstly, he has no religious axe to grind, an approach singularly unusual in studies of Mother Teresa. Indeed, a number of people have already criticized his book, based only on reading a few press releases, because they assume it will be critical of Mother Teresa. At the same time, Dr Alpion has sometimes been made to feel uncomfortable over the four years he has been researching the book. In the context of such strong feelings, his more balanced approach is welcome and, indeed, when he has lectured to secular or religious audiences on Mother Teresa, he has invariably been well received by both. Even if they have not agreed with all his interpretations of her life and significance, they have acknowledged his scholarship and his capacity to listen and engage. Secondly, Dr Alpion has had a lifelong interest in the media and uses a variety of mediums (photography, film, television and radio, and the press) from various parts of the world, especially India and the Balkans, as well as in the West, in producing this book. His research has also involved interviews with a large number of people working within both the religious and the secular media and this is clearly evident in the text. Thirdly, and I, perhaps unsurprisingly, think most importantly, his current experience as Lecturer in Sociology and Media Studies in the Department of Sociology at the University of Birmingham, in the UK, informs this study. His move from a Ph.D. in English Studies to an academic career in Sociology and Media Studies means that he has brought a critical eye to the literature on celebrity culture, a literature which has grown rapidly, as indeed has the cult of celebrity itself, over the past two decades. Dr Alpion's knowledge of the celebrity literature is amply reflected in this book. Although the book is not designed to test academic theories of celebrity, his knowledge of the academic literature ensures that this book presents an original perspective on Mother Teresa's life. In a way, then, and implicitly rather than explicitly, this book addresses the question of why when the name of Mother Teresa is entered into a Google search it produces well over four million hits.

I urge you to read this book; you will find it interesting and rewarding. It will give you a new and more balanced insight into the identity and impact of one of the most prominent figures of the twentieth century.

Professor David Marsh
Head of Sociology, The University of Birmingham, UK
January 2006

Introduction

One of the most common assumptions about famous people is that there is not much about them that the public does not already know. This is probably true in the case of contemporary celebrities who are manufactured daily by the media. This book, however, is not about that kind of celebrity. Concentrating on the life, personality, work and legacy of Mother Teresa, the study aims to highlight some erroneous approaches and hasty conclusions apparent in the celebrity discourse about this world-famous nun. No matter how much Mother Teresa had in common with some well-known people, I argue that the Albanian-born Roman Catholic missionary was a unique celebrity.

Mother Teresa is one of the most written about individuals to have hit the international headlines in the last quarter of the twentieth century. Books about her life and work run into the hundreds. Considering the vast literature that already exists on this renowned religious personality, I was not surprised by the reaction of some of my friends and colleagues when I informed them a few years ago of my intention to write a book about her. 'Why do you want to write a book on Mother Teresa?' they asked me bewildered. 'What could you possibly say about her that has not already been said?'

Fame is a fickle game. Few can play it and not get hurt. Mother Teresa, her friendly biographers maintain, did not chase fame. The nun was spotted by the Indian media initially in the late 1940s when she was about to set up her order of the Missionaries of Charity. From that time onwards, she gradually became a media fixture in India, her adopted country, and throughout the world. This was quite a significant 'accomplishment' considering that her vocation was different from careers that typically lead to fame and fortune. Mother Teresa and her work became famous because of the media. Her rise to prominence was carefully engineered and monitored by public relations experts and spin doctors both in the East and in the West.

In this fame-making process Mother Teresa was hardly passive. Over the fifty years she was in the public eye, the celebrity nun played a key role in promoting not so much herself as her religious cause. Mother

Teresa matured constantly as a PR expert throughout her life in the lime-light. She was apparently capable of exerting a form of control over the media like few other influential people. No matter how popular Mother Teresa eventually became, she would have never been able to keep the media in check on her own. Various political, religious, nationalist and business circles around the world developed a calculated interest in this Roman Catholic missionary. They made sure that she had all the publicity and media immunity necessary so that she could continue to serve them and their causes without any hindrance.

As a result of my research, I have concluded that Mother Teresa became increasingly aware that she was being used, but she did not seem to mind as long as the growing publicity she received helped her to achieve her main goal in life, which was not necessarily to serve the poorest of the poor. The media were often deceived, or so it would seem, as to what exactly Mother Teresa stood for, but the publicity game went on regard-less. Thanks to constant selective media coverage, Mother Teresa became the epitome of love and compassion for humanity and one of the most outspoken defenders of life. The media also turned Mother Teresa into the world's most celebrated 'social worker', an accolade which the nun strongly resented.

One of the main aims of this book is to explore how Mother Teresa became famous, how she handled fame and why she succeeded where many celebrated people from the world of politics, entertainment and sport fail so often, some of them spectacularly. I found the answer to these and other important issues in Mother Teresa's private life. This is not to say that this book is a biography. The biographical approach I follow throughout the study is largely determined by the often eclectic and selective nature of most of her existing biographies. In spite of numerous biographical works on her published since 1969, a 'complete' biography of Mother Teresa has yet to be written. Even the best of her authorized and unauthorized biographies tend to offer only a partial pic-ture of her life. The current study is partly intended to fill in the gaps, some of them surprisingly huge, in the literature about the nun. Moreover, it is hoped that the emphasis I put on some key moments in Mother Teresa's life in Skopje and Calcutta will inspire future biographers and scholars to study further and more impartially every stage of her life and work.

Thus far almost anyone who has written about Mother Teresa has done so for one of two completely different purposes: either to praise or condemn her. Since her death in 1997, some biographers like Anne Sebba (1997) and Emma Johnson (2003) have tried to offer a more balanced portrait of the nun. Important as such attempts certainly are, they have not been able to appease the opposing camps. Not many modern celeb-rities have generated as much heated debate, controversy and hostility between their devout admirers and staunch opponents as Mother Teresa did when she was alive, as well as after her death. There seems to be no end to the often bitter dispute between the two warring parties about her 'saintly' or 'evil' nature. The forgiving nun has some of the most intolerant and unforgiving supporters and opponents.

This study attempts to keep clear of such partisan approaches. I neither glorify nor condemn Mother Teresa. The main purpose of the book is to explore the nun's initiation into, attitude towards and relationship with celebrity culture, fame and the media. Throughout the six chapters I map out Mother Teresa's rise to fame and the key role others and she herself played in creating, promoting and censoring her public image.

In the course of the project, while conducting field work in several countries I came across many of Mother Teresa's friends and foes. I met and talked to anyone who was willing to share their views with me. What they knew about Mother Teresa was all I cared about; they were entitled to love or hate her as long as they did not try to convince me that they alone knew the 'real' Mother Teresa. And I certainly was not out to make converts. My direct and open approach won me many useful contacts from both 'warring' camps. In many cases we agreed to disagree but this never stopped us from arguing and exchanging views. I often felt like a mediator between two bitterly opposed factions.

What I knew about and thought of Mother Teresa when I began the project did not matter to me. If my initial perception of the nun would in the end prove to be naïve, right, or wrong was also irrelevant. I wanted to find some answers which would please no one exclusively, including myself, and yet be partially acceptable to both antagonistic camps. This does not necessarily mean that I was after a compromise. Quite often in the book those who admire Mother Teresa uncritically may think that I am on their side, just as on some occasions those who bitterly oppose the nun may wrongly conclude that I am one of them. From the first I tried as hard as I could to be not so much detached and dispassionate about the topic – research devoid of keen interest and passion is either impossible or not worth undertaking in the first place – but open to whatever suggestions and views I would come across. The only thing that I was keen to avoid from the start was the temptation to see Mother Teresa either exclusively as a saintly person or as a thoroughly demonic force. What I was after was an understanding neither of the otherworldly nun and selfless humanitarian nor, to use one of Germaine Greer's phrases about Mother Teresa, of the 'religious imperialist'.[1] My initial and only purpose was, and remained to the end of the study, to get to know the human being behind the many Mother Teresas we have been presented with over several decades.

Some loyal friends and fierce opponents of the nun were at times not very diplomatic in their letters and emails to me. Occasionally, I was the target of abuse and insults from people who often chose to remain anonymous. They, as well as those critics who identified themselves, often jumped to conclusions about the 'irreverent', 'blasphemous' or 'complimentary' study on the basis of scraps of information from media reports and articles that appeared in several countries following a University of Birmingham press release issued in October 2004. Some admirers and opponents of the nun inferred what the book was about without reading the manuscript, at a time when I myself did not quite know the direction the project was heading in.

The overwhelming majority of Mother Teresa's friends and opponents I came across during numerous interviews, conversations, talks and lectures, however, did not hasten to draw conclusions about the study or my intentions. They were always willing to share with me their memories, feelings and thoughts about the woman who had obviously made quite an impact on them, and in some cases even more than they were aware of or prepared to admit. They gave me the benefit of the doubt and became increasingly forthcoming, especially when they became more confident that I was interested in conducting impartial research.

The biographical and historical approach employed throughout the study proved instrumental in understanding both Mother Teresa and the national, political and, most importantly, the religious milieux that influenced her throughout her life. It is hoped that the content and discourse analysis of a large number of writings about the nun, as well as the information from the correspondence and interviews conducted with people who knew her well, will offer readers an opportunity to see her in a fresh light without the characteristically uncritical devotion or the uncompromising hostility that prevails in and undermines many biographies, hagiographies and critical works, where the opportunity to draw independent conclusions is taken away from readers from page one. This book is intended to help readers, no matter how much or how little they know, or what they think of Mother Teresa, to understand and not judge her.

In the first chapter I approach Mother Teresa's celebrity status in the context of contemporary celebrity culture. After highlighting the changes Western celebrity culture went through from the start of the seventeenth century, I explore the impact of the nineteenth-century Graphic Revolution on fame and fandom. Also in this chapter I identify three approaches to Mother Teresa's celebrity status (subjectivist, structuralist and poststructuralist) and the major players that turned the nun into a media and humanitarian icon, as well as assess the role she played in creating, preserving and protecting her public image.

The second chapter approaches Mother Teresa the celebrity in a Balkan context. Of particular interest in this part of the book is the information about and the analysis of the efforts made by various ethnic, national, religious and political circles to appropriate or share the nun with other parties for their own purposes. I also take issue with some admirers and critics of Mother Teresa who ascribe to her the mantle of patriotism.

The third chapter draws attention to the lack of information in Mother Teresa scholarship about her Skopje years (1910–1928). In this part of the study I identify some inaccuracies about her life recorded in many books written by her close friends, colleagues and opponents since the early 1970s. Finally, the chapter highlights the partisan approaches apparent in most of the works about the nun.

The fourth chapter centres on the role Mother Teresa herself seemed to have played either directly or indirectly in keeping out of her biographies some important information about her early life in Skopje. The chapter also explores some of the reasons the nun apparently had for not wishing to talk about her family and Albanian nationality throughout her long life in the limelight. This is the first time Mother Teresa's reticence about her family has been the subject of an academic study.

Mother Teresa's extraordinary sacrifices cannot be properly understood if they are not seen in the context of her exemplary attachment to the figure of Jesus and, equally importantly, the unique circumstances in which she became so close to her saviour. This is the main theme of chapter five. In this part of the book I also make a connection between Mother Teresa's attachment to Jesus and our obsession with celebrities.

Chapter six traces Mother Teresa's expectations and disappointments during the 1929–1948 period in India. Like her Skopje years, this stage of her life has been largely ignored by many of her biographers. The reason I pay particular attention to those years is that they reveal the extent to which Mother Teresa tried and failed to obtain the support of some of her religious superiors in Calcutta for her own understanding of Christian missionary work in the new India that was emerging in the late 1940s. In this part of the book I also identify what Mother Teresa had in common with and set her apart from past and contemporary missionaries. Finally, I assess the reasons why the Vatican decided to give Mother Teresa and her order of the Missionaries of Charity preferential treatment in the early 1960s.

This book offers a fresh perspective on the extent to which celebrity culture permeates every aspect of our lives. Mother Teresa is one of the pioneering religious personalities in modern times to understand and use to great effect the power of the media to promote religion. I hope that the attention I pay to her personal life, relationship with the media and public image will encourage other media studies scholars to approach her and other celebrities from different walks of life to explore further the vagaries of stardom and celebrity culture.

As always, famous people continue to play an important role in our lives. Celebrity culture is the modern form of religion. The gods of today are not very different from ancient deities. Nor are we very dissimilar to early worshippers. Unlike the gods of antiquity, though, our idols are constantly prone to scrutiny. We have the means to create and know them better than our predecessors ever could. I do not know if it wise to know 'gods' and 'goddesses' intimately. If we really want to be acquainted with our 'godly' role-models, however, it is always advisable to know them thoroughly.

Some are born great, some achieve greatness,
and some have greatness thrust upon 'em.
William Shakespeare

The celebrity is a person who is known for his
well-knownness.
Daniel J. Boorstin

In the future everyone will be world-famous
for fifteen minutes.
Andy Warhol

1 Mother Teresa and celebrity culture

i. The democratization of fame

In this chapter I assess Mother Teresa's celebrity status in the context of contemporary celebrity culture. In the first part of the chapter I identify some of the changes 'fame' and 'status' went through in the West from the start of the seventeenth century. I then assess Mother Teresa's fame from three perspectives: subjectivist, structuralist and post-structuralist. Of particular interest in this chapter is the origin of the discourse about Mother Teresa's saintly nature and the information provided about those who originated, endorsed and sustained it. Also in this chapter, I identify what Mother Teresa had in common with celebrities from the world of entertainment, politics and sport as well as what set her apart from them.

As a species, we have always been and will always be preoccupied with fame. Distinguishing ourselves, craving for and securing recognition and acknowledgement, is neither a 'sin' nor a 'virtue': fame-seeking is an innate human drive. There has never been a society without famous people and, as Thomas Carlyle once put it, '[t]he History of the world is but the Biography of great men'.[1]

In pre-industrialized societies 'fame' and 'status' were almost synonymous and they were usually inherited, but there were cases when 'commoners' too earned them as a result of achievements and heroic deeds that elevated them above the rest of the populace, thus legitimizing their rise to power and prominence. From the first half of the seventeenth century, the period which saw the emergence of newspapers in some Western European countries as a novel means of disseminating the news, and especially from the mid-nineteenth century onwards, thanks to the development of other technologies – dry-plate photography, telephone, phonograph, the roll film, radio, motion picture, television and the Internet – that facilitated the continuous distribution of information at a much greater speed and to an ever-expanding audience, the notions of 'fame' and 'status' underwent significant denotative and connotative changes.

Technology paved the way for the democratization of fame, and the media heightened further two of our basic instincts: eagerness to know as much as possible about other people's personal lives, and craving to convince the world as much as ourselves of our importance as individuals. It is hardly surprising that gossiping and mimicry found a new lease of life in the media age.

Being famous in the industrialized world gradually came mainly to mean being in the public eye. Capitalism produced a new brand of famous person: the celebrity. In his acclaimed 1962 book *The Image: A Guide to Pseudo-Events in America*, Daniel J. Boorstin defined the modern-type celebrity as 'a person who is known for his well-knownness'.[2]

In true capitalistic fashion, the media industry manufactures celebrities by the bushel. So much so that it would be no exaggeration if we described them as constituting a social class of their own. Andrew Smith goes even further in his article 'All in a good cause?' which appeared in the *Observer* on 27 January 2002. In his view, Live Aid in 1985 demonstrated the truth that 'a new social world had been made, in which there were only two categories of people – the celebrity corps and what Liz Hurley would later notoriously characterize as "civilians", i.e. the rest of us'.

In a media-saturated world where the attainment of celebrity status is seen as an end in itself and where, for better or for worse, celebrities are such influential role models for an ever-growing fandom, there is always the possibility of either equating fake prominence with genuine greatness or ignoring some of our real heroes.

Concentrating on the figure of Mother Teresa, this chapter identifies some of the approaches and flaws apparent in the contemporary celebrity discourse. Although she was a global 'celebrity', there are very few references in the academic debate about Mother Teresa to the nature of her celebrity status and her relationship with the media. This is even more surprising considering that, as a rule, Mother Teresa experts approach her more or less in the same way as we would normally approach celebrities from the fields of theatre, cinema, television, music, politics and sport.

Mother Teresa became a global celebrity when she started making headlines as a Nobel Prize laureate. Reporters were among the first to see and treat Mother Teresa as a star. 'How wonderful to see the world press for once spellbound by a true star,' an editor of the Norwegian paper *Aftenposten* exclaimed in December 1979, 'a star without false eyelashes and makeup, without jewels and fur coats, without theatrical gestures.'[3]

Mother Teresa is yet another example of the extent to which celebrity culture has permeated every aspect of life. The nun's relationship with the media also reveals that, like any famous person, religious personalities often employ the press and every other medium of mass communication with dexterity and, at times, unscrupulously, to reach out to their intended audiences.

In spite of the similarities between her and many celebrities, Mother Teresa was a media icon with a difference. The main aim of this chapter is to identify some of these differences and highlight the uniqueness of this celebrated nun in a world that abounds in big names.

Mother Teresa was one of the most written about and publicized women in modern times. Except for Pope John Paul II, she was arguably the most famous religious celebrity in the last quarter of the twentieth century. After her death, as during her life, Mother Teresa continues to generate a huge level of interest and heated debate from those who either praise or criticize her. The ongoing argument about whether or not the celebrity nun deserves her fame or notoriety is further proof of our increasing fascination with media celebrities from every walk of life.

ii. Sanctified by the media

People approach Mother Teresa's celebrity status mainly from three different perspectives: subjectivism, structuralism and post-structuralism. The employment of these approaches indicates the complexity of the media icon called Mother Teresa and the 'liquid' nature of the notion of celebrity nowadays.

Subjectivists maintain that talent, which eventually leads to fame, is innate and God-given. In Mother Teresa's case, this attitude is apparent in the numerous books, authorized and unauthorized biographies, pictorial histories, television programmes, films (documentary, feature and animated), plays, novels, poems, paintings, musicals and sculptures that often bear the signature of her friends, colleagues, admirers and supporters all over the world. In the media, this interpretation surfaced when she was first spotted by the Indian Catholic press in Calcutta shortly after she had set up the Missionaries of Charity order in 1950. Referring to this time, the reporter Desmond Doig, an Indian Catholic of Anglo-Irish origin, remarked in 1976 that twenty-seven years earlier he was tipped off by a Catholic functionary and fellow journalist to watch the European nun because 'she's quite extraordinary. She's going to be a saint.'[4]

In the first instance, the myth about Mother Teresa's 'sainted' status was apparently started by Mother Teresa herself, something, which, as will be explained later in this chapter, she came to regret. Mother Teresa always maintained that she received the first call from God to serve the poor some time in 1922 before her twelfth birthday.[5] A quarter of a century later she claimed she was the recipient of another call, which she would refer to as 'the call within a call'. On 10 September 1946, during a train journey she heard God 'calling me. The message was clear. I must leave the convent to help the poor by living among them.'[6] This, Mother Teresa believed, 'was an order. To fail it would have been to break the faith.'[7]

Even when she became world famous, and was aware that her words were likely to be scrutinized by her friends and foes alike, Mother Teresa would not hesitate to express in public her belief that she was somehow in direct contact with God and the Ancient Fathers of the Church. One of her preferred parables involving herself was the 'encounter' with Saint Peter at heaven's door. Peter had tried to keep her from going in, saying 'I'm sorry. We have no shacks in heaven.' Upset by the doorman saint's 'irreverence', the saint-to-be had responded: 'Very well! I will fill heaven with the people from the slums of the city, and then you will have no other choice than to let me in.'[8]

Mother Teresa accepts that the holy 'encounter' took place when she was delirious and suffering from a very high fever. One does not have to be a psychoanalyst or an atheist to conclude that, like the second call in 1946, her 'audience' with Peter could have been triggered by her poor health and agitated state of mind. Unfortunately, we do not know much about the exact state of Mother Teresa's health when she received the first call. Like most of her first eighteen years in Skopje, even this life-changing incident remains something of a mystery. What is widely known, though, is that throughout her childhood Mother Teresa was frequently ill and confined to her bed. She suffered from malaria and whooping cough and also had a club foot.[9] Her parents were constantly concerned because of her illnesses, especially her mother who thought 'she would lose her because of her fragile health'.[10] Mother Teresa's health did not get any better in India. She was often sick, especially in 1946. This is what Sister Marie Thérèse recalls about that year: 'We were careful of her. I don't know whether she realized it, but we were. . . . When it came to the work and the running around, our Superiors took extra care with her.'[11] She was apparently so sick that her friends feared she would be stricken with tuberculosis. As a precaution, she was asked to stay in bed for three hours every afternoon. Seeing no improvement, she was directed to go to the hill station of Darjeeling to recuperate. On the way there the sick and tired Mother Teresa had her second 'encounter' with God.

Seen in the context of the Holy Scriptures, Mother Teresa's paranormal experiences are similar to what many prophets, apostles, disciples and saints before her have apparently gone through. Mental anguish and poor health frequently seem to have paved the way to 'revelations'. Jews and Muslims, for instance, maintain that prophets such as Moses and Mohammed suffered from depression when God communicated with them directly.

Different people approach and interpret 'holiness' in different ways. In the case of devout believers, a person's sanctity is measured not so much by their ability to perform miracles as by their absolute faith in the strange ways God works through some chosen individuals. This is one of the key themes in Saint Paul's first letter to the Corinthians:

> Now concerning spiritual gifts, brothers and sisters, I do not want you to be uninformed. . . . Now there are varieties of gifts, but the same Spirit; and there are varieties of services, but the same Lord; and there

are varieties of activities, but it is the same God who activates all of them in everyone. To each is given the manifestation of the Spirit for the common good. To one is given through the Spirit the utterance of wisdom, and to another the utterance of knowledge according to the same Spirit, to another faith by the same Spirit, to another gifts of healing by the one Spirit, to another the working of miracles, to another prophecy, to another the discernment of spirits, to another various kinds of tongues, to another the interpretation of tongues. All these are activated by one and the same Spirit, who allots to each one individually just as the Spirit chooses. . . . And God has appointed in the church first apostles, second prophets, third teachers; then deeds of power, then gifts of healing, forms of assistance, forms of leadership, various kinds of tongues. Are all apostles? Are all prophets? Are all teachers? Do all work miracles? Do all possess gifts of healing? Do all speak in tongues? Do all interpret? But strive for the greater gifts. And I will show you a still more excellent way.[12]

Those who are not very religious, on the other hand, are eager to find some more down-to-earth explanations about Mother Teresa's 'audiences' with God or the Old Fathers of the Church. Failure to provide some rational accounts has shrouded the nun's figure in mysticism and mystery in the eyes of many secular beholders who respect her. While Mother Teresa's religious admirers consider her skill in 'paranormal' communication as an undeniable proof of her 'divine' nature, others who are not religious and who do not necessarily object to her work and legacy could well perceive it as evidence of mental disturbance.

My intention here is not to approve or disapprove of the opposing interpretations of Mother Teresa's 'paranormal' abilities. Instead, I intend to offer a middle way which will hopefully be useful in approaching her figure and legacy without preconceptions and eventually in helping to clear away the supernatural fog her figure, intentions, work and legacy seem to have been shrouded in for quite some time. It is my belief that the more details we know about the personal lives of influential people, especially if they are invested with 'supernatural' powers, the easier it will be to answer some of the puzzling questions about them in particular and human nature in general.

Considering how much Mother Teresa was immersed in literature (secular and religious) from a young age,[13] her strong ambition to become a writer, and the obvious creative flair she displayed in the poems she wrote in Skopje,[14] and in numerous letters she sent from India to her family and friends in the Balkans from 1929 onwards,[15] it is not difficult to see how the educated, enthusiastic and imaginative young woman, who turned into a devout nun, could have occasionally blurred reality with fantasy, especially when she was suffering from recurring bouts of ill health.

A string of coincidences also seems to have strengthened Mother Teresa's conviction that God intervened to help her in fulfilling her vocation as Jesus's special 'envoy' to alleviate the suffering of the poor. In her speeches, press conferences and books penned by her, or by her admirers on her behalf, she would often mention moments of crisis when things had finally, out of the blue, turned out to be all right. Food, money, clothes and shelter were apparently made available to Mother Teresa and her sisters and brothers when most needed and least expected. Mother Teresa never saw such occurrences as mere coincidences.[16] Neither did her supporters and admirers, whose numbers grew as a result of witnessing her 'divine' ability to seek and always secure God's help.

As the news about Mother Teresa's extraordinary ability to secure God's intervention for the sake of the poor at the eleventh hour began to spread, she came to be seen as the modern personification of a shamanic figure *par excellence*. Likewise, her determination to *care* for the sick was gradually but steadily perceived and interpreted as a miraculous power to *cure* them. In the Roman Catholic Church, anything belonging to or that has been touched by a saint or a person about to be proclaimed a saint – bones, strands of hair, the remains, vials of blood, burial site, possessions, clothes, books, letters, pictures and statues – is called a 'relic' and is venerated and cherished dearly by their brethren after their death.[17] In Mother Teresa's case, however, her sanctity took root and flourished during her lifetime. Rich and poor, intellectuals and uneducated people, believers and non-believers, Catholics and followers of other faiths who had been in contact with her or had only heard about her were gradually falling under her spell. Mother Teresa's letters and gifts to her admirers were treated by them as 'relics' even while she was alive.

Following her 1968 BBC interview with the journalist Malcolm Muggeridge, the nun's reputation also began to spread across 'secular' and 'rational' Western Europe. Many people who met her in the late 1960s and early 1970s did not know what to make of her. There were some, however, who felt spell-bound in her presence, and their numbers grew throughout the 1980s and 1990s.[18] Stories about Mother Teresa's positive impact on people's lives mushroomed not only among Catholics but also among non-Catholics and the secular-minded.[19] The Mother Teresa 'fan-club', it appears, was and remains a very broad church.

Mother Teresa's opponents, on the other hand, find stories about her 'supernatural' abilities ridiculous and bizarre. They are particularly keen to make fun of the incident involving the controversial BBC journalist Malcolm Muggeridge who in 1969 went to Calcutta to prepare a documentary about Mother Teresa. Referring to the incident in his 1971 book *Something Beautiful for God: Mother Teresa of Calcutta*, Muggeridge explains that filming inside Nirmal Hriday (Bengali for 'the place of the pure heart'), the Home for the Dying Destitute, which Mother Teresa had founded in Kalighat in 1952, proved problematic because the place was dimly lit. Although he was reluctant, the cameraman Ken Macmillan eventually had a go. Confident that he would fail to record anything inside the building, Macmillan also took some film outside.

But the cameraman had obviously worried in vain. Much to his and Muggeridge's surprise, when the film was processed in London, they noticed that 'the part taken inside was bathed in a particularly beautiful soft light, whereas the part taken outside was rather dim and confused'.[20] Both Muggeridge and Macmillan were delighted with the unexpected result but not for the same reason. For Macmillan there was no mystery involved. He had taken delivery of some new film made by Kodak shortly before going to Calcutta. This is Macmillan's reaction to the pleasant surprise:

'That's amazing. That's extraordinary.' And I was going to go on to say, you know, three cheers for Kodak. I didn't get a chance to say that though, because Malcolm, sitting in the front row, spun round and said: 'It's divine light! It's Mother Teresa. You'll find that it's divine light, old boy.' And three or four days later I found I was being phoned by journalists from London newspapers who were saying things like: 'We hear you've just come back from India with Malcolm Muggeridge and you were the witness of a miracle.'[21]

Muggeridge did his best to spread the news about the 'miracle'. He was so eager to tell people about his 'divine' experience that it soon turned almost into an obsession. In his own words, '[i]t so delighted me that I fear I talked and wrote about it to the point of tedium, and sometimes of irritation'.[22] But who can blame Muggeridge for getting carried away? After all, miracles are not daily occurrences, not even for journalists. And since not many people were with him in Calcutta to witness the miraculous event for themselves, Muggeridge naturally saw it as his own sacred duty to describe the paranormal encounter as vividly and accurately as possible to humanity at large:

I myself am absolutely convinced that the technically unaccountable light is, in fact, the Kindly Light [Cardinal] Newman refers to in his well-known exquisite hymn. . . . Mother Teresa's Home for the Dying is overflowing with love, as one senses immediately on entering it. This love is luminous, like the haloes artists have seen and made visible round the heads of the saints. I find it not at all surprising that the luminosity should register on a photographic film. The supernatural is only an infinite projection of the natural, as the furthest horizon is an image of eternity. . . .

One thing everyone who has seen the film seems to be agreed about is that the light in the Home for the Dying is quite exceptionally lovely. This is, from every point of view, highly appropriate. Dying derelicts from the street might normally be supposed to be somewhat repellent, giving off stenches, emitting strange groans. Actually, if the Home for the Dying were piled high with flowers and resounding with musical chants – as it may well have been in its Kali days – it could not be more restful and serene. So, the light conveys perfectly what the place is really like; an outward and visible luminosity manifesting God's inward and invisible omnipresent love. This is precisely what miracles are for – to reveal the inner reality of God's outward creation. I am personally persuaded that Ken recorded the first authentic photographic miracle.[23]

Muggeridge's interpretation of the 'miracle' and his unashamedly partisan portrayal of Mother Teresa's image and work in his 1969 television documentary, the 1971 book and numerous interviews undoubtedly heightened his 'celebrity' status. His career as a journalist was also given an unexpected boost. This was hardly surprising. After all, Muggeridge had scooped the 'miracle' story of the twentieth century. It is not very often that a reporter has the chance to offer his contemporaries the opportunity to see with the naked eye what countless generations have hoped for in vain. Not many mortals have been blessed to witness a miracle since Moses split the Red Sea, Jesus walked on water, and Mohammed ascended to and returned from heaven. Muggeridge must have really felt like the chosen one.

Muggeridge's 'miracle claim' and the noise he made about it caused some embarrassment to the Catholic Church. None the less, the story stuck. Muggeridge the journalist had paved the way for the elevation of Mother Teresa to the position of a 'living saint'. On 29 December 1975, four years after the publication of Muggeridge's saint-making book *Something Beautiful for God*, *Time* magazine accompanied Mother Teresa's portrait on the front cover with the caption 'Messengers of Love and Hope – Living Saints'.

The news about the miracle called Mother Teresa was music to the ears of a largely sceptical, but willing-to-be-deceived, secular Western audience. It is always good to know that we are not a God-forsaken race, that there is still hope for redemption, that we are being looked after by a divine power, that we have the means of finding proof about the existence of our heavenly Father and communicating with him, if not on a one-to-one basis, at least through the mediation of a nun called Mother Teresa.

In 1962 Daniel J. Boorstin remarked:

We need not be theologians to see that we have shifted responsibility for making the world interesting from God to the newspaperman. We used to believe there were only so many 'events' in the world. If there were not many intriguing or startling occurrences, it was no fault of the reporter. He could not be expected to report what did not exist.[24]

In a way, the newspaperman has been reporting 'what did not exist' since the dawn of the modern press. Reporting the real and the unreal, or what Boorstin calls 'pseudo-events', was a seminal feature of the news industry from the start. Boorstin rightly laments that 'pseudo-events' seem to have taken over, but he apparently did not foresee the extraordinary length some journalists would go to and the sources and the means they would employ to 'invent' them. In the case of the 'divine light' recorded in the Home for the Dying, we apparently discovered yet another potential of the media: the ability to produce miraculous pseudo-events. If God was indeed dead, thanks to modern technologies we could reincarnate him, and if he never existed in the first place, we can literally invent him. Apparently, we have not only the mental gift to imagine miracles but also the means to materialize them.

Technology obviously does not necessarily make myths distant and irrelevant. On the contrary, it manufactures them as commodities that are increasingly in demand. As Christopher Hitchens puts it, 'modern technology and communications have ensured . . . that rumour and myth can be transmitted with ever greater speed and efficiency to the eyes and ears of the credulous'.[25]

The fact that Mother Teresa herself was instrumental in creating the myth about her 'paranormal' abilities does not necessarily belittle the significance of her work in Calcutta. Nor does the endorsement of her saint-like status by devout Catholics and a 'sensationalist' journalist like Muggeridge make her lifetime devotion to Jesus and to the poor less appealing to millions of people who do not necessarily believe in miracles allegedly recorded by Kodak. If Mother Teresa's saintly nature is a matter for debate, her commitment to her vocation and to the poor was exemplary.

This is one of the reasons why the Indian media, both Catholic and non-Catholic, were keen to support and advertise her work from the start. And not only the Indian media. From the 1950s onwards, many leaders in West Bengal and India were willing and eager to fully endorse and sponsor Mother Teresa's brand of charity work. Politicians such as the Chief Minister of West Bengal Dr Bidhan Chandra Roy and Indian prime ministers like Jawaharlal Nehru and his daughter Indira Gandhi would often employ the Bengali and Indian press to put and keep Mother Teresa constantly in the spotlight. Thanks to numerous Indian leaders' direct interest in her, the Indian political establishment and the Indian media acknowledged Mother Teresa as a 'living saint' before she caught the lenses of the European and American media, even before the miracle-spotter Muggeridge. In July 1961 Mother Teresa made headlines in the Indian press thanks to her good friend Dr Roy. Interviewed on his eightieth birthday, the senior and much respected politician surprised his fellow countrymen by the unexpected tribute he paid to the Catholic nun. 'As I climbed the steps of the Writers' Buildings leading to my office,' he told a *Calcutta Statesman* reporter, 'I was thinking of Mother Teresa who devotes her life to the service of the poor.' The same paper commented that 'Dr Roy felt that Mother Teresa was doing magnificent work. She served those who were most miserable and found no place in hospitals, and among them were lepers and cholera patients.'[26] Asked by a Christian audience in the late 1960s what he thought of Mother Teresa, Dr Zakir Hussain, the Muslim president of India, replied: 'In your lexicon I believe this woman is a saint.'[27]

Mother Teresa's 'saintly' nature was also apparently acknowledged by less distinguished Indians. One of the parables most frequently mentioned by Mother Teresa's admirers regarding the difficulties she encountered in her work at the beginning of her religious order is about an incident which occurred at the Home for the Dying shortly after it was opened. Having received complaints from fanatic Hindus that the patients who died in the home, which was set up in the two halls adjoining Calcutta's famous temple in Kalighat, were baptized by Mother Teresa's sisters in their final moments and then buried as Christians, the city's Chief Medical Officer and a senior police officer went there to investigate the issue for themselves. The story goes that the officers found Mother Teresa so engrossed in her work that it took her some time to notice them. When she eventually became aware of their presence, she offered to show them her work, an offer which the Indian officials politely declined. Turning to the crowd of Hindu believers who were waiting in anticipation outside, the police officer is reported to have said: 'Yes, I will send this woman away, but only after you have persuaded your mothers and sisters to come here to do the work that she is doing. This woman is a saint.'[28]

The Indians have a long-established veneration for holiness. They hold in especially high esteem those who devote themselves to others. This explains to some extent why those Indians who came to know Mother Teresa in person, were familiar with her work and helped her in any way they could, had no hesitation in taking to their hearts a white woman and a Catholic missionary.[29] They acknowledged and appreciated from the first her selflessness and devotion to the poor, the orphans, the old and the infirm, who had been abandoned by their families and ignored by neighbours. The local Indians did not need the intervention of politicians or the intrusion of the media to be convinced that Mother Teresa was 'one of them'.

In his 2005 collection *The Argumentative Indian: Writings on Indian History, Culture and Identity*, Bengali-born Nobel Prize-winning economist Amartya Sen attributes India's ability to accommodate different faiths, cultures, traditions and customs mainly to his country's rich argumentative tradition. This could well be the case but, like every other civilization past and present, India and Hinduism also have a long tradition of intolerance both towards the 'native other' and towards foreigners. Hindus, like Ancient Greeks, have traditionally looked down upon aliens. In the words of the renowned Indian diplomat, writer and columnist Pavan K. Varma:

> The violence and bigotry traditionally inflicted by high-caste Hindus on members of their own faith, the low-caste Shudras, has no parallel in any other religion. Nor is Hinduism particularly welcoming to outside influences. We need only recall that until recently Hindus considered all foreigners to be *mleccha*, inherently unclean, and regarded those who ventured to foreign lands – as Mahatma Gandhi famously did when he left for England to study law in 1888 – as having polluted themselves.[30]

For a foreigner like Mother Teresa to have made friends among Indians of all faiths, especially Hindus, from the start of her lonely venture into the slums of Calcutta is proof of her humility and ability to convince her Indian acquaintances and friends that, although a stranger, she had their best interests at heart. The nun's success also proves the Indians' gratitude to outsiders like her who are always sensitive to local culture and tradition. Mother Teresa may not have been as well-known and admired across all sections of Indian society as her staunch supporters often maintain in their writings, but those who knew and backed her certainly respected her as one of their own. More importantly, such helpful people did not expect any public recognition for their support. Their cooperation with Mother Teresa was unconditional.

Some of India's political and civic leaders also showed a keen interest in Mother Teresa from the start of her religious congregation in 1950. Indian politicians at local and national level were interested in ensuring that the 'saintly' Mother Teresa was known by as many people as possible in Calcutta and throughout India. It was equally important that the news about her was spread around the world. The leaders of India could see the value of presenting the nun as a foreign 'saint' among the 'welcoming' and 'open-minded' Indians and they used the media very effectively to achieve their aims.

Their efforts were soon to produce dividends. The Catholic nun proved very helpful to the political establishment in India in the wake of independence from Britain and separation from Pakistan in 1947, and the civil war that led to the creation of Bangladesh in 1971. Through Mother Teresa, Indian politicians aimed at highlighting the new India's 'secularism' and promoting the Indians as a tolerant and welcoming nation. Likewise, successive Indian governments backed by the Indian media used Mother Teresa to push forward with their progressive reforms at home to better the lives of millions of citizens traditionally abandoned and shunned by the class-conscious and caste-ridden Indian society. The message of the Indian politicians who supported Mother Teresa to their conservative countrymen could not have been any clearer: if a white

Western woman, a Roman Catholic nun, could show so much love and affection for India's abandoned children, lepers, untouchables and the dying old, Indians too were surely capable of finding enough love, compassion and tolerance in their hearts to show the same noble sentiments. After all, Mother Teresa was hardly saying or doing something the Indians themselves had not heard or done before. With her charity work, she was rendering her contribution, small as it was, towards keeping alive a not-much-publicized Calcuttan and Indian tradition furthered by 'home-grown' humanists like the 1913 Nobel Prize laureate for literature Rabindranath Tagore, Mahatma Gandhi (another great twentieth century media icon), and several of her contemporaries such as Pandurang Shashtri Athavale and Acharya Shri Chandananji. In the words of an Indian journalist in the late 1970s, Mother Teresa and her Sisters:

> with their serene ways, their saris, their knowledge of local languages … have come to symbolise not only the best in Christian charity, but also the best in Indian culture and civilisation, from Buddha to Gandhi, the greatest saints, the seers, the great lovers of humanity with boundless compassion and consideration for the underprivileged: what Shakespeare called the 'quality of mercy'.[31]

The founding fathers of modern India aimed at building what Jawaharlal Nehru, the country's first prime minister, called in his 'tryst with destiny' speech to the Constituent Assembly in New Delhi on 14 August 1947, 'the noble mansion of free India where all her children may dwell'. This, Nehru believed, could be achieved by taking and fulfilling the pledge that '[t]he service of India means the service of the millions who suffer. It means the ending of poverty and ignorance and disease and inequality of opportunity'. This was a noble sentiment and a praiseworthy ambition but also a rather tall order in a country where poverty has traditionally been seen as a deserved punishment for a sinful existence in a previous life and as an opportunity for the rich to gain points through almsgiving. Dealing with and eroding the entrenched Indian caste system was a challenge the new leaders of India had to tackle very carefully because they did not want, nor could they afford, to alienate powerful sections of Indian society.

In India, however, the 'segregation' and 'discrimination' of human beings are not allegedly endorsed only by Hinduism. Like the Hindus, a large number of followers of Christianity and Islam across India have traditionally been in favour of the caste system. India will become a 'noble mansion' for all its citizens when the caste system that treats at least one third of the country's population as less than human comes to an end.

The negative impact of the caste system was obvious to the leaders of new India in the second half of the twentieth century. Getting rid of the caste system was undoubtedly a mammoth task, which Nehru and other politicians of his generation, including the Bengali Communists who reigned in Calcutta for most of the last quarter of the twentieth century and who are still in power, were aware that they could not accomplish. They were also adamant that they would not be able to tackle this issue on their own. This is the reason why they were eager from the first to use whatever help they could get, even from abroad, and from anyone who was sensible enough to tread carefully in the new, complicated political-nationalistic-religious reality of India. This is where Mother Teresa proved very useful to the emerging post-independence Indian political establishment, and where she excelled from the first. The tact with which she dealt with sensitive issues relating to Indian politics, religions, customs and tradition won her the increasing backing of several Indian leaders and of those sections of the Indian media that were open minded and courageous enough to promote and offer support publicly to a white woman and a Roman Catholic nun at a time when any foreigner or foreign influence was frowned upon. It was mainly thanks to this home support from rank and file Indians, as well as friends in high places, that Mother Teresa came to be seen throughout India as the embodiment of 'love', which St Paul defines in his first letter to the Corinthians as the 'still more excellent way'.

In the late 1960s and throughout the 1970s Mother Teresa became the personification of human compassion not only in India but also throughout the world. Millions of people, irrespective of their colour, creed, nationality, social status, political beliefs and financial position, apparently saw in her work the answer to some of their problems. The nun, it appears, came to be regarded as a modern sage who had found a purpose in life which had nothing to do with materialistic values. Through her much publicized simple life, her strong faith in God, her belief in the goodness of human nature, her humanitarian work and her veneration for life, many people in India and especially in the West seemed to have discovered for themselves a new purpose in life. In a materialistic world, many apparently believed they had to be grateful to Mother Teresa for showing them a different and equally satisfying way of living. Western individualism and materialism were single-handedly challenged by a tiny and unpretentious nun who became an idol for the poor as well as for the rich, for believers as well as non-believers.

That such a 'saint' could flourish in India was an excellent advertisement for the new India and her new leaders whose pride in their country did not turn them into blinkered nationalists eager to shun any good foreign influence that could help them in their efforts to set the country on the course of economic and social progress and emancipation. To Mother Teresa's good fortune, chief minister Roy and prime minister Nehru did not seek to hide their country's problems; nor did they see poverty as an Indian stigma that had to be kept away from the eyes of the world, especially of the colonial West. Mother Teresa was lucky

Numerous saints have flourished and flourishing in India — Sai Baba etc. vide Mark Tully

to start her charity work and religious order at a time when West Bengal and India were governed by open-minded leaders who were great Indian patriots with an internationalist vision. It was no coincidence that in his famous 1947 speech Nehru spoke of taking 'the pledge of dedication to India and her people and to the still larger cause of humanity'. If a Western 'saint' could facilitate their work at home as well as improve the image of India abroad, then so be it. This explains, to some extent, why a foreign Christian became a celebrity in India and why she enjoyed such unprecedentedly high levels of support for so long.

If Mother Teresa was a natural pragmatist, her influential Indian backers obviously never lagged far behind her. In this give-and-take silent pact the 'saint' and the Indian 'saint-makers' from the fields of politics, media, religion and business were all winners. For everyone concerned this seemed like a perfect match. Like any match, however, it did not have the blessing of everyone.

iii. The 'Conspirators' and the 'Simpleton'

Mother Teresa's relationship with the media has not been a long and uninterrupted honeymoon. One of the earliest critical newspaper articles about her appeared in the *Boston Globe* on 16 October 1983. The author of the uncomplimentary feature, Sylvia Whitman, had spent a couple of months as a volunteer in Calcutta a year earlier. In her piece, Whitman takes issue, although indirectly, with the way the vulnerable people in the care of Mother Teresa and her sisters were treated. The media criticism of Mother Teresa began in earnest, however, only in the early 1990s. In April 1992, for instance, *The Nation* ran Christopher Hitchens's article 'The Ghoul of Calcutta', which has set the tone for much of the criticism against the nun ever since. In addition to reporters like Hitchens, the list of Mother Teresa's opponents includes theologians like Dr Ken Matto, and academics such as the feminist scholar Germaine Greer. These and other critics of the nun find absolutely nothing positive in her work in India and throughout the world. Like other fierce adversaries, they also adopt an essentially structuralist approach when assessing Mother Teresa's celebrity status, as well as the scope, intentions and the consequences of her work.

Contrary to the subjectivists, the structuralists investigate celebrity 'as the expression of universal structural rules imbedded in culture',[32] arguing that well-known people are manufactured and expected to serve the powers that make them famous. In the case of Mother Teresa, her structuralist opponents argue, her role as a fabricated media icon was manifold: to legitimize the exploitation of the poor, spread Christianity in non-Christian lands, preach a fake Gospel, perpetuate the humiliation of third-world countries, present as normal the subjugation of women by men, and help the West to ease its guilty conscience about its colonial legacy in India and other developing countries.

Structuralist interpretations of Mother Teresa's figure are often based on conspiracies. Christopher Hitchens, for instance, believes that she was essentially a fundraiser for the Vatican. This, he argues, is the reason why she was willing to be seen more often than not in the company of a dictator like 'Baby Doc' Duvalier of Haiti, an alleged fraudster like the American businessman Charles Keating, or a shady media mogul like Robert Maxwell. Hitchens is one of the first journalists to express concern, and perhaps not without reasons, about the millions of dollars donated to Mother Teresa to help the poor which allegedly remain still unaccounted for. Hitchens's criticism of Mother Teresa, however, is undermined seriously because it is not always based on impartial research. Throughout his 1995 book *The Missionary Position: Mother Teresa in Theory and Practice*, Hitchens expects the reader to accept without question his guilty verdict on Mother Teresa and be shocked by the 'incriminating' evidence he has collected and presented much in the fashion of tabloid journalism. The only 'reliable' information Hitchens uses in his 1995 book to discredit Mother Teresa comes from *In Mother's House*, the unpublished manuscript of Susan Shields, a former member of the Missionary of Charity,[33] who left the order in May 1989, almost a decade after joining it. As far as Hitchens is concerned, Mother Teresa was the personification of evil and those who do not agree with him are either 'stupid' or as 'evil' as she was.

Hitchens's scathing criticism of Mother Teresa as a conspiratorial religious figure can be matched only by the vitriolic attacks against her by the Indian physician Dr Aroup Chatterjee. In contrast to Hitchens, Chatterjee occasionally gives Mother Teresa, albeit half-heartedly, some credit for her charity work in Calcutta, especially during her anonymous years. All the same, Chatterjee's well-researched 2003 book *Mother Teresa: The Final Verdict* also abounds in conspiracy theories. Chatterjee argues passionately in this work, as well as in much of his writings on the nun, that those who initially made her a public face in the West were very much part of a carefully crafted conspiracy against India and especially against West Bengal and its capital Calcutta. He singles out mainly three chief 'conspirators': the British journalist Malcolm Muggeridge, the former American Secretary of Defence who later became President of the World Bank Robert Strange McNamara, and the French author and script-writer Dominique Lapierre.

Chatterjee is adamant that Muggeridge, McNamara and Lapierre bore strong personal grudges against the city of Calcutta and its people. In the case of Muggeridge, argues Chatterjee, he disliked the former imperial city for its independence movement, liberal humanism, emancipated and proud middle-class women, and early attachment to Marxism. On a personal level, Muggeridge allegedly despised Calcutta and its people because he could never forgive the sophisticated Bengali intellectuals for patronizing him during the several years he was posted there as a journalist.

As for McNamara, Chatterjee insists, the American politician-businessman never forgave the Calcuttans for the massive demonstrations they held to protest his visit to the city as Secretary of Defence during the Vietnam War. The third conspirator, Lapierre, argues Chatterjee, found it impossible to stomach the humiliation he had experienced in Calcutta when he was shooting *City of Joy* on location in 1991, a film which, Chatterjee believes, has further tarnished the image of Calcutta in the West. In the words of the film's producer Jake Eberts, the cast and the crew were faced all the time with 'riots, firebombs, government protests, lawsuits and crowds marching in the streets'.[34] Calcuttans made it clear to Lapierre and his team that they would not tolerate easily their collective humiliation in the eyes of the world.

If one is to take seriously all the 'facts' recorded meticulously by Chatterjee, it is not very difficult to see how people like Muggeridge, McNamara, and Lapierre were allegedly intent on paying the Calcuttans back for the personal insults they had received there. Interestingly enough, notes Chatterjee, all the 'conspirators' were 'evangelical type Christians' or born-again Catholics who apparently have never thought highly of India and the Indians. Moreover, Chatterjee believes that these powerful, 'malicious' *sahibs* (his preferred term for the white 'enemies' of his city), discovered in Mother Teresa the ideal 'tool' and the perfect 'simpleton' to get even with Calcutta.

Chatterjee rightly argues that Muggeridge and McNamara were instrumental in securing the much-coveted Nobel Prize for Mother Teresa in 1979. It is very doubtful she would have ever been awarded the distinguished prize if these two allies had not been able to secure the energetic support of several American senators such as Pete Domenici, Mark O. Hatfield and Hubert Humphrey. By the time these and other influential political players supported her nomination for the Nobel Prize initially in 1978 and then again in 1979 they had already been involved in fundraising activities for Mother Teresa. It is interesting to note that it was around this time that Mother Teresa modified her stance on the sensitive issue of abortion to coincide completely with the views of Muggeridge and of his powerful American friends.

What Chatterjee fails to acknowledge, however, is that far from being a 'simpleton saint', Mother Teresa was a very shrewd practical woman. She played the game of her 'conspirator' backers from the fields of the media, politics and film for as long as they helped her to achieve her main goal in life: Mother Teresa went to India to serve Jesus. If Mother Teresa was indeed used by some individuals, institutions and countries, one should also bear in mind that she used her users just as much.

Bengali and Indian intellectuals like Aroup Chatterjee, Krishna Dutta, Sunanda K. Datta-Ray, Dhiru Shah and Rajeev Srinivasan who are critical of Mother Teresa,[35] obviously believe she played a major role in creating and sustaining the unsavoury image of Calcutta in the West. While I do not hold Mother Teresa on her own responsible for Calcutta's negative media coverage, I fully understand Chatterjee's and his fellow Indians' consternation. The depiction of what was once one of the most fascinating cities of India as 'hell on earth' reveals some of the weakest aspects of the Western media: its partiality, sensationalism and tendency for selective information about those 'alien' parts of the world that we often tend to humiliate at worst and patronize at best. Calcutta, Bangladesh, Ethiopia, Columbia, or countries and regions that are not that distant like Albania and the Balkans become newsworthy in the West mainly for reasons related to floods, famine, epidemics, drugs, human trafficking, economic crises, political unrest and ethnic tensions.[36] Not many newspapers and TV networks in the West seem to be interested in reporting past and present achievements of the 'wretched' nations of the world, whether they are in Eastern Europe, Asia, Africa, or Latin America. The media are largely responsible for the biased and often negative image we in the West have about the undeveloped and developing world.[37] In our psyche, most of the nations living in such regions are doomed to vegetate, and we are their only hope to improve somehow their wasted lives and meaningless existence.

In this context, Chatterjee and other Bengali and Indian critics of the 'white saviour' Mother Teresa are right to be upset about the constant negative media coverage their city has been exposed to for so long. What they also should bear in mind, however, is that Mother Teresa did not have any hidden agenda against their city as such. In her interviews, speeches and books she never singled out Calcutta as being the poorest place on earth. Nor did she ever make any disparaging remarks against its people. On the contrary, she always commended them for their religious tolerance and generosity. More importantly, whenever she spoke about the poor of Calcutta she also referred to the poor in other countries, in both the developed and the undeveloped world.

By the time the world press focused its cameras on Mother Teresa of Calcutta in the late 1960s and throughout the 1970s, in spite of its unparalleled economic and cultural heritage in India and throughout the period of the British Empire, her adopted city had already been stigmatized in the West. The writings of colonial figures and writers such as Robert Clive (1725–1774), Rudyard Kipling (1865–1936) and, more recently, Margaret Rumer Godden (1907–1998) make only a small part of the huge archive of unsympathetic literature about Calcutta. Western reporters have been drawing for decades upon this far from flattering literature to present this part of India as the epitome of poverty and human depravity. The situation has not changed for the better even today and it seems that the tabloidization and degradation of the city of Calcutta and of its proud citizens will continue to go unchecked for quite some time.

One could argue that Calcutta's 'unsavoury' reputation in the West was the price this corner of India and its people had to pay for the headaches they caused the British Empire from the eighteenth century onwards. Moreover, the intellectuals of Calcutta apparently did not do themselves any favours in the eyes of the West with their open sympathy for Marxism throughout the twentieth century. During the Cold War, the Western media would openly demean any regime and country adopting or showing sympathy for Marxism. While all East European countries have been eager to wipe out any trace of their Communist legacy following the domino-effect collapse of their Communist governments in the late 1980s and early 1990s, Calcutta is one of the few places outside the former Soviet Union where Communism and Marxism still appear to be popular. Anyone visiting Calcutta during elections would think that the city is the unacknowledged headquarters of the world Communist movement. There are not many metropolitan centres in the world today where statues of Marx, Engels, Lenin and Stalin continue to lord over parks and streets as in Calcutta. It appears that, for the Bengali Communists and Marxists, the defeat of Communism in Eastern Europe is something that has nothing to do with them.

Perhaps Communism can still deliver something in Calcutta. Perhaps this was one of the reasons why, as will be seen in chapter four, Mother Teresa was always on very good terms with the Communist government of West Bengal, something which, incidentally, has not often been reported in the Western media. Whatever role Communism does play at the moment or is likely to play in the future in a place like Calcutta, the 'outmoded' ideology makes this poor city even more 'interesting' in the eyes of Western 'tourist' reporters who have always had a special knack for reporting to their largely unsuspecting and credulous audiences and readers back home only the exotic and the outlandish.

Some Indian intellectuals believe that the West would not have been able to demean the city of Calcutta to the extent that it obviously has unless Western propaganda had found 'collaborators' from within India. The Atlanta-based Indian writer Dhiru Shah, for instance, blames the 'westernized'/'Anglo-Americanized' Indians, some of India's 'selfserving', 'greedy' and 'selfish' politicians, some sections of the Indian press and 'the indifferent majority' for presenting Mother Teresa as the only person in India who '[was] engaged in caring for the poor and helpless folks'.[38] Aroup Chatterjee holds that his native Bengal and Calcutta have been stigmatized by the Indian political establishment because they envy the Bengalis for their pride, cultural heritage and achievements.[39] Chatterjee and other Indian scholars who hold this view are keen to mention the remark made by the Indian nationalist leader Gopal Krishna Gokhale: 'What Bengal thinks today, India will think tomorrow.' In contrast to Chatterjee, the veteran Indian journalist Sunanda K. Datta-Ray believes that the citizens of Bengal and especially of Calcutta, where he grew up, have lost their sense of pride and dignity. In his words, '[n]o other city would so gladly offer its dying to be stepping stones in a relentless ascent to sainthood'.[40] Datta-Ray is especially critical of the Indian and Bengali media for in his view not having the courage to show to the Indian nation and the world the 'real' Mother Teresa. He is especially bitter about an incident in the early 1970s when he was asked by Doordarshan, the state-run Indian broadcasting company, to interview the nun in celebration of a papal award. As he had not met her before, he asked her during their preliminary discussion what distinguished her from other 'social workers':

> Mother Teresa was horrified. She was not doing social service. She was 'helping the poor' because 'our lord' had told her to do so for the sake of her soul. She stressed the difference between social service as an end for those who are helped, and service for the helper's spiritual welfare. 'So the good work you do is for your own sake?' I asked. 'The beneficial effect that it has is only incidental, the real purpose is your personal salvation?' Mother Teresa did not disagree.
> As I spent the evening talking to her workers at the Nirmal Hriday home – Mother Teresa had wisely advised me to become familiar with her work before the interview – I could not help dwelling on what she had told me. It would be central to our discourse on television, for I realised that it revealed her and her mission, as well as her relationship with Calcutta, in an altogether new light. So did Mother Teresa. Doordarshan telephoned early next morning to say that she had called to tell them that she would not be interviewed by me. She had chosen her own interviewer: my friend and colleague, Desmond Doig, her biographer. If Doordarshan refused, there would be no interview.
> Doordarshan, being Doordarshan, had already capitulated. Calcutta was the ideal setting for an [sic] European in search of salvation.[41]

This 'capitulation' of the Indian media, as well as of the Indian film industry, is very much lamented to this day by several Indian journalists, intellectuals and film-makers who complain that they are subjected to pressure and censorship if they attempt to portray Mother Teresa differently from the officially endorsed version. There have even been cases where journalists and film-makers have been threatened with the sack if they publicize their iconoclastic work on Mother Teresa.[42] India may indeed be the world's most populous and dynamic democracy, but Indian society, it seems, is still riddled with censorship.

Mother Teresa's popularity in India and the reluctance of some Indian officials to tolerate any public criticism of her can also be explained by the fact that this country treats its celebrities like deities. The Indians tend to venerate especially their fellow citizens who receive their 'laurels' or some degree of acknowledgement in the West. In India, home-grown international celebrities from the world of politics, cinema, business and, in the case of Mother Teresa, religion, seem to be beyond reproach. They are seen as a valuable part of the national heritage, as proof of India's ability to produce outstanding individuals. As for some of Mother Teresa's Indian critics, they hold that she was offered star treatment in India not only because she was known and venerated worldwide but also because she was white.

Some of the conspiracy theories which attribute blame to Western countries, Western media, the Catholic Church, Indian politicians and the Indian media are certainly far-fetched. It is absurd to think that Mother Teresa could generate so much support because of a global conspiracy against India, the Bengalis or the city of Calcutta. The nun was not supported by the capitalist West to spite the Marxists of Calcutta. Nor was she deemed an ideal candidate for the Nobel Prize, as Chatterjee argues, because she was originally from Albania, which in the 1960s had officially adopted atheism. The fact of the matter is that, contrary to the version of events presented by the Enver Hoxha regime throughout the Cold War, Albania on its own was never considered such an important member of the Communist bloc that it warranted the West's special attention.[43] Chatterjee is right when he argues that giving the Nobel Prize to a deeply Catholic nun from Albania would very effectively cock a snook at socialist governments world-wide.[44] This, however, was hardly the only, or even the main reason, why Mother Teresa's work was acknowledged at such a high level.

Considering the constant attention the Indian and world media paid to Mother Teresa's charity work in Calcutta after she was awarded the Nobel Prize in 1979, it was inevitable that the city's image would suffer. This, however, does not justify the predominantly negative picture of Mother Teresa that Chatterjee and other Indian and Western critics depict relentlessly in their writings. While the 'divinity' of Mother Teresa is to some extent the outcome of Mother Teresa's own words about herself as well as the end-result of the efforts of many people, countries, institutions (political, religious, business, media) that apparently took a lasting and calculated interest in her persona and work, it would be unfair to brush aside as insignificant, and even worse as devious, the almost seven decades of her life she spent trying to help the poorest of the poor in person, through her sisters, brothers and co-workers, or by bringing them to the attention of those who have the power and the resources to do something to alleviate their hardship. Mother Teresa succeeded in her attempts to make the Indians as well as millions of people outside India feel ever more responsible for the unfortunate human beings marginalized by society. The Indian critics of Mother Teresa who see her as almost a demonic figure would be able to assess her work more objectively and perhaps even start to appreciate her if they did not let national pride get in the way. No matter what 'flaws' Mother Teresa might have had, she certainly loved India as no other country in the world, including her native Albania.

iv. The celebrity with no private life

What is interesting about some of the opponents of Mother Teresa is that they are inclined to discredit her not directly, but by discrediting those who supported her. This is particularly the case with adversaries like Christopher Hitchens and Aroup Chatterjee. They dig deep into the private lives of anyone who helped the nun to become an international celebrity. The numerous derogatory comments that Hitchens and Chatterjee make in their books against Malcolm Muggeridge, Robert S. McNamara, Dominique Lapierre or Ronald Reagan are at times rather too personal and insulting. While both critics have raised some serious issues about the motives and nature of Mother Teresa's work in and outside India, their uncompromisingly hostile attitude towards her and those who supported her has undermined considerably the value of their criticism. Likewise, some Indian opponents of the 'Saint of the Gutters', as the Indian press often refers to Mother Teresa, have ended up producing, either on purpose or unwittingly, what one could consider 'muck-raking' criticism.

The personal attacks mounted on Mother Teresa's supporters are partly related to their allegedly chequered pasts as well as their not-so-holy intentions in financing, endorsing and promoting the work of this particular Christian missionary. One could interpret such attacks as an indication of the pent-up frustration and failure of Mother Teresa's committed opponents to uncover something embarrassing and humiliating about the nun herself. The unprecedented media attention Mother Teresa generated for almost fifty years in India and throughout the world was bound to expose many personal details about her. Being a celebrity, it was inevitable that her life would become 'public property', that people would want to know as much as possible about the woman behind the nun.

The vast literature on this religious celebrity, however, would disappoint anyone hoping to find there revealing details about the private Mother Teresa. Accounts of her personal life remain rather sketchy even in the best authorized and unauthorized biographies. Both her subjectivist admirers and her structuralist opponents have failed to produce a complete biography of Agnes Gonxhe Bojaxhiu. As for those who approach her figure from a post-structuralist position, they too have been unable so far to 'uncover' the woman behind the missionary. While Mother Teresa was undoubtedly a 'media star', analysing her life along the straightforward post-structuralist lines employed when commenting on the lives of stars from the fields of the media, sport, music and cinema remains problematic.

The star discourse emerged for the first time in the United States in the early 1910s when interest in actors went beyond their screen roles. John Belton holds that:

> [a]ctors develop a persona or portrait of themselves out of the personalities of the various characters they have played over the course of

their careers and out of elements of their personal lives that have become public knowledge.[45]

With the press becoming ever more inquisitive and intrusive, many famous actors found it impossible to keep details of their personal lives out of the public gaze. Media played a crucial role in the transformation of actors into stars. As Christine Gledhill notes, '[a]ctors become stars when their off-screen life-styles and personalities equal or surpass acting ability in importance'.[46] As a result of the information about the actors' personal lives made public by the media, the attention of many film fans shifted from the screen characters to the real people who portrayed them. This important shift was possible because of the emergence of what Richard deCardova calls the 'star scandal' discourse.[47]

The unprecedented interest the public started showing in the stars' intimate lives transformed not only the relationship between actors and their admirers, but also redefined the notion of fame for screen actors. The 'star scandal' thus became an irreplaceable stepping stone to fame (or infamy) and celebrity status not only in twentieth-century America and other developed countries but also across the developing world.

While the 'star scandal' obviously plays a crucial role in the lives and careers of stars from the world of entertainment, politics and sport, it hardly had any significant impact on the celebrity status of Mother Teresa. This does not mean that she was and remains immune from controversial stories. On the contrary, thanks to the relentless efforts of opponents like Hitchens and Chatterjee to reveal the 'real' Mother Teresa, the controversial has always been an important part in the often heated debates about her. Claims that Mother Teresa accepted preferential treatment in India and overseas, that she travelled in luxury, that she was treated in expensive clinics and mishandled millions of dollars are a familiar theme in the ever-growing critical literature about her. In spite of such sustained iconoclastic attacks on her figure, during her lifetime and after her death her image has hardly been dented seriously. So far her avowed opponents appear to have been unable to produce the 'killer' evidence that would irreparably damage Mother Teresa's reputation.

The main reason why Mother Teresa has apparently remained immune for so long from the 'star scandal' is because, unlike most stars, she does not seem to have suffered from the tensions resulting from the dichotomy between the *public face* a celebrity has to promote all the time, and the *private self*, or what Chris Rojek calls, the 'veridical self',[48] which the star tries to protect fanatically but often without success. In Mother Teresa's case, the private and the personal appear to have been one and the same thing. Although, like any other international 'star', she was constantly under media 'surveillance', throughout her long public life Mother Teresa never had to lash out at any photographer as the actor Johnny Depp did in London in 1999: 'I don't want to be what you want me to be tonight.'

It appears that Mother Teresa was unique among twentieth-century celebrities in that she could be in public what she was in private. This was quite an achievement for Mother Teresa and for those who supported and promoted her in a world that teems with paparazzi who are always scandal-hunting and thus undermining the careers of all sorts of famous people, including religious celebrities.

As a seasoned public figure Mother Teresa apparently succeeded where many media stars usually fail. Not only did she seem able to establish very good contacts with journalists, but she also appeared to have cast a spell on them. For her devoted supporters, the reporters' veneration for Mother Teresa was, and remains, yet another proof of her 'saintliness'. Bob Geldof, however, found 'nothing other-worldly or divine about her'[49] when he met her in 1985. If Bob found anything extraordinary about his 'saintly' fellow charity worker, it was her skilful handling of the media. She struck him as 'outrageously brilliant'[50] in the way she handled reporters: 'She made them laugh and she defined the terms of the questions they could ask her.' 'The way she spoke to the journalists,' concluded Geldof, 'showed her to be as deft a manipulator of media as any high-powered American PR expert.'[51]

To a large extent, Mother Teresa's good relations with the media and her ability as a 'deft manipulator' were made possible and tolerated mainly because of the high moral ground she occupied as a result of her charity work and simple preaching for almost seventy years in India and throughout the world. Mother Teresa was very much aware of this 'moral ground' which, to quote Geldof, 'gave her the right to march up to airlines and ask for a free ticket to Washington, and once she arrived, to ask to see the President of the United States knowing he dare not refuse her'.[52]

No political, religious and business support would have kept Mother Teresa in the public eye for five successive decades unless the propaganda machine and the news industry had paid exclusive attention to her humanitarian work. The nun's status as an exemplary media icon is likely to remain secured for as long as the media focus exclusively on her selflessness and devotion to 'human debris'. It is mainly thanks to the media that the celebrity Mother Teresa has entered the consciousness of our age as the epitome of compassion for humanity.

Whether she deserves this status or not is something that will continue to divide her admirers and supporters in the years to come. What is certain, however, is that in our sceptical age nobody's sanctity can be taken for granted for too long, not even the sanctity of a media untouchable like Mother Teresa.

The history of mankind is the history of its great men: the important thing is to find these out ... clean the dirt from them ... and place them on their proper pedestals.

Thomas Carlyle

Patriotism is when love of your own people comes first; nationalism, when hate for people other than your own comes first.

Charles de Gaulle

Lying is a form of our [Serbian] patriotism and is evidence of our innate intelligence. We live in a creative, imaginative and inventive way. In these lands every lie becomes a truth in the end.

Dobrica Ćosić

2 The Balkans appropriation of Mother Teresa

i. The main claimants

No matter what interests various countries, governments, institutions, political and religious leaders, businessmen and reporters, especially those hailing from the West, had and still have in the image and legacy of Mother Teresa, they would invariably give the impression that their admiration and adoration for the nun comes mainly from her charity work to benefit the 'throwaway' people in India and elsewhere. While it is true that many people admired and continue to admire her for just that, many more Mother Teresa fans have declared their attachment to her, especially since her death, mainly because of what she allegedly did for them. This is particularly the case in the Balkans, where the nun's admirers mushroomed suddenly in the wake of the global recognition she received as a result of the Nobel Prize in 1979. From that moment, the international celebrity Mother Teresa was seen by many parties in the Balkans as a god-send, especially by her fellow Albanians and the Macedonian Slavs, most of whom were blissfully unaware of her before the flashing cameras of the world media embellished her with the publicity halo which in the Balkans has a magic effect. This chapter traces Mother Teresa's reception in and the impact of her fame on the Balkans throughout her life as an international celebrity and especially since her death in 1997.

In the summer of 2003 an unholy war broke out between the Albanians and the Macedonian Slavs over the filiation of a sainted woman. The decision of the Government of the Republic of Macedonia to erect a monument dedicated to Mother Teresa, not very far from the centre of Rome, aroused the Albanians' suspicion and jealousy.

This was not the first time that the Albanians felt they were being robbed of 'their' Mother Teresa; some of their neighbours had apparently tried to appropriate her almost immediately after the Albanian Catholic nun was discovered by the BBC's Malcolm Muggeridge in 1968. When Mother Teresa was awarded the Nobel Prize for Peace in 1979, the competition between several Balkan countries to claim the celebrity nun as their own 'daughter' began in earnest. According to Albert Ramaj,[1] the Croats were the first to claim that she 'belonged' to them. On 5 August 1990, Mother Teresa was made Honorary Citizen of Zagreb. The Croatian Government issued her with a Croatian passport, which was presented to her by the country's ambassador in India in the early 1990s. The Croats, most of whom are Roman Catholics, base their argument mainly, if not exclusively, on the fact that Mother Teresa apparently spoke Serbo-Croat better than Albanian. Several Slav reporters are keen to emphasize that, while she was fluent in Serbo-Croat, she spoke little or no Albanian;[2] something strongly contested by the Albanians. Mother Teresa apparently retained a good command of Serbo-Croat because in India she was in contact with priests from the former Yugoslavia.

The issue of what languages Mother Teresa could and could not speak or write has been mentioned occasionally by her biographers Eileen Egan and Kathryn Spink. Both writers were very close to the nun for many years. Referring to Mother Teresa's meeting with an Albanian diplomat at the Albanian Embassy in Rome, probably in the late 1960s, Egan, who was accompanying Mother Teresa, remarks in her 1986 biography:

> Mother Teresa fastened her tawny eyes on him and said simply in her native tongue, '*Sou de Schipteru.*' (I am from Albania.) This was literally correct since she could no longer say she was Albanian, having acquired Indian citizenship.
>
> The Embassy employee looked from Mother Teresa to me as though unable to credit his senses and then said a few brusque words which we took to be an invitation to enter the building. . . . The three of us settled into the large chair around a low coffee table and Mother Teresa said once more, '*Sou de Schipteru.*'
>
> The man replied with a burst of speech while Mother Teresa struggled to form a few words. A blush rose and covered her face; she turned to me smiling ruefully. 'I can't find the words in my mother tongue. It's too far back.'
>
> At that point, I thought I had better explain our presence, since the Albanian was looking uneasy.[3]

I am not sure what Egan means by Mother Teresa's 'native tongue' but *Sou de Schipteru*, which the nun is attributed to have uttered twice, is not the Albanian for 'I am from Albania.'[4] Hence, Egan's explanation about the connotation of Mother Teresa's statement, after she utters it for the first time, 'being literally correct', is irrelevant.

Egan then explains that she came to the rescue of the embarrassed Mother Teresa and the baffled Embassy employee; at her intervention, the conversation between the three was soon conducted in English. As the *attaché* walked the two women to the door, however, Egan remarks that he and Mother Teresa talked in Serbo-Croat.

Egan dwells on the issue of Mother Teresa's linguistic skills, or lack of them, also when describing an informal gathering in Oslo in 1979:

> At the afternoon liturgy in the chapel of St. Joseph's Institute, presided over by Bishop Nikola Prela of Skopje, Mother Teresa joined with the congregation, chiefly immigrants or guest workers from Yugoslavia, in the responses, '*Gospodine smiluj se, Kriste smiluj se.*' (Lord have mercy, Christ have mercy.) When called upon to speak to the congregation in Serbo-Croatian, she had to pause halfway through her talk. She smiled and asked for help with some words. The language of her schooldays was too infrequently used to allow for speedy recall. She took time to write a short message in Albanian, which she could still write but had forgotten how to speak. 'My fellow-countrymen,' she wrote, 'the Albanians are always in my heart. I pray that God's peace may come into our hearts, our families, and the entire world. Please pray for our poor and also for me and my Sisters. I do pray for you.' Instead of signing herself, 'M. Teresa, M.C.,' she signed it with her family name, 'M. Teresa Bojaxhiu.'[5]

In her 1998 biography of Mother Teresa, Kathryn Spink remarks that the correspondence with her mother and sister in Tirana was the means by which the nun 'kept up her knowledge of the Albanian language',[6] a correspondence that was suspended for a while under Albania's Communist regime. Spink suggests clearly that in the early 1960s Mother Teresa's knowledge of Serbo-Croat was good enough to use it in her correspondence. In 1962 the nun received a letter from a priest in the town of Ohri in Macedonia informing her of what had happened in Skopje since her departure in 1928. Mother Teresa wrote back to thank the priest in Serbo-Croat: 'I thought that the people of Skopje had completely forgotten Agnes, as you are the first to write to me in such a long time.'[7]

From the accounts offered by Egan and Spink, it is difficult to create a clear picture of the extent to which Mother Teresa had remembered or forgotten her native Albanian and the Serbo-Croat language which she had studied at school. Like most of her biographers, they obviously did not consider the issue of the languages the nun spoke during the first eighteen years of her life in Skopje important enough to deserve more than a brief mention.

One of the few biographers of Mother Teresa who is keen to highlight that she had a good command of Albanian (both spoken and written) is her Albanian friend Lush Gjergji.[8] According to Gjergji, the nun spoke Albanian, her native language, very well, but was not very confident of her ability to use literary Albanian in public.[9] Gjergji maintains that Mother Teresa could write Albanian with ease, which is obvious from several letters she sent as a missionary to her mother, siblings and Albanian friends and relatives. Gjergji has included facsimiles of letters written by the nun in Albanian in several of his books about her.[10] Mother Teresa obviously wrote letters in Albanian throughout her life.

Like the Croats, the Serbs have allegedly made some attempts to prove that Mother Teresa was originally from Serbia. The Serbs and those who support their claim apparently read too much into the fact that her brother was called Lazar.[11] For the Serbs, the name 'Lazar' is very dear because it reminds them of one of their leaders and saints, whose death in 1389, as we will see later in this chapter, was instrumental in laying the foundations of the myth about the Serbian nation being the main defender of Christianity in the Balkans against Islam.

'Lazar' or 'Lazarus', however, is hardly an 'authentic' Serbian proper name. The name had been in use among the Albanians and other European peoples several centuries before the Serbs settled in the Balkans and converted to Christianity. So, for instance, 'Lazarus' is mentioned in the New Testament in reference to two people, a character in one of Christ's parables and the brother of Martha and Mary of Bethany who was raised from the dead. The name Lazarus has also been known in Western Europe apparently from the first century AD. The Bishop of Aix, believed to have been consecrated at Marseilles in 407, was also called Lazarus.

The name 'Lazar' remains popular to this day among the Albanians, especially those adhering to the Catholic faith. Considering that Mother Teresa happened to be a Roman Catholic, that she came from an Albanian patriotic and religious family that took pride in their devotion to the fatherland and their ancient attachment to Catholicism,[12] and that she was called Agnes, the name of several Catholic saints and martyrs,[13] it is unlikely that her parents would have named their son after a Serbian Orthodox saint. According to Mother Teresa's brother, he was named 'Lazar' after his grandfather on his father's side, which is further proof of how popular this name was among the Albanian Catholics.[14]

The Serbs and the Croats obviously do not have any credible evidence to claim Mother Teresa as their 'own'. Both these Balkan claimants, however, have changed her Albanian family name 'Bojaxhiu' to 'Bojadžijević',[15] which has always enraged the Albanians.

Shortly before the beatification of Mother Teresa in Rome in October 2003, the Vlachs also intensified their efforts to prove that she belonged to them.[16] The Vlachs are an old nomadic European people who call themselves Aromani (meaning 'Romans'), Romani or Rumeni. They live in small groups across the Balkans, mainly in Romania, Bulgaria, Serbia, Albania, Macedonia and Greece, and speak a Latin language which, in spite of some similarities, is separate from the Romanian language used by the northern Vlachs. In the Balkans, the Vlachs are recognized as an ethnic community only in the Republic of Macedonia. This, according to Albert Ramaj,[17] could have been a calculated concession on the part of the Macedonian state in the wake of the collapse of the former Yugoslavia to weaken the position of the Albanians who, after the Macedonian

Slavs, constitute the second largest ethnic population in the country. Ramaj also suggests that by officially acknowledging the Vlachs as an ethnic community, the Macedonian Slavs hoped they would find it easier to claim that some important historical Albanian personalities were of Vlach origin.

Ramaj's interpretations may seem rather far-fetched, but the fact of the matter is that, since the official recognition of the Vlachs as an ethnic community in Macedonia, some Macedonian Slav intellectuals, politicians and reporters have shown a tendency to present as Vlachs an increasing number of distinguished Albanian leaders, writers and intellectuals. This tendency, the Albanians argue, is obvious especially in the case of the claim made by some Macedonian Slav and Vlach scholars that Mother Teresa's father was a Vlach,[18] a claim which was immediately refuted and ridiculed by the Albanians, much in the same way as they had done with the efforts of the Croats and the Serbs to 'appropriate' the celebrity nun.[19] The Vlachs, who adhere to the Orthodox faith, have yet to explain how Mother Teresa's 'Vlach' father happened to be a Roman Catholic.

As far as the Macedonian Slavs are concerned, the Vlachs living in Macedonia are essentially Slavs, something which apparently 'legitimizes' their claim that Mother Teresa's father too was a Slav. This, they argue, entitles them to get a piece of the nun in spite of the fact that, like the Vlachs, they too do not share Mother Teresa's Catholic faith. Despite these incongruities, the Macedonian Slavs are determined to stick to their claim that she was not Albanian, at least not completely, something which, they believe, gives them every right to claim and honour her as one of their own as well as enable them to dampen the Albanians' euphoria about 'their' global star.

The monument the Macedonian government decided to dispatch to Rome was the latest link in the long chain of honours the establishment in Macedonia had been bestowing for several decades upon 'their' Mother Teresa. On 26 June 1980, only six months after she was awarded the Nobel Prize for Peace, the government of Macedonia made Mother Teresa an honorary citizen of Skopje.

The Albanians have always been uncomfortable with what they consider as the Macedonian Slavs' excessive veneration for Mother Teresa, but the monument was apparently the last straw. What upset the Albanians most was not the monument itself (after all, the Macedonian Slavs had already dedicated a statue to Mother Teresa in Skopje shortly after her death in 1997), but the Cyrillic inscription which was allegedly intended to accompany the monument in Rome: 'Macedonia honours her daughter Gonxhe Bojaxhiu – Mother Teresa, Skopje 1910 – Calcutta 1997'.

To prevent such an 'injustice', thirty-eight noted Albanian intellectuals and politicians wasted no time in dispatching a letter to the Mayor of the Eternal City, Walter Veltroni. The Albanians also asked the Holy See to intervene on their behalf. In their letter to Veltroni, the Albanians emphasized that the Former Yugoslav Republic of Macedonia had no right 'to usurp the figure and deeds of Mother Teresa' simply because Skopje happened to be her native city. Mother Teresa was born there to ethnic Albanian parents on 26 September 1910. At that time Skopje was still under the authority of the Ottoman Empire. As for Macedonia, Yugoslavia and Albania, such independent 'states' did not exist in 1910.

Either because he heeded the Albanians' advice not to be 'part of this project [Macedonian monument of Mother Teresa] which falsifies history to cash in politically', or simply because he wanted to avoid yet another typical Balkan squabble, Mayor Veltroni was sympathetic to the Albanians' 'predicament' and so, much to their delight, the Macedonian Slavs' 'elaborate scheme' to 'steal' Mother Teresa from them, her 'genuine' ethnic brethren, was nipped in the bud.[20]

Naturally, the Macedonian Slavs felt that the West had once again misjudged them for reasons they could not, and still do not, understand. The Balkans is a breeding ground for conspiracy theories, but the Orthodox Macedonian Slavs were quick to profess publicly that their intention to honour Mother Teresa with a monument at the heart of Catholic Rome had no hidden agenda. Tome Serafimovski, the sculptor of the controversial statue, and Risto Penov, the mayor of Skopje, denied there was any catch. Both of them, incidentally, have made public their doubts about Mother Teresa's Albanian origin.

Mother Teresa preached peace, understanding, tolerance and forgiveness in India and throughout the world for most of the twentieth century, but she apparently failed to inject some neighbourly spirit into her own native Balkans. In their bitter row over her 'blood type', some Albanians and Macedonian Slavs showed how intolerant they are. In their attempts to appropriate her for themselves or challenge the other party's copyright claim, they missed a unique opportunity to celebrate and commemorate together the life, work and legacy of their internationally renowned fellow citizen, the only twentieth century world figure from the Balkans to present this traditionally troubled region in a new and promising way.

ii. The Albanians and their international highflyers

Like any nation in the Balkans, indeed throughout the world, the Albanians are very proud of their historical figures. Being the direct descendants of the Illyrians, they take pride in several famous ancient kings like Bardhyllus and Glaucius and Queen Teuta. Following their defeat by the Romans in about 165 BC, however, the Albanians began to take pride especially in compatriots who achieved success outside of Albania. The Albanians are keen to mention that many Roman and Byzantine Emperors such as Diocletian, Julian, Claudius, Constantine the Great, Justinian I and Anastasius were apparently of Illyrian origin. They also mention with pride that at least half a dozen pontiffs, including the eighteenth century Pope Clement XI (né Giovanni Francesco Albani), were Albanians or of Albanian descent.[21] While the Albanians never fail to blame the five-century-long Turkish occupation of their country, they always mention with pride that they allegedly gave the Ottoman Empire twenty-six grand viziers (prime ministers) as well as some of its greatest architects. According to the well-known French memoir writer Laure Junot, Duchess d'Abrantès (née Permon) (1784–1838), the renowned French statesman and historian Adolphe Thiers (1797–1877), the French linguist and ethnographer Robert D'Angely (1893–1966), and Napoleon Bonaparte are also of Albanian origin.[22] Nowadays the Albanians take pride in modern celebrities of Albanian origin among whom they are keen to mention the Hollywood brothers, James and the late John Belushi, the 1998 Nobel Prize Laureate in Medicine, Ferid Murad, and the writer Ismail Kadare, several times Nobel Prize nominee and the first winner of the Man Booker International Prize in June 2005. The list of the Albanian celebrities is quite impressive for such a small nation.[23]

Most of the internationally renowned figures of Albanian origin in the past (as well as today) had an acute awareness of their European identity. This is one of the reasons why they could integrate so well in the Western and Eastern parts of the Roman Empire. The Albanians retained their European consciousness especially throughout the 500 years of Turkish domination, during which time many of them looked towards Istanbul for jobs and career opportunities much in the same way as numerous talented and ambitious Albanians and other Eastern Europeans look nowadays towards London, Paris, Berlin and New York. The Albanian-born ruler of Egypt, Mohammad Ali (1769–1849), the founder of the 1802–1952 Albanian dynasty of Egypt, is one of the best examples of the extent to which famous Albanians who served or opposed the Ottoman Empire always looked to Europe as a source of inspiration. Ali was instrumental in opening Egypt up towards Western Europe, something he was able to do by taking advantage of the legacy of Napoleon's brief but significant expedition to Egypt and by sending many promising Egyptian students to France, hoping that they might acquire there the education, culture, skills and awareness that would enable them to retrace their own Pharaonic roots. And the gamble paid off. Upon their return, Ali's students became the key figures of the Egyptian Renaissance as a result of which the Egyptians rediscovered their Pharaonic past and established enduring ties with the West.[24]

Another internationally famous military figure and statesman of Albanian origin who played a similar, if not more important, role in orienting his country towards 'rational' Europe was Mustafa Kemal Atatürk (1881–1938), the founder of modern Turkey. Kemal was instrumental in abolishing the Caliphate in 1924, making the army the guardian of secularism, lifting the ban on alcohol, closing religious schools and replacing the Islamic *Sharia* law with several European countries' legal, penal and commercial codes. Kemal was the driving force behind the emancipation of women. It was mainly thanks to his intervention that the Arabic script was replaced by the Latin alphabet. Kemal was also the founder of Turkish democracy and the inspiration behind the impressive transformation that Turkey went through in the early decades of the twentieth century from a humiliated former superpower to a new, vigorous and ambitious state with clear aspirations to join the family of Western European nations.

Like her famous compatriots Mohammad Ali and Mustafa Kemal Atatürk, Mother Teresa was always aware of her Albanian and European identity, in spite of the fact that, as we shall see later on in the book, she went to extraordinary lengths to present herself as a Catholic nun who had gone 'native' in her adopted country, India. Like Ali and Kemal, she was also highly motivated and had a very practical mind. Unlike Ali and Kemal, however, Mother Teresa was essentially a spiritual human being, and the source of her spirituality came exclusively from the Catholic interpretation of the New Testament endorsed and championed by the Vatican.

While in the past many successful Albanians outside Albania always saw themselves as essentially European, some of them hardly did anything to benefit their country of origin directly. Mohammad Ali, Mustafa Kemal and Mother Teresa are some of the more recent and best-known examples of this trend. These three Albanian international personalities were almost completely disengaged from Albania throughout their careers. Like numerous successful expatriates over the past two millennia, Ali, Kemal and Mother Teresa devoted their lives wholeheartedly to the causes they embraced or invented for themselves, causes which had nothing to do with Albania as such. For them, the Albania they or their predecessors left behind was a distant and alien country. Some famous Albanians apparently did not even know anything of their Albanian origin until they were told about it. For the sake of promoting their careers and in order to achieve their highly ambitious and egoistic targets, many successful Albanian military, religious and political figures abroad even chose to keep quiet about their Illyrian-Albanian-Balkan roots; at times, indeed, they had no qualms about denying their ethnic origin and nationality altogether. More recently this tendency has manifested itself among some Albanian athletes in Greece who, much to the consternation of their countrymen, have opted to take Greek names, apparently as a precondition to be allowed to compete in Olympic Games and European and world championships as members of the Greek national team.

This is not to say that no famous Albanian abroad tried to benefit the Albanian nation in one way or another. Their numbers, and the contribution they made to the progress of Albania, however, were hardly significant, especially bearing in mind the huge positive impact some of them had on other countries, virtually changing the course of their history. The only notable exception to this pattern of detachment was the renowned military strategist Gjergj Kastrioti (1403–1468) who devoted his entire life to Albania. He will be discussed shortly.

While some famous Albanians obviously failed to show any particular interest in their country of origin, their countrymen never stopped admiring them. Taking pride in stars of Albanian origin is, and will probably remain for quite some time, a much-loved Albanian national pastime. While the Albanians tend to cherish any international acknowledgement, no matter how small or trivial, they have a preference especially for prizes awarded in the West. As far as these devoted fans are concerned, any expatriate who is famous in the West automatically qualifies to be considered the pride of the Albanian nation. This, to some extent, explains why they display such a fierce loyalty and attachment to the figure of Mother Teresa and why some of them appear to be reluctant to share her with their neighbours, especially the Macedonian Slavs.

iii. Balkan heroes of mixed ethnicity

Present-day Macedonians, like the Albanians, have a long tradition of 'worshipping' their famous countrymen. Macedonia's main hero-celebrity, of course, remains King Alexander III (356–323 BC), usually known as Alexander the Great. After Alexander, no other Macedonian hero has achieved a comparable iconic status. This is perhaps why the Macedonian Slavs depend so much on him and evoke his name and deeds any time they deem it necessary to remind their neighbours and the world of their status as a nation.

Much to the Macedonian Slavs' irritation, 'their' Alexander has always also been claimed by other nations in the Balkans, mainly the Albanians and the Greeks. It is not my intention here to affirm or contradict any Balkan party's claim on Alexander's ethnicity. I simply argue that the ethnicity of ancient heroes is not a very clear-cut issue.

As a rule, during the time of Alexander, the royals were of mixed blood. In the ancient world marriage was a very effective way for rulers to strengthen their position at home, secure borders, and enter into mutually beneficial military and commercial agreements with neighbouring countries and beyond. Alexander himself and his father were products of calculated marriages.

A great deal about Alexander's personal life remains a mystery to this day, and as such is open to speculative and sensational interpretations, such as that seen in the 2004 film *Alexander*, directed by Oliver Stone. However, at least one thing about him is indisputable. Historians largely agree that while Alexander's father Philip II was Macedonian, his mother Olympias was an Illyrian princess. Does this make Alexander an Illyrian? Perhaps not. This, however, does not mean that the Illyrians had no right to claim him as one of their own, or that Alexander did not see himself as being part Illyrian. Philip's mother was also an Illyrian princess.

As with Alexander, Philip's Illyrian blood-line did not necessarily make him an Illyrian. The Illyrians, however, believed that they had every reason to take pride in such royal connections, and rightly so. Seeing the great leaders Philip and Alexander had become, the Illyrians were certainly proud of their extraordinary grandsons. In Alexander's case their pride was twofold; after all he was both their grandson and great-grandson.[25]

The legend of Alexander was kept alive over the centuries by the Illyrians and their descendents, the Albanians. So much so that Alexander has always been an inspirational figure for many Albanian leaders in the past. That Alexander holds a special affection in the Albanian national consciousness is also evident from the fact that the Albanian currency is called 'Lek', which is short for 'Aleksandër'/'Alexander'.

Alexander, however, was a 'mongrel', not only in terms of his blood-relations but also in terms of his education. One of his teachers, Aristotle, introduced him to his *Morals* and *Politics*. Alexander remained to the end of his life passionate about Homer's *Iliad*, and the work of Aeschylus, Euripides and Sophocles. Equally important is the lifelong attachment to and envy Alexander developed for Greek mythological figures like Hercules and Perseus. The Macedonian Slavs and the Albanians who have been competing for quite some time over their exclusive right to claim Alexander as one of their own should perhaps note that he was not very particular about earthly relatives. This Macedonian king was obviously more interested in finding for himself a divine connection. Alexander was obsessed with the idea of immortality and he believed he could achieve it, not by conquering the world, although he made sure that he explored this avenue as few other military figures before or after him, but by establishing a godly origin. His immersion in Greek culture offered him what he believed was the answer to his quest for immortality: a divine genealogy. His 'divinity' was finally acknowledged 'officially' by the accommodating pharaonic priests who greeted this already 'Son of Zeus' as 'Son of Ammon-Ra' at the oracle of the ancient Egyptian deity in Siwah in present-day Libya in 331 BC. One could argue that the Greeks as well as the Egyptians are as equally entitled as the Macedonians and Albanians to claim the cosmopolitan Alexander as one of their own.

Alexander is not the only Balkan hero whose origin remains a bone of contention for several parties in the Balkans. The ethnicity of numerous less ancient famous figures is often equally bitterly contested. So for instance, the Greeks, the Bulgarians and, more recently, the Macedonian Slavs have yet to agree on the descent of the two brothers from Thessalonica, Cyril and Methodius, who in the ninth century started evangelizing as Byzantine Christian missionaries among the Slavs. Likewise, Bulgarian and Macedonian Slav historians still cannot find a consensus on the lineage of the nineteenth-century revolutionary Goce Delčev.

The Balkan tendency to appropriate historical figures and contest their ethnic roots and belonging is also manifested in the ongoing controversy about the origin of the Albanian hero Gjergj Kastrioti, also known as Skanderbeg. Gjergj Kastrioti was the son of Gjon Kastrioti, a fifteenth-century Albanian ruler, who opposed the Ottoman invasion. Following his father's defeat, Gjergj and his brothers were taken hostage by the Sultan. During his time in Turkey, Gjergj excelled himself as the leader of several military campaigns. In recognition of his achievements, the Sultan made him a General and bestowed upon him the title 'Iskander Bey', or 'Lord Alexander', in honour of Alexander the Great.

In spite of the recognition and privileges he received in Istanbul, Iskander Bey or 'Skanderbeg', as the Albanians came to address him, returned to Albania where he led a successful resistance against the Ottomans for twenty-five years. His defiance of the Ottomans was important not only for Albania and the Balkans, but also for Europe. Skanderbeg did an inestimable service to dithering Catholic Europe at a time when militant Islam was a real threat to the West. Were the Albanian castle to fall, the English knight John Newport wrote in 1456, 'the invasion of Europe is certain because no other power would be able to mount the same resistance'. Unfortunately, Western Europe failed to return the favour to Skanderbeg when he needed support. Frustrated with the chronic indecision and shifty attitudes of the Church leaders when it came to offering help to his army, Skanderbeg told a Cardinal in Rome on 17 February 1467: 'I should have fought against the Church first then the Sultan.'[26] Pope Pius II and other pontiffs had no hesitation in giving Skanderbeg the title *Athleta Christi* (Champion of Christ), but this athlete of Christendom was often left on his own to run the European resistance against the Ottomans. No wonder that when he died in 1468 not just Albania, the Balkans and the Papal States but the whole of Catholic Europe felt vulnerable.

The appeal of heroes like Skanderbeg is so strong that they are always bound to find admirers and followers beyond their own 'ethnic' group. In this long process of admiration and imitation, their partial and at times complete appropriation by peoples and countries other than their 'own' gradually becomes inevitable. The interest that those highly ambitious and successful individuals generate through countless generations across several nations at different stages in history is testimony to their exceptional charisma, power and, above all, their apparent ability to defy oblivion, our deadliest enemy, through their immortal fame. These heroes, their lives and their achievements that seem to outlast nations, cultures and civilizations are visited and revisited indefinitely in the hope that they will give up at some point the secret of how they could achieve so much within a human being's limited lifespan and, in the case of Alexander, in just 33 years. They and their deeds are the nearest thing that can make us believe that, small and insignificant as we humans appear to be in the cosmic order of things, our potential is limitless.

As time goes by, what we know about heroes like Alexander and Skanderbeg is no longer history; these historical figures turn into legends. As is often the case, legends and historical facts are not always compatible. Which is just as well. Alexander and Skanderbeg would cease to be what they are if reality and fantasy, fact and fiction, historical detail and pure imagination did not intersect so effortlessly. Without undermining their historical achievements, what is important in the end about such heroes, what makes them unique, is that we have made them what they are, and they are what we want them to be. This is one of the reasons why they constantly generate heated debates, unconfirmed doubts and endless controversies. Without this elusiveness, ancient heroes would lose their ability to be reincarnated by different parties that want to keep them 'alive' for various reasons at specific stages in their history.

Famous ancient people can be a bone of contention between various regions of the same country.[27] Hero appropriation becomes more of a serious problem, however, when it involves different nations. In such cases efforts to appropriate each other's heroes result in international tensions because they are often seen as (and at times are) an orchestrated attempt to fabricate history. So, for instance, according to uncorroborated speculations, Skanderbeg's family allegedly had a 'foreign' connection. Even if such an 'alien' link proves to be true, this would not make him less Albanian, and it certainly does not prove that he was a 'Slav' – Macedonian, Serb, Bulgarian – as some Balkan scholars and politicians hypothesize. In September 2004, Eleonora Petrova-Mitevska, a member of the Macedonian parliament, declared that 'Gjergj Kastrioti Skanderbeg is Macedonian and he has fought to protect Macedonian history and territories'.[28] While it is true that Skanderbeg's resistance was intended to protect the Balkans from the Turks, he did not do this simply because he allegedly had a Slavic connection. When Skanderbeg was alive, the Macedonia that Petrova-Mitevska has in mind had hardly produced an independent culture, tradition and resistance of its own worthy of tempting Turkish Sultans to travel all the way from Istanbul to destroy them. As we will see shortly in this chapter, the Macedonian Slav identity is a much later creation.

Petrova-Mitevska's gaffe enraged the Albanians. Several Albanian politicians in Macedonia wasted no time in responding in kind to their 'not very learned' Macedonian colleague, arguing that her remarks were further proof of some Macedonian Slav politicians' and intellectuals' attempts to fabricate the history of modern Macedonia by appropriating Albanian historical figures.[29] The incident, which did not help the already tense ethnic relations between the Macedonian Slavs and the Albanians in Macedonia, reminded the two 'camps' once again of their other row about the origin of Mother Teresa which had started in the spring of 2003 and is still ongoing.

iv. The Macedonian Slavs and Mother Teresa

The controversies between the Macedonian Slavs and the Albanians over the origin of Alexander the Great, Skanderbeg and Mother Teresa could be interpreted as signs of an identity crisis which the new state of Macedonia is going through in the wake of its independence in the early 1990s. While it has been widely acknowledged that the Illyrians were the ancient predecessors of the Albanians, the present-day Macedonians' claim that they are the descendants of the ancient Macedonians remains wishful thinking. The Slavs started settling in the Balkans from the third to the seventh century AD. Ancient Macedonia itself was colonized by the Slavs in the seventh century AD. Ethnically, culturally and, more importantly, linguistically speaking the Macedonian Slavs have little connection with the ancient Macedonian ethnicity, culture and language. Ancient Macedonia had its beginnings in the eighth century BC, began to flourish in the fifth century BC, reached its zenith during the reigns of Philip II and Alexander, and ceased to have any significance as an ancient power after 146 BC when it became a Roman province.

Following the collapse of Rome, Macedonian territories came under the authority of the Byzantines, Bulgarians, Greeks, Albanians, Turks and Serbs. Present-day Macedonia emerged as an independent state in 1991 following its secession from the former Yugoslavia. The christening of this new country 'Macedonia' did not go down very well in the Balkans. Bulgaria and Greece, for instance, have traditionally seen Macedonia as part of 'their' territories, which explains why these two countries, especially Greece, took issue not only with the name of 'Macedonia' but also with its very existence as an independent state. This is a dispute which, if it gets out of control, could easily destabilize an already tense Balkans.

While the new Macedonia that emerged after the collapse of Yugoslavia is officially a multi-ethnic state, it is the Macedonian Slavs who still have the final say on how the country is run. In an effort to present themselves as a nation that can be taken seriously in the region and beyond, the Macedonian Slavs pay too much attention to the 'Macedonian identity', which essentially means Macedonian Slav identity. This policy has hardly endeared non-Slavic communities to the Macedonian Slavs, especially the Albanians who, according to figures released in December 2003 by the Macedonian Institute for Statistics, make up 25.17 per cent of the country's population.[30]

The discriminatory practices apparent in governmental departments, police force and education were some of the causes of the armed conflict in spring 2001 between the Macedonian state and Albanian guerrilla fighters, who demanded equal rights for the Albanian population. The prompt intervention of the international community fortunately avoided the escalation of the conflict, but this country may face further difficulties. The raging war of words on the ethnicity of Mother Teresa and Skanderbeg indicates that the two major ethnic groups in the Republic of Macedonia are becoming increasingly sensitive about and over-protective of their cultural heritage, history and heroes.

The row over Mother Teresa's origin is particularly interesting in view of the fact that, unlike Alexander the Great and Skanderbeg, she did not live in the distant past. One would normally assume that in Mother Teresa's case there should be no room for biographical ambiguities because everything about her life and work can be easily traced and verified. Many people who knew her intimately as a child, as a young girl and as a nun are still alive and they can clarify any detail about her life and work that has been reported inaccurately either by mistake or on purpose.

Determining Mother Teresa's ethnic origin should not be difficult also because, unlike her two illustrious Balkan expatriates, Alexander the Great and Skanderbeg, she was not royalty. Nor did she come from an ancient aristocratic family that had to use inter-ethnic marriages to consolidate, maintain or expand its power and influence.

This does not mean, however, that Mother Teresa was a 'commoner', or a Balkan 'peasant', as most of her Western and Indian friends and opponents maintain indirectly or openly in their books. Both parents of the 'plebeian' nun came from well-to-do families that had earned their fortune through hard work over several generations.[31] It is true that her parents' marriage was an arranged one, and that their families' wealth and social status played a role in bringing them together.[32] Both parents, however, were born in Albania and were Albanians. Mother Teresa's brother Lazar Bojaxhiu emphasized all the time that his parents and their descendants were Albanians from Kosova, his mother's family being originally from Novosela near the town of Gjakova, and that of his father from Prizren.[33]

For reasons which will be explained later in this chapter and in chapter four, Mother Teresa herself was never keen to mention her nationality when she talked to the press. There were occasions, however, when she made it absolutely clear that she was Albanian. So, for example, when she was awarded the Nobel Peace prize in Oslo in 1979 she told the curious international media during one of the ceremonies that '[b]y blood and origin I am *all Albanian*' (emphasis added).[34] Considering that Mother Teresa's brother and, more importantly, Mother Teresa herself were always consistent about their Albanian origin, it makes no sense to argue that her descent is far from clear. Surely Mother Teresa was the best authority on the issue of her ethnic origin.

The Macedonian Slavs have always been aware of the fact that, as far as her ethnicity is concerned, Mother Teresa never pretended that she was anything other than Albanian. All the same, this has not stopped some of them casting doubt on her Albanian roots. Macedonia has its fair share of Mother Teresa experts among the Macedonian Slavs and the Albanians who have recently tried hard to find in a few hand-picked letters, speeches and remarks of Mother Teresa crumbs of evidence of her 'lifetime' attachment and devotion either to Macedonia or Albania. Some Macedonian Slav artists, scholars, reporters and politicians, who have taken a keen interest in and have written widely on her, such as Tome Serafimovski, Jasmina Mironski and Stojan Trenčevski,[35] the president of the association 'Skopje Woman Mother Teresa', are keen to score points over their Albanian rivals not only with regard to the fact that, in their view, she spoke little or no Albanian but, more importantly, that during one of her visits to Skopje she refused to give a straightforward answer when asked repeatedly if she was Albanian, Macedonian, Vlach, Serbian or of any other nationality. 'I am a citizen of Skopje, the city of my birth,' she told the reporters eventually, 'but I belong to the world.' During the same visit, referring to the 1963 earthquake, which had almost flattened her native city, she remarked: 'It may look completely different, but it is still my Skopje.'[36]

For a devoted Roman Catholic like Mother Teresa, 'my Skopje' did not necessarily mean the capital of the predominantly Orthodox Christian Republic of Macedonia. Nor did she refer to the city of her birth as 'my Skopje' purely because it had been inhabited by Albanians since ancient times. The possessive adjective 'my' in this case refers to the Skopje of her childhood memories, something she was keen to emphasize repeatedly:

> If there were not so much concrete we could be walking on the pavements of the streets where I spent *my childhood*. I am glad to see these places again. At least for a short time I am back in *my childhood*. (emphasis added)[37]

More importantly, perhaps, Mother Teresa referred to the city of her birth as 'my Skopje' because of its sixteen centuries of documented Catholic legacy. Ancient Skopje was one of the region's thriving cities during Roman and Byzantine times. The Illyrians, like the Greeks, came into contact with Christianity during the Apostolic age. In 'The Letter of Paul to the Romans', the apostle states that 'from Jerusalem and as far around as Illyricum I have fully proclaimed the good news of Christ'.[38] The ancestors of the present-day Albanians were among the first Europeans to convert to Christianity. As early as the first century AD, they had established in the city of Dyrrachium (present-day Durrës) one of the world's earliest bishoprics. By the end of the third century AD, the Albanians were Christianized. This means that they became Christians over a century before the pagan Roman conquerors underwent their 'conversion of convenience',[39] and at least six centuries before any of the neighbouring Slav nations, including the Macedonian Slavs, decided to adopt Europe's 'official' religion.

Mother Teresa's Skopje had its own bishop by the fourth century AD, and since then some of the Albanians in the town have remained faithful

to the teachings of Christ. Skopje's loyalty to Christianity, obviously, made
the city of her birth very special to the devoted Albanian Catholic nun
because it symbolized her own people's exemplary attachment to Christ.
It was primarily in this respect, one could argue, that Skopje had a special
place in her heart, and why she, it is claimed, called herself a 'Skopjanka',
someone from Skopje.[40]

For some Macedonian Slavs, however, an Albanian Mother Teresa
apparently was and still remains unacceptable for several reasons. Like
the Serbs, the Macedonian Slavs have considered the Albanians a millen-
nium-old obstacle to the colonization of some parts of the Balkans.
Throughout their long struggle for national survival, though, the Albanians
have never considered the Macedonian Slavs a serious threat. Their greatest
danger has always come from the Serbs whose dream of colonizing the
Albanian territories started as early as the ninth century. The following
discussion on Serbia's territorial ambitions over lands populated by the
Albanians may seem like an unnecessary digression from the topic in question and from the main focus of the book but is vital to an understanding
of the reasons why the Macedonian Slavs, like the Serbs, are far from
happy to admit that Mother Teresa was Albanian, and are determined to
'prove' the Albanians wrong.

Finding a 'final solution' to the Albanian 'obstacle' that has always
undermined Serbia's overt ambition for absolute control over the southern
Balkans has consistently been at the heart of the Serbian expansionist
policy. This is articulated very clearly in 'The Expulsion of the Albanians'
memorandum. This revealing document, which represents the 'bible' of
the uncompromising Serbian colonialist policy, was penned by Vaso
Čubrilović, a Serbian academic and statesman who was a member of the
group that plotted the assassination of Archduke Franz Ferdinand in 1914.
The memorandum was presented to the government of Milan Stoyadinovic
(1935–1939) in Belgrade on 7 March 1937. Incidentally, this Serbian-
born prime minister and academic was one of several Serbian politicians
and intellectuals who ardently admired and supported both Hitler and
Mussolini. After criticizing in his memorandum what he calls 'the slow
and cumbersome strategy of gradual colonization'[41] his country had
followed in the past, Čubrilović puts forward a detailed strategy according
to which Serbia would eventually get rid once and for all of the Albanians
by deporting them *en masse* to Turkey and expelling the rest of them to
Albania proper. He is confident that only 'the brute force of an organized state'[42] and 'coercion by the state apparatus' would 'make staying
intolerable for the Albanians'[43] in their ancient homeland in Kosova. The
ethnically cleansed Albanian lands, he goes on, would then be populated
with 'arrogant, ireascible and merciless' Montenegrins,[44] who would
eventually develop 'a less local and more broad-minded, Serbian out-
look',[45] and Serbian 'colonists' from impoverished parts of Serbia. Only
by completely eradicating the Albanian population in Kosova, would Serbia

finally consolidate its absolute control over 'this strategic point', which, to a large degree, determines 'the fate of the central Balkans'.[46] Equally important for the Serbs, notes Čubrilović, is fulfilling the ambition to establish territorial contact with the Macedonian Slavs:

> From an ethnic point of view, the Macedonians will only unite with us, if they receive true ethnic support from their Serbian motherland, something which they have lacked to this day. This can only be achieved through the destruction of the Albanian wedge.[47]

Čubrilović's 1937 memorandum was followed by other similar and at times more vicious plans proposing even the complete elimination of the Albanian state, an idea first put forward in the London Treaty of 26 April 1915. Such plans were formulated during World War II by several Serbian intellectuals and politicians including Ivan Vukotić, Stevan Moljević, and the 1961 Nobel Prize laureate for literature Ivo Andrić.[48] Čubrilović himself submitted a second memorandum on 3 November 1944, this time entitled 'The Minority Problem in the New Yugoslavia', arguing that '[t]he democratic federation of Yugoslavia will only achieve peace and ensure its development if it can be made ethnically pure'.[49] As in the first memorandum, Čubrilović is adamant that the only way to do this is to follow the example of the Third Reich in dealing with the 'alien element'. According to Čubrilović, all minorities in Yugoslavia 'deserve to lose their right of citizenship'.[50] Čubrilović believes that the expulsion of ethnic minorities, especially of the Albanians in Kosova, would be carried out efficiently only by the military. In his words, 'the army must be brought in, even during the war, to cleanse the regions we wish to settle with our own people, doing so in a well-planned but ruthless manner'.[51] By now Čubrilović is careful not to give the impression to fellow Slavic nations, especially Croatia, that he has only the interests of Serbia at heart.[52] Although this demagogue is eager to sound more like a 'Yugoslav' citizen than someone masterminding Serbian expansionist policy, he makes no secret of his ultimate goal, which is Serbia's ethnic conquest of Kosova.[53] Only by completely colonizing all the Albanian lands in the south of the Balkans on behalf of Serbia, Čubrilović concludes, '[are we] to reach our goal of linking Montenegro, Serbia and Macedonia'.[54]

Like most other Slavs living in the republics comprising the former Yugoslavia, the Macedonian Slavs were also unhappy with the influence the Serbs wanted to exert in the running of the federation that emerged after the Second World War. Unlike other fellow Slavs, however, the Macedonian Slavs were more inclined to put up with 'the jailer of the other Yugoslav nations', as Serbia was often referred to within the federation and internationally,[55] because of the Serbs' uncompromising stance on the issue of the complete colonization of the Albanian lands south of their border. As far as the Macedonian Slavs are concerned, a Kosova without Albanians would weaken significantly the Albanian community in the Republic of Macedonia. The Macedonians Slavs have never been able to implement any plan to ethnically cleanse the Albanians living in Albanian lands in the Republic of Macedonia on the scale and with the openness pursued for so long by the Serbs. On the other hand, like the Serbs, they have always been eager to denigrate the Albanians and anything Albanian. The official, degrading discourse employed by numerous Serbian leaders, epitomized in the racist remarks of the Serbian prime minister Vladan Djordjević (1844–1930), who saw the Albanians as 'pre-humans',[56] is also present in the rhetoric of some Macedonian Slav and Montenegrin politicians and intellectuals, the main aim of which is to deny Albanians their Illyrian descent[57] and present them as 'uncivilized'.

By demonizing the Albanians relentlessly, the Serbian-led Slavic coalition hoped that the Western powers would in the end allow them to eliminate completely this non-Slavic nation. After all, by getting rid of the Albanian 'savages', the Serbs and their fellow Montenegrin and Macedonian Slavs were apparently doing a huge favour to Western Europe. It was imperative that the West should perceive these three allies' colonization of the Albanian lands as 'absolutely necessary' to avoid an 'imminent danger' awaiting Europe by the 'non-European' Albanians.

To achieve this ambitious task, the Serbian politicians needed something of an ideological footing. The Serbian army and its Slavic mercenaries could not do the job properly unless their brutality was backed up with 'scholarly' and 'scientific' arguments that 'justified' the disintegration, assimilation and finally the elimination of the Albanian nation as a must to safeguard not so much Serbia's interests but the very future of Western civilization.

Vaso Čubrilović believed that 'the expulsion of the Albanians as quickly as possible and resettlement by our colonists'[58] required 'close collaboration between the government, private initiative and scholarly institutions'.[59] He was adamant that Serbian intellectuals in particular had a vital role to play in 'selling' Serbia's colonial policy to the Serbian people and, more importantly, to Western Europe as perfectly 'rational'. In a tone which is both admonishing and inviting, in his 1937 memorandum Čubrilović drew attention to the fact that Serbian educational and research institutions

> have begun to lose the prestige they once had. . . . Many billions would have been saved in this country, many mistakes would have been avoided in our government policy, including our colonization policy, had the problems been studied seriously and objectively in advance by competent scholars before they were taken up for solution. Our policy of colonization, likewise, would have acquired a more serious approach, greater continuity and effective application, had the opinions of experts and scholars been sought in advance. To start

with, the Royal Serbian Academy of Sciences and the University of Belgrade ought to take the initiative to organize *scientific studies of the whole problem of colonization* in our country. This would be feasible for many reasons. At the university we have experts on every aspect of colonization. Teachers and academicians at the university are independent scholars, less subject to external political influence. They already have good experience in such fields and their scholarly work is a guarantee of objectivity. They should, therefore, take the initiative of setting up a *colonization institute*, the task of which would be to pursue *colonization studies*. (emphasis added)[60]

As is obvious from Čubrilović's assessment, Serbian academics have always been loyal adherents and nurturers of the Serbian dream of domination of the Balkans. In Čubrilović's own words, his scholarly fellow countrymen 'already have good experience in such fields'. Being a university professor himself, Čubrilović was, of course, speaking as a well-informed insider. What Čubrilović was asking of his colleagues now was that they be much more active and sophisticated during the renewed and well-funded campaign to present all non-Serbs living in territories ruled by Belgrade, especially the Albanians in Kosova and across Yugoslavia, as racially inferior, cultureless and historyless.

The constant onslaught on Albanian history, language, culture and tradition waged by numerous Serbian, Montenegrin and Macedonian Slav scholars, the attempt to present the Albanians as a nation with no heroes of their own, and the claim that most noted Albanian national leaders, poets, artists, linguists and scientists are not of Albanian origin,[61] were meant to further humiliate this ancient and proud nation.

This carefully orchestrated propaganda campaign to besmear the Albanians has been constantly challenged but never more seriously than in the case of Mother Teresa. Her emergence as an international humanitarian icon inevitably shattered as never before the Serbian myth that the Albanians were 'barbarians'. How could someone like Mother Teresa, who came to epitomize the best of human spirit in a century dominated by savage wars and bloodshed, come from 'Albanian stock'? Surely, a nation of 'thieves', 'hooligans', 'thugs', 'arsonists', 'kidnappers', 'drug-dealers', 'rapists', 'human traffickers', 'terrorists' and 'pimps' (some of the derogatory terms used by Serbian and Macedonian propaganda to demonize the Albanians) who have always caused 'problems' among the Slavs in the Balkans, 'initiated' the disintegration of Yugoslavia, and are currently posing a grave danger to Western civilization with their 'obvious' links to the international mafia, could not produce a dove of peace like Mother Teresa. It was only logical, therefore, that Mother Teresa was not, could not, and should not be Albanian. If she could not be a Macedonian Slav, a Serb or a Croat, she must certainly be a Vlach, a Roma, a Venetian – anything but an Albanian.

Mother Teresa was and appears still to be unacceptable to the Serbs and the Macedonian Slavs not only for her humanitarian spirit but, more importantly, also for her staunch faith. The Serbs' vitriolic attacks on Albanian culture, history, language, tradition and personalities, attacks which, as Čubrilović admits with disturbing frankness, after 1878 included 'secretly razing Albanian villages and urban settlements to the ground' with 'great practical effect',[62] have somehow served their purpose to alienate some European countries from the Albanians. Such acts of vandalism, however, were never deemed effective enough to completely demonize the Albanians in the eyes of all the European nations. For the Albanians to be seen as a constant 'grave peril' to Europe, they had to be presented as a 'mob' that 'endangered' the very 'essence' of modern European 'identity': Christianity.

Many Serbian scholars in conjunction with the Serbian Orthodox Church believed that they had finally found in Islam the most efficient weapon with which to humiliate the unruly Albanians and alienate them forever from Europe. The plan was simple but had far-reaching consequences. The Serbs were to present themselves as a nation with a biblical mission in the second millennium, a mission which included stopping the advance of the Ottomans and, more importantly, crushing a 'demonic' people like the Albanians, who were 'dangerous' to Europe not only because they were 'uncivilized', but also because they were not Christians, and, even worse, because some of them had committed the dreadful sin of apostasy. Obviously, the Serbs were indispensable if Christianity were to remain Europe's uncontested religion.

The myth of the Serbs as defenders and martyrs of the Christian faith has its roots in the misrepresentation of an important event in the history of the Balkans, the Battle of Kosova. This infamous battle is in essence a remarkable show of unity on the part of several Balkan rulers determined to oppose the advance of the Ottomans in the Balkans. The Balkan rebels must have caused the Turkish Sultan quite a headache to have made him order and lead himself a fearsome punitive expedition against them. The major battle between Murat I's army and the Balkan alliance troops took place on the Plain of Kosova in June 1389. In spite of their unity and valour, the Balkan coalition proved to be no match for the mighty Ottoman army.

The Balkan resistance this time was led by Prince Lazar of Serbia, but the alliance itself included many nationalities from the region, including the Albanians.[63] For several centuries to come, this fourteenth-century battle was a bitter memory for many Balkan nations, a painful reminder of a common defeat against a common enemy. In the nineteenth century, however, Serbian nationalists and the Serbian Orthodox Church, helped by some collectors of Serbian epics and poets such as Vuk Karadžić and Petar II Petrović-Njegoš, claimed that the battle was a key event only in the history of the Serbian nation. This meant that the 1389 defeat ceased to be a Balkan defeat; instead it became exclusively a Serbian defeat. This battle, the Serbs have claimed for more than a hundred years, is testimony to the Serbian nation's suffering in the name of Christ.

The conversion of some Albanian rulers to Islam in the wake of the 1433–1468 Skanderbeg-led Albanian resistance was used by some nineteenth-century Serbian politicians, scholars and leaders of the Serbian Orthodox Church to present the Albanians as non-Christian, and as such a non-indigenous European people. According to the new Serbian version of the Battle of Kosova, the Albanians had not fought alongside the Serbs against the Turks but on the side of the Turks against Prince Lazar's army. Serbian propaganda was eager to paint all Albanian Muslims as Turks or Islamicized Serbs, and every Albanian national movement as an Albanian attempt to establish a Muslim state at the heart of Christian Europe. The Serbs employed the rhetoric of the crusaders to give legitimacy to their colonization policy across Albanian lands.

That the Serbs waged terror against the Albanians not simply because they allegedly wanted to defend Christianity but primarily because they intended to colonize their lands is obvious from the brutality they showed at the start of the twentieth century against both Muslim and Catholic Albanians. Attempts were made to coerce Albanian Catholics to renounce Catholicism and convert forcibly to the Orthodox faith. Faced with conversion or death, some Albanian Catholics apostasized; those who refused were massacred.[64] As in similar earlier campaigns, the Serbs appropriated Albanian churches and other religious sites, thus reinforcing the myth that Kosova was the cradle not just of the Serbian nation but more importantly of their proverbial devotion to Christianity. The Orthodox Serbs' employment of 'religious rhetoric to justify the defence of "sacred" Serbian interests,' holds Noel Malcolm, is 'a classic example of religion being mobilized and manipulated for ideological purposes'.[65]

This mobilization and manipulation of religion was apparent throughout the existence of Yugoslavia. Some Albanians in the Yugoslav federation were rather naïve at times in seeing Islam as 'their' national religion, but they were also conveniently 'helped' by the Yugoslav authorities, especially the Serbs, and the Macedonian Slavs to distance themselves from Christianity and stick to 'their' Islamic 'roots'. So, for instance, while on the one hand the Albanians in the post World War II Yugoslavia were constantly prohibited from baptizing their children with Albanian names, on the other hand, they were always encouraged to use Muslim names instead. Likewise, throughout the twentieth century, while Serbian and Macedonian governments constantly forbade the Albanians from opening schools in their native language, they would welcome any effort on the part of the Albanians to build mosques or open *madrasas*. In a Yugoslavia that followed an openly discriminating policy in employment towards the Albanians, becoming an *imam* was one of the few career opportunities open to many young Albanians. According to Sokol Shameti, this is the main reason behind the surplus of *imams* in Macedonia.[66] The 'traditional good will' of the Yugoslav, Serbian and Macedonian authorities towards the Albanians' 'religious sentiments' explains why in Albania proper, in contrast to Kosova and Macedonia, Islam is not, and never has been, seen as an integral part of Albanian national identity, but mainly as a legacy of the Ottoman occupation.

The Serbs mobilized and manipulated religion, especially throughout the 1990s when the Serbian ultranationalists led by Slobodan Milošević were largely responsible for the disintegration of Yugoslavia. In his 1984 address to the members of the League of Communists at the University of Belgrade, Milošević made it clear that he foresaw a leading role for the Serbian Orthodox Church in interpreting the interests of the Serbian nation. As in the past, throughout the wars that engulfed Yugoslavia at the end of the twentieth century, it was the Serbian Orthodox Church that originated and sustained the discourse according to which the Serbs were the 'martyred Christians' of the Balkans whom Europe must listen to and help. The Serbian Orthodox Church was instrumental in generating the 'promised land' theme employed constantly by Milošević and his team of fanatic nationalists during the Kosova war of 1999 in an attempt to present their ethnic cleansing policy against the Albanians as a God-given mission to defend not just their Christian heritage in Kosova but also the whole of Christendom from the Muslims.

As during the time of Čubrilović, even when Yugoslavia was falling apart, fanatical Serbian nationalists and the Serbian Orthodox Church relied heavily on their traditional allies, Serbian academics. Several Serbian scholars and journalists-turned-politicians like Dobrica Ćosić, Vojislav Koštunica and Vuk Drašković remain staunch supporters of the now-discredited thesis regarding the legitimacy of the Serbs' claim over Kosova as the holy cradle of Serbia.

Much to the Serbs' disappointment, the Europe of the 1990s had changed considerably from the Europe that at the beginning of the twentieth century had kept quiet about or, even worse, condoned the atrocities committed by the Serbian army against the Albanians. The intervention of the international community to stop the ethnic cleansing of Kosova in 1999 indicated that the Western powers were no longer duped by, and some were unwilling to have anything to do with, Serbia's rhetoric and colonization policy in the southern Balkans, at least not publicly. Eighty-six years after the dismemberment of the Albanian nation at the London Conference in 1913, a dismemberment which came about partly as a result of Serbian propaganda about the 'danger' the Albanian Muslims apparently posed to Christian Europe, the West finally decided not to ignore any longer the Albanians' plight. Obviously, the Albanian question had never been an Islamic question in the first place.

Following the example of the extreme Serbian nationalists and of the Serbian Orthodox Church, many Macedonian Slav politicians, religious leaders, intellectuals and reporters were eager to present the Albanian guerrilla fighters during the 2001 conflict not as frustrated individuals who were fed up with being treated as second-class citizens in their own country and were determined to put an end to institutionalized discrimination and racism, but as Islamic terrorists. Human Rights Watch expressed concerns about 'endemic police abuse' against the Albanians in Macedonia in 1996, 1998 and again in 2001.[67] Like the Serbs, the Macedonian Slavs failed in their attempts to convince the Western powers that the outraged Albanians in Macedonia were Muslim separatists. Partly because of the pressure from the international community and partly because it was obvious that they could not put down on their own the growing Albanian armed resistance, the government of Macedonia had no option but to sign the Ohri Peace Agreement in August 2001.

Even after the agreement, many Macedonian Slav intellectuals and politicians kept on 'warning' Europe of the Islamic 'danger' coming from the Albanians. Unable to provide any valid proof of their accusations, they tried hard to establish a link between the Albanians in Kosova and Macedonia, the Albanian state and Al-Qaeda in the wake of the terrorist attacks against the United States of America on 11 September 2001. Often during his trial at The Hague, where he was held accused of committing crimes against humanity, Slobodan Milošević tried, albeit without success, to 'enlighten' the UN tribunal regarding the notion that the Albanians and Osama Bin Laden are 'inseparable'. Milošević also claimed that his trial would fuel terrorism (read Islamic terrorism) in the Balkans.[68] Articles of a sensationalist nature penned by several Western writers have been used unscrupulously in Serbian and Macedonian Slav propaganda as 'absolute proof' that the Albanians are 'guilty' as charged.[69]

The news from the Vatican that Pope John Paul II was to beatify Mother Teresa in October 2003 obviously upset those Serbs and Macedonian Slavs who had been trying hard to vilify the Albanians, especially the guerrilla fighters in Kosova and in Tetova in Macedonia, as Muslim terrorists. As far as those who generated, used or hid behind the Serbian and Macedonian Slav propaganda were concerned, a Catholic nun like Mother Teresa, who was venerated as a 'saint' by millions of Christian and non-Christian believers and secular people worldwide when she was alive and who was well on the road to canonization only six years after her death, was not, could not and, more importantly, should not be Albanian.

Mother Teresa's Albanian origin, especially the fact that her parents came from an ancient Catholic Albanian family in the Albanian town of Prizren in Kosova, made a farce of the claim made by extremist Serbian nationalists and the Serbian Orthodox Church that the Albanians in Kosova were all Muslims. Likewise, the fact that she was born to Albanian parents settling down and prospering amidst the ancient thriving Catholic Albanian community in Skopje meant that the ultranationalists among the Macedonian Slavs and some leaders of the Macedonian Orthodox Church, too, had to reconsider their long-held line about the Albanians in Macedonia being non-native or all Muslims.

That some Macedonian Slavs were and still are far from happy to admit that Mother Teresa was Albanian is apparent by the fact that in many conferences, symposiums, exhibitions, radio and television programmes and documentaries, books and CD-ROMs dedicated to her in Macedonia, her Albanian roots are almost completely ignored. In most cases, her ethnicity is mentioned mainly to emphasize that she was of a mixed-ethnic origin. To this day, Mother Teresa's name in the monuments dedicated to her in Skopje is written only in Cyrillic or English. Even her original Albanian name 'Gonxhe Bojaxhiu' is inscribed in English as 'Gondza Bojadziu'.

Only recently, as a result of the pressure exerted by Albanian politicians and intellectuals in Macedonia, and because their attempts to present Mother Teresa as a non-Albanian did not have any impact on the West's perception of her, some Macedonian Slav politicians have started making a few condescending remarks about Mother Teresa's Albanian origin. It is obvious that the Macedonian government can no longer afford to ignore the Catholic nun's Albanian roots.

For an impoverished country like Macedonia that is eager to join the European Union as soon as possible, Mother Teresa is seen as excellent PR, a means of showing Europe that freedom of religion and other civil and political rights are allegedly guaranteed by the Macedonian state equally to all ethnic groups in the country, including the Albanians. Mother Teresa, some Macedonian Slav politicians apparently believe, can help them to improve the country's recently tarnished image. And they may be right. The saint might not have seen herself as a Macedonian Slav, or a representative of the Republic of Macedonia when she trotted the globe as an international religious and media celebrity, but she can still be useful after her death to the former Yugoslav Republic of Macedonia, or the FYROM, as this country is still bizarrely known internationally. This is one of the reasons why in April 2006 the Macedonian parliament approved the 'Mother Teresa Award', which will be given to distinguished personalities for their contribution to humanitarian work and culture.

v. The Albanians and Mother Teresa

Many Albanians apparently needed a figure like Mother Teresa during the 1990s. Known to the world mainly as economic migrants fleeing from poverty in Albania, and as political refugees escaping from Serbian prosecution in Kosova, the Albanians found in the person, faith, celebrity status and charity work of Mother Teresa a source of immense pride and inspiration. They felt that she had somehow restored their dented dignity. Through her, the Albanians could tell the world that they should not be judged only on the basis of their poverty, that poor as some of them are, they are also an immensely spiritual and humanitarian people who 'can produce inspiring figures of world stature'.[70] Those who look down upon them only have to look at the consistency with which Mother Teresa devoted herself to Christianity and the poor of Calcutta and the world. As far as ordinary Albanians are concerned, it was no accident that a saintly figure like her was Albanian. How exactly her Albanian roots influenced Mother Teresa, however, is something that her devoted Albanian admirers have yet to explain.

But while the pride that ordinary Albanians derived from Mother Teresa in the late 1980s and throughout the 1990s was both therapeutic and genuine, the keen interest that several Albanian circles took in her was apparently motivated by the intention to further their political, nationalist and religious causes. The growing attention Albanians began to pay to their famous expatriate, especially after her first visit to Tirana in 1989, has been noted by several Mother Teresa scholars in the West. 'Within a year of her visit,' notes Emma Johnson, 'she had become a national hero in Albania, praised by both Christians and Muslims, and was featured on Albanian postage stamps and in its history books.'[71]

Albania's 'love affair' with the religious Mother Teresa, paradoxically enough, was initiated by the country's atheistic leaders in the late 1980s. Mother Teresa appears to have tried several times from the early 1960s onwards to obtain permission from the government of Albania to visit the country. Her requests, however, were allegedly turned down every time because of Enver Hoxha's insistence on keeping her away. Following Hoxha's death in 1985, his successor Ramiz Alia gradually changed the long-held officially hostile attitude towards Mother Teresa because he obviously believed his government could benefit by being friendly to the nun. By allowing her to visit Albania in 1989, the country's new Communist leader wanted to send out a signal to the West that, although he had been handpicked for the post by an atheist predecessor, he was still capable of and willing to steer Albania into a completely new direction of multi-party politics and religious tolerance. By the same token, Alia apparently saw the visit as another chance to warn hardliners in the Politburo that some radical changes, especially restoring freedom of religion, were not only inevitable but also imminent. To avoid open confrontation with the die-hard Communists, however, Alia was keen to present Mother Teresa's belated homecoming as a 'private visit'.[72]

Bearing in mind how hostile Enver Hoxha had allegedly been towards Mother Teresa, Alia was apparently eager that the nun's first visit should be perceived as being strictly for private reasons. Apparently he did not want to alienate Hoxha's widow, Nexhmije, who remained a very influential political figure in Albania until the disintegration of the Communist regime in 1991. How exactly Nexhmije reacted to Alia's plan to allow Mother Teresa to visit the country in 1989 is anybody's guess. Nor is it known how the nun ended up sending flowers to the grave of her 'committed adversary'. If Mother Teresa did indeed visit Albania in 1989 allegedly only to visit the graves of her mother and sister, who had passed away in 1972 and 1973 respectively, one would assume that an international religious and media icon like her would have been wise enough to avoid honouring in public a leader that many Albanians and most of the world saw as a dictator. It is possible that Nexhmije gave her consent to Mother Teresa's visit on condition that the nun pay her respects at her husband's grave. It is also likely that Mother Teresa agreed to pay a visit to Hoxha's grave as a gesture of gratitude to her hostess. After all, the invitation to visit the country was issued in Nexhmije's name.

So far no evidence has been found that Nexhmije herself had anything to do with her husband's alleged stubbornness not to allow Mother Teresa to visit Albania during his reign. Following their first encounter in 1989, Nexhmije has maintained that she has never had anything against the nun. On the contrary, according to the Italian journalist Riccardo Orizio, who met Hoxha's widow in prison shortly after the collapse of Communism, she spoke warmly about the nun. In his 2002 book *Talk of the Devil: Encounters with Seven Dictators*, Orizio quotes Nexhmije as saying: 'we liked Mother Teresa. You know, she felt at home here [in Albania].'[73] Nexhmije even claims that Mother Teresa was impressed with the efforts of the Communist government to benefit Albania. In her words, Mother Teresa was a 'true patriot' and a 'great Albanian'[74] who 'came with an open mind and praised our achievements'.[75]

Following Mother Teresa's 1989 visit, all Albania's politicians – those in power, and those who were trying to come to power – were eager to make public as often as possible their huge admiration for the country's newly discovered 'patriot', and took every opportunity to honour her accordingly. According to a 1992 presidential decree, Mother Teresa was entitled to travel on an Albanian diplomatic passport, if she chose to. The Communist-turned-democrat president Ramiz Alia created the 'Mother Teresa Prize' to be awarded to distinguished humanitarian and charity workers. On 27 November 1996, another Albanian president, Sali Berisha, awarded Mother Teresa the Order of 'The Nation's Honour'. The Albanian political establishment intensified its efforts to honour Mother Teresa especially towards the end of her life, and immediately after her death. The Albanian government announced three days of national mourning when the nun passed away on 5 September 1997. Shortly after her funeral, Rinas, the country's only international airport, was christened 'Mother Teresa Airport'. In Tirana, the central hospital and one of the main squares were also named after her.

Partly because of the Macedonian Slavs' efforts to appropriate her and ascribe her a non-Albanian origin after her death, and partly because they wanted to restore Albania's damaged reputation in the wake of the much publicized disturbances resulting from the collapse of the fraudulent pyramid schemes in the late 1990s, the Albanians' veneration for Mother Teresa turned almost into a national obsession in the months prior to her beatification in 2003. The Albanian government set up a 'special commission' headed by a minister of state to organize the activities before and after the beatification. Highly publicized events about Mother Teresa – conferences, symposiums, exhibitions, screening of documentaries and feature films, album promotions and concerts – were held everywhere. Albanian diplomats hosted numerous events about the nun in several countries.

On the eve of the beatification the 'special commission' announced plans to put a statue of the Albanian Catholic nun in one of the squares of the capital, and made a recommendation to President Alfred Moisiu to honour the Missionaries of Charity. Numerous politicians, intellectuals, writers, poets, composers, singers, instrumentalists, painters and, of course, a whole battalion of media people were keen to do and to be seen to be doing their bit so that not only the Albanian nation but, more importantly, the whole world, would see how dear Mother Teresa was to Albania. To honour their 'sainted' expatriate, some 2,000 people took part in a 'people's marathon' in Tirana in autumn 2003. And as if all these public manifestations of love and adoration were not enough, the Albanian government declared 19 October, the beatification day, a public holiday, and the October 2003–October 2004 period, the 'Year of Mother Teresa'.

The Kosova Albanians did not lag behind in their reverence for Mother Teresa. In fact, they have been even swifter to honour and appropriate her as an Albanian 'heroine' than their countrymen in Albania. As in Albania, the public adoration for Mother Teresa in Kosova grew especially in the 1990s. In 1990 the Mother Teresa Charity Organization was founded in the capital of Kosova, Prishtina. In the same year, Mother Teresa was made an honorary member of the Academy of Sciences and Arts of Kosova. Shortly before Mother Teresa's death, the then Kosova Albanian leader, Ibrahim Rugova, made her an Honorary Citizen of Kosova.

Anne Sebba believes that the Albanians took such a keen interest in Mother Teresa in 1989 because '[a]t first, officialdom described her simply as a well-known benefactress of Albanian origin, and many ordinary Albanians thought she was a wealthy expatriate returning to dispense money'.[76] Also, according to Sebba, the Albanians' excessive public adoration for the nun during the 1989–1997 period was motivated by their intention to persuade her to choose Albania as her final resting place. The biographer claims that, in 1995, there was even talk of Mother Teresa's 'apparent, but unlikely, wish' to be buried in Albania, something which 'would of course dramatically change the country's familiarity with tourism. Making Albania into a pilgrimage country might be the greatest gift Mother Teresa could give them'.[77]

The Albanians, especially those adhering to the Roman Catholic faith, were eager to know where Mother Teresa wanted to be laid to rest from the moment she became internationally famous. This was one of the questions she was asked by a fellow Albanian priest at a ceremony organized in her honour as a Nobel laureate in Oslo in December 1979. 'I have never thought about this,' Mother Teresa replied. 'No one, until now, has asked me about this. Let them bury me anywhere, they can do whatever they want with my body.'[78]

According to Lush Gjergji, when he asked Mother Teresa shortly before she passed away in 1997 where she wished to be buried, she had replied: 'In my country, but this is most unlikely. The Indians will never accept this'.[79] Whether or not the Indians would have refused to respect Mother Teresa's wish to be buried in Albania, in Skopje or in Kosova is difficult to say. Perhaps we also will never know if it was entirely up to Mother Teresa as to where she was to be buried. In the end Calcutta was chosen as the nun's final resting place, a decision which, according to Sebba, was motivated primarily by Mother Teresa's knowledge that her sisters would always tend her grave lovingly.[80]

Many celebrated Albanians living abroad over the past few centuries have publicly expressed their wish to be buried in Albania, but Mother Teresa, it seems, was not one of them. Her decision not to be buried in Albania, Kosova or Macedonia was seen by some of her countrymen in the Balkans as 'unpatriotic'.

While Mother Teresa's choice of Calcutta as her burial ground was another testimony to her attachment to the people of the city and of the India she undoubtedly loved and served for almost seventy years, the main reason why she decided to be buried in the subcontinent was primarily linked with her lifetime mission to serve Jesus. No matter how much or how little Christianity takes root in India in the future, Mother Teresa's grave is likely to remain for a long time to come a sacred spot for Christians, especially Catholics, worldwide, a frontier that will constantly invite and inspire future devout followers of Christ to keep on spreading his teachings there and in other parts of the world. Considering how much Christ meant to her, it is unlikely that she needed anyone to enlighten her as to the lasting service she would do to her Master, as she often called Jesus, by choosing Calcutta as her final resting place.

Aroup Chatterjee maintains that Mother Teresa had wanted (or expected) to be buried in Calcutta in the grounds of St John's Church in Sealdah, where many of her nuns are laid to rest. Her wish, however, was not fulfilled. On 9 September 1997, four days after her death, Calcutta's Catholic establishment announced to the media that Mother Teresa would be buried inside Mother° House on Acharya Jagadish Chandra Bose (Lower Circular) Road because 'they were worried that her grave would be desecrated'.[81] If Mother Teresa was indeed as dear to the

Calcuttans when she was alive as the Catholic and the world media often claimed throughout her life, the fears of the Calcutta Church leaders about the desecration of her grave seem to suggest that her reported 'immense popularity' in the city was perhaps somehow inflated.

One could argue that the desecration of her grave could have been a possibility even if she had been buried in the Balkans. In this region, as elsewhere in the world, deceased public figures are not always allowed to rest in peace. And not only the great and the good. Ethnic and religious hatred in this region has also never spared the ordinary dead. One of the infamous instigators of this irrational hatred, Čubrilović, would stop at nothing to ethnically cleanse Kosova of the Albanians. One of the 'practical' and 'effective' ways he recommended in 1937 to get rid of the Albanians once and for all included 'the demolition of their cemeteries'.[82]

The fact that Mother Teresa decided to be buried neither in Kosova, her parents' original home, nor in Skopje, her native city, indicates that she apparently had no intention of becoming another bone of contention for the Albanians, the Serbs and the Macedonian Slavs after her death. Her grave in Kosova or Macedonia would have been seen by the fanatical Serbian and Macedonian Slav nationalists as a mecca of Albanian patriotism. After all, some Albanians in Kosova and Macedonia had already started seeing and selling her as a national icon throughout the 1990s.

The question remains: would the famous nun's grave have been free from the risk of desecration had she been buried in Albania? Perhaps yes, but there have also been cases in Albania when the graves of well-known personalities have come under attack. So, for instance, in 1944 the Communists destroyed the impressive mausoleum of the Queen Mother, which King Zog had commissioned immediately after her death in 1934.[83] Shortly after Mother Teresa sent flowers to Enver Hoxha's grave in 1989, his statue was dragged through the streets of Tirana and his remains disinterred from the Nation's Martyrs Cemetery. If some Albanians could be so publicly disrespectful to their King's dead mother, who had stayed away from politics, and to an allegedly 'much-loved' leader like Hoxha, who, despite his many grave faults, had certainly devoted his life to his country in one way or another, what guarantees could Mother Teresa possibly have had that her grave in Albania would not generate controversy, or even worse, be desecrated? In spite of the fact that she was so popular among the Albanians in Albania, Kosova and Macedonia from the early 1990s until her death in 1997, she apparently had no reason to believe that such respect would last for ever after she was gone, especially in view of her official stance towards Kosova and Albania, an issue which will be addressed in more detail at the end of this chapter and in chapter four.

Mother Teresa is still venerated by ordinary Albanians of all faiths, but the enthusiasm with which Albanian politicians spoke about her in public on the eve of the beatification in October 2003 had waned considerably a year later. On the first anniversary of her beatification, many Albanians had forgotten that 19 October was meant to be a national holiday.[84] But it soon transpired that they were not being irreverent on purpose. The Albanian government had apparently simply failed to remind the people in advance of the significance of this particular date, a mistake which, of course, did not escape the attention of some politicians of the opposition, who used it to score points on behalf of their own parties. The Albanian authorities themselves were surprisingly reluctant to organize any public event to bring to an end what was announced with so much pomp and media hype twelve months earlier as the 'Year of Mother Teresa'. A couple of Albanian dailies published scathing comments about the Albanian politicians' obvious lack of interest to show up at any ceremony dedicated to the nation's saint on 19 October 2004, while a year earlier, they – friends and foes alike – had stampeded in droves towards the Vatican to attend the beatification ceremony.[85]

The Albanian media also expressed disappointment and even anger that, a year after the beatification, the Albanian government had not yet decided where to erect the monument dedicated to Mother Teresa.[86] The statue was finally unveiled on 9 December 2004 in the presence of no less than six Balkan presidents and the Prime Minister of Norway, who had come to Tirana to attend a summit on inter-religious and inter-ethnic dialogue.[87] The unveiling ceremony, however, was criticized by the Albanian media and several intellectuals for being too formal.[88] The Albanian government, it appears, did not bother to advertise the event in advance to attract the attention of ordinary Albanians. On the inauguration day, only a select group of Albanian and foreign dignitaries had the privilege to be in the company of the saint of the poor. The official ceremony was apparently seen by some Albanian politicians as yet another chance to show that, despite the criticism they had received earlier, they continue to hold Mother Teresa very dear, and are always delighted to express their veneration for her in public, especially in ceremonies attended by heads of state. These Albanian politicians would never miss a chance to flag up the nun's nationality and humanitarian work in the company of foreign dignitaries in Albania and abroad.

Like the Albanian politicians, the Albanian Catholic Church is using the figure of Mother Teresa for its own purposes. The leaders of the Church apparently believe that the sainted sister can be very useful in bringing this institution closer not only to the Catholics but also to people of other faiths. One effective way of doing this is by highlighting time and again the nun's 'devotion' to Albania. The official line of the Church is that Mother Teresa cared as much for her fellow Albanians as for the poor of India and the world, a line which has been proven 'infallible' in view of the evidence collected over the years. One such 'indisputable' piece of evidence was recovered immediately after Mother Teresa's death. When the Archbishop of Albania, Rrok Mirdita, returned from the nun's funeral in Calcutta in September 1997, he brought with him a rug, which some Albanian women apparently gave Mother Teresa as a present when she visited Albania in 1989.[89] Mother Teresa, we are told, prayed on this rug for eight years until the last moments of her life. The talismanic rug, which is now on display at St Paul's Cathedral in Tirana, is apparently seen by some of Mother Teresa's ardent admirers as a sign that she had always been a 'confirmed patriot'.

Mother Teresa's 'patriotism' is one of the preferred themes in Lush Gjergji's work on the nun. Gjergji is keen to emphasize that in his many meetings with Mother Teresa she constantly professed to him her 'undying love' for Albania and the Albanians.[90] That her own country and people were always in her mind, he argues, is exemplified especially by her words about the disintegration of law and order in Albania in the spring of 1997. Mother Teresa's 'actual' words, scribbled in March 1997, have been turned into a poem – 'Për Shqipërinë Time'/'For My Albania' – by the Albanian poet Visar Zhiti. The same poet has also versified Mother Teresa's last prayer 'Dua të kthehem në Shqipëri'/'I want to come back to Albania' which, according to Gjergji, the ailing nun wrote on 27 August 1997, only a few days before she passed away.[91]

An unbiased reader, who is familiar with Mother Teresa's writings, would notice in these 1997 prayers/poems no departure from her lifetime discourse in terms of themes, tone or choice of words. They reveal Mother Teresa as she always was: an exceptionally devoted Roman Catholic nun who was also worried about what was going on in Albania. As always, however, even in these two works, she finds the root of the problem in people's tendency to stray away from God. Her final wish was to have twelve statues of saints in Albania and another dozen in Kosova so that her nuns could pray for the 'd/evil' to leave her country. Even in such 'patriotic' pieces, Mother Teresa makes it abundantly clear that her main and only wish is 'to serve the poorest of the poor', and she advises 'her' Albanians 'to see God in our neighbour'.

The 'patriotism' she appears to show exclusively in her prayers is one of the reasons why the Albanian Catholic Church is eager to present her in a more down-to-earth way. All the Albanian nationalist movements over the centuries have been supported by leading Albanian clerics of all faiths: Christianity (both Orthodox and Catholic), Islam and Bektashism. The Albanian Catholic Church, in particular, takes enormous pride in what it is keen to present as its official motto: 'Fe dhe Atdhe' ('Religion and Fatherland').

In spite of many Albanian clergymen's devotion to the national cause, in a multi-faith country like Albania religion has never been a crucial nation-forming factor. This is a major difference between Albania and some countries in Western Europe and especially in the Balkans. As Paulin Kola observes:

having been at the receiving end of repeated invasions by countries more powerful than themselves, the Albanians remained fragmented and unable to establish a unifying central authority that would command their collective allegiance. What the Albanians conspicuously lacked was a central religious authority that might, as in the case of their neighbours, have been instrumental in establishing the psycho-social prerequisites for a nation-state.[92]

The Albanians still suffer from the lack of such a 'central religious authority' and will continue to suffer in the future not necessarily because they are a multi-faith nation, but because the religious bodies in Albania apparently pledge allegiance first to their 'mother' religious institutions abroad. The attempt by the enlightened patriotic clergyman Fan S. Noli to establish the Albanian Orthodox Autocephalous (Independent) Church in 1922, for instance, was a start in the right direction. To this day, however, Noli's example has not been followed by leading figures of other faiths who have yet to understand the significance of establishing independent Albanian religious institutions.

Albanians of all faiths have traditionally venerated any fellow clergy-man who has given priority to the national cause. Such spiritual-patriots have become the pride of the nation, hardly needing any endorsement by their own church or brethren.

Mother Teresa has constantly provided her Catholic admirers in Albania with abundant proof of her absolute devotion to Catholicism. This is the reason why, like other Albanians adhering to the Catholic faith in Kosova and Macedonia, they too are full of praise for the nun. The Albanian Catholics are also eager to follow the official line of the Albanian Catholic Church regarding Mother Teresa's so-called undisputed attachment to Kosova and the Albanian nation. They are aware, however, that in order for her to match the equation 'Religion plus fatherland equals a perfect Albanian Catholic', she has to be seen as the epitome of Albanian patriot-ism by the whole Albanian nation.

Like the Catholic establishment in Albania, the Albanian Catholics know that 'patriotism' is not one of the easily recognized virtues of Mother Teresa. This explains their failure to argue convincingly why they consider her to be a great patriot. No matter how impressed the Albanians are by Mother Teresa's Nobel Prize, there is no guarantee that they will take her to their hearts for very long. Unless Albanians acknowledge Mother Teresa as a great patriot, her appeal will eventually fade away. Only patri-otism will retain the brightness of Mother Teresa's sainted halo amongst all Albanians.

This explains why any time Albanian Catholic orators mention Mother Teresa's exemplary devotion to Christ, they are equally keen to remind their audiences of their celebrated sister's 'patriotism'. One of the preferred 'parables' about Mother Teresa's 'dedication' to 'her' nation concerns her meeting with the US president Bill Clinton at the beginning of 1997. In that gathering attended also by Ibrahim Rugova, she is reported to have said to Clinton in the presence of several world leaders: 'Mr President, this [pointing to Rugova] is my brother – the leader of Kosova which is suffering. Please take care of him and my people.'[93]

Mother Teresa needed the support of powerful people just as powerful people needed the endorsement of the 'living saint'. The nun was very close to some White House residents, including the Clintons, who were always keen to be seen in her company. For Bill Clinton, who had to seek public redemption for his often un-presidential behaviour, playing host to such a virtuous public figure was quite a character reference. No wonder Clinton is eager to remind people of his friendship with the nun. On one occasion, Clinton is reported to have told some Albanians that in ordering the NATO attack on Yugoslavia in March 1999, he had finally kept a pledge given to Mother Teresa, who had asked him to help her people. Good will is crucial in international politics, but it would be naïve to think that the West intervened in Kosova because a nun, be that Mother Teresa, put in a good word to the most powerful man in the world. It would take more than gesture politics to sort out the problems of the Balkans, especially the long-term future of Kosova.

For the Albanian Catholic Church, securing the pan-national endorsement of Mother Teresa's 'patriotism' is of vital importance because this would elevate considerably the status, bearing, and the appeal of this institution in Albania, a country which has only recently rejoined Christendom officially. Mother Teresa personally made an inestimable contribution towards returning Christ to Albania. For many years, the devoted nun had served as the West's unofficial ambassadress to Communist Eastern Europe and other troubled spots around the world, and as the Vatican's irreplaceable envoy to several Christian and non-Christian countries. Mother Teresa proved useful to the Vatican especially in the case of Albania which, in 1967, became the only officially atheistic state in the world. After all, the famous nun did not visit her country of origin in 1989 entirely or mainly for private reasons. Of course, she wanted to pay her long-overdue last respects to her mother and sister, but she would not have consented to pay the controversial visit to Enver Hoxha's grave for this reason only. She agreed to honour Hoxha first and foremost as a concession she had to make for the sake of serving Christ and the Vatican.

The Albanian Catholic Church has always been aware that Mother Teresa's much-publicized closeness with and services to the Vatican would not necessarily endear her to all Albanians, especially the secular-minded and those adhering to other faiths. History has taught the Albanians that foreign countries and religious institutions, including the Vatican, have not always tried to establish their influence in Albania with this small country's best interests at heart. The Vatican's close connections with various colonial powers that have occupied Albania proper and other Albanian territories over the centuries is a detail not easily missed by the Albanians. This remains one of the reasons why, in spite of the enormous pride the Albanian Catholic Church derives from Mother Teresa's great services to the Vatican, this institution is often eager to advertise the saintly Mother Teresa among the Albanians as a patriot.

Considering the interest some Albanian political, nationalist and religious circles apparently have in Mother Teresa, it is not surprising that they depend so much on the Albanian media to send out the intended messages to the Albanians. Many Albanian reporters have written very positively about Mother Teresa's personality and legacy because they genuinely believe she was a positive force in the twentieth century, and more importantly because she embodied some of the virtues of the Albanian nation.

Like many of their colleagues in other former Communist countries, Albanian journalists are often under the pressure of the government, businesses, various institutions and influential individuals to write favourably or negatively about, or ignore completely, certain people and events. The days when the state had absolute power over the media in Albania came to an end with the advent of the multi-party system in the early 1990s. Albanian journalists were soon to learn, however, that democracy does not necessarily put an end to censorship. This is not to say that the Albanian government or the Albanian Catholic Church exerted any pressure as such on editors and reporters to write favourably about Mother Teresa. Stories praising the Catholic nun were run regularly by the Albanian media after her first visit in 1989. Mother Teresa's 'patriotism', however, became a much-preferred theme and at times the dominant one in the Albanian media when the Serbs, the Croats, the Vlachs and especially the Macedonian Slavs apparently tried to take her away from the Albanians in the months before the beatification in 2003.

The bitter debate about Mother Teresa's ethnicity started in earnest when the Skopje-based Albanian newspaper *Fakti* broke the news about the Macedonians' efforts to 'usurp' Mother Teresa. *Fakti* stood by its story, in spite of several official denials from Sašo Čolakovski, the Macedonian government's spokesperson, and from some civic leaders, that there was no malign intent in the proposal to donate to Rome a copy of Tome Serafimovski's bronze statue of Mother Teresa which was already erected in Skopje. In no time, many Albanian and Macedonian Slav politicians and intellectuals entered a war of words. This was apparently a good opportunity to flaunt Albanian and Macedonian Slav patriotism.

It is difficult to prove whether or not the Macedonian Slavs were planning to inscribe on the statue the now infamous words 'daughter of Macedonia'. What is certain, however, is that since the moment when *Fakti* uncovered the Macedonian Slavs' 'hidden agenda', the Balkan media has been at the forefront of the vicious campaign for 'exclusive rights' to Mother Teresa's figure.

The Albanian media, in particular, have been keen throughout the 1990s to present Mother Teresa as an exclusively Albanian celebrity. Many newspapers, radio and television channels, and websites appeared to be working in unison with Albanian politicians and the Albanian Catholic Church, especially from September 1997 to October 2003, to highlight what an extraordinary patriot Mother Teresa had been throughout her life.

Eager to publicize sensationalist stories and in an effort to endear Mother Teresa to the Albanian public, most of the Albanian dailies were ready to publish any letter written by the nun in which she referred to Albania. In 2003, some of Mother Teresa's letters, which had already been published in some of her biographies since the 1980s, were hailed by editors as great discoveries. Some newspapers were especially keen to get hold of any scrap of information to cement the myth of the nun's attachment to Albania. On 15 October 2003, for instance, *Korrieri* published the original English version of Mother Teresa's letter to Ramiz Alia of 16 August 1989:

> Dear Mr President of our dear country Albania,
> After many years of prayers and desire to visit my oen [sic] country after visiting so many through out [sic] the Eorld [sic], at last the good God gave this beautiful gift to come and to see my people. My oen [sic] family lived here for many years and they also died here, so I eas [sic] able to visit their graves. I hope together ee [sic] eill [sic] do something beautiful for God and for our people.
> God bless you,
> M. Teresa, me [sic][94]

Most of the spelling mistakes are apparently as a result of the editor's failure to use the letter 'w', which is not in the Albanian alphabet, instead of 'e'. The editor also appears to have been unaware of the fact that Mother Teresa used to scribble immediately after her signature not 'me' but 'MC', an abbreviation which stands for her Missionaries of Charity order. As for the translation offered by *Korrieri* alongside the original, it apparently betrays the journalist's poor command of English and equally poor translating skills. In the so-called 'përpiktë'/'exact' Albanian translation provided, the phrase 'our dear country Albania' becomes 'vendi *im* i dashur Shqipëria' [*my* dear country Albania'] (emphasis added), and 'throughout', preceding 'the world', is translated inaccurately. This compound English word is written as two separate words ('through' and 'out') in the letter, and the emphasis in the translated version is put on 'out', apparently to suggest that, in the case of Mother Teresa, any place outside Albania meant 'jashtë' (abroad) and not 'home'. The author of the article, it seems, wanted to make as much as possible of the presence of the emphatic 'own' between 'my' and 'country', to highlight how much Albania and Albanians meant to Mother Teresa.

That the reporter is eager to enlighten the readers as to Mother Teresa's exceptional love for Albania is also seen from the unnecessary clarification provided in the Albanian translation after the phrases 'my own country' and 'my people'. Having translated 'my own country' as 'vendi im' and 'my people' as 'populli im', the journalist explains that in these two cases, the Albanian pronoun 'im'/'my', really means 'i saj'/'her'. The journalist obviously felt it was necessary to alert the newspaper's 'ignorant' readers to this 'shrewd' connotative nuance as a means of facilitating their understanding of the nun's 'complicated', 'highly intellectual' and unmistakably 'patriotic' letter.

Towards the end of the article, feeling obviously vindicated, the reporter concludes that as far as Mother Teresa was concerned, there were no uncertainties regarding her relationship, spiritual or otherwise, with Albania and the Albanian people. Surely, the nun had clarified such issues many years before the Balkan debate about her ethnic origin had started.

Considering that the Albanian media, the Albanian Catholic Church, the political establishment in Albania, Kosova and Macedonia and numerous intellectuals were trying to present Mother Teresa as Albania's modern 'national hero', something of a contemporary kindred spirit of Skanderbeg, who is the only undisputed Albanian national hero, it would hardly be surprising if some of the 'errors' in *Korrieri* were indeed intentional. After all, similar inaccuracies in translation and fanciful comments on what Mother Teresa wrote or 'implied' in her letter to the Albanian leader surfaced in other Albanian newspapers and on several Albanian websites.[95] Like their *Korrieri* colleague, numerous Albanian journalists were eager to paint Mother Teresa as the 'patriot saint' of the Albanian nation. In their haste, however, they got wrong even some of the most publicized facts about her early life. So, for instance, the author of the article 'Albania to Celebrate Mother Teresa's Beatification', which appeared in the *Southeast European Times* on 4 August 2003, claimed that the nun 'lived for more than 17 years with her mother, sister and brother in Tirana'. This reporter obviously did not know that Mother Teresa's first visit to Tirana took place in 1989 at the age of 79. Around the same time, another Albanian journalist wrote that Mother Teresa was awarded an 'Oscar' for Peace in 1979, which is an easy mistake to make considering the media hype surrounding the Nobel Prize and Oscar recipients. Some Albanian admirers of Mother Teresa apparently were in a hurry to advertise not so much this Roman Catholic nun's humanitarian work as the fact that one of their expatriates had become a global star and, more importantly perhaps, that such an international celebrity had always been 'attached' to Albania.

vi. Mother Teresa and the Indians

But if the Albanians and the Macedonian Slavs are so touched by 'their' Mother Teresa's 'attachment' to them, and therefore entitled to make so much noise about the nun's occasional use of 'my' in reference to Albania and Skopje, then imagine what the Indians could do to 'copyright' her. After all, she spent in India not only a few days, as is the case with Albania, or eighteen years, as in Macedonia's case, but almost seventy successive years. The long time she spent in India is one of the reasons why Mother Teresa used for her adopted country an endearing diction that she never employed for any other country or people, including 'her' Albanians and Macedonian Slavs.

India had fascinated Mother Teresa for some time before she decided to go there as a nun in 1928. She grew even more attached to this vast, fascinating and populous country as soon as she arrived in Calcutta, West Bengal, on 6 January 1929. From 1948, the year when she left the Loreto order to work in the slums of Calcutta, her identification with India and the Indian people became complete. In the same eventful year, she replaced the dark habit she had been wearing for twenty years as a European nun, with the white sari of a poor Indian woman. From 1960, the year she made her first trip outside India, she was always keen to show to the world how much she had absorbed India and Indian culture. The white Catholic nun who always dressed and *namasted* (greeted) her admirers around the world like an Indian, saw herself as a natural international spokeswoman of India and the Indian nation. '*We* in India love *our* children,' (emphasis added) she told the national convention of the National Council of Catholic Women in Las Vegas in October 1960.[96]

That Mother Teresa saw herself primarily as an Indian is also obvious from her correspondence with several leaders of India. Her Indianness and devotion to India are seen especially in the letter she sent to the Indian prime minister Morarji Desai and the country's parliamentarians in 1978. In her message, the nun expresses her concern about 'The Freedom of Religion Bill' proposed in the Indian Parliament. The following are some of the selected excerpts from this long letter. I have italicized the words and phrases that, in my view, reveal her attachment to India and the Indian people:

Dear Mr Desai and Members of *our Parliament,*
After much prayer and sacrifices I write to you, asking you to face God in prayer, before you take the step which will destroy the joy and freedom of *our people. Our people,* as you know better than I – are God-fearing people. . . . I love *my people* very much, more than myself. . . . *Our people* in Arunachal are so disturbed. All these years *our people* have lived together in peace. . . . Who are we to prevent *our people* from finding this God who has made them – who loves them – to whom they have to return? You took over your sacred duty in the name of God – acknowledging God's supreme right over *our country* and her people. It was so beautiful. But now I am afraid for you. I am afraid for *our people*. . . . You do not know what

abortion has done and is doing to *our people*. . . . Mr Desai and Members of Parliament, in the name of God, do not destroy the Freedom *our country and people* have had, to serve and love God according to their conscience and belief. Do not belittle *our Hindu Religion* saying that *our Hindu poor people* give up their religion for 'a plate of rice'. . . . I have always made it my rule to co-operate whole-heartedly with the Central and State Governments in all undertakings which are *for the good of our people*. . . . Why are we [Christian missionaries] not with *our poor* in Arunachal? . . . The Catholics of *our country* have called an All-India day of fasting, prayer and sacrifice on Friday, 6th April to maintain peace and communal harmony and to ensure that India lives up to its noble tradition of religious freedom. I request you to propose a similar day of intercession for *all communities of our country* – that *we may obtain peace, unity and love*; that *we become one heart*, full of love and so become the sunshine of God's love, the hope of eternal happiness and the burning flame of God's love and compassion, in *our families, our country* and in the world.

(sd.) M. Teresa MC
God bless you.[97]

The bill's main target was to restrict the Christian missionaries' activities in India. Mother Teresa was, of course, upset by this, but in her letter she does not speak only on behalf of her religious order, the Christian missionaries, the Indian Christians or the Christian community in Arunachal Pradesh, which by then had already started suffering the consequences of the Indian government's attempts to keep Christianity in check.

As is obvious from the letter, Mother Teresa's language and tone are not those of an outsider and certainly not of a concerned European tourist, but of a 'native' Indian. The letter is so skilfully peppered with the singular and plural first personal pronouns 'I' and 'we', as well as the possessive adjectives 'my' and 'our', that no politician nor any non-Christian in India would have had any reason to question the author's sincerity or, even worse, accuse her of having a motive other than protecting the civil rights of all Indians, and of praising as well as urging India's politicians to preserve the country's long-standing tradition of religious tolerance.

Mother Teresa's heart-felt plea to prime minister Desai is one of the many passionate letters she addressed to India's leading politicians throughout her long stay in India. Her correspondence with the Indian leaders is yet further proof of her exceptional devotion both to the country and to its people. By the time she wrote the 1978 letter, Mother Teresa was already an important figure in India. A year later, the Nobel Prize added weight to her opinion on an international scale. Even when she became an almost unparalleled media celebrity and the epitome of human compassion, she never ceased considering herself primarily an Indian.

As Anne Sebba rightly notes, although several countries awarded Mother Teresa honorary citizenship, she identified herself most closely with India.[98] Echoing the same sentiment, an Italian nun posted at the Missionaries of Charity home in Skopje, who apparently was baffled by the bickering between the Albanians and the Macedonian Slavs about 'their' Mother Teresa on the eve of the beatification, remarked pointedly that the founder of her religious order felt the strongest affinity with another part of the world entirely. The same nun also declared that Mother Teresa 'felt more Indian than any other citizenship'.[99]

Mother Teresa, it appears, was not a very eloquent public speaker but she always knew how to win the hearts and minds of leading politicians and ordinary people in India. The Indians have seen numerous Christian missionaries over the centuries but none like Mother Teresa who declared with pride: 'Ami Bharater Bharat Amar' ('I am Indian and India is mine').[100] And she obviously meant what she said. After all, she never deserted the Indians in her lifetime and, naturally, chose to be buried in their country.

vii. Mother Teresa and the Balkans

Considering her lifetime devotion to India, it is difficult to see how several Balkan peoples, especially the Albanians and the Macedonian Slavs, could claim that Mother Teresa belongs exclusively to them, or that she was an Albanian or Macedonian Slav 'patriotic' figure. A typical definition of a 'patriot' would be someone who loves his/her country, feels very loyal towards and is willing to sacrifice him/herself for it. It is not my intention to question Mother Teresa's love for her country, whatever 'her country' meant in her case. Nor am I insinuating even for a moment that the nun's loyalty towards her own country was in any way dubious. What I would like to take issue with here is the irresponsible way many politicians, religious figures and reporters in the Balkans, especially among the Albanians and the Macedonian Slavs use words like 'patriot' and 'patriotism' in reference to Mother Teresa.

If the Macedonian Slavs, for instance, are right when they claim that she was a Macedonian Slav 'patriot', a spirited woman like Mother Teresa would not have hesitated even for a single moment to call upon the leaders of the world publicly, especially the Western leaders, most of whom she knew personally, to officially recognize 'her' new country. By the same token, if Mother Teresa was indeed such a great Albanian 'patriot', as some Albanian politicians, clerics and reporters maintain, or 'a guardian angel for Kosova and the Albanian nation', as Ibrahim Rugova, the late Albanian President of Kosova, called her immediately after her death,[101] she certainly had many chances throughout the long time she was in the public eye to make it abundantly clear where exactly she stood regarding her commitment to the national cause. Mother Teresa was fully aware of her significance and influence and, if she was indeed a 'patriot', as some

Albanians apparently understand this word, she would certainly have been gutsy enough to talk in public about injustices suffered by the Albanian nation since 1913 onwards. More importantly, perhaps, a 'patriotic' Mother Teresa would not have remained silent all her life about the mistreatment of her fellow Albanians in Kosova, Montenegro and Macedonia.

The Macedonian Slavs and the Albanians, however, are not alone in attributing to Mother Teresa qualities she obviously did not have or claim. The nun's 'patriotism' and especially her alleged involvement with Balkan nationalist causes invented and propelled by some of her Albanian and Macedonian Slav admirers and zealots have also been noticed by Christopher Hitchens, a Washington-based English journalist, who has gained himself a reputation for his abrasive and outspoken style of writing. In Hitchens's list of celebrity 'crooks', Mother Teresa comes top. He remains as hostile to the 'saint' from the Balkans now as when she was alive. In the controversial programme *Hell's Angel*, shown in Britain in 1994 on Channel 4, his image-smearing book *The Missionary Position: Mother Teresa in Theory and Practice*, which appeared in the following year, and in numerous articles and interviews,[102] Hitchens attacks Mother Teresa, for being, in his view, among other things, a friend of dictators and swindlers, a proselytizer, Calcutta's main image-wrecker, and the West's tool to salve its guilty conscience about 'the wretched of the world'. If Hitchens had his way, Mother Teresa should have been prosecuted for 'crimes against humanity'.[103]

Hitchens cannot see how the nun could speak so openly about and be taken seriously regarding issues such as abortion and family planning considering that she was not married herself and never had children. Following this logic, it could equally be said that Hitchens himself has no right to talk about theology or comment on religious people considering his hostile attitude towards religion. 'I'm an atheist,' he told Matt Cherry of *Free Inquiry* magazine during an interview published in the Fall 1996 issue. 'I'm not neutral about religion, I'm hostile to it. I think it is a positively bad idea, not just a false one. And I mean not just organized religion, but religious belief itself.'[104] Hitchens would reiterate the same intolerant views almost a decade later in a conversation with his 'rival' brother Peter Hitchens and Ian Katz, the *Guardian* features editor: 'I can't stand anyone who believes in God, who invokes the divinity or who is a person of faith. I mean, that to me is [sic] horrible repulsive thing.'[105]

Hitchens's extreme dislike for religion and people of faith has undermined considerably some serious issues he raises and valid points he makes regarding the nature and intention of Mother Teresa's activities in India and around the world. His uncompromisingly biased attitude towards the nun also does not allow him to differentiate between her relationship with the Vatican and her fellow Albanians. As is often the case in Hitchens's works on, or rather 'against', Mother Teresa, his abrasive style of writing is a poor substitute for the absence of balanced research. That he does not seem to have made a serious effort to understand the nun is also obvious from the claim he makes in his 1995 book that she was involved in the cause of 'Greater Albania'. 'Agnes Bojaxhiu,' postulates Hitchens, conveniently using Mother Teresa's original name, 'knows perfectly well that she is . . . a fund-raising icon for clerical nationalists in the Balkans.'[106] Hitchens offers no evidence whatsoever to substantiate his conclusion that Mother Teresa herself was implicated in the Albanian nationalists' cause. 'In Tetova,' he notes, 'the Albanian centre of western Macedonia, and in Kosovo too, local zealots speak of Greater Albania as the response to Greater Serbia, and they flourish their pictures of Mother Teresa.'[107] The 'zealots' Hitchens refers to were peaceful demonstrators who were trying to attract the attention of the West to the violation of some of their basic human rights by the Serbian and Macedonian governments. The protesters were not flourishing pictures of an ultranationalist saint, which in the Balkans are in abundance, but the pictures of an internationally venerated woman who had come to symbolize forgiveness, compassion, tolerance and understanding. As the Albanians in Kosova and Macedonia were soon to realize, the pictures of their famous compatriot, which were used with the hope of highlighting their plight throughout the 1990s when Yugoslavia was dying a violent death elsewhere, were not of much use in their non-violent efforts for justice.

Hitchens also ignores the fact that Mother Teresa herself had nothing to do with the flourishing of her pictures. As is so often the case in the West, celebrities in the Balkans, especially those who do not live there, have no control over their memorabilia. Fans as a rule do not consult with their chosen celebrities when they decorate rooms with their posters or wear t-shirts bearing their faces and names. In this case, Mother Teresa was as helpless and vulnerable as any other star; her name and image were used by whoever thought they could benefit from them.

Hitchens does not find Mother Teresa 'guilty as charged' only with regards to her 'involvement' in the cause of 'Greater Albania'. He also implies that the nun was such a great Albanian 'patriot' that she was also prepared to serve the Communist government of Albania. According to Hitchens, the fact that she paid homage to and placed a wreath by the grave of Enver Hoxha in 1989 proves that '[a]n Albanian Catholic nationalist . . . might, on "patriotic" questions, still feel loyal to an ostensibly materialist Communist regime'.[108]

Hitchens apparently comes to the conclusion that the 'saintly' Albanian Catholic nun committed the dreadful 'sin' of patriotism simply because her father Nikollë Bojaxhiu, a charismatic and successful businessman, happened to be an ardent Albanian patriot. Hitchens seems to believe that anyone coming from a patriotic family should also be a patriot. The axiomatic conclusion 'like father, like daughter', which Hitchens obviously has in mind, was never true in Mother Teresa's case, however. Her father's patriotic views did not and could not have had any impact on her partly because he died when she was only nine years old and partly because, in the wake of his sudden death, the Bojaxhius' immediate concern was not the fate of the Albanian nation but how to earn a living. Shortly after Nikollë's premature demise, 'his business partner appropriated the assets of the business and the family was left with nothing but their shelter'.[109] As we shall see in the coming chapters, immediately after her father's death, Agnes fell under the spell of religion, not of patriotism or nationalism; and more importantly, when she became famous she was far from eager to reveal her father's attachment to and ultimate sacrifice for the national cause. As a matter of fact, talking about her father in public was a taboo that Mother Teresa never broke.

Hitchens is right when he concludes that in the Balkans, 'yesterday as today, allegiance to the Church was more than a merely confessional matter. It was, and is, imbricated with a series of loyalties to nation, region and even party.'[110] His singling out of the Balkan peoples for their 'strange' inclination to link religious loyalty to nationalistic, regional and political causes, however, betrays a tendency apparent in the studies of many other Westerners who in the past as well as nowadays fail to recognize that, at least in this context, the Balkans is hardly any different from the rest of the world. Considering Hitchens's British-American-Jewish background, one would expect him to know that a truism like the imbrication of religion with nationalistic, regional and political loyalties has been one of the factors determining the establishment, survival and achievements of Britain, the United States and Israel. The Balkans has its own characteristics that single this region out from the rest of Europe, and not always for good reasons, but the imbrication Hitchens has in mind is certainly not what makes this corner of Europe 'bizarrely' unique. If Mother Teresa mixed religion with politics, she made sure that such imbrication never included Albania, Macedonia or the Balkans. Like many other Mother Teresa supporters in the Balkans who claim that she was a patriot without explaining why they think so, her committed adversary Christopher Hitchens has yet to come up with some credible evidence to substantiate his claim that she was 'a keen nationalist'.[111]

Mother Teresa may indeed have been, to quote Hitchens, 'a primitive sermonizer',[112] but she obviously had more vision and far-sightedness than some her erudite adversaries, Hitchens included, with regard to how to be of service to those unfortunate fellow humans who, for no fault of their own, have been stripped of any shred of dignity. One only has to visit Calcutta to realize that, in spite of her efforts and dedication, Mother Teresa was unable to have an overall impact on the city. What once was a proud imperial metropolis of impressive parks and architectural wonders, has turned into a wretched place. You do not have to wander far to find the impoverished people of this crumbling city; its poverty and squalor confront you almost everywhere. Unlike most Westerners visiting Calcutta, including myself, who after witnessing a shocking reality hasten to fly back home to our comfortable lives, Mother Teresa decided to stay among those unfortunate human beings throughout her adult life. It is true that she did not do this only or primarily to help the poor, but it is also true that many unfortunate people did and continue to benefit to this day in Calcutta because of the work she started in the slums of this city in the late 1940s. If I had to choose between those who help the poor for the sake of certain religious purposes or those who confine their contribution to human 'debris' to the writing of some controversial articles or booklets rubbishing the work of such selfless religious 'social workers', I am in no doubt as to whose side I am on, especially after visiting Calcutta myself.

Mother Teresa is criticized not only for not doing enough to eradicate the poverty of Calcutta, which, in my view, would be an impossible task even if there were numerous Mother Teresas and religious orders like the Missionaries of Charity, but also for condoning poverty and siding with the rich. If her opponents expected her to be a revolutionary, or a leftist of the Hitchens type, they are talking about another Mother Teresa altogether. In spite of the fact that what she tried to do, and to some extent was successful in doing, was down to her revolutionary stamina, she certainly did not belong to that group of revolutionaries who ask victims of poverty, war, negligence and 'tradition' to raise up and threaten those in power who, if they so chose, could certainly do something to better the lives of India's and the world's countless *misérables*. Mother Teresa would always ask the poor to forgive and the rich to give. If this nun was guilty of not preaching hatred, then pacifism is certainly a virtue.

Public figures like Mother Teresa are often condemned and vilified whether or not they are reticent or take a stand, challenge taboos and show compassion and tolerance towards their own adversaries. To explain this point, let me concentrate on one of the nun's most 'controversial' decisions: paying her respects to the tomb of Enver Hoxha. The wreath she sent to Hoxha's grave could well have been one of the conditions she had to meet in order to be allowed to visit Albania, but it hardly represents, as Hitchens maintains, an act of 'self-prostitution' for 'the worst of Communism'.[113] For less sarcastic people than Hitchens, who are not inclined to see things in life either as completely good or completely evil, her decision to send flowers to the resting place of a controversial figure like Hoxha could be interpreted as a well-calculated and well-meaning public gesture. By 'honouring' Hoxha, Mother Teresa apparently intended to send a message not only to 'her' Albanians but also to other nations in the Balkans and across Eastern Europe, that they should learn to forgive. The last thing the impoverished Albanians needed when they were on the verge of a national crisis was to be reminded, let alone urged, by

an internationally venerated religious and humanitarian icon like Mother
Teresa that they should be intolerant and seek revenge for their sufferings during the reign of Hoxha and of those who succeeded him after
his death.

Mother Teresa was not above or beyond politics, which explains
why she remained to the end of her life a powerful political as much as
a religious figure. The unassuming nun was a political force many would
have preferred to have on their side rather than as an adversary. She was
a fiercely loyal friend and a reliable ally to numerous political and business leaders, including some very controversial ones across the world who
had helped her to carry out her lifetime mission to promote Christianity.
She spoke out in several cases on politically sensitive issues one does not
usually associate with a nun. She would not hesitate to make her often
controversial views clear, whether following the Bhopal tragedy in India
in 1984 or during several conflicts in the Middle East and elsewhere in
the world. Understandably, her 'undiplomatic' public involvement in such
highly publicized and contentious affairs earned her many enemies and at
times even alienated some of her closest political allies, including some
figures within the Catholic Church.

Never throughout her many years as an influential religious and political
force, however, did Mother Teresa intervene in Balkan politics. When it
came to the Balkans, the actively political Mother Teresa was surprisingly
inactive. She always maintained a silence that many people in her native
region, including some of her Albanian admirers, found puzzling and even
disturbing. Nothing could detract her from her stubborn disengagement
from the political, ethnic and religious conflicts in the Balkans. And, much
to the dismay of the Albanians, she was certainly resolute in her life-long
decision to keep quiet in public about the treatment of her fellow countrymen in Kosova and Macedonia, especially throughout the turbulent 1990s.
She was determined to keep aloof from anything that could 'compromise'
her non-interventionist stance in the Balkans, in spite of the fact that at
times this contradicted openly the policy of her Missionaries of Charity
worldwide. And yet, during her lifetime, and to the present day, no
Albanian politician, cleric, reporter or scholar has ever questioned in public
the carefully crafted myth of Mother Teresa's 'patriotism', nor made even
a half-hearted attempt to argue that, at least on some occasions, her
engagement in Albania and the Balkans could have been perfectly justified
on humanitarian grounds, especially in the spring of 1990.

In March and April 1990 many Albanian children in Kosova suddenly
fell ill. The Serb-run health service was apparently completely unprepared
for the emergency situation. The Kosova Albanians claimed that the
Serbian authorities were unwilling to intervene because the epidemic itself
was allegedly caused by the Serbian Secret Police that is known to have
possessed and used chemical warfare agents including Sarin and Tabun.[114]
The alleged intoxications took place when the Serbs started implementing

their new segregation policy in the elementary and secondary schools in Kosova. The news of the mysterious poisoning of 7,000 Albanian children in nurseries and schools did not take long to reach the West, but the international community was unable to react accordingly because, at that time, Kosova was hardly anyone's priority.

Disturbed by the West's reluctance to intervene, the Albanian community in the United States collected some financial and medical supplies to come to the aid of the children of Kosova.[115] In spite of their efforts, the Albanian Americans were allegedly unable to convince the Serbian authorities to allow them to send the financial and medical assistance to Kosova. The UN was asked to act as a mediator, but the organisation apparently declined to be involved.

Finally, a request was made to Mother Teresa's Missionaries of Charity hoping that her sisters would agree to distribute the humanitarian aid in Kosova. The response from Mother Teresa, or rather from those who spoke for her, was not long in coming but it was hardly what the anxious Albanian Americans had been expecting. The Missionaries of Charity refused to assist them, arguing that Mother Teresa and her order were not involved in politics or politically motivated charity missions. This was very disheartening for the Albanian Americans who had requested her help, particularly because the nun was deemed to be an impartial figure widely respected in the West and in the Balkans.

Apparently, this incident is not known to many Albanians and the Albanian media. As for those few who knew about it, they chose to sweep it under the carpet. Once again, the Albanians preferred to keep quiet for the sake of preserving a myth about a world celebrity who happened to be Albanian.

Lush Gjergji claims that the alleged refusal of the Missionaries of Charity to distribute the medical supplies in Kosova in 1990 'was in keeping with her [Mother Teresa's] lifetime policy of non-involvement in political conflicts'.[116] There were occasions, however, when Mother Teresa apparently was not very worried about compromising her 'non-involvement' policy when it came to saving the lives of innocent victims, especially children, elsewhere in the world. She and her sisters are known to have been very active in helping those who were caught up in several sensitive and highly publicized inter-ethnic, political, religious and international conflicts in India, Pakistan, Jordan or Northern Ireland, to name but a few.[117] Mother Teresa did not hesitate to publicly associate herself with and do everything she could to alleviate the sufferings of some of the most discriminated against and marginalized people in the world, whether they were Indian outcasts, Australian Aborigines or African Americans.[118]

Mother Teresa was never known as someone who shunned controversy. Eleven years before the poisoning of the Albanian children took place in Kosova, she received a request, also from America, to undertake a humanitarian mission. This time those who needed her help were not

Albanian American citizens but the families of the American hostages who were held in Teheran. The concerned relatives asked if she would personally intervene on their behalf with the Iranian government to release their loved ones. Mother Teresa, who at that time was in Oslo collecting her Nobel Prize, had no hesitation in undertaking the task. She assured the anxious families that she would personally try to contact the Iranian authorities as soon as she arrived in Italy. The following is Mother Teresa's own account of the meeting she had with an Iranian diplomat in Rome on 13 December 1979:

> I went to the Embassy and told the man that I had been asked to see him about the American hostages. I told him, 'I know nothing. I have been too busy to read anything. I come to you as a mother would who longed for her children. People have appealed to me to do this. I am willing to go to Iran or to talk to Ayatollah on the telephone. Meantime, we will be praying.' The man said he would look into the matter.[119]

Less than three years after this peacemaking effort, Mother Teresa put herself in grave danger volunteering to save the lives of 64 mentally ill children in Beirut in the midst of the civil war. Against the advice of her nuns and church leaders, she crossed the front line not once but twice. Her heroic efforts and success in 1982 impressed everyone who saw her in action or watched the PBS documentary about the incident. In the words of an eyewitness:

> What stunned everyone was her energy. She saw the problem, fell to her knees, and prayed for a few seconds, and then she was rattling off a list of supplies she needed. . . . We did not expect a saint to be so efficient.[120]

Mother Teresa's decision not to be involved in the distribution of medical supplies to the Albanian children of Kosova in 1990 does not mean that her commitment to help the needy children around the world had weakened in the wake of her bravery in Beirut. The nun remained to the end of her life an avid supporter of vulnerable children across the world. On 2 January 1991, less than a year after the poisoning of the children in Kosova, she wrote compassionately both to George Bush Sr and Saddam Hussein begging them with her 'whole heart' 'to be reconciled with one another'.[121] Mother Teresa pleaded 'on bended knee' to the two leaders

> for the poor and those who will become poor if the war that we all dread and fear happens . . . for the innocent ones . . . for those who will be left orphaned, widowed, and left alone because their parents, husbands, brothers and children have been killed . . . for those who

will be left with disability and disfigurement ... for those who will
be left with no home, no food and no love. Please think of them as
being your children.[122]

Mother Teresa makes it clear in her letter to the two presidents that
everyone should do their bit to stop the war because when people 'suffer
... we will be the ones who are guilty for not having done all in our
power to protect and love them'.[123]

In spite of my efforts to date, I have failed to find a similarly inspired
message among the letters she sent to politicians in the Balkans and especially to the leaders of 'her' Albania and Macedonia. Did Mother Teresa
ever write to Enver Hoxha pleading with him to stop persecuting, jailing
and executing those who did not agree with his policies? Did Mother
Teresa ever contact the leaders of the former Yugoslavia in writing begging
them to treat the Albanians in Kosova, Montenegro and Macedonia as
equal citizens? Did Mother Teresa ever send a message to Slobodan
Milošević imploring him to stop butchering the women and children of
Sarajevo? Did Mother Teresa ever put pen to paper entreating Franjo
Tuđman to stop the killing and the expulsion of innocent Serbs from
Croatia?

Mother Teresa was often found in the company of some world leaders
whose record of crimes is as bad as that of the dictators that ruled the
Balkans in the second half of the twentieth century. The Balkan nun
allegedly had quite an impact on some cruel heads of states across the
world, who would listen sympathetically to her requests, even demands,
either because they had fallen under her spell, or because they could ill
afford to ignore the woman widely acknowledged as a living saint.

Mother Teresa does not seem to have had quite the same impact on the
leaders of her native Balkans, or perhaps she never tried hard enough to
see if they, too, would listen sympathetically to her pleas on behalf of the
innocent victims of war and persecution, especially the children. Perhaps
she did not contact them because she did not believe they would listen to
her. Perhaps she knew that some of them were too arrogant to heed anyone's
plea or advice. Or perhaps she did not want to be snubbed publicly.

The Balkans has indeed produced its share of brutal and insensitive
leaders, but heads of state in this region are also traditionally known for
their sense of inferiority towards the West. It would have been no surprise
if some of them thought twice before ignoring outright someone like
Mother Teresa. They knew that being disrespectful or insensitive to a plea
from the 'saintly' nun would have certainly brought unwanted bad publicity to themselves, their parties, their governments and their countries.
The Balkans is a region where now as well as in the past image, especially
in politics, is everything.

It is not that Mother Teresa was absent altogether from the Balkans.
On the contrary, she visited the region on several occasions especially

after she gained international fame. She started opening houses for her sisters in different Balkan countries from 1979 onwards and their number increased considerably towards the end of her life. Most of her visits to the region were to inspect her houses or open new ones. One of the reasons why Enver Hoxha allegedly would not allow her to visit Albania was because she had asked to open a house for her sisters. Apart from 'reinstating' Christ in Albania, the main purpose of her first visit to Tirana in the late 1980s was to open a house. She had made this objective very clear to Ramiz Alia from the first when he indicated that he was willing to allow her to visit the country. Referring to this issue, Kathryn Spink notes that:

> [e]ven before the lifting of the ban she had made approaches to the Albanian Government under Mr Ramiz Alia, telling him as always that she and her Sisters wanted only to bring tender loving care for the people of Albania. 'The President told me that to open a house there I would have to break the law', she would confide with mischievous satisfaction in February 1992. 'I told him, "Then I am ready to break the law."' The idea of being a law-breaker for God was one which obviously amused her.[124]

Mother Teresa finally succeeded in opening her first house in Albania immediately after her first visit in 1989. Her sisters now operate in Tirana and several other towns and cities across the country. Mother Teresa was obviously prepared to intervene in Albania only for the sake of promoting Christianity.

It would be wrong to interpret Mother Teresa's insistence on having representatives of her order in Albania as proof of her patriotism. As far as Mother Teresa was concerned, the notion of patriotism was alien to her.

By the time she went to Rome to intervene on behalf of the Americans to try to resolve the hostage crisis in 1979, Mother Teresa had never made any efforts to use her influence as an international public figure to put any pressure on the government of Enver Hoxha to stop persecuting its political and religious adversaries in Albania. When she was asked, also in 1979, if she had ever spoken about the situation in Albania to the Pope, whom she had met on several occasions, Mother Teresa replied: 'I have not discussed with the Pope about Albania because I did not think it was necessary and also because he was far too concerned about our poor people.'[125] By 'our poor people', Mother Teresa meant those she and her sisters were helping in India and other countries. Mother Teresa would discuss Albania with the Pope only when the pontiff deemed it appropriate. Albania was not important to the pontificate when Mother Teresa was awarded the Nobel Prize in 1979, and as such she was not advised to make any efforts to approach the Albanian government directly at that time. By the late 1970s, the Vatican had other plans for Mother

Teresa; her role was to act as that institution's public envoy to other socialist countries. Mother Teresa was actively carrying out such a role when she went to Oslo to collect the Nobel Prize. Lush Gjergji, who was with her during that time, remembers how on one occasion she interrupted her breakfast to meet two reporters from a socialist country. Before leaving the table she had asked her fellow Albanians to pray for her meeting. When she returned Mother Teresa told her company that the meeting had been 'very fruitful'.[126]

Considering how actively involved Mother Teresa was in politics, one could easily ask why she always kept herself away from Balkan politics. As will be seen later in the book, Mother Teresa apparently had several reasons for not becoming involved in Balkan politics, and more importantly for not being seen as an Albanian patriot. Those Albanians and Macedonian Slavs who highlight her 'patriotism' seem to forget that the nun sacrificed so much in her life – family, marriage, children – not for the sake of her country, but because she felt she had a calling. They also ignore the fact that her 'calling' had nothing to do directly with Albania, Macedonia and the Balkans. Mother Teresa did not want anyone to accuse her of being an Albanian patriot, an issue that will be covered in detail in chapter four.

Mother Teresa's relationship with and distance from her native Albanians and the peoples of the Balkans, the battle between several Balkan nations to appropriate her, and the Albanians' noise about her 'patriotism' reveal how complex a figure the nun was. The vast literature on Mother Teresa has so far shed hardly any light on these important aspects of her life and personality. Mother Teresa scholarship has also been unable until now to address the significance of the nun's Albanian and Balkan roots. This is hardly surprising, though. As we will see in the following chapter, most Western and Indian writers are interested in Mother Teresa for reasons that have hardly anything to do with where she came from.

The childhood shows the man,
As morning shows the day.

John Milton

The Child is Father of the Man.

William Wordsworth

Our whole life is but a greater and longer
childhood.

Benjamin Franklin

3   The forgotten years

i. The saint without a nation

This chapter traces the extent to which Mother Teresa's first eighteen years in Skopje have been studied or ignored by her biographers, especially those writing for a Western audience. The texts studied include works written from the early 1970s to the present. Considerable attention is paid to the literature about the 1910–1928 period originating from the Balkans. The textual analysis provided is intended to explore some of the motives for the attention, or lack of it, several Mother Teresa experts pay to her early life, family, ethnicity and nationality. The works analysed are seen in the contexts of the time when they were written, the nature of the authors' interest in Mother Teresa and their affiliations to certain religions, countries, nationalities and ethnic groups.

Some of the issues that come to mind with regard to most internationally known figures are their nationality and ethnic origin. This is certainly the case with most past and present Nobel Peace Prize recipients. It is difficult to separate well-known leaders and human rights activists from their own countries or peoples. So, for instance, Mohamed Anwar Al-Sadat is inseparable from Egypt, Lech Walesa from Poland, Menachem Begin, Yitzhak Rabin and Shimon Peres from Israel, Aung San Suu Kyi from Burma, Fredrik Willem De Klerk and Nelson Mandela from South Africa, Yasser Arafat from Palestine, and John Hume and David Trimble from Northern Ireland. Nationality and ethnicity appear to be strong identifying signifiers also for the Nobel Peace laureates of the cloth. The Reverend Dr Martin Luther King Jr, is always associated with the United States of America, just as Archbishop Desmond Mpilo Tutu is with South Africa, and the 14th Dalai Lama (Tenzin Gyatso) with Tibet.

The 1979 winner of the Nobel Peace Prize, however, seems to be an interesting exception to the axiomatic conclusion about the association between someone's place of birth and their celebrity status. Mother Teresa is probably one of the few twentieth-century dignitaries – religious or otherwise – whose country of origin and ethnicity are little known to many people. Throughout her lifetime and after her death her identity was and remains strongly associated with India. Considering the long time she spent in India, it is no surprise that several authors have attempted to study her figure and legacy in the context of her adopted country. Many of them make this clear in the titles of their studies where the word 'India' figures conspicuously.[1]

Most people who have written books and produced biographies (pictorial, authorized and unauthorized) and films (documentary, feature and animated) on Mother Teresa, however, tend to accompany her name in the titles of their works especially with that of the city which became her home for some seventy years as a missionary. This tradition has its genesis in 1971 when Malcolm Muggeridge published his seminal work *Something Beautiful for God: Mother Teresa of Calcutta*. Since that time 'Calcutta' has become a fixture in the titles of numerous works on Mother Teresa.[2] Some writers like Edward Le Joly (1985) and Sunita Kumar (1998) prefer to call their works on the nun simply *Mother Teresa of Calcutta*, with no other trimmings in the title.

Over the years, most of the nun's numerous ghost-writers have acknowledged her 'authorship' simply as 'Mother Teresa'. Some of them, however, feel that it is necessary to clarify that the 'author' of their works is not just any 'Mother Teresa' but *the* 'Mother Teresa of Calcutta'. This tendency, which began in the 1970s, became more apparent in the 1980s and the 1990s and has continued after her death.[3]

Mother Teresa has been identified with Calcutta not only by the authors who admire her. Several of her critics also mention Calcutta in the titles of their works to highlight the alleged negative impact she started having on this city from the late 1960s when she first attracted the attention of the Western media. In April 1992, for instance, *The Nation* ran Christopher Hitchens's article 'The Ghoul of Calcutta'.

As for Mother Teresa's native country and her ethnic roots, however, they are never mentioned in the title of any work about her. It appears as if Mother Teresa of Calcutta had no country of origin or ethnicity in the conventional sense or, perhaps, no original homeland or ethnic connections worth mentioning. Apart from being 'Mother Teresa of Calcutta', the only other 'identity' ascribed to Mother Teresa is that of a Roman Catholic.

Mother Teresa's 'lack' of a conventional nationality is an indication of her popularity and enduring appeal, something which her supporters are always eager to emphasize. How such a highly publicized religious woman ended up with no definite national identity, though, is an issue they are not very keen to explore. The nun's numerous sympathetic image-makers of different religious, political and ethnic denominations apparently find in her an idealist who, like Stephen Dedalus, James Joyce's hero of the 1916 autobiographical novel *A Portrait of the Artist as a Young Man*, aimed at and apparently managed to rise above and 'fly by' the restricting 'nets' of nationality, language and politics.[4] Unlike Joyce's artistic *doppelgänger*, however, Mother Teresa could reach out to people and celebrate life from within the 'net' of religion. With her lifetime commitment to help the poorest of the poor in a predominantly Hindu country like India, she succeeded in proving to a materialistic and largely sceptical West that religion can be used to improve people's spiritual and material well-being. The nun also showed that rather than dividing people, faith can bring together communities across the cultural, ethnic, religious, economic and political divide.

ii. Missing facts

Mother Teresa may indeed, to use a cliché, belong to India, but she was not an Indian. It is also important to emphasize that she had a separate identity from her fellow European Catholic missionaries in India. As stated earlier, Mother Teresa was an Albanian Catholic nun born and raised in Skopje, the capital of the recently independent state of Macedonia. This particular biographical detail has been acknowledged in Mother Teresa scholarship even before the bitter Balkan row over her ethnicity on the eve of the beatification. Mother Teresa's Albanian origin is mentioned in many books on the nun, whether they are penned by Indians or Westerners, friends or opponents, Christians or non-Christians, believers or non-believers. What Mother Teresa experts fail to acknowledge, however, is the significant role ethnic roots and national identity played in her life. These remain topics of merely casual interest in Mother Teresa scholarship to this day.

Agnes Gonxhe Bojaxhiu lived in Skopje up until 26 September 1928 when she left for Dublin to train as a nun. She would not return to her native city for almost half a century. An informed and impartial Mother Teresa scholar, however, would easily notice in the kind of Christianity she preached and in the charity work she carried out in India and throughout the world that, in a sense, she seemed never to have left Skopje. As we shall see later in this chapter and in the coming chapters, she carried with her much of the teachings that her parents, relatives and priests gave her in Skopje during her childhood and youth.

Most of Mother Teresa's biographers pay no attention to her early years. This is particularly the case with Western and Indian experts. Many of them have not cared to visit her birthplace, and very few have made any attempts to interview the people who knew her during the 1910–1928 period.

Mother Teresa scholars who pay some attention to her early life and ethnic origin come mainly from the Balkans. Many of them are Albanians and Macedonian Slavs. As a rule, the Balkan writers are interested in the nun's childhood and youth mainly because they apparently want to claim the famous nun as their own. This explains why Mother Teresa experts mushroomed in this region immediately after she was awarded the Nobel Peace Prize in 1979 and before the beatification in 2003.

Balkan biographers of the nun have failed to have any impact on the Mother Teresa literature produced in the West and India. Nor has the recent Balkan row over her ethnicity induced the large number of her non-Balkan sympathetic hagiographers and biographers, or her opponents, to pay attention to the years she spent in Skopje. Most of them are simply not interested in the formative stage of Mother Teresa's life or in the significance of her Albanian roots.

Mother Teresa is probably one of the most publicized twentieth-century figures and, with the exception of Pope John Paul II, certainly the most famous religious celebrity of our time. She was thrown into the limelight initially in 1950 when she was spotted by the Indian Catholic press in Calcutta. Both Catholic and non-Catholic Indian outlets ensured that she was constantly in the public eye, first in West Bengal and gradually throughout India. Thanks to the constant attention of the Indian media industry, and the equally constant backing of the Indian political establishment, Mother Teresa's popularity in the subcontinent grew increasingly throughout the 1950s and especially after she became a world celebrity.

Several Indian journalists who covered Mother Teresa before she became famous in the West and thereafter would occasionally refer to her ethnicity. Some of them reported that the nun was originally Albanian. In most cases, however, they would simply remark that Mother Teresa was a Yugoslav nun. When she was alive, as a rule, Indian reporters and biographers were not interested in her life before she set foot in their country. For most Indian writers Mother Teresa apparently had only one identity – that of a European Roman Catholic. As for her country of origin, ethnicity and, indeed, the first eighteen years of her life in Skopje, they were ignored almost completely. This trend has hardly changed in the literature on Mother Teresa that has come out in India in the wake of her death in 1997.

Mother Teresa's name and fame reached Western Europe not via India and the Vatican but through the United States. She was initially noticed by the American Catholic media apparatus towards the end of the 1950s. Catholic Americans took her to their hearts because of her services to the Catholic Church in a predominantly non-Catholic country like India. Several White House administrations like that of President Reagan, American multinationals, like the now-defunct Union Carbide, and American businessmen like the financier Charles Keating, found in Mother Teresa a staunch ally in their hour of need.[5]

Mother Teresa's first visit to Europe since 1928 took place in 1960. By that time, however, she was still relatively unknown in Europe. European media started to pay attention to Mother Teresa mainly in the late 1960s.

Like her Indian admirers, Western journalists and writers have never shown any interest in highlighting Mother Teresa's ethnic roots and country of origin. This is obvious especially in the media coverage she received in Britain from 1968 when she was interviewed by Malcolm Muggeridge of the BBC. In 1969 Muggeridge made a film about Mother Teresa, choosing for a title one of her 'catchphrases' *Something Beautiful for God*. Two years later Muggeridge published a book on Mother Teresa – *Something Beautiful for God: Mother Teresa of Calcutta* – which proved to be one of the most influential image-making works on her. Since then she has been the subject of numerous books and television programmes. Even by the time she became world famous, her Albanian origin and early years were hardly of interest to the nun's biographers, whose number would increase considerably after she was awarded the Nobel Prize.

Mother Teresa's life may indeed have been 'public property'[6] when she was alive. Strangely enough, however, unlike other international celebrities, in spite of the intense global media attention she received from the late 1970s until the end of the 1990s, nothing of importance was ever reported about her childhood. This particular period was largely ignored and continues to be ignored in the ever-growing Mother Teresa literature intended primarily for Western readers. While the Western public is spared no minute details about almost every aspect of the charitable work carried out by Mother Teresa and her sisters and brothers of the Missionaries of Charity, the information about her as a child, as well as details about her schooling, social life and, equally important, about her parents and siblings remain sketchy, fragmented and, in most cases, missing altogether, even in some of the best biographies.

One of the reasons why, perhaps, some biographers skip Mother Teresa's early life completely or depict a very sketchy picture of her childhood and youth is because they are apparently not fully aware of the importance of studying every stage of her life in offering as complete a portrait as possible of the person she really was. A considerable number of her early biographers had not written a proper biographical work or a book prior to taking upon themselves the task of chronicling her life. This is how Kathryn Spink records her gratitude to Mother Teresa about twenty years after the nun had given her the consent to write about her:

> [Mother Teresa] gave me her permission to write, telling me that I did not have to ask, and adding that she hoped that I was not putting any of my own money into the venture. Apparently, Nobel laureate though she was, she had no inkling that her consent to that, my 'real' first book with all its defects and limitations, would be enough to launch my career as a writer.[7]

Mother Teresa launched, and probably will continue to launch, the careers of many other inexperienced biographers.

Of course, not every biography of Mother Teresa should cover her entire life. It is perfectly normal for some biographers to concentrate on certain stages of her life and work and either ignore or mention the others only in passing. This is often the case with biographies of famous people. What separates the biographies of Mother Teresa from the biographical works on other well-known personalities is that, so far, almost none of her numerous biographers has made the nun's early years the sole or the main topic of their work. Even books with promising titles such as David Porter's *Mother Teresa: The Early Years* (1986) and Claire Jordan Mohan's *The Young Life of Mother Teresa of Calcutta* (1996) would disappoint anyone expecting to find there a systematic and detailed account of Mother Teresa's childhood and youth. Rather than chronicling the early life of Agnes Gonxhe Bojaxhiu, Porter and Mohan are more interested in covering her life story after she left Skopje in 1928.

The tendency to pay little attention to Mother Teresa's early years is apparent not only in these works. Even the most prolific and seasoned Mother Teresa experts, Kathryn Spink included, fail to cover at length the nun's early life. In this context, in Mother Teresa scholarship, the word 'biography' is often a misnomer. Most of her biographies are simply hagiographies. As for Mother Teresa's opponents, they make casual remarks not so much about her early life as to the fact that she was Albanian. Even in this case, her 'Albanianness' becomes an issue only when, like Christopher Hitchens, they want to highlight how 'devoted' she was to Albania and the Albanian national cause, or, like several Indian critics, they argue that, coming from a poor country like Albania, she should have tried to help her own impoverished compatriots first before taking it upon herself to alleviate the sufferings of vulnerable Indians.

On the whole, the literature on Mother Teresa bears the signature of her Catholic colleagues, friends, admirers and followers, which explains to some extent the predominantly devotional nature of their work. In spite of the fact that so many books have been churned out on this particular nun, it is still too early to talk about a dispassionate and objective Mother Teresa scholarship. A few publications that appeared throughout the 1990s, and especially some that have come out in the wake of her death, however, are clear indications of a welcome tendency to study her life and work in a more detached way.

Even in this emerging non-partisan literature on Mother Teresa's person and legacy, there is no difference in the attitude towards her early life. Mother Teresa appears to be one of the public figures of our time about whom we seem to know almost everything as an adult but hardly anything of importance about her first eighteen years. So much so that it seems as if this religious celebrity was born at eighteen.

iii. A catalogue of biographical inaccuracies

The little information Indian and Western writers provide about Mother Teresa's years in Skopje from 1910 to 1928 is full of inaccuracies. On the whole, Mother Teresa experts, who show no particular interest in her early years, also display some confusion about Agnes Gonxhe Bojaxhiu's actual birthplace as well as about the geography and history of the Balkans. In his article '"Mother" Teresa', Ken Matto locates her place of birth 'in what is now Yugoslavia/Bosnia'.[8] According to David Porter, the nun was born 'in Skopje in Serbia'.[9] On the opening page of his book *Life Stories: Mother Teresa*, Wayne Jackman observes that the town where Mother Teresa was born was 'Skopje in Macedonia'.[10] In her study *Mother Teresa: The Nun Whose 'Mission of Love' Has Helped Millions of the World's Poorest People*, Charlotte Gray notes that Mother Teresa was born 'in Skopje, Albania'.[11]

The fact of the matter is that Mother Teresa was not born in Bosnia, Serbia, Macedonia or Albania, as we understand these terms now, or indeed as they were understood in the 1910s. Some opponents and admirers apparently fail to notice that for some five centuries before, and at least two more years after Agnes Gonxhe Bojaxhiu was born, Skopje was administered by the Ottoman Empire. The 'states' of Bosnia, Macedonia and Albania did not exist in 1910. As for Serbia, this Balkan country had not yet occupied Mother Teresa's native city by the time she was born, nor did the European powers recognize the authority of the Serbian state over Macedonia during the eighteen years Mother Teresa lived in Skopje. To this day, Serbia has no legitimate territorial claim over Skopje or the new state of Macedonia.

Historical and geographical inaccuracies of the same nature also surface in Richard Tames's book *Mother Teresa*. According to Tames, the Skopje of 1910 was 'in the small kingdom of Serbia'.[12] The kingdom of Serbia had no control over Skopje or 'Macedonia' throughout the long presence of the Ottomans in the Balkans. Under the Turks, Skopje was included in the *vilāyet* (the Turkish for 'administrative province') of Kosova, which was one of the four *vilāyets* populated by the Albanians. The other three administrative provinces in the Albanian lands were those of Shkodër, Janinë and Manastir.

This is not the only inaccuracy recorded in Tames's book. In the opening pages of this work we are offered some information on the whereabouts of the shrine of the Madonna of Letnice. By all accounts, this religious place was very important to Mother Teresa throughout the first eighteen years of her life. Tames locates this well-known church not in Letnice, Kosova, but in another part of the Balkans altogether: 'The Bojaxhiu family prayed together every day, celebrated all the religious festivals and made a pilgrimage each year to the shrine of the Madonna of Letnice in the mountains of Montenegro.'[13] The picture used to illustrate the location of this place of pilgrimage has this caption: 'Montenegro, a beautiful setting for the shrine of the Madonna of Letnice'. In her 2003 book on Mother Teresa, Emma Johnson also wrongly notes that the Madonna of Letnice shrine is in the mountains of Montenegro.[14]

Tames and Johnson obviously thought that since this place of worship is situated in a place called *crne gore*, which in Serbo-Croat means 'black mountain', and since there is a small state in the Balkans of the same name, then it stands to reason that the Bojaxhius went on their annual pilgrimage to Montenegro.

A few biographers make no reference at all to Mother Teresa's ethnic origin. Wayne Jackman (1993), for instance, mentions nothing about her being Albanian, not only in the opening chapter where he records some details about her parents and siblings, but also throughout the whole book.

It is not uncommon for Mother Teresa to be given a 'collective' and inaccurate ethnicity and nationality. In several publications she is referred to as a Yugoslav nun, who was born 'in Skopje, Yugoslavia'.[15] Mother Teresa biographers like Malcolm Muggeridge, Georges Gorrée, Jean Barbier, Desmond Doig, Kathryn Spink, Eileen Egan and Kathleen Egan apparently fail to notice that there was no such place as 'Yugoslavia' at the time Mother Teresa was born. In its embryonic form, Yugoslavia emerged only in December 1918, and even then its official name was the 'Kingdom of the Serbs, Croats and Slovenes'.

The fact that Mother Teresa was occasionally identified by the Indian and Western media as a 'Yugoslav' nun has led some people to believe that she was a Slav. This is how the Indian biographer Navin Chawla presents the relationship between the nun and Pope John Paul II in his 1992 book:

> Quite understandably, her relations with the Head of the Catholic Church, Pope John Paul II, are very good. She invariably refers to him as 'Holy Father' and looks upon him as a real father. She admires his simplicity. She deeply appreciated his offering a place to the Missionaries of Charity in the Vatican, where they have set up a soup kitchen for the destitute of Rome. Not only does it serve as an acknowledgment of the presence of the poor, it has helped to demystify the aura of the Vatican as an oasis of great splendour and wealth. *Whether the fact that both are Slavs – he is Polish and she is a Yugoslav Albanian – has contributed to their mutual understanding and respect is a matter for conjecture.* The Pope certainly holds her in great regard, and admires her for her outspoken defence of the Church's traditional values. (emphasis added)[16]

Chawla is right about Karol Wojtyla (the original name of Pope John Paul II) being a Slav. The 264th pontiff was a Pole who loved Poland dearly and who did everything he could to help his nation overthrow Communism. Like several other Mother Teresa biographers, however, Chawla obviously does not know much about the ethnic map of the Balkans. Agnes Bojaxhiu was not a Slav, nor are her fellow Albanians. This explains why, in contrast to other nationalities living in the Yugoslav state that emerged in the second decade of the twentieth century, the Albanians living there became officially Yugoslav citizens not from the start but in 1928. Even when they were recognized by law as 'Yugoslavs', they were soon to learn that their new citizenship was hardly a passport to equal rights. It was mainly because of their non-Slavic origin that the rulers of Belgrade treated the Albanians as second-class citizens from the inception of the federal state of Yugoslavia in the late 1910s to its collapse in the early 1990s.

Chawla is also wrong about Mother Teresa's Venetian connection. Both Mother Teresa's parents were ethnic Albanians. Contrary to Chawla's claim, the nun's mother did not come 'from *nearby* Venice'[17] (emphasis added). Chawla's conclusion about the vicinity of these two European metropolises is wrong not only in geographical terms, though. Venice is also a long way from Skopje in terms of differences apparent in the languages the inhabitants of the two cities speak, as well as in their ethnicities, nationalities, cultures, traditions and religious affiliations.

Most acknowledged biographers of Mother Teresa mention that she was Albanian but they refer to this fact very briefly, almost casually. So little is mentioned about her Albanian roots, parents, siblings, relatives and, indeed, about her eighteen years in Skopje that one has the impression that any information on this part of her life is hardly important. In many books, Mother Teresa's life from 1910 to 1928 is summed up in a very brief entry in the 'Important Dates'/'Date Chart'/'Chronological Table' appendix. This is then followed by another entry referring to the year 1928:

1910 Born in Skopje.
1928 Travels to Ireland.[18]

1910 Aug 26: Agnes Gonxha Bojaxhiu born in Skopje, Albania.
1928 Sept 15: Agnes leaves Skopje to join the Sisters of Loreto in Ireland.
      Dec 1: Sister Mary Teresa (Agnes) sails for India.[19]

1910 (27 [sic] August) Agnes Gouxha [sic] Bojaxhiu is born.
1928 Goes to the Loreto convent in Ireland and then to Darjeeling, India, to train as a nun.[20]

Apparently, these authors, and they are by no means the only ones,[21] felt that nothing significant enough happened in Mother Teresa's life in Skopje from 1910 to 1928 to justify even a brief mention. As for those biographers who refer to her early years, in most cases they sum them up in one or two sentences and at most in one single paragraph. Malcolm Muggeridge, for instance, mentions only in passing Mother Teresa's early life and origin in *Something Beautiful for God*. So casual are his remarks about such seemingly 'irrelevant' biographical details throughout the book that one has the impression that he could have just as well ignored them completely.[22] This is what he has to say in the *27 August 1910* entry in the 'Chronological Table' at the end of the book, before jumping to the next entry dated *29 November 1928*:

> *27* [sic] *August 1910* Born of Albanian parents at Skopje, Yugoslavia. There were three children, one boy and two girls. She attended the government school.[23]

Muggeridge's lack of interest in Mother Teresa's early years seems to have set a trend for the many books that appeared soon after the publication of *Something Beautiful for God*. The following are some of the many similar sentences and paragraphs in later works regarding Mother Teresa's life from 1910 to 1928:

> The daughter of an Albanian chemist, Agnes Gonxha Bojaxhiu was born on 27th [sic] August 1910 in Skopje, Yugoslavia.[24]

> *27* [sic] *August 1910* Born Agnes Gonxha Bejaxhiu [sic], of Albanian parents at Skopje, Yugoslavia. There were three children, one boy and two girls. She attended the Government (Gimnaziya) school.[25]

> [Mother Teresa] was born on 27th [sic] August, 1910, in Skopje, Yugoslavia, of Albanian parents. Her name then was Agnes Gouxha [sic] Bojaxhiu. Her father was a grocer and Agnes was one of three children – two girls and a boy. She attended the local Government (Gimnazija) school . . .[26]

> Mother Teresa was born Agnes Gonxha Bojaxhiu in Skopje, Albania, on 26 August 1910, the youngest of three children. She had a comfortable childhood – her father was a building contractor and importer, her mother was strict but loving with a deep faith. After her father's premature death, life became harder and to support her family Agnes' mother set up a business selling clothes and embroidery.[27]

The quotes, which are more or less replicas of each other both in terms of the details they provide and their length, hardly justify John Cairns's claim that 'most of Mother Teresa's biographical details are now well known'.[28] This may be true for Mother Teresa's life from September 1928, when she left Skopje, to the end of her life in September 1997 but this is certainly not the case for the 1910–1928 period. To sum up the first eighteen years of a public figure of Mother Teresa's international standing in some few eclectic, rather picaresque, and inaccurate facts and figures like her father's professions (chemist, grocer, building contractor and importer), two different dates of birth (26 and 27 August), and several countries of birth (Albania, Macedonia, Serbia, Bosnia, Yugoslavia), is to oversimplify, if not vulgarize, the very notion of 'biography'.

Some Mother Teresa biographers do refer very briefly to her childhood in Skopje. Their interest in this early stage of her life, however, seems to be motivated mainly by their desire to highlight how deeply steeped in religion she was as a little girl as well as how devoutly Catholic her parents were, especially her mother. The exclusive attention and importance most Western and Indian biographers attach to Mother Teresa's religious background is such that one wonders if they would have chosen to refer at all to her early years if it were not for highlighting this specific aspect of her life in Skopje. To illustrate this point, here are again the same previously quoted sentences about her childhood, only this time I have also included the information about Mother Teresa's allegedly too religious childhood that follows immediately in each case:

> The daughter of an Albanian chemist, Agnes Gonxha Bojaxhiu was born on 27th [sic] August 1910 in Skopje, Yugoslavia. As a young girl she was pious and well-behaved, and would have made someone a good wife, if at the age of twelve she had not become aware of another calling. Six years later some Jesuit fathers told her about the Sisters of Our Lady of Loreto in Calcutta. *And that was it!* (emphasis added)[29]

> 27 [sic] *August 1910* Born Agnes Gonxha Bejaxhiu [sic], of Albanian parents at Skopje, Yugoslavia. There were three children, one boy and two girls. She attended the Government (Gimnaziya) school. While at school, she became a member of the Sodality. At that time, Yugoslav Jesuits had accepted to work in the Calcutta Archdiocese. The first group arrived in Calcutta on 30 December 1925. One of them was sent to Kurseong. From there he sent enthusiastic letters about the Bengal Mission field. Those letters were read regularly to the Sodalists. Young Agnes was one of the Sodalists who volunteered for the Bengal Mission. She was put in touch with the Loreto nuns in Ireland as they were working in the Calcutta Archdiocese.[30]

> [Mother Teresa] was born on 27th [sic] August, 1910, in Skopje, Yugoslavia, of Albanian parents. Her name then was Agnes Gouxha [sic] Bojaxhiu. Her father was a grocer and Agnes was one of the three children – two girls and a boy. She attended the local Government

(Gimnazija) school and whilst there became a member of a Catholic association for children known as the Sodality of Mary. At the age of twelve, Agnes was already convinced that she had a vocation to the religious life. She was caught in a wave of enthusiasm for the missions and for the work of spreading the Gospel, an enthusiasm inspired by the writings of Pope Pius XI and endorsed by the institution of the Feast of Christ the King. It was at this time that the Yugoslav Jesuits had agreed to work in the Calcutta Archdiocese and one of the first to arrive there was sent to Kurseong. From there he wrote fervent and inspiring letters about the work of the missionaries among the poor and the sick, and the child Agnes responded with the unshakeable conviction that her calling was to become a missionary.[31]

Mother Teresa was born Agnes Gonxha Bojaxhiu in Skopje, Albania, on 26 August 1910, the youngest of three children. She had a comfortable childhood – her father was a building contractor and importer, her mother was strict but loving with a deep faith. After her father's premature death, life became harder and to support her family Agnes' mother set up a business selling clothes and embroidery. In her teens, Agnes became a member of a young people's group in her local parish called the Sodality and through the activities there, guided by a Jesuit priest, Agnes became interested in the world of missionaries.[32]

It is true that Mother Teresa came from a religious background. Her father Nikollë was 'a faithful member of the Church'.[33] He was close to several Catholic archbishops in Skopje and was always very generous to the church, even more so if he happened to like the local priest. This was especially true in the case of the Albanian Archbishop Lazar Mjeda, who started working in Skopje in 1909. Several biographers of Mother Teresa have been keen to emphasize that Nikollë and the priest were close friends. Their friendship was the main reason why, to quote David Porter, Mother Teresa's father was 'even more generous towards the church than he would naturally have been'.[34] Nikollë was 'a personal friend' of this particular priest, but their friendship was not motivated only by the fact that they shared the Catholic faith. Lazar Mjeda was the brother of the promising Albanian classical poet Ndre Mjeda (1866–1937). As a young man, Ndre Mjeda had studied theology, rhetoric, Latin, Italian and literature in France, Spain, Croatia, Italy and Poland. It was as a student and later as a lecturer in music, philosophy, philology, logic and metaphysics in Italy and Poland during the 1880–1898 period that this talented writer wrote some of his best poetry, such as the poems 'The Nightingale's Lament' and 'Skanderbeg's Grave'. In these and other works, the poet expresses his love for Albania and how much he misses it in exile, and evokes the figure of the Albanian national hero.

As a token of appreciation for his generosity towards the church in Skopje, Lazar Mjeda gave Nikollë some 'good books', which included his brother's works. It is during this time that Agnes Gonxhe Bojaxhiu is known to have started enjoying reading poems written by Ndre Mjeda and other Albanian poets.[35] Ndre Mjeda's nostalgic and patriotic work made a very strong impression especially on Nikollë who, like the poet, often travelled abroad and was strongly attached to his country. Nikollë was also something of an artist himself; he enjoyed singing and was an active member of a Skopje brass band. For a devoted patron of arts and an ardent Albanian patriot like Nikollë, it was only natural that he should express his wish to help financially not only Lazar Mjeda but also his brother Ndre. Nikollë's generosity left a lasting impression on the archbishop which is obvious from the way he expressed his gratitude to his affluent friend: 'May God reward you and your family in this life and in the afterlife for everything you have done for me, for the church and for the Albanian people.'[36]

That Nikollë was far from a religious fanatic can also be seen from Mother Teresa's and her brother's recollections of him. The siblings would remember three things about their father: his generosity towards the poor, his gift as a story-teller, and his disciplinarian nature. None of these features appeared to have been motivated or influenced exclusively by his devotion to Catholicism. His generosity, for instance, was a manifestation of his humanitarian spirit for which he was well-known in his city. As a member of the Skopje City Council, he was in a unique position to know which religious and secular institutions, businesses and individuals needed financial support. Being wealthy, Nikollë could, of course, afford to be more generous than his fellow Albanians (both Christians and Muslims) and citizens of other ethnicities and faiths. He became very popular in Skopje not only as a benefactor of the church but also for sponsoring important projects that improved significantly the city's cultural life and infrastructure. His popularity was enhanced especially as a result of his generosity towards the poor and the old who had either been abandoned by their own children or were forsaken by relatives and neighbours.

Nikollë was keen to instil in his three children feelings of respect and love for ordinary human beings. This is the reason why he and his wife often welcomed to their house poor people to whom they were not related, and introduce them to their children as 'relatives'.[37] It was during these early years that Mother Teresa was taught not so much from the pulpit as around the family table that the poor, the vulnerable, the infirm and the dispossessed were not some 'human debris' to be kept at arm's length. Nikollë apparently wanted his children to learn to share their wealth with those who were not as fortunate as them. Mother Teresa never forgot his advice: 'My daughter, never take a morsel of food that you are not prepared to share with others.'[38] Her brother Lazar would also always remember that, when he was little, his father would often give him instructions to send parcels of money, clothes and food to the poor.[39] Nikollë made sure that the poor who knocked on his door for help were not disappointed even when he was not at home. This is the reason why he left extra money with his wife when he was away on business.

Nikollë, the benefactor, was not a religious preacher. When he returned home from foreign trips he would always delight his children with stories. Neither Mother Teresa nor her brother, however, is known to have said anything about such memorable story-telling sessions being about religion or religious places abroad. Had Nikollë ever mentioned anything about any place of worship he had visited in countries like Italy and Egypt, where he is known to have travelled often, his children would have certainly remembered such a thing, and if either Mother Teresa or Lazar had even slightly referred to his father's 'preaching' ability, this was certainly something Mother Teresa's admiring biographers would have gladly recorded in their work.

The third facet of Nikollë's personality, his disciplinarian nature, was also not an expression of his religiosity. Mother Teresa's father was quite an advanced man for his time. Not only did he allow his two daughters to go to school, he was also keen that they should get the best education possible. Sensing perhaps a propensity for waywardness in his son, he would often reprimand him for not paying enough attention to his studies. In the evening he would usually go up to Lazar's room to ask him if he had behaved himself with friends and teachers and to test his knowledge of the subjects he was taking at school. Interestingly enough, Nikollë never seems to have advised his three children to behave themselves in a way that becomes a Catholic. More important for this disciplinarian but much-loved father, who always helped out the poor without drawing attention to himself, was that his children should never let him down. Being aware of how much he was respected in Skopje, he would often advise them to bear in mind his status, or as he used to put it: 'Never forget whose children you are.'[40]

While Mother Teresa's sympathetic biographers have failed to offer any strong evidence to prove what a strict religious father Nikollë was, they nearly always emphasize that her mother Drane was an exceptionally strict Catholic. I will discuss in detail in chapter five the extent to which religion was important in Drane's life after she lost her husband and the impact her faith had on her children, especially on her youngest daughter Agnes. For the time being, suffice it to say that it appears that Drane was not any more religious than other Catholic Albanian women in Skopje throughout the time her husband was alive.

When Nikollë was alive Drane did not have his active social life, but nor was this wealthy woman cut off from the world. Being aware of how fortunate they were, she and her husband would often visit the church to express their gratitude to God for their prosperity. It would be wrong, however, to conclude, as many biographers have so far done, that Drane attended the church when her husband was alive simply because she was a devout adherent of the Catholic faith. In those days, the church was not only a place of worship but also an important venue for people to meet and attend activities which were not always of a strictly religious nature. The Bojaxhius' local church was well-known for organizing cultural events, especially concerts. For wealthy people like Drane and Nikollë, frequent visits to the parish church were also motivated by the wish to offer help to the needy. Church was the perfect venue for a generous couple like them to receive information about the people who needed support and how they could be reached. The church was also very important to Mother Teresa's parents in trying to achieve their aim of bringing up their children as responsible citizens. Drane and Nikollë took their three children to service regularly, and encouraged them to participate in charity events.

The Bojaxhius were also attached to the church because of music, which played an important role in their daily life.[41] Like their father, the three children were passionate musicians. In the words of one of their childhood friends, Agnes in particular 'had real talent for music' and played the mandolin well.[42] The church offered Agnes and her siblings a very good opportunity to pursue their musical talent. They were always active in the concerts and festivals organized by the church. Agnes and her sister were members of the church choir, and they were known as the 'two nightingales of the church', Agnes being the soprano and Age the contralto.[43]

Nikollë and Drane were also keen for their children to go to church regularly because it was a place where they were taught by the clergy to take pride in their Albanian identity and the history of the Albanian nation. Local priests would often talk to the children about Albanian literature and the Albanian national hero Skanderbeg.[44]

It is also important to emphasize that both Nikollë and Drane taught the children by their own example how to be of help to those who were poor and vulnerable. Mother Teresa's parents were the first Samaritans she encountered in her life. Many years later when she wandered through the streets of Calcutta offering comfort to the old and the abandoned, she was hardly doing something new. As a little girl, she had regularly accompanied her mother in similar charity missions through the streets of Skopje.

The charitable Mother Teresa was not born during the weeks she spent in the Irish convent in 1928, nor when she was first exposed to the shocking squalor of Colombo, Madras or Calcutta. The real genesis of the Mother Teresa many people in Calcutta, across India and throughout the world came to know and admire in the second half of the twentieth century is found in the little and unpretentious Balkan town of Skopje. Being brought up by devoted, demanding and open-minded parents, listening to the preaching of several devout Albanian and Slavic Catholic priests, enjoying the company of Albanian, Croat, Slovene, Hungarian, Italian and Jewish friends,[45] growing up in a thriving multi-ethnic, multi-religious and multi-cultural community – the Bojaxhiu children obviously had a very healthy beginning in life. This kind of childhood was bound to have a positive impact on them, especially on the more sensitive Agnes. The tolerant views and attitudes towards people of different ethnicities and religions she displayed as a nun and as a charity worker were sown during her early years in Skopje. Georges Gorrée and Jean Barbier's conclusion that once 'some Jesuit fathers told her about the Sisters of Our Lady of Loretto in Calcutta. And that was it!,'[46] is rather hasty and simplistic, and as such misleading. There was no 'And that was it!' in Mother Teresa's life. An interpretation like this ignores, belittles and trivializes the huge impact her family, the local church and a multi-culturally diverse city like Skopje had on Mother Teresa throughout the 1910–1928 period and beyond. Mother Teresa's decision to become a nun was not taken suddenly and certainly not in a hurry. Exceptional individuals like her do not embark on a life mission on a sudden impulse.

The huge formative impact her background had on Mother Teresa has been largely ignored or is mentioned only in passing in the vast literature on her intended mainly for Western and middle-class Indian readers. Up until the mid-1980s not many people in India and the West knew much about Mother Teresa's ethnic, cultural and national roots. From then onwards, details about her early life began to appear in some texts. In most cases, however, this flimsy information is presented more in the form of parables about a legendary figure who seemed to have lived and worked in a very distant, almost mythological past, than as well-researched biographical details about the life of one of the most influential twentieth-century figures. So far, biographers of Mother Teresa refer to the city of Skopje mainly to highlight its exotic nature, or to introduce readers to some equally exotic and 'primitive' aspects of Mother Teresa's fellow countrymen like *besa* (Albanian for 'promise/word of honour'), and the 'blood feud', which to this day remain some of the most preferred themes for most Western writers and researchers interested in Albania and the Balkans. In a half-hearted and unsuccessful attempt to find some explanation for Mother Teresa's devotion to Christ in the essentially 'folkloric' nature of her people, Eileen Egan is keen to highlight in the opening chapter 'The Strands of Life' of her 1986 biography that 'ineradicable aspect of Albanian identity deeply imbedded in her character. It throws a vivid light on the reality of a rare woman.'[47] This aspect is, of course, *besa*, to which Egan returns in the second chapter 'The Call Within a Call':

> It is a concept deep in the consciousness of Albanians that refers to the absolute sacredness of the word of honor, the inviolability of the pledged word in daily life. The concept ... is contained in the word *besa*.

As Mother Teresa explained it to me, should a family promise hospitality to someone and he came to claim it, the family would provide it and protect that person at any cost. The cost might be heavy indeed if the person claiming hospitality were, as often happened, a hunted man stalked by seekers after retribution or vengeance. The pledge would be fulfilled even in the extreme situation that word came that the guest had been involved in the death of a member of the host family. As she was explaining *besa*, one could transport oneself back to the beleaguered people of Albania, engaged not only in resistance to occupation, but also in feuds among themselves. Their very lives depended on no document, no treaty, but hung by the slender thread of a simple word of honor.[48]

Egan does not make it clear if she asked Mother Teresa about the concept of *besa* or if the nun had initiated the discussion herself. Albanians often like to talk to foreigners about their ancient national virtue of *besa* and their proverbial hospitality, especially to those foreigners with a special interest in the exotic. It would not be surprising if Mother Teresa preferred to talk to her Western biographers about Albanian ancient customs. There are indications that, at least in private, she took pride in her Albanian roots, and would often talk about her nation's virtues. And not necessarily only to her Western friends with an eye for the exotic. She appears to have also talked about Albanian traditions, especially the concept of *besa*, to her fellow nuns. One of the questions asked by Mother Teresa's sisters attending my lectures at St Xavier's College in Calcutta on 1 July 2005 was about the significance of *besa* in the context of Mother Teresa's devotion to Jesus.[49]

No matter how much or how little Mother Teresa liked to talk to her Western friends and fellow sisters about *besa*, it would be naïve and inaccurate to try to interpret her attachment to Christ exclusively or mainly in the light of the ancient Albanian custom of honouring a pledge. It is true that Mother Teresa's devotion to the Catholic faith is a modern example of the determination on the part of some of her fellow Albanians to adhere to Christianity. On the other hand, Mother Teresa's lifetime attachment to Jesus can be best explained not so much in the context of an exotic national custom or tradition such as *besa*, but of a complex set of personal circumstances, something which is discussed at length in the next chapter. Fanciful and exotic theories and explanations as to how and why an Albanian girl chose to become a nun are unlikely to satisfy those who admire Mother Teresa but do not necessarily share her faith, or any faith for that matter. The importance that Egan attaches to the Albanian concept of *besa* to explore and explain the unique nature of Mother Teresa's bond with Jesus is misleading and not very useful even for those followers of Catholicism whose admiration for Mother Teresa does not stop them from searching for a rational explanation for her initial attachment and lifetime devotion to Jesus. Egan's attempts to explain the 'unexplainable' are also disappointing because her references to *besa* are inconsequential in the context in which the term crops up in her 1986 biography. Such haphazard references indicate once again how superficially Mother Teresa's background and her years in Skopje have been treated even by some of her best-known biographers and friends. Fantasy and speculation have not always served Mother Teresa experts well, especially those who have been and still remain indifferent to her Skopje years. A full-length study of the nun's early life has still to be written, and if such a work could be penned by a dispassionate scholar, it could prove very useful in understanding and reinterpreting some key aspects of Mother Teresa's faith and journey from 1928 when she left Skopje for Ireland and then for India. A biography of Agnes Gonxhe Bojaxhiu's life in Skopje would be an enlightening introduction to the life of the nun Mother Teresa.

iv. Different audiences, same purpose

The little information on Mother Teresa's early years that surfaces in the works of her Western and Indian biographers comes mainly from books written by Balkan authors. One of the nun's most prolific biographers in the Balkans is Dr Lush Gjergji. Although he has written many works on Mother Teresa, Gjergji remains one of her least-known biographers in the West.

Gjergji is an Albanian living in Kosova. By his own account, his interest in Mother Teresa began in 1962, and he met her for the first time in Rome in 1968. Gjergji is one of the first biographers to have recognized the need to study Mother Teresa's early life in Skopje. After years of research, in 1980 Gjergji produced his first book on the nun entitled *Nëna jonë Tereze* ('Our Mother Teresa'). In the 38-page opening chapter 'Fëmijëria e Nënës Tereze' ('Mother Teresa's Childhood'), Gjergji provides for the first time some interesting details about the Bojaxhiu family and Agnes's parents, siblings and friends. More importantly, Gjergji was able to shed some light for the first time on the nun's health, dreams, ambitions, frustrations and talents as a little girl and as a young woman.

To write the introductory chapter Gjergji did what no other biographer of Mother Teresa had done before: he contacted several people who had known Mother Teresa at one stage or another from 1910 to 1928. Gjergji found of particular interest the information he collected about Mother Teresa from the conversations he had with her friend and relative Lorenc Antoni (1909–1991) in the late 1970s. Antoni was a distinguished Albanian composer from Prizren, Kosova. He and Mother Teresa had grown up together. Antoni's recollections offered Gjergji a clear picture of Mother Teresa during her years in Skopje. Equally important is the fact that Antoni had preserved the diary he had kept as a young man. In this diary he had often referred to Agnes, her interests in books, her early passion for writing, and her friends. He had also recorded in his journal the moment she confided to him her decision to become a nun, and her departure from Skopje in 1928.

Around the same time that he interviewed Antoni, Gjergji travelled to Italy to meet Mother Teresa's brother Lazar, who had been living there since 1939. Lazar told Gjergji even more interesting details about his younger sister, especially about her relationship with him and the other members of the family. Thanks to the information provided by Antoni and Lazar, Gjergji learned some very down-to-earth details about the woman who by that time had already been elevated to the status of 'living saint'.

The third and most important source of information for Gjergji's first book was, of course, Mother Teresa herself. Gjergji found the biographical details he had collected from the nun, Antoni, Lazar and several of her childhood friends very useful in highlighting what he calls Mother Teresa's 'home front'.[50]

Gjergji's first biography of Mother Teresa, especially the opening chapter containing the information on her early years in Skopje, understandably attracted the attention of several European publishers. Soon after the publication of the Albanian edition in 1980, his book was translated into several languages: Serbo-Croat in 1982, Slovenian and Italian in 1983, French in 1985, Spanish in 1988, Hungarian in 1990 and English in 1991. More recently the book has been translated into Dutch and Polish. Since the publication of his first book on Mother Teresa, Gjergji has published at least nine more works about her. He is also the author of many articles and has given numerous radio, television and newspaper interviews on the woman he was close to for almost thirty years.

In spite of his lifetime dedication to researching Mother Teresa's early years, Gjergji's work in the West has often been ignored, casually referred to and, according to him, on one occasion plagiarized.[51] The reasons for this kind of reception and treatment are manifold. For a considerable number of Western writers, Gjergji has only one identity; they refer to him in most cases as a 'cousin' of Mother Teresa.[52] The truth, however, is that Lush Gjergji is not even remotely related to the famous nun.[53]

In several cases, Western authors tend to ignore Gjergji's work because they see him primarily as a 'journalist' and a 'priest',[54] or, as Christopher Hitchens puts it rather unceremoniously, 'one of Mother Teresa's Albanian co-religionists'.[55] The fact of the matter is that Gjergji is not only a journalist, or an ordinary priest, but also an academic with a Ph.D. from the University of Rome *La Sapienza*. His work on Mother Teresa and other stimulating subjects related to Christianity, especially Catholicism, and the culture, history and tradition of Kosova, Albania and the Balkans, have been well-received not only by his fellow Albanians but also by his peers and the general public across the Balkans. He is respected in Kosova by his fellow Albanians whether they adhere to Islam or Christianity. Following the example of 'the mother of my dreams',[56] as he refers to Mother Teresa, Gjergji has been preaching tolerance, forgiveness and understanding among all the peoples in the Balkans throughout his life as a priest and writer.

One of the reasons why Western writers ignore Lush Gjergji's work on Mother Teresa is because his interest in the nun's image and work is motivated primarily by their common religion and nationality. Gjergji is certainly keen to present Mother Teresa as an epitome of an Albanian Roman Catholic as well as a great Albanian patriot, thus conforming to the official line of the Albanian Catholic Church about her, a line which Gjergji himself has worked hard to create and sustain from the late 1970s onwards. That Gjergji was keen to sell Mother Teresa to the Albanians as a great patriot and her family as an example of Albanian patriotism is obvious in his 1980 book. In this work Gjergji pays particular attention to Lazar Bojaxhiu's account of his father's devotion to Albania. In the same book, Gjergji is keen to highlight that the Bojaxhius were a family of patriots even before Nikollë was involved in patriotic activities. This is seen in Gjergji's effort to attach a patriotic connotation to the root of the family name 'boja-xhiu', which in Albanian means someone who decorates houses using paint. 'Boja' is the Albanian for 'paint' and 'ink'. According to Gjergji, in the case of the Bojaxhius, 'boja' could mean 'blood', signifying the commitment of Mother Teresa's ancestors to and the blood they have shed for the Albanian national cause.[57] Aware of the far-fetched nature of this interpretation, Gjergji is quick to note that this view is held by 'others'. These 'others', however, are identified neither in any of the later editions of his 1980 work nor in other books he has written on the nun where he has included the same piece of information. In his 2000 book *Nëna e Dashurisë* ('Mother of Love'), for instance, Gjergji argues that in the case of the Bojaxhius, the root-word *boja* connotes 'the blood shed for faith and country'.[58]

Gjergji's inclination to highlight constantly the patriotic background of Mother Teresa's family as well as her own 'commitment' to the Albanian nation intensified especially prior to and after her death in 1997, partly because of the efforts of some nationalistic and ethnic groups in the Balkans to appropriate her, partly because some of them started claiming more forcefully than ever before that she was not completely Albanian, and partly because of his intention to promote further the image and standing of the Albanian Catholic Church as an essentially Albanian patriotic institution. It could be argued that Gjergji's intention to depict and promote the nun as a modern Albanian national heroine is one of the reasons for some of the inconsistencies apparent in a couple of his publications.[59]

In spite of Gjergji's efforts, the myth of Mother Teresa's 'patriotism' has yet to take root among all Albanians, including those living in his native Kosova. The Kosova Albanians certainly speak very highly of the nun for her humanitarian work in India and throughout the world.[60] Many of them, however, remain sceptical of accounts of her inflated patriotism, and are rather uncomfortable with the sustained efforts made by Gjergji and the Albanian Catholic Church to emphasize towards the end of her life and prior to her beatification that she was a nun devoted to the Albanians in Kosova as much as to the poor of the world.

Of particular interest is the opinion of several Albanian intellectuals in Kosova, and especially of some academics at the University of Prishtina who are disenchanted with and rather irritated by the myth of Mother Teresa's 'patriotism' endorsed and promoted by the Government of Kosova, the Kosova media and several Catholic writers. So far, however, the official line on Mother Teresa's 'commitment' to the Albanians of Kosova has never been contested by any Kosova Albanian academic. It will take some time for Kosova Albanian scholars and the media to overcome their timidity and express openly their views, even when they clash with stereotypical policies reeking of false and drummed-up patriotism. In spite of their obvious frustration and irritation, at the moment it seems that not many Albanian academics in Kosova, Macedonia as well as in Albania are prepared to be seen as 'unpatriotic'.[61]

In spite of the theme of Mother Teresa's 'patriotism' evident in Gjergji's work, on the whole his discourse on the nun's life in general, especially about her first eighteen years in Skopje, is more or less of the same nature as the discourse employed by her Western biographers about her life and work in India. If Gjergji's work should not be taken very seriously because, as David Porter puts it, 'his main reason for writing was to give Albanians an account of their most distinguished Christian sister',[62] then almost every Catholic biographer and writer, including Porter, who has shown and continues to show interest in Mother Teresa has committed more or less a similar 'sin'. Their attachment to Mother Teresa was and is still motivated primarily by the intention to give the followers of the Christian faith, especially the Catholics, an account of their most distinguished twentieth-century Christian sister. In this context, most Western writers are drawn to Mother Teresa mainly for the same reason that initially urged a priest from the Balkans to write about her in the first place. Publicizing Mother Teresa, and through her, the ethics, validity and power of Catholicism remains the main drive behind numerous publications bearing the signatures of a large number of Western and non-Western Catholic writers, of whom Lush Gjergji is one.

Some Western biographers of Mother Teresa tend to ignore the writings of Lush Gjergji because he apparently wanted to appropriate her on behalf of a certain ethnic group or country in the Balkans. By the same token, the tendency of Western writers to ignore the first eighteen years Mother Teresa spent in Skopje could also be interpreted as an attempt on their part to 'appropriate' and present her as an almost exclusively

Western Catholic figure. The little or no attention many Western writers pay to her ethnic roots, childhood and youth could also be seen as an attempt on the part of the West to appropriate and monopolize this media and religious icon mainly because of the humanitarian aspect of her work.

While few can deny that Mother Teresa stood for something good, noble and humane, the Western and Indian discourse is not prepared as yet to acknowledge properly that her goodness had its genesis in a country like Albania and in a region like the Balkans, which are traditionally perceived in the West as trouble spots. Many people believe that Mother Teresa was the epitome of the most celebrated Catholic virtues such as tolerance and forgiveness. An impartial study of her early life would also clearly indicate that she saw evidence of and absorbed such virtues initially from her fellow Albanians and the other ethnic and religious communities as she was growing up in Skopje from 1910 to 1928.

The vast literature on Mother Teresa in the West offers a fascinating account of the life and work of one of the most celebrated personalities of the twentieth century. This literature, however, hardly covers the first eighteen years she spent in her native city. This early stage has largely been and is still being ignored by most Western biographers partly because apparently they are not interested in Mother Teresa's life prior to her important decision to become a nun in 1928, and partly because researching this part of her life would mean studying and perhaps getting bogged down in the often complicated ethnic, religious, national and cultural history of the Balkans.

In spite of some praiseworthy attempts on the part of several Balkan writers such as Lush Gjergji and Albert Ramaj to study her early life, the 1910–1928 period has yet to attract the attention of Mother Teresa scholars. Even in Gjergji's and Ramaj's work, the information on Mother Teresa's early years is not always presented according to the requirements of a modern biography. The Albanian and Macedonian Slav biographers have yet to write a full-length biographical study of Mother Teresa's early years. This can be successfully achieved only if due attention is paid to every member of her family, every aspect of her life at home and in the local community, her early interests, ambitions, achievements and frustrations and more importantly to the nature and history of her relation with the local church. Only through a systematic study bearing these and other issues in mind would one hope to find out how and when Agnes Gonxhe Bojaxhiu became devoted to the figure of Jesus.

In order to carry out a study of such magnitude the Balkan biographers of the nun would have to get rid first of their biases towards ethnic and religious 'rivals' and be generous enough to include in their work some bits of information about Mother Teresa herself or some members of her family that for one reason or another may sound controversial. Biographies that are written either to completely praise or completely condemn famous people are distorted portraits. There are many biographers, some of them in the Balkans, who apparently know more about Mother Teresa than they are prepared to disclose. Gjergji, for instance, probably knows more about the nun's early years than any other biographer. So far, however, much of his work on Mother Teresa has been essentially of a devotional nature. Unless he decides to write at length about the child and young woman called Agnes Gonxhe Bojaxhiu, his work will continue to be undermined by what Christopher Hitchens calls its intriguing 'fragmentary character'.[63]

Gjergji's selective recording of details from Mother Teresa's early years, and the apparent lack of communication and co-operation between the Mother Teresa scholars from the West, the Balkans and India have resulted in a rather incomplete and fragmented portrait of Mother Teresa. A complete and unbiased biography of Mother Teresa is impossible without a thorough study of her first eighteen years in Skopje. This part of her life would certainly shed considerable light not only on several individuals and events that had an impact on her childhood and youth, but also on the history and the people of the city of Skopje.

Mother Teresa was very much influenced by her parents, relatives and friends in Skopje, some of whom were not Albanian. The genesis of her humanitarian spirit is undoubtedly found in the healthy neighbourly spirit of this cosmopolitan city where, contrary to some long-held erroneous perceptions in the West and the Balkans, people of several ethnicities, nationalities, faiths and cultures could, and obviously can again live in harmony with each other. Mother Teresa seems to have been very much a product of a tolerant environment where individuals and communities co-existed and thrived without being a threat to each other or being perceived as such.

Incorporating the formative 1910–1928 period in future biographies of Mother Teresa would hardly diminish her achievements as a religious figure. In studying her early life, we would in fact identify and celebrate some of the virtues of the peoples of the Balkans, virtues which we in the West, in India and other parts of the world do not very often hear about. While Mother Teresa is certainly one of the most valuable assets of the Roman Catholic Church in the twentieth century, she also remains the best proponent of peace, understanding and tolerance to have emerged from the often troubled, discordant and intolerant region of the Balkans in modern times.

While he was still speaking to the crowds, his mother and his brothers were standing outside, wanting to speak to him. Someone told him, 'Look, your mother and your brothers are standing outside, wanting to speak to you.' But to the one who had told him this, Jesus replied, 'Who is my mother, and who are my brothers?' And pointing to his disciples, he said, 'Here are my mother and my brothers! For whoever does the will of my Father in heaven is my brother and sister and mother.'

Matthew 12: 46–50

To endure is the first thing that a child ought to learn, and that which he will have the most need to know.

Jean-Jacques Rousseau

Thank God for the maladjusted child.

Martin Luther King, Jr

4 Mother Teresa's attitude towards her early years

i. Thou shalt ... thou shalt not

Considering the lengthy period Mother Teresa remained in the public eye and how much was written about her during her lifetime, it is interesting to explore the extent to which she was aware of the little attention her friends and opponents alike paid to her early years. Equally important is to see what she thought about the obvious lack of interest that even some of her most trusted biographers showed in her childhood and youth, and indeed if she had anything to do with the information blackout on her formative years in the vast literature published about her from the early 1950s until her death. These and other related issues are the focus of this chapter.

The obvious lack of biographical information on Mother Teresa's first eighteen years in Skopje becomes even more intriguing considering the extent to which she was often involved personally in generating the vast literature on her. Mother Teresa appears to have always been willing to co-operate with anyone interested in writing sympathetically about her and her work. Numerous authors have reported that she always welcomed their suggestions for book proposals. One of the first people to have expressed his wish to write a book about the nun was her old friend Edward Le Joly. This is how Le Joly presented his request to her in the mid-1970s and how she responded to it:

> 'Mother, I have to ask you a favour; may I write a book on you and the Missionaries of Charity? Will you allow me to do so? We have worked many years together. I intend to write from the spiritual angle, to show your motivation, the hand of God directing and protecting your Congregations.'
>
> 'Yes, Father, write about us, You have known us well, you have been with us from the beginning. We have the same ideas.'[1]

Le Joly's *We Do It for Jesus: Mother Teresa and her Missionaries of Charity* came out in 1977. The book is significant because it was apparently through this work that the nun gave the clearest indication yet to friendly colleagues and strangers interested in writing favourably about her and her order that they would always have her full support. In 1979 her fellow Albanian Lush Gjergji also sought her permission to write about her. Not very modestly perhaps, Mother Teresa had replied: 'Write, write as much as possible about me and my work.'[2] Gjergji notes that Mother Teresa was especially keen that her countrymen wrote about her, and that she admitted this openly.[3] Every time Mother Teresa encouraged her admirers – Albanian or otherwise – to write about her, she would never forget to make a rather self-contradictory clarification: 'Write not about me but about God, and if God wants to speak to my people through me, I am always ready to be of service to God.'[4]

In 1980 Mother Teresa gave her consent to another admirer, Kathryn Spink, to go ahead with her plans to write a book on her. According to Spink, the nun had told her that she did not have to ask for her permission.[5] Spink was understandably grateful to the accommodating nun who soon became her 'friend and mentor';[6] after all, with her generosity, Mother Teresa had helped this admirer to launch her career as a writer.[7] Since the publication of her first book in 1981, Spink has become one of the most prolific biographers of Mother Teresa.

Mother Teresa was happy to co-operate not only with Christian admirers, mainly Catholics, who were interested in publicizing her and her work, but also with people of other faiths, especially with Hindus. In 1986, for instance, she would delight another novice writer, this time an Indian civil servant by the name of Navin Chawla, when she replied positively to his request to write a book on her. 'I would not have attempted this book,' Chawla wrote upon completion of his work, 'had Mother Teresa not blessed the idea. Throughout the five years that I have taken to research and write it, she has given me her complete support and trust, answered innumerable questions and always made time for me.'[8] Chawla was right to be grateful to Mother Teresa as she gave him not only 'her support and trust'. He mentions several times in his book, which was published in 1992, that the nun would ask him time and again about the progress he was making with the project. There is even a slight hint that Chawla was becoming rather uncomfortable[9] with her constant inquiries, something which Mother Teresa seems to have noticed herself at some point. This is perhaps one of the reasons why when the book was finally completed she told him: 'I have never given to anyone else this kind of opportunity.'[10] Chawla duly mentions several times that Mother Teresa helped him enormously throughout the long period he was engaged with the project. In the Prologue to his book, for instance, he notes that:

[o]ver the next four years she [Mother Teresa] reposed her trust in me and gave me a letter addressed to all her Sisters, permitting them

to show me their work and answer my questions; I used this letter frequently on my travels. I went often to Calcutta ... whenever I arrived in Motherhouse, she would say, 'Acha, so you have come?', and proceed to help me with the odd letter of introduction or answer my latest volley of queries.[11]

Chawla was also keen to record his gratitude to Mother Teresa and her sisters in the Epilogue. In one of the meetings he told her:

that while I did not wish to burden her with the rest, it would help considerably if she would designate someone to provide me with information or settle my doubts when she was away. Her organisation was growing at such a fast pace that statistics, names and places were constantly in danger of becoming dated. Besides, as a Hindu, there were occasional aspects of her faith where my understanding was incomplete or inadequate. Mother Teresa nodded ... and, after a moment's thought, suggested Sister Joseph Michael. . . . In the course of the last eighteen months, this Sister, with her gentle smile, made time for me, often at short notice. She gave me letters of introduction to the Superiors in the Mission houses I wished to visit, without which they would not have answered my questions.[12]

Chawla was not the only biographer of Mother Teresa to have enjoyed her full support. Several writers had previously worked closely with her and, perhaps, even more closely than Chawla. The nun is not known to have ever refused her co-operation to anyone interested in praising her and her work.

Mother Teresa apparently had a direct say in what her biographers could and could not write about her. Her claim that she had never read a single book about her or her work[13] was perhaps true. It is also true, however, that she did not have to read some of them because she had already had a chance to peruse them herself or had them read to her before they were sent off to print. Audrey Constant, the author of *In the Streets of Calcutta: The Story of Mother Teresa* (1980), proudly admits that '[w]hen I wrote the story (which I did with the help of the Sisters of Charity) Mother Teresa herself amended the manuscript and she wrote in a copy of the book and sent it to me'.[14] While Constant enjoyed having Mother Teresa's assistance only through correspondence – she apparently never met the nun while writing the book – Chawla had the opportunity to see her in person on several occasions and even read her some paragraphs from his work. Chawla remembers how during one such 'tutorial' in the parlour of 'Mother House' in Calcutta, '[l]istening intently, she [Mother Teresa] nodded a few times in emphatic approval. Finally, she said in her simple way, "Very good, very good. Get it published everywhere!" '[15]

Shortly after Chawla completed the biography, Mother Teresa worked closely with Lucinda Vardey and John Cairns who also were interested in writing a book on her. In the words of Cairns:

> [d]uring the following months, we were offered more and more support with the project by Mother Teresa and her community and began by talking to Mother Teresa at great length on a wide range of subjects. We then discussed her approach and the work of the Missionaries of Charity with specific sisters and brothers in India and in the West, whom Mother introduced. . . . Finally, Mother Teresa and her Order saw and approved the text and wished it well.[16]

In view of the nun's direct and close collaboration with numerous biographers, it is not surprising that many people, including her ghost-writers, assume that most of her biographical details are well-known.[17] This is hardly the case, though. Peter Dawn's *Mother Teresa: Apostle of the Unwanted*, which appeared in 1969, is one of the earliest books on the nun. Since then so many works have been written on Mother Teresa that compiling a complete bibliography would be quite a daunting task even for her most enthusiastic title-spotters. Some of the biographies of the nun have been hailed by their authors and reviewers as 'meticulous', 'thorough', 'balanced', 'exhaustive', 'comprehensive', 'fact-filled', 'genuine', 'excellent', 'luminous', 'revealing', 'in-depth', 'a definitive account' and even 'complete'. Thus far, however, in spite of some serious attempts to offer an informed and impartial picture of this famous woman, attempts which have intensified especially after her death in 1997, it would be impossible to claim that any book has succeeded in giving us the 'complete' and the 'real' Mother Teresa. Perhaps, such a book will never be written. Perhaps, such a book cannot be written. And there are people who obviously believe that such a book should not be written.

To have a better understanding of 'heroes' like Mother Teresa, to make sense of their work, commitments and achievements, one is inclined to show an interest in every stage of their lives. Those who immerse them-selves in the vast literature on Mother Teresa with the hope of finding there in-depth information about her as a child and a young woman in Skopje, are bound to be disappointed. Mother Teresa's early life has always been, and to some extent remains to this day, *terra incognito*.

ii. Intriguing reticence

Considering that Mother Teresa often had the final say on what should and should not go into the numerous books devoted to her, one would normally ask why she herself did not draw the attention of her biogra-pher-friends to her Skopje years. It was unlikely that such admiring, grateful and obliging scribes would have turned down her request if she had asked them to highlight further this formative stage in her life.

One could easily notice how little Mother Teresa talks about her early years even in some of the authorized biographies which she apparently edited herself. Here are some comments the nun made over the years about her family, parents and siblings:

'We were a very happy family, full of joy and love, and a peaceful childhood . . .'[18]

'It was a happy family. I had one brother and one sister . . .'[19]

'Mine was a happy family. I had one brother and one sister . . .'[20]

The above statements and similar ones appear in books written by her close friends and admirers from 1980 onwards. What is obvious about them is the scarcity of information and lack of details about the nature of her relationship with her mother, father, sister and brother. It appears Mother Teresa did not tell anyone much about them. Most of the information available about her immediate family and early years comes from her brother Lazar.

Mother Teresa's consistent reticence about her family and early life is not only surprising but also intriguing. This becomes even more obvious in view of the fact that every time she referred to her 'happy' family she would immediately add something else, which would in fact reduce somehow the significance of her affirmation of happiness in Skopje.

The nun left her 'authorized' biographers in no doubt that she was reluctant to say anything specific about her family and her life in Skopje. 'I do not like to talk about it. It is not important now,' she is reported to have said many years after leaving her native town in 1928.[21] This statement is recorded, either in direct or indirect speech, in almost all the books about her. As to where, when, in what circumstances and to whom she first uttered these words it is difficult to say.

Aware of the fact that the obvious absence of Mother Teresa's early years could be considered a weak point in their research, some authors note that their biographies are neither 'traditional'[22] nor 'complete'[23] because 'Mother Teresa herself has consistently refused to talk about her childhood. She dismisses it as unimportant.'[24]

Mother Teresa, it appears, considered her 'happy' childhood so unimportant that not only was she reluctant to talk about it, but she also did not seem to have been concerned if the little information recorded by biographers was presented inaccurately. That she was '[s]o unconcerned . . . about accuracy in relation to the chronicling of her own life'[25] is obvious from the numerous discrepancies reported over the years about her and the members of her family. I will concentrate here primarily on some of the inaccuracies included in books penned by close friends and admirers of Mother Teresa. The authors in question had unprecedented access to the nun throughout the time they were researching her life and work. This means that most of the biographical details about Mother Teresa's early life came from her.

In Mother Teresa's case, biographical inaccuracies are apparent in information about her date of birth, place of birth and her original name. Even some of her closest friend-biographers such as Malcolm Muggeridge, Desmond Doig, Lush Gjergji and Kathryn Spink record Mother Teresa's birthday as 27 August 1910.[26] This inaccurate date is included mainly in works published throughout the 1970s and the 1980s. Some of Mother Teresa's friends like Spink have corrected the mistake in their later works, thus recording the proper birthday, which is 26 August 1910. The wrong date of birth, however, appears even in publications that have come out after Mother Teresa's death. Gjergj's 2000 biography *Nëna e Dashurisë* ('Mother of Love') is one such case.[27]

As we have already seen in the previous chapters, while some writers agree on Mother Teresa's Albanian origin, they do not seem to be of the same mind when it comes to her exact place of birth. The nun appears to have been born all over the Balkans: Albania, Macedonia, Serbia, Bosnia and Yugoslavia. The complicated history of the Balkans over the last six centuries has certainly contributed to the confusion about Mother Teresa's birthplace. The region's intricate history, however, can hardly be blamed for some glaring mistakes recorded in several works. Some biographers' knowledge of the geography, history and political map of the Balkans is so poor that it beggars belief. So, for instance, having dutifully drawn the reader's attention in her 1998 biography of Mother Teresa to the fact that her friend's date of birth was not 27 August 1910, Kathryn Spink remarks with authority that the nun 'was none the less actually born in Skopje, Serbia, on the previous day'.[28] The statement about Skopje being in Serbia is hardly the most inaccurate thing Mother Teresa's friends have reported about the Balkans. Lucinda Vardey's knowledge of the peninsula, for instance, is even worse than Spink's. A couple of years earlier, eager to highlight the importance of the nun's first visit to Albania in 1989, Vardey notes that in '1991 [sic] Mother Teresa returned for the first time to her native Albania (Serbia) [sic] and opened a home in Tirana'.[29]

Such guesses about the nun's place of birth are perhaps best ignored, like several other biographical inaccuracies present in other works on Mother Teresa. Spink's remark that Skopje is in Serbia and Vardey's observation that Albania also is in Serbia, however, are included in books penned by writers that Mother Teresa apparently was closely associated with personally. After all, Spink claims that her book is 'An authorized biography' and Vardey's remark is included in *A Simple Path*, a work which has been ascribed to Mother Teresa. I am not saying that Mother Teresa herself wrote Vardey's book or every publication attributed to her. The nun obviously had numerous ghost-writers. As trusted friends of Mother Teresa, however, one would think Spink and Vardey would not have included any biographical details in their work prior to checking them first with her. Moreover, as we have already seen a few pages earlier, Mother Teresa 'saw and approved the text' written by Vardey and her team before it was submitted for publication.

As in the case of her date and place of birth, biographers have hardly been any more consistent with the spelling of Mother Teresa's original name. The nun's family name 'Bojaxhiu', for instance, has been recorded as Bejaxha[30] and Bejaxhiu.[31] As for 'Gonxhe' (the Albanian for 'rosebud'), the name that was given to Mother Teresa at baptism, this has been spelt as Concha,[32] Ganxhe,[33] Gonxha[34] and Gouxha.[35] In most cases, the various spellings of Mother Teresa's baptismal name appear in works written by biographers who were very close to her.

Most Western biographers believe that Mother Teresa was given the name 'Gonxhe' when she was baptized a day after she was born on 26 August 1910. Her Albanian friend, Lush Gjergji, however, maintains that the nun was actually born on 27 August and the baptism ceremony itself took place a week later, which is also the time when her family decided to call her 'Gonxhe'.[36] Eileen Egan, on the other hand, records 26 August as Mother Teresa's birthday, maintaining that the nun once told her that the date usually given as that of her birth, August 27, was in fact the date of her baptism.[37] It is obvious that Mother Teresa's friendly biographers fail to agree on certain facts about her early life, something which is rather odd considering how close some of them were to her for many years. Kathryn Spink, another trusted biographer, speculates that the fact that the nun allowed some writers to give 27 and not 26 August as her birthday indicates that '[t]he date which marked the beginning of her Christian life was undoubtedly the more important to Mother Teresa'.[38]

Equally odd are some conflicting details recorded by several intimate friends of Mother Teresa about her parents. So, for instance, Eileen Egan who was one of the nun's must trusted companions for several decades, maintains that Drane, Mother Teresa's mother, was originally from 'the Venetian region'. Considering Egan's mistaken belief that Kosova's capital Prishtina was originally called Prizren,[39] one is bound to be sceptical about some of the details she provides regarding Mother Teresa's early life. As noted earlier, Lush Gjergji is adamant that while the nun's mother was born in Prizren in Kosova, her family came originally from the Gjakova region, also in Kosova. Gjergji bases his claim on the information he gathered from Mother Teresa's brother Lazar in Italy in the late 1970s.

In the case of Mother Teresa's father, even some of the biographers who were very close to the nun fail to agree as to what exactly his trade was. Nikollë is said to have been a merchant, an entrepreneur, a grocer, a building contractor, a wholesale importer of foods and a pharmacist.[40] Mother Teresa, as will be seen later in the book, was very fond of her father. Lush Gjergji maintains that she remembered him with fondness to the end of her life.[41] Why such a loving daughter allowed her friends to paint such a blurred portrait of her father is something that her scribes have yet to explain.

Anne Sebba draws attention to two more inconsistencies, one of which is about the year when Mother Teresa's father died. Sebba notes that while Eileen Egan maintains that Nikollë died in 1919, aged forty-five, David Porter does not give a date but implies 1918.[42] Lush Gjergji is more specific about the time of death; he believes Nikollë passed away in the autumn of 1918.[43] Sebba has no explanation for the two different years given for the death of Mother Teresa's father but she attempts to make some sense of the other inaccuracy that concerns both the nun's mother and her only sister:

> When I visited Tirana in 1995 I went to see the mixed-religion cemetery where Mother Teresa's mother and sister Age are buried. . . . According to the women's simple marble gravestones, Drana, or Roza as it says, lived from 1889 to 1972. This would mean that she was just fifteen when she gave birth to her first child – perhaps fourteen at the moment of conception – and was some fifteen years younger than her more worldly husband. This would not have been particularly unusual for the time and the place. Many Albanian girls were betrothed in infancy. . . . But Age's gravestone gives her dates as 1913–73, clearly a non-sense as all the accounts – and there is photographic evidence too – are agreed that she was six years older, not three years younger, than Agnes.
>
> I have puzzled over this. Perhaps the marble-carvers in Tirana are not concerned about accuracy. Perhaps Drana's birth date as carved is as wrong as her daughter's. But, if so, why has Mother Teresa, who has visited these graves in recent years and has approved the crosses now placed over them by her Missionaries of Charity, not had such inaccuracies rectified? In 1991 she had one of the graves resited so that both were closer in the same cemetery. Three years later she attended an informal ceremony to bless the graves. . . . Is it possible that someone, and not necessarily Mother Teresa herself, thought it best not to advertise to the world that Mother Teresa's mother had conceived at such a tender age and therefore deliberately falsified the dates? And suppose this were the case, might one not therefore praise Mother Teresa as a dutiful daughter for going along with the deception in order to protect her mother's memory? Both tombstones were originally organised by the Albanian Catholic opera singer, Maria Krja [sic]. . . . The dates, she insists, were the same as those found on Age's identity card.[44]

Other writers before Sebba had noticed inaccuracies in Mother Teresa's biographical details. While doing research for his book *Mother Teresa: Her People and Her Work*, which came out in 1976, for instance, Desmond Doig had the opportunity to read a note that Father Julien Henry, a close friend of Mother Teresa by the time she was working hard to set up her Missionaries of Charity order in the late 1940s, had made in one of his large, cloth-bound notebooks. The note in question refers to the moment when Mother Teresa left the Entally convent in 1948 and is written in the name of 'The Society of the Missionary Sisters of Charity' and 'Agnes Concha Bejaxha'. 'The name as written in Father Henry's book and the name as spelled in articles one has read,' Doig remarks in his biography, 'are at variance. I may be forgiven for not checking at the source but, in truth, I would not dare ask Mother Teresa. I can hear her saying so distinctly, "It does not matter. It is of no importance." '[45] Doig obviously belongs to the group of the docile biographers who believed that they should pay attention only to those aspects of Mother Teresa's life and biographical details that met with her approval. This trend did not change among the nun's sympathizers during her lifetime. Even after her death in 1997, there is hardly any friend or colleague of Mother Teresa who has published anything critical of her, in spite of the fact that, in private, some of the people who knew her well and have not lost their admiration for her, are critical of some of her views and policies, especially her unrelenting opposition to abortion and contraception.[46]

Anne Sebba's *Mother Teresa: Beyond the Image* (1997) is certainly a welcome attempt to approach Mother Teresa's figure and legacy not only with the purpose of praising her but also of offering a critique of who she was and what she stood for. But then Sebba is not a Catholic. On the other hand, like most Catholic biographers of the nun, Sebba also makes no attempt to inquire into the reasons behind the nun's persistent reticence regarding numerous inaccurate personal and family details recorded in her biographies, and her alleged total lack of interest in her first eighteen years in Skopje.

iii. Swapping nationality for religion

Almost every book on Mother Teresa written by her colleagues and admirers draws attention to the fact that she was not eager to talk about herself. Several half-hearted attempts have been made to explain why this public figure was not particular about revealing any details about her personal life. The most common explanation is that the nun was so reticent about her past because she had nothing interesting to tell. This hasty assumption is made mainly by biographers whose only purpose in writing about her is to praise her for her exemplary religious devotion. Mother Teresa's life, David Porter maintains, 'is not a sensational epic. It explodes no myths. It gives no earth-shaking revelations.'[47] Kathryn Spink also considers the nun's background as 'essentially "ordinary"'.[48] The theory about the so-called ordinariness of Mother Teresa's life is advocated also by more critical writers. In the opening pages of her 1998 biography Anne Sebba is keen to emphasize that:

> [b]iographically speaking, Mother Teresa's life is not interesting; there is the same straightforward religious faith that guides her in every-thing, and a list of awards won goes nowhere towards explaining either the inner motivation of my subject or the response of the rest of the world. Mother Teresa, it appears, has suffered from none of the inner conflict that give [sic] the best biographies their dramatic tension.[49]

Those who sing only praise to Mother Teresa or who are only slightly critical of her maintain that, in spite of its 'non-eventness', her early life is still 'a remarkable story'.[50] And the only thing which apparently makes Mother Teresa's life remarkable is her exemplary attachment to Jesus. Those who uphold this interpretation are keen to point out that even on those rare occasions when she spoke about her early life in Skopje, she did so apparently only to emphasize the important role religion played in her family. 'I remember my mother, my father and the rest of us praying together each evening,'[51] the nun once reminisced. It is this 'strictly' reli-gious background, the nun's ardent supporters are keen to point out, which turned the 'ordinary' little girl Agnes Gonxhe Bojaxhiu into the religious icon Mother Teresa. Why the other two Bojaxhiu children did not turn out to be as religious as Gonxhe is something her biographers fail to explain. Aware that most books on the famous nun, especially those penned by Catholic writers, are more like hagiographies, some of Mother Teresa's devotees are keen to emphasize that this is exactly how it should be. In a self-vindicating tone, Kathryn Spink, for instance, admon-ishes in her 1998 authorized biography the restless prying critics who try to find in Mother Teresa's early life what apparently is not there:

> Those who have sought to find in Mother Teresa's life complex psycho-logical explanations have been consistently frustrated. Hers is a life not devoid of controversy – perversely it is not unheard of for church men and women to be the ones who do not want to hear talk of Mother Teresa – but it is a life of extreme simplicity as far as ques-tions of motivation are concerned. Unsatisfying though it may seem to some in the century of Freud, her life is full of areas which do not admit of rational enquiry, and the answer to such questions is almost invariably 'for Jesus', 'for love of God'. 'If you remove Jesus from my life,' she once told a group of reporters, 'my life is reduced to a mere nothing.'[52]

No one who has written up until now about Mother Teresa, not even her most committed adversaries like Christopher Hitchens and Aroup Chatterjee, has ever suggested that she was not an exceptionally devoted nun. No one has ever denied that it was as a result of her absolute devotion to 'orthodox' Catholicism that Mother Teresa was perhaps unaware of how irrational and embarrassing her behaviour and views were at times even to some of her close friends and allies within the Catholic Church.[53]

The fact that Freud and his literary contemporaries like James Joyce and D. H. Lawrence drew attention towards the end of the nineteenth century and in the early decades of the twentieth century to the significant role early years play in our lives does not necessarily mean that others before them had not tried to explain human behaviour along the same lines. Freud, Adler, Jung and many other psychoanalysts, psychologists and artists throughout the twentieth century did not invent the subconscious; they only made us more aware of its significance and articulated it as never before. Ignoring and ridiculing any attempt to see the life of our 'heroes', whether it be a 'saintly' figure like Mother Teresa or anyone else, from a psychoanalytic perspective, ignoring completely such a long heritage of thorough and groundbreaking research on issues as diverse as the interpretation of dreams, fantasies and visions, nervous disorders, psychopathology, psychic determinism, hysteria, individual psychology, birth order, parental neglect, childhood development, inferiority complex, overcompensation, the ego, the personal and the collective unconscious, introversion and extroversion, and the Electra Complex, is to trivialize a significant stage in our eternal quest to understand who we are, to define what makes us human and, equally important, to fathom what the future has in store for a species like ours.

Theories that the genesis of Mother Teresa's extraordinary devotion to Jesus was of an 'otherworldly' nature and so can never be explained rationally, represent a line of argument that some people obviously prefer to follow and they are certainly entitled to. The same 'privilege', however, should also be granted to those whose views on the origin and nature of the nun's attachment to Christ are not necessarily or entirely inspired and endorsed by Catholic or Christian orthodoxy. The best biographies of saints over the centuries, especially Catholic saints, often pay due attention to the early years of these exceptionally spiritual beings. In his spiritual autobiography *Confessions* (written from AD 397–400), Saint Augustine, for instance, pays special attention to certain key moments from his early life with the purpose of highlighting their formative impact on him. Why is it then we should make an exception in the case of Mother Teresa? Why this spirited, dogmatic and well-orchestrated campaign to protect this nun from the inquisition of the 'prying' minds that try to find some down-to-earth explanations about the source and nature of Mother Teresa's extraordinary faith in Divine Providence? The 'protection' that some of her over-zealous minders offer to 'their' Mother Teresa reeks of the obscurantism that has often undermined in the past not only the Catholic Church but also other Christian sects and religions.

While there is no doubt that religion was the most important driving force in Mother Teresa's life, as will be seen in chapter five, the nun was not a 'born' Christian devotee. No matter how religious her family was, her extraordinary attachment to Christianity did not necessarily start when she prayed with her parents and her siblings. The figure of Jesus made a lasting impact on the impressionable little Agnes not during the 1912–1918 period, as most of her uncritical biographers hold, but in 1909. The nun was being sincere when she stressed, at times to the point of exaspera-tion, that the reason she did not want to talk about her family was because '[t]he important thing is to follow God's way, the way he leads us to do something beautiful for him'.[54] No one can doubt even for a moment that when she said that Jesus was everything to her, that was exactly how she felt throughout her life as a nun. Such a lifetime attachment to Jesus, however, did not start shortly before she left Skopje in 1928, during the weeks she spent in Dublin that same year, or on the ship that carried her from Ireland to Calcutta, where she arrived in the early days of 1929. Mother Teresa's extraordinary religious affiliation reached a fervent point in Skopje at a particular moment in her life, a moment she was not willing to talk about either because she was apparently not capable of articulating it herself, or because she did not want to talk about it as it was too disturbing for her, or because she thought that her interpretation would be misinterpreted, or because she could sense that her story would not be welcomed by some parties for various reasons that will be identified and explored shortly in this chapter.

If we approach Mother Teresa's life dispassionately – that is, not only with the purpose of proving that she was (or was not) Albanian, a great Albanian 'patriot', a proud 'Skopjanka', a 'Macedonian daughter', the Vatican's most important 'asset' in the twentieth century, 'a religious imperialist', a friend of the poor, the lepers and the outcasts in India or a handy 'tool' in the hands of various Indian governments, but simply to study her as a human being – we will eventually 'discover' how consistent and complicated a person she was all her life. This 'new' Mother Teresa would be simultaneously a good Albanian, a proud Skopje citizen, a devoted servant of the Holy See and a committed friend of India. Our tendency to appropriate her for national, political and religious motives, as well as to attack her for these and other reasons means that Mother Teresa found it impossible to please all those who were interested in her. In order to remain in the public eye for the sake of achieving her main and only target, a target which took her several years to clarify in Skopje, she had to prioritize to whom she had to belong first and foremost. Understandably, her choice was determined by her commitment to the figure of Jesus. Mother Teresa would learn very early in her life as a celebrity that she had to choose to ignore, or at least to pretend to ignore, some people and periods in her life, as advised either directly or indirectly by those who catapulted her to international fame. In this complicated game of going along with other people's and institutions' choices and agendas, Mother Teresa, it appears, had no choice but to sacrifice, at least in public, her affinity for the Albanian nation and the Balkans.

More importantly, as a result of some careful calculations, she also chose to keep quiet about one of the most important stages in her life, her first eighteen years in Skopje. It would be absurd to think that she refused to talk about such years because there was nothing worth talking about. Mother Teresa herself never said that her life in Skopje was insignificant, only that she did not want to talk about it. If, indeed, nothing important happened to her from 1910 to 1928, she could have easily stated this very clearly, at least once. While Mother Teresa never made such a statement, she always insisted, and in some cases rather nervously, that she would rather avoid talking about her childhood and family altogether. The nun's edginess regarding this issue was noticed from the first by some of her loyal biographers. 'About this book,' she told Edward Le Joly when he was writing his biography in the mid 1970s, 'I must ask you, nothing personal.'[55] The nun's request must have impressed Le Joly very much since he opens the work with the following statement: 'This book is not a complete biography of Mother Teresa – she does not want one to be written.'[56]

While Mother Teresa was always eager that people wrote about her and her work, what she was very much against was any attempt to write about her early years in Skopje. David Porter's statement that 'Mother Teresa's interest in her own biography is minimal'[57] does not necessarily mean that she did not want people to write about her and her work. On the contrary, as we have already seen in this chapter, she was always eager to welcome suggestions to write about her from numerous colleagues and strangers. What Mother Teresa was obviously not interested in disclosing anything about was her life prior to the year 1928 when she left Skopje for good. Those who wanted to obtain any information about this particular period of her life would find the usually accommodating nun very reluctant to talk. As far as this issue was concerned, no degree of persistence on the part of her colleagues and admirers who kept on writing about her for almost five decades would persuade her to talk about her early years. There were cases when she would even be harsh with anyone who would not take no for an answer. 'Over the years,' notes Spink, perhaps reflecting on her own experience, Mother Teresa 'had been consistently terse in her response to questions which endeavoured to probe her personal life and motivation.'[58] Eventually, all her friends who wrote about her had to accept that her personal life was the only area about which she would always remain reticent. Even in those rare cases when she agreed to talk about her past, she never told biographers what they did not already know. As Navin Chawla notes:

> To inquiries about her life in Skopje, the influence of her mother and her separation from her family when she was only eighteen, her answers were desultory, her heart not in the conversation, her smile leading one away to the work of her community and to her current occupations.[59]

Mother Teresa's reluctance to talk about her early years and especially her family is rather strange considering how eager she was to remain in contact with her mother, her sister and her brother until they died. The nun wrote often to her mother and sister for many years after she parted company with them in Zagreb in 1928. During the Second World War, communicating with family and friends became very difficult. Her communication with her mother and sister, who had moved to Tirana before the war broke out, was also almost non-existent for many years after the war ended. In spite of her efforts to visit them in Albania and her attempts to arrange for them to be allowed to move to Italy, the three women could never meet again. As for her brother Lazar, Mother Teresa kept regularly in contact with him as from 1960, the year she met him in Rome for the first time in almost a quarter of a century, up until he died.

No matter how much she loved her family and the members of her family obviously loved her, Mother Teresa was still reluctant to talk about them. Her friendly biographers are keen to mention every time how much importance Mother Teresa always attached to family values, how she tirelessly asked people to love and respect their parents and family members, but they fail to give a cogent answer to the apparent 'contradiction' between Mother Teresa's discourse and her attitude towards her own family. Mother Teresa's opponents are keen to use this and other 'contradictions' to prove that she was not prepared to practise what she preached.

Mother Teresa's admirers and opponents have failed to approach the nun's early life and her 'contradictions' dispassionately. They draw hasty conclusions about her without paying much attention to her personality and her family circumstances. The main reason for this is that, for friends and foes alike, Mother Teresa has always been an 'ordinary' human being from an 'ordinary' family background, and her early life the epitome of simplicity. This 'simpleton' called Agnes Gonxhe Bojaxhiu was apparently injected by God with an extraordinary dose of spirituality when she was a child for reasons known only to God.

Mother Teresa, however, was hardly ordinary. Nor were her parents and siblings. She refused to talk about her family members not because she wanted to hide her 'humble' roots. As far as her family background was concerned, Mother Teresa did not suffer from an inferiority complex. On the contrary, as will be seen in chapters five and six, she would often remonstrate in private if anyone made any derogatory remarks about her background. If she decided to keep quiet about her early life and some members of her family, she obviously had some very strong reasons for this. Many areas of her life are in need of 'rational inquiry', but none more so than her early years and the motives she had for categorically refusing to talk about her family.

iv. The Muggeridge effect

Mother Teresa's encounter with Malcolm Muggeridge in the late 1960s is important for several reasons, especially regarding the information this journalist reported (or did not report) about her childhood and family background. If we pay attention to the 1968 interview, the television documentary shot on location in Calcutta the following year and the book *Something Beautiful for God: Mother Teresa of Calcutta* that came out in 1971, we would easily notice that the three pieces do not reveal much about Mother Teresa's family or her first eighteen years in Skopje. If we concentrate on the book, for instance, we find there nothing by Mother Teresa in direct speech about her parents, siblings and her Skopje years. The only direct remarks she makes are recorded in the 'interview' section of the book. Asked by Muggeridge where her original home was when the feeling that she had to dedicate herself to the poor people first came to her, Mother Teresa replies:

> In Skopje in Yugoslavia. *I was only twelve years old then. I lived at home and with my parents*; we children used to go to a non-Catholic school but we also had very good priests who were helping the boys and the girls to follow their vocation according to the call of God. It was then that I first knew I had a vocation to the poor. . . . Yes, in 1922. . . . *At the beginning, between twelve and eighteen I didn't want to become a nun. We were a very happy family.* But when I was eighteen, I decided to leave my home and become a nun, and since then, this forty years, I've never doubted even for a second that I've done the right thing; it was the will of God. It was his choice. (emphasis added)[60]

Those who are not very familiar with the details of Mother Teresa's life, based on the picture painted by the nun here – presuming that this is exactly what she said without any deletion or editing by Muggeridge – would think that both her parents were alive in 1922 when Agnes was twelve. The fact of the matter is that by 1922 her father Nikollë had been dead for at least three years. The Bojaxhius were indeed very happy when Nikollë was alive. While it is true that Drane took very good care of her children after her husband's untimely death, the tragedy scarred the young family for ever. Strangely enough, Mother Teresa does not mention her father's demise during the interview. This is in fact the only time she makes a reference to him in Muggeridge's book.

Muggeridge alerts the reader from the start that *Something Beautiful for God* is tantalizingly short on biographical details. 'I should explain, in the first place,' the opening sentence of the book reads, 'that Mother Teresa has requested that nothing in the nature of a biography or biographical study of her should be attempted.'[61] This is a request that, as we have already seen, became something of a fixture in almost all biographical works authored by her colleagues and admirers after the publication of Muggeridge's eulogizing work. I do not doubt that this was exactly what Mother Teresa herself had requested from Muggeridge. What I would like to explore here is the significance of this statement in the context of the time when it was made and to whom it was made. This is how Mother Teresa explained her strong aversion to biography in a letter to Muggeridge at the time he was writing the book:

> Christ's life ... was not written during his lifetime, yet he did the greatest work on earth – he redeemed the world and taught mankind to love his Father. The Work is his Work and to remain so, all of us are but his instruments, who do our little bit and pass by.[62]

Mother Teresa's statement suggests two different things, which seem to both contradict and complement each other at the same time. At first, she appears to draw a parallel between Jesus's life and that of her own. Those who do not know much about the nun's unique attachment to the figure of Jesus could well interpret the first part of her statement as a rather brazen attempt to convince people of her self-importance and that, like Jesus, she also was somehow a divine creature. Anyone wanting to write about her personal life would have plenty of time to do so after her death because, as in the case of Jesus, people would always be eager to know as much as possible about her.

It is difficult to say what exactly Mother Teresa's colleagues made of her remarks when she apparently 'equated' herself with Jesus, especially in the early days when she was not widely known. Some of her friends apparently realized that she was not claiming that she was a 'divine' creature. Her remarks, rather, were an indication of her exceptional immersion in the figure of Christ. This is certainly how Edward Le Joly interpreted her 'narcissistic' discourse. In his own words, '[s]he is Paul writing to the Colossians: "There is only Christ: He is everything and he is in everything."'[63]

Muggeridge himself appears to have seen Mother Teresa's reference to Jesus, especially the second part of the statement, as an expression of her modesty, and as a plea to him and others interested in her and her work not to pay attention to her because she was hardly important. Over the years Mother Teresa grew very fond of her catchphrase: that she felt 'like a pencil in God's hand' – words which her devoted biographers and ghost-writers have over-quoted in an attempt to emphasize the extraordinary efforts the nun made to efface herself for the sake of Christ.[64]

Muggeridge had apparently become very religious by the time he met Mother Teresa in the late 1960s. This and the nun's impact on him, especially the role she obviously played in convincing him to convert to Catholicism, are well documented. What is surprising, however, is that during the early years of their 'friendship', especially from 1968 to 1971, he was far from a devout Catholic. As he puts it in the book:

> in my unspoken dialogue with Mother Teresa, I conclude that I could not in honesty seek to be received into her Church; not even to please her – something that, in the ordinary way, I would go to almost any lengths to achieve.[65]

No matter how much Muggeridge had fallen under Mother Teresa's spell by the time he was writing her biography, it would be naïve to conclude that that was the only reason he apparently agreed so readily to her request not to write about her personal life. A well-educated person like Muggeridge, who would time and again emphasize the significant formative impact his early years and his charismatic father had on him,[66] would have hardly agreed to such an 'unreasonable' demand simply to please a nun who, in his view, was 'not particularly clever, or particularly gifted in the arts of persuasion'.[67] For an inquisitive and 'trenchant newspaperman' like Muggeridge, who had 'skewered Britain's sacred cows (including both Winston Churchill and the Royal family in the days when they were still off-limits)',[68] his readiness to accommodate Mother Teresa's strange demand so readily could only mean that in this particular instance, like her (although not necessarily for the same reasons), he too was not interested in revealing the person behind the persona.

While Muggeridge's two television programmes and the book on Mother Teresa certainly paved the way for her to become a global media phenomenon, it would be wrong to assume that she was the only beneficiary in this publicity game. Muggeridge too benefited from Mother Teresa's rise to fame. The level of interest the public showed in Muggeridge's 1968 tele-conversation, 1969 documentary, 1971 book and numerous interviews gave a new impetus to his career as a journalist and a writer. In this context, it could be argued that Muggeridge had every reason to be grateful to the unassuming nun, and was happy to show his gratitude to her by consenting to her request not to write about her personal life.

But Muggeridge was no grateful fool. He was aware that granting such an unreasonable demand to his interviewee so readily would most certainly invite severe criticism and ridicule from his enemies. To wrong-foot anyone who would accuse him of hypocrisy and inconsistency, Muggeridge tried to offer some justifications for respecting Mother Teresa's 'wishes in this, as in all other matters'.[69] This time, however, even his characteristically acerbic commentary could not help him prepare a sound self-defence. When he resorts to philosophizing, Muggeridge, the witty journalist, sounds more like a mediocre preacher. In a desperate attempt to convince first himself and then the sceptical readers and his adversaries, the veteran journalist draws attention to a philosophical truism which he seems to have invented himself:

> It is, of course, true that the wholly dedicated like Mother Teresa do not have biographies. Biographically speaking, nothing happens to them. To live for, and in, others, as she and the Sisters of the Missionaries of Charity do, is to eliminate happenings, which are a factor of the ego and the will. . . . So, when her vocation came to her as a schoolgirl, the only impediment was precisely this [her] loving, happy home which she did not wish to leave. Of course the vocation won, and for ever. She gave herself to Christ, and through him to her neighbour. This was the end of her biography and the beginning of her life; in abolishing herself she found herself, by virtue of that unique Christian transformation, manifested in the Crucifixion and the Resurrection, whereby we die in order to live.
>
> There is much talk today about discovering an identity, as though it were something to be looked for, like a winning number in a lottery; then, once found, to be hoarded and treasured. Actually, on a sort of Keynesian principle, the more it is spent the richer it becomes. So, with Mother Teresa, in effacing herself, she becomes herself.[70]

For Muggeridge, it is obvious that it makes no sense to explore the circumstances in which the schoolgirl Agnes Gonxhe Bojaxhiu decided to leave everything that was dear to her in Skopje in order to become a nun in a mysterious corner of the world thousands of miles away from her family and country. The matter-of-fact manner in which Muggeridge refers to this turning-point in Agnes' life could well give the impression to those who do not know much about Albania and the Balkans of the 1920s that becoming a nun, or at least thinking about it, was a stage that every young Christian girl from the region would normally go through.

Muggeridge's remarks on the unnecessary attention people apparently pay to 'identity' today are hardly the best examples of his ability to produce acerbic commentary either, something which is noticeable also in his criticism of celebrity culture. In admonishing those who highlight the significance of identity, Muggeridge is in fact contradicting his own views on and contribution to celebrity culture. In the second paragraph of the same work he is eager to point out that, in his view, Mother Teresa 'is a unique person in the world today; not in our vulgar celebrity sense of having neon lighting about her head'.[71] By trivializing the issue of Mother Teresa's own identity before she left Skopje, Muggeridge became one of the first biographers to install the neon lighting about the nun's head. Some flimsy celebrities are reluctant to talk about their identity because they apparently have none to declare, or rather none interesting enough to be taken seriously. In contrast to this mass of 'famous' but nevertheless 'unidentifiable' individuals, Mother Teresa certainly had an important and complex identity. Unfortunately, she chose not to talk about it throughout her life as a public figure, and not necessarily only or mainly for the reasons she herself gave to Muggeridge and other writers, or for the reasons they provided.

Unlike most friendly and 'unsuspecting' biographers of Mother Teresa who maintain that she did not want to talk about her family because personal details were apparently intrusive for a spiritual creature like her, Muggeridge, it appears, had other reasons for not showing interest in the nun's early life and roots. The usually inquisitive journalist admits from the start that he was hardly persistent when in the nun's company in finding out about her personal life, and that his interest in her childhood, parents and home was 'desultory'.[72] Muggeridge does not say where, when or how often he asked Mother Teresa about her family and early years. From a couple of hints in the text we can only assume that any time the question of her family arose during their meetings, Mother Teresa spoke with fondness about her parents and home.[73] Her words, however, are not presented in direct speech; they are reported by Muggeridge as casual matter-of-fact remarks, as if they did not matter and could have well been left out altogether.

Mother Teresa did not take to Muggeridge when they first met in London in 1968. According to Aroup Chatterjee, Muggeridge got impatient with her because she turned up late for the interview: 'The seasoned television presenter and man of the world adopted an avuncular attitude towards this shy and wispy nun, who was also younger.'[74] Muggeridge at first believed that his interviewee was an 'Indian nun from Calcutta'. He apparently discovered that Mother Teresa was Albanian during the televised conversation. When he learned this, however, Muggeridge did not express any great desire to know more about her background. We do not know exactly what Mother Teresa and Muggeridge talked about before and after the interview. What we know for certain is that she was hardly jumping for joy when she was told that Muggeridge was planning to interview her again, this time not in London but in Calcutta. In Muggeridge's own words, 'in the first instance [Mother Teresa] resisted our coming with cameras at all'.[75]

For Muggeridge, there was nothing strange in Mother Teresa's reluctance to co-operate with him for a second time. As far as he was concerned, it was only natural that 'an obscure nun of Albanian origin' who had been 'very nervous – as was clearly apparent – in front of the camera, somewhat halting in speech'[76] during the 1968 televised interview would not want a repeat of the same ordeal. After all, Muggeridge postulates, Mother Teresa had 'a deep-seated and well-founded suspicion of the whole filming procedure which had to be overcome by, among other things, a charmingly persuasive letter from Cardinal Heenan'.[77]

Like Muggeridge and 'all the professionally concerned', Mother Teresa could not have predicted the huge impact the 1968 interview would have on her life and work. All the same, she understood well enough the significance of giving an interview to such a powerful and respectable international broadcasting corporation as the BBC. Her nervousness in front of the camera in 1968 is something one would normally expect even from more seasoned media celebrities. After all, as Muggeridge rightly notes, the interview gave Mother Teresa an opportunity '[to] reach English viewers on a Sunday evening as no professional Christian apologist, bishop or archbishop, moderator or knockabout progressive dog-collared demonstrator ever has'.[78]

It would be wrong to interpret Mother Teresa's nervousness during the first meeting with Muggeridge, however, only as a sign of how overwhelmed she was because she was being interviewed by the BBC. While it is true that Mother Teresa was not widely known in Europe prior to the first interview with Muggeridge, it is also true that she was hardly a media novice either. When the 'obscure' Albanian missionary met the worldly British journalist in 1968, she was already a media celebrity in India and the United States. Nor was Mother Teresa star-struck by Muggeridge, who was so self-conscious of his journalist-celebrity status; something which she had noticed not only during their first encounter in London but also when they met in Calcutta the following year. Referring to the nun's attitude towards him in 1969, Muggeridge observes: 'I may add that Mother Teresa was not at all dazzled by whatever tin-pot reputation I might have as a communicator whose words had made a certain impact here and there, and who was known accordingly.'[79]

What Muggeridge apparently failed to notice was the fact that the proud nun might have found his haughty attitude in London far from tolerable. Muggeridge was infamous for his caustic remarks, sarcasm and intellectual arrogance.[80] He would have certainly had no qualms in making this 'nonentity', the 'inarticulate' nun, aware of his important status and showing off some of his expertise in and devotion to Christianity. After all, when they first met, religion had already become 'Malcolm's theme to the exclusion of almost everything else'.[81]

Muggeridge's brand of militant Christianity, however, did not have much in common with the charitable Christianity Mother Teresa had been preaching and practising in India since the establishment of the Missionaries of Charity order in 1950. As far as Muggeridge was concerned, admirable as the nun's 'faith in action' certainly was, it still lacked the necessary ingredient of 'religious militancy', as he apparently understood the term. He obviously believed that the charitable nun was not doing enough to spread Christianity in a non-Christian country like India. That Muggeridge did not appear to have approved entirely of Mother Teresa's essentially charitable work is clear also from the following comment he made during the televised interview in 1968:

> Mother Teresa, will you explain one thing for me? The inspiration from your work comes from the Mass, from your Catholic devotions, from your religious life. Now then, when you have people helping, don't you feel that you must put them in the way of having this same help?

To which Mother Teresa responded: 'Everyone, even the Hindus and the Mohamedans, has some faith in their own religion, and that can help them do the works of love.'[82] The nun's reply, however, did not necessarily please Muggeridge who could not help asking: 'Is that enough?' For someone like Muggeridge, who by that time was becoming increasingly intolerant of other faiths and cultures, Mother Teresa's relaxed attitude towards other religions meant that she was not militant enough and, worse, that she was showing signs of liberalism, which Muggeridge abhorred.[83] The 'journalist monk' was obviously far from happy with the 'media saint'.

Disappointed as he was by Mother Teresa's 'lack of militancy' and her obviously tolerant approach to creeds other than Christianity in India, Muggeridge could still see her potential to propagate his own right-wing ideas. He became particularly aware of the nun's marketability in the wake of the unexpected impact the 1968 televised interview had on the British public.

The viewers' response made Muggeridge reconsider an important aspect of Mother Teresa's life to which he had not initially paid much attention: her East-Europeanness. This does not mean that he developed a sudden affection for Mother Teresa's country, Albania, or the Balkans. Nor was he eager to help her fellow countrymen in Albania get rid of its Communist and atheistic rulers. Muggeridge was not known for liking small and poor countries like Albania. According to Aroup Chatterjee, Muggeridge was also 'deeply anti-Semitic'.[84]

Muggeridge appears to have had a particular aversion towards Albania, something he had made public as early as the late 1940s. In September 1949, he attended a party in London together with some of Britain's leading intellectuals and writers. The purpose of the party was to introduce them to the members of the Albanian National Committee, an organization founded in Paris earlier that year by some Albanian *émigré* leaders, and to give them some publicity. The committee was expected to replace Tirana's Communist government once it was toppled by the Western-backed home-grown resistance.

Thanks to Muggeridge, however, not only did the party fail to achieve what its organizers had expected, it also turned into a complete public relations disaster. As Nicholas Bethell puts it in his 1984 book *The Great Betrayal: The Untold Story of Kim Philby's Biggest Coup*, 'The whole atmosphere was spoilt ... by Malcolm Muggeridge who declared in a loud voice that Albania was a ridiculous country anyway that ought to be partitioned as soon as possible between Greece and Yugoslavia.'[85]

It appears that Muggeridge's outburst was not just a whim. By that time, Britain and America were sponsoring and co-ordinating the efforts of Albanian political immigrants to destabilize the Communist regime in Albania. Being an MI6 agent[86] himself during those years, Muggeridge's far-from-diplomatic remark could well have been an indication of the frustration he and his intelligence paymasters must have felt as a result of the persistent failures of their covert operations in Albania.

Muggeridge obviously believed that, as an Eastern European, Mother Teresa could be very helpful, especially in view of the fact that, as Aroup Chatterjee puts it, 'he had been a champion of Catholicism in eastern Europe, and was connected with underground Catholic groups that worked behind the iron curtain, financed with large chunks of money laundered by the CIA and the Vatican'.[87] Having initially flirted with socialism himself, a flirtation that had its genesis in the impact that his father, a Labour MP, had had on him in his early years, Muggeridge eventually developed a phobia about Communism and especially the Soviet Union. With money coming from the CIA, he is alleged to have launched a campaign in the mid-1950s aimed at disrupting the visit to London of the Soviet leaders Nikita Khrushchev and Nikolai Bulganin.[88]

As will be seen later in the book, Mother Teresa would soon be influenced by Muggeridge's political and militant brand of Christianity. During 1968–1971, however, she was apparently suspicious of him and the motives behind his interest in her and her work in Calcutta. It is very likely that in the early years of their co-operation, Mother Teresa did not know much about Muggeridge. Her friends and mentors in the Vatican and London, like Cardinal Heenan, however, certainly knew what he stood for, and they probably advised her that while she had to be cautious with him, it would also be unwise not to benefit from the promotion she herself, her religious order and more importantly the Catholic Church would get from co-operating with him and the BBC.

No matter how useful Muggeridge proved from the first in turning Mother Teresa into a media star in the West and how close they became in the following years, it is obvious that the nun never came to trust this particular journalist enough to share with him intimate details about her personal life, especially about her early years in Skopje. Had she told Muggeridge at any stage some of the information about her family that will be mentioned shortly in this chapter, the nun's image would have been seriously tarnished, perhaps beyond repair. A journalist like Muggeridge who, as was evident from the 1949 London party, had a reputation for behaving quite recklessly at times, was most likely to have revealed certain details about Mother Teresa and her family that she and those who backed her, especially the Vatican, did not want to become public knowledge. Muggeridge certainly believed that the nun he made famous served him well. Little did he know, apparently, that he was as much used by Mother Teresa as he obviously benefited from her.

v. Mother Teresa's 'weakest links'

Mother Teresa, it appears, had several strong reasons not to reveal things about her early years and family members to the unpredictable Muggeridge or to any of her admiring biographers. In the case of Muggeridge, her reticence may not have been caused by his openly anti-Albanian feelings. After all, it is quite possible that Mother Teresa did not know that he loathed Albania and the Albanian nation when they first met in London in 1968. On the other hand, she must have known, probably from the information received from those who made the arrangements for her first BBC interview and those who intervened to convince her to co-operate with Muggeridge in Calcutta in 1969, where he stood with regards to Communism.

This is not to say that Mother Teresa herself did not share Muggeridge's strong aversion to Communism and the Communist governments that were in power in at least one sixth of the globe for the most part of the twentieth century. Unlike Muggeridge, however, she had very good reasons to be reticent in public about how she felt about Communism and certain Communist governments.

No matter how much Mother Teresa might have hated in private Communism as an ideology and as a social system, she always enjoyed very good relations with Indian Communists. Paradoxical as it may seem, Communists appear to have been among the nun's most steadfast friends in her adopted country, especially in the state of West Bengal. The Communist Party of India (CPI) was set up in 1920. The splitting up of the CPI in 1964 resulted in the formation of the Communist Party of India (Marxist). The late 1960s saw West Bengali Communists hold important posts in this state's governments. In 1967 and 1969, for instance, Jyoti Basu, one of India's most prominent Marxist leaders in the second half of the twentieth century, became Deputy Chief Minister in West Bengal's United Front governments. In 1977 Basu was elected the Chief Minister of West Bengal, this time for the Left Front government, a post which he held until he retired in 2000.

Mother Teresa is known to have been very close to Jyoti Basu. The partnership between a devout Catholic nun and an equally devout Communist leader may seem, and perhaps was, odd, but one has to see it in the context of the complex socio-economic-political situation of West Bengal in the last four decades of the twentieth century in order to make sense of it. In addition to Calcutta's long tradition of being one of India's most vital intellectual centres, the city's growing poverty in the twentieth century was one of the main reasons Communist ideas took root there in the early decades of the twentieth century. Basu's long reign as the Chief Minister of West Bengal (a record that has yet to be matched in India), for instance, was down not only to his skilful political manoeuvering, but also to his government's progressive programmes, which were intended to address sensitive and urgent social issues and improve the lives of the poor, the disposed and especially of the untouchables. The plight of the untouchables remains one of the most sensitive and shameful issues in contemporary India and has yet to be addressed properly by the Indian political establishment and society at large, or by the international bodies that concern themselves with human rights issues.

Mother Teresa's charitable mission in India was never geared towards the eradication of poverty or achieving social justice. Nor was it her intention to challenge the caste system. This missionary was never a revolutionary when it came to how society, including Indian society, should be run. Her efforts to help the poorest of the poor in Calcutta were not something new, but they took on quite a symbolic significance considering she was a foreigner, a Catholic and a woman. These 'qualifications' were bound to endear her to the West Bengali Communists; they certainly made her very special in the eyes of their Marxist leader Jyoti Basu. Referring to Mother Teresa's unique and enduring friendship with Basu, this is what Navin Chawla notes in a tributary article about the nun that appeared in the Indian national magazine *Frontline* in 2000:

> He [Jyoti Basu] is, perhaps, the only person for whom Mother Teresa invariably prefixed the words 'My friend' before she took his name. It was well known in Calcutta that Mother Teresa could walk into his office at any time. And I am informed that he only said 'Yes Mother', and gave her whatever she wanted because it was invariably for the poor. When Jyoti Basu asked her to do something for the mentally-disturbed women inmates locked up in the Calcutta Jail, Mother Teresa asked for land. Here, in the middle of the Tengra slums she constructed a number of buildings to house the sick and mentally disabled women and to provide for their rehabilitation.[89]

Jyoti retained his respect for Mother Teresa after she passed away. The Archbishop of Calcutta, Henry D'Souza, made particular mention in his concluding address at the Netaji Indoor Stadium on 13 September 1999 of Basu's help in making the state funeral arrangements. Basu himself arrived at the stadium after the religious ceremony and offered a wreath. This was a gesture which the Indian media interpreted as 'a statement of the relationship the Left Front Government had established with Mother Teresa over the years: cooperation and support for her public work and a conscious distancing from the religious aspects of her work'.[90]

In 1999, Basu's friendship with the nun received another public acknowledgement and endorsement when he was selected by Mother Teresa's ninety-first birthday celebration and millennium award ceremony committee to be the recipient of the award for the year 1999–2000. This was the first time a leading personality was recognized on the late nun's birthday for his contribution to society, a move which is expected to become a tradition in Calcutta.

Considering the fact that following Basu's retirement the Marxists and leftists of Calcutta have hardly shown the same fondness towards Mother Teresa's image and work,[91] one could conclude that the friendship between the veteran Marxist and the Catholic nun was largely the result of the meeting of two practical and pragmatic individuals who were wise enough to leave their political and religious differences aside when it came to helping the poorest of the poor. Jyoti did not become less Marxist and Mother Teresa less Catholic because they could work together. Their co-operation proves that only those who put others first can overcome differences, even when they seem irreconcilable. Mother Teresa worked with many such 'irreconcilable' allies, whose friendship and support she continued to cherish throughout her life. Her loyalty to them was exemplary and she often went to great lengths not to hurt them. Not many public figures have Mother Teresa's courage to stand by her friends in their hour of need and even fewer would be brave enough to 'defend' them in public when they fall from grace.

The long-term and productive relationship Mother Teresa had with Basu, however, was not the only or the main reason why she never made any statement against Communism or the Communist government in West Bengal. Her persistent reticence had more to do with her intention to avoid annoying Tirana's Communist rulers. Mother Teresa is not known to have publicly criticized even in the slightest way the Albanian Communists, especially Enver Hoxha, at any time throughout the many years she was a public figure. She kept quiet even when Hoxha's repressive measures against a number of Catholic priests and clerics of other faiths was condemned by the West in the late 1960s.

Mother Teresa's persistent silence about Tirana's Communist rulers was noticeable especially when she became internationally famous. When she received the Nobel Prize for Peace in Oslo in 1979, a journalist asked her bluntly at a press conference what she thought about religious persecution in Albania. Even on this occasion, when the attention of the world's press was focused on her as never before in her life, Mother Teresa did not condemn the Communists. Her reply on this occasion was: 'I don't know what to say since I don't know what is happening there. I can say only one thing. My Albanian people are always in my heart.'[92] The nun chose to be meticulously diplomatic with her comments about Tirana's Communist regime even when she was interviewed by Albanian journalists. Also in 1979, during an interview which appeared that year in the Kosova magazine *Drita*, Lush Gjergji asked Mother Teresa to comment on the plight of 'the Albanian brothers on the other side of the border who have no religious rights whatsoever'.[93] Her reply to Gjergji was almost identical to the one she had vouchsafed earlier in Zagreb and Oslo: 'I have no opinion on this matter as I do not know what is happening there.'[94]

Mother Teresa's persistent refusal to criticize, let alone condemn openly, Hoxha's atheistic government when she became world famous baffled international reporters and annoyed her fellow countrymen, especially those who had left Albania when the Communists came to power. But while the world's media were soon convinced by the 'reasonable' explanations provided by the Vatican propaganda machine as well as by the nun herself – mainly that she was not a political figure and as such had no interest in politics – her compatriots felt they were let down by the only Albanian international personality whose open criticism of the Communist regime would have certainly attracted worldwide attention and condemnation as never before for violations of human rights in Albania. Confused by and even angry with Mother Teresa's ongoing reluctance throughout her life as a much-venerated religious and media icon to denounce the Communists, many Catholic Albanians in the United States wrote letters of complaint to the *Albanian Catholic Bulletin*, an annual journal that first appeared in San Francisco in 1980, and which 'began as almost the only concentrated effort anywhere in the world to present the dire situation of religion in Albania in its true light'.[95]

Like many fellow Albanians abroad, Mother Teresa was perfectly aware of what was happening in Albania. One of the main reasons she would constantly refuse to be drawn into making a public statement condemning Enver Hoxha and his Communist government was because she had to consider the safety of the two members of her family living in Albania until the early 1970s. Her sister Age had moved from Skopje to Tirana in 1932. Two years later she was joined there by her mother Drane. Mother Teresa was under no illusion as to how cruel the Communists could be to relatives of those labelled 'enemies of the state'. Had she been even slightly critical towards them, her sister and mother would have most certainly been imprisoned or interned like many other people who had crossed Tirana's Communist rulers.

Many biographers of Mother Teresa often comment on the brutality of the Albanian Communist government towards Albanian Catholics.

While it is true that many Albanian Catholic clerics were imprisoned and some were even executed, it would be wrong to claim that the Communists' wrath was directed only towards Catholic priests.[96] As Finngeir Hiorth observes in his 1990 article 'Albania: An Atheistic State?':

> [a]lthough the oppression of the Catholic Church was particularly savage, the Communists in no way were lenient in their attitude to the Orthodox and the Muslims. In a few years the church leadership of the Orthodox Church was virtually eliminated. Similar purges took place in the Muslim community.[97]

It is also equally important to emphasize that the Communists treated with brutality not only those members of the clergy who did not applaud the policies of the Albanian Communist Party but also anyone who thought or acted differently. Enver Hoxha was often exceptionally cruel also with Communist colleagues who disagreed with him.

While very few people today in Albania, even among the remnants of die-hard Communists, would try to defend the often barbaric ways Hoxha's government used to eliminate its enemies, it would be wrong to try to exonerate, or worse present as a martyr of the nation, every person that suffered under the Communists, and this includes some clerics. While the execution of opponents was a loathsome practice in Communist-ruled Albania, it is hard to dispute that some of the individuals who were arrested and eventually executed collaborated openly with the occupying Italian and German armies. This group of collaborators included priests, some of them adhering to the Catholic faith. Some Albanians, it appears, have still to come to terms with the fact that during the Second World War some of their fellow countrymen, including priests of all faiths, did commit treason.

Hoxha was certainly not prepared to tolerate any challenge to his authority, whether this came from religious or lay people and organizations. On the other hand, it appears that the Catholic Church in Albania and some Albanian Catholic priests were not prepared to put the interest of the country above the interest of the Vatican. The repeated calls of the Communist government to the Catholic Church in Albania to sever relations with the Vatican were rather hasty and perhaps absurd. The Communists' efforts to have a say in nominating the leaders of the Catholic Church, however, were not as blasphemous as they are made to be by some overzealous Albanian Catholic writers. The Communists were not the first 'outsiders' to insist on having a say when appointing high-ranking church officials. The Albanian Catholic Church is known to have sought approval from Istanbul for the appointment of its bishops throughout the nineteenth century, when Albania was under Turkish rule. Tirana's Communist rulers were certainly wrong if they insisted on being consulted on the appointment of all bishops but not on the appointment of the

Head of the Albanian Catholic Church. Such 'interference' on the part of the State was neither wrong nor unprecedented.

'Interferences' of this nature are common practice in several Western countries today. The post of the Archbishop of Canterbury, for instance, is important in England and not only in religious terms; this particular position is equally important politically. This explains why the appointment of the leader of the Church of England is not an issue that rests entirely with this institution's General Synod. For a high office of such national importance it stands to reason that both the British Prime Minister and the British Monarch should have a say on who is appointed as the shepherd of the Anglican congregation. On 9 July 2002 the Church of England's General Synod voted overwhelmingly in favour of allowing the Prime Minister Tony Blair and Queen Elizabeth II to continue having the ultimate say in choosing its bishops following a warning by senior clerics that 'a move to allow it to appoint its own leaders would undermine its position as the established church'.[98] The current system was inaugurated by Henry VIII in legislation dating back to 1533 and reinforced by the Act of Supremacy of 1588. No educated reader needs to be reminded of the benefits Britain enjoyed in the wake of Henry VIII's decision to become the head of his country's church. In the words of the bishop of Durham, Michael Turnbull, 'God has called the Church of England to exercise servanthood and mission in partnership with the state'.[99] England did not become a godless country because of its independence from the Vatican, nor has the Anglican Church become less religious because politicians and monarchs together have been having the final say for almost five centuries as to who becomes the Archbishop of Canterbury.

In order to consolidate its independence after World War II, and in the interests of national unity, it was and still remains imperative for Albania that the Catholic Church and all other religious bodies in Albania (the Orthodox Church and the Muslim Community) affirm their independence from 'mother churches' outside Albania. Having failed so far to declare their religious independence, the Albanians are one of the last peoples in the region who have yet to understand the significance of having national churches that put the interest of the Albanian nation before the interests of 'foreign' churches. Albanians would be more religious if the motto of their spiritual institutions changed from 'Religion and Fatherland' to 'Fatherland and Religion'.

We can only speculate as to whether Hoxha would have still declared Albania an atheistic state, as he eventually did in 1967, if religious leaders had been more forthright. He could well have done so. There have been cases, however, when Communism and religion have co-existed. Mother Teresa spent most of her life in a country where these two 'antagonists' have a long tradition of co-existence. Unfortunately, this was not what happened in Albanian from 1944 until the end of the 1980s. The Communists' impatience and some religious leaders' inflexibility brought about a shameful and painful tragedy whose victims included not only numerous priests of all faiths but also hundreds and thousands of ordinary believers.

Some Mother Teresa experts are keen to insinuate that the Communists were especially cruel towards the nun's relatives in Albania. In her 1986 biography, Eileen Egan includes some comments made, probably in the early 1970s, by Mother Teresa's brother on a clipping from an Italian newspaper:

> This is what is happening in Albania. A priest has been shot for baptizing a baby. His name was Father Stephan Kurti, and he was a distant relative of ours. The sister of our grandmother married a Kurti. He was imprisoned after the war as an anti-Communist and then freed for good conduct. In 1965 over two thousand mosques, churches and religious buildings, Orthodox and Catholic, were demolished or used as warehouses or museums. For protesting the demolition of Catholic churches, he was imprisoned again. A woman in the prison camp, who had given birth to a child, asked him to baptize it in secret. He agreed, even though by the law of 1967, this could be dangerous to his life. He was tried by a 'people's tribune' in a desecrated Catholic church.[100]

The prosecution and the execution of the priest and the alleged mistreatment of anyone in Albania related either directly or remotely to Mother Teresa's family, however, had nothing to do with the nun herself. Her religious activity and publicity do not seem to have angered the Communists to the extent that they would seek revenge by mistreating any of her relatives as they often did in the case of the next of kin of many Albanian political emigrants. Interestingly enough, as far as Mother Teresa's mother and sister were concerned, the Communists apparently did not maltreat them. On the contrary, as the case of her sister Age reveals, they even apparently allowed her some 'privileges' they would certainly not have granted to the siblings of anyone who was publicly critical of the regime. During the early years of the Communist government, Age worked as a translator of Serbo-Croat in the Yugoslav Embassy in Tirana. She was later employed as a translator and broadcaster for Radio Tirana, a mouthpiece of the regime whose staff were always vetted very carefully.[101] Far from allegedly living in constant fear of persecution, Age also appears to have had quite an active social life. According to her brother Lazar, she was a member of the Radio Tirana Choir until her retirement.[102] Equally important is the fact that Age and her mother were not shunned by friends, even those who were on very good terms with the regime. They were particularly close to the famous Albanian Catholic opera singer Marije Kraja, who is also known to have organized their funerals.[103] A well-known artist like Kraja was certainly aware that she would put not only her career but also her life in jeopardy if she was seen in the company of people who were regarded with suspicion by the regime, let alone if she was publicly involved in their burial. Lush Gjergji is also keen to emphasize that the Communists mistreated Mother Teresa's mother and sister, but, like other biographers, offers no conclusive evidence to back up his claim.[104]

Mother Teresa herself would often express concern about Drane and Age. 'My mother and sister,' she wrote to a priest in Ohri in 1962, 'are still in Tirana. Only God knows why they have to suffer so much. I know that their sacrifices and prayers help me in my work. It is all to the greater glory of God.'[105] As in other cases, though, even in this letter Mother Teresa does not make any specific accusations against the Communists for mistreating her loved ones. So far, Mother Teresa's published private correspondence does not show that she had any proof that the Tirana regime ever mistreated Drane and Age apart from the authorities' refusal to allow the two women to leave Albania and settle in Italy.

Most of Mother Teresa's biographers base their thesis about the prosecution of her family by the Communists on the fact that the nun was never 'allowed' to see her mother and sister. What they fail to mention is that up until 1960, as far as Mother Teresa was concerned, meeting with her mother and sister does not seem to have been her top priority.

Mother Teresa's first trip outside India since she arrived there in 1929 took place in 1960 when she went to Las Vegas to attend the national convention of the National Council of Catholic Women. On her way back to Calcutta, she and Eileen Egan, who accompanied her, stopped in Rome. In her biography, Egan makes several references to the meeting between the nun and her brother Lazar. The last time the two siblings had seen each other had been over three decades earlier. Egan, who witnessed the reunion, notes: '[t]here was sadness in being completely cut off' from their mother and sister in Albania.[106] During this meeting and in several other meetings Mother Teresa and Lazar had throughout the 1960s they never expressed any concern about the safety of their mother and sister in Tirana. Nor did they ever claim, in the wake of their deaths in the early 1970s, that the Communist government had mistreated Drane and Age. It is worth noting that in the correspondence between Mother Teresa and her family made public so far neither party makes any direct accusation of brutality or mistreatment. Their mother was eager to leave Albania not so much to escape persecution but because she wanted to see Lazar's family and Agnes again before she died.[107]

Referring to the 1960 meeting between Mother Teresa and Lazar, Egan remarks that the siblings concluded that there was 'no way' for them to come into 'direct contact' with their mother and sister in Tirana or 'to bring them out of Albania'. By that time Mother Teresa had no intention of contacting the Albanian authorities herself. Even her stopover in

Rome was not motivated only by the purpose of being reunited with her long-lost brother, or discussing with him how to help Drane and Age to leave Albania. As Egan puts it:

> For Mother Teresa, coming to Rome to ask that the 'little Society' in Calcutta be placed directly under the See of Peter was a climactic event in her religious life.
>
>   The constitutions having been written, Mother Teresa would now make personal and formal application for recognition of the Missionaries of Charity as a society of pontifical right. If the Holy See agreed, the Society would then no longer be under the protection of the archbishop of Calcutta but directly under Rome. Only with this recognition could the Sisters begin to move out from India to other countries.[108]

Like many other friendly colleagues and biographers of Mother Teresa, Egan blames the Albanian leaders for never allowing the nun to see her mother and sister. On the other hand, like other uncritical Mother Teresa experts, Egan does not offer much evidence of the nun's efforts to contact the Albanian government personally. Egan mentions only one case when Mother Teresa herself went to the Albanian embassy in Rome, probably in late 1968. Even in that meeting, the nun apparently did not request permission to go to Albania, but pleaded with the Albanian government to allow her mother and sister to leave the country and settle in Italy.[109]

Mother Teresa's admiring biographers also fail to emphasize that the nun was not always keen on writing to Drane and Age, certainly not regularly. In one of her letters to Lazar, written perhaps in the late 1960s, Age expressed her dismay and disappointment in Mother Teresa for not writing to her 'for a very long time. It appears she is too busy to think about me.'[110] In her letter to Lazar of 14 December 1971, Age informs him again that she and her mother 'have not received a single letter from Ganxhe', adding with a touch of irony that 'being busy with her big projects she does not seem to think to bother about us'.[111] This letter was written at a time when Drane's health had deteriorated seriously. Mother Teresa does not seem to have written to Age any more regularly even after Drane's death on 12 July 1972. On 27 May 1973 Age complains once again to Lazar: 'I have not received any letter from Ganxhe. It appears she has started to forget her sister.'[112] Age died three months later.

Speculation about why Mother Teresa could never see her mother and sister is rife. There are rumours that the Albanian leaders apparently demanded money from her in return for allowing Drane and Age to leave Albania, and that she would be allowed to visit them in Tirana provided she stayed in the country for good. While I have been unable to find any evidence corroborating the first claim, the second 'theory' appears in Kathryn Spink's 1998 biography. Mother Teresa, maintains Spink:

explored the possibility of going to Albania herself before her mother died, but was given to understand that whilst permission would be granted for her to go to Albania no guarantee could be given that she would be allowed to leave again afterwards.[113]

Spink does not say how she came across this information. In general, Mother Teresa's biographies tend not to acknowledge their sources. This is one of the reasons why some incidents mentioned in the literature on Mother Teresa cannot and perhaps will never be authenticated or corroborated.

It appears we will never know the extent to which Mother Teresa herself tried to persuade the Albanian government prior to the death of her mother and sister to allow her to see them or to issue them with visas to leave Albania. We are on much safer ground, however, if we say that Mother Teresa seemed to have depended more on some of her powerful acquaintances and friends across the world to convince and perhaps put pressure on the Albanian government to allow her mother and sister to travel to Rome. During the meeting with her brother Lazar in Rome in 1960, Mother Teresa is reported to have pointed out that they had friends all over the world. 'Do not lose heart,' she encouraged him once, 'I hope we can do something through them.'[114] Several world leaders, such as the American president John Kennedy, the French president Charles de Gaulle, the Indian prime minister Indira Gandhi, and the Secretary-General of the United Nations U Thant, apparently tried and failed to reunite Mother Teresa with her mother and sister.[115]

The issue as to why Tirana's Communist government was apparently reluctant to the end to allow Mother Teresa's mother and sister to leave the country, or why Mother Teresa appears to have hesitated to approach the Albanian officials herself, preferring instead to use her powerful contacts as mediators, would become less of a mystery if the nun's biographers paid more attention to the figure of her brother Lazar. We do not know much about him and the little we are told in books on Mother Teresa is not very helpful in creating a clear picture of him. The information about him and his life is patchy and fragmented. The first biographer to mention Lazar is Lush Gjergji. In the opening chapter of his first book on the nun, Gjergji often refers to the meeting he had with Lazar prior to Lazar's death in 1981. While Gjergji found Lazar very helpful in collecting for the first time some valuable information about Mother Teresa's first eighteen years in Skopje, he does not tell us much about the interviewee himself. Gjergji is especially reticent about Lazar's life in Italy.

Lazar was three years older than Mother Teresa. After completing his secondary education in Skopje in 1923,[116] he was offered a scholarship to study at a military school in Graz, Austria, for a year. He returned to Skopje in 1924 but left the family shortly afterwards. This time he is believed to have moved to Tirana to begin his studies at the Military

Academy. Upon graduation he joined the Royal Albanian Army. It is difficult to say how he fared in the Albanian army. According to David Porter, by the time he completed his studies in 1928, Lazar was Second Lieutenant.[117] Eileen Egan maintains that he was made a lieutenant, and was soon to become an equerry to King Zog.[118] According to documents made available in 2005, Lazar appears to have had a very successful military career in Albania. There is even talk that he was promoted to General.[119]

It is difficult to prove whether or not Lazar was a general in the Royal Albanian Army. His 'generalship' is probably another attempt on the part of the Albanian media to ennoble as much as possible Mother Teresa's family status. What is known for certain is that Lazar left Albania in 1939. No biographer of Mother Teresa discloses any information about why exactly the nun's brother left the country in that particular year. Eileen Egan is as reticent as any other Mother Teresa expert on this issue, but she remarks that Lazar fled Albania 'after the defeat of the Albanian army in 1939', perhaps implying that he was one of the Albanian officers who mounted a resistance to Mussolini's invading army.

It appears, however, that Lazar was *not* one of those Albanian officers and civilians who resisted the occupation of the country when they were abandoned by King Zog, who fled Albania having safely packed in the boots of the royal motorcade the country's gold reserves. Like his King, Lazar wasted no time in leaving Albania. Obviously, Lazar did not run away because he believed that his life would be in danger under the Italians. If that were the case, he would have chosen to emigrate to any country but Italy. For reasons which are not known yet, however, Italy was his place of exile.

In his 1990 biography of Mother Teresa, referring to this moment in Lazar's life, Lush Gjergji simply states that he went to Italy, where he remained throughout and after the war. In another book, which appeared a decade later, Gjergji makes a slight but nevertheless important change to his earlier statement. According to him, 'Lazar Bojaxhiu went to study in Italy in 1939'.[120] Gjergji offers no explanation as to why Lazar chose to go to Italy to pursue his studies precisely in that momentous year in the history of Albania. Nor does he mention Lazar's exact place of study in Italy, who sponsored his studies and when (or if) he completed the course. Gjergji also does not provide any details about Lazar's activity after the completion of his studies and throughout the six years of the Second World War. Referring to his studies abroad, Lazar is known to have said that after his course in Vienna, 'I was supposed to go … to Saint-Cyr, but I had seen Italy and I had such a passion for it that I went to the military academy in Turin'.[121] Lazar does not say when exactly he went to and for how long he stayed in Graz, Vienna and in Turin. Considering that Lazar completed his studies in Vienna either in 1924 or 1925, it is difficult to conclude if his words mean that he furthered his studies in Turin immediately after completing the course in Graz or some years later. Lazar is not known to have made any specific reference to any studies in Italy in 1939.

From the information provided in Gjergji's several books on Mother Teresa one could conclude that the nun's and her brother's portraits are rather sketchy. Gjergji appears to leave out in his biographical writings certain bits of information which he perhaps thinks would not work very well with Albanian readers. Like most Western biographers, Gjergji is keen to quote Mother Teresa as saying '[w]e were a very happy family, full of joy and love and with a peaceful childhood'.[122] Unlike them, however, Gjergji always leaves out the second part of Mother Teresa's statement recorded in several books written by non-Albanian biographers: 'I do not like to talk about it. It is not important now.'[123] Instead, he comments on the significant role her loving family and so-called peaceful childhood had on the life and work of Mother Teresa.

Gjergji is not the only friendly biographer of Mother Teresa who is reticent about certain details in the nun's life as well as about some obvious gaps in the life of her brother. The same tendency is obvious in most biographies of Mother Teresa penned by her Western friends. In the uncritical literature on the nun, her brother's significance is reduced to some occasional and at times incoherent remarks he apparently made about himself, his family and his famous sister to trusted biographers like Lush Gjergji and Eileen Egan.

One of the few Mother Teresa experts to pay some attention to Lazar's activity in Italy is Anne Sebba. According to Sebba, Lazar 'had joined the Italian army after the Italian occupation of Albania in 1939 and after the Second World War was condemned to death *in absentia* by a military tribunal in Tirana'.[124] Unlike most biographers of Mother Teresa, Sebba includes some bibliographical references in her 1997 book on the nun. Regarding the issue of Lazar's involvement with the fascist army, however, Sebba too fails to disclose any source of information. From the above statement it is difficult to conclude whether Lazar joined the Italian army in Albania in 1939 or whether he did so when he arrived in Italy. Sebba does not refer to this aspect of Lazar's life in her book again.

By his own account, Lazar was a colonel in Mussolini's army.[125] It appears his collaboration with the fascists in Italy was very high profile considering that when the war was over 'a band of [Italian] partisans had decided to shoot him'.[126] Had he been in Albania at the end of the Second World War he would not have fared any better either. In Lazar's own words, '[t]he Albanian or Italian partisans would have killed me except for my wife'.[127] This statement is included in Eileen Egan's 1986 biography of Mother Teresa. Egan also describes how 'Lazar's courageous Italian wife, Maria ... had thrown herself across her husband's body so that she would have to be shot first',[128] an account which she obviously heard from Lazar himself. We do not know what Lazar had done to anger the Italian partisans so much that they wanted to subject him to a summary execution; Egan attributes their behaviour to the 'chaos' that apparently engulfed Italy at the end of the war. Nor are we informed as to why the Albanian partisans were so hostile to Lazar, what exactly he was accused of and, equally important, what strong evidence the Albanian government apparently had to justify its terribly harsh verdict.

Like all other biographers who mention Lazar in their works, Egan vouchsafes no personal opinion or criticism of him regarding his obvious links with the Italian fascists throughout the war. On the other hand, like several other friendly biographers, she is always ready to condemn the Albanian Communist government for its 'heartless' behaviour towards Lazar, his family in Albania and his world-famous sister. Egan apparently believed that the Communists should have treated Lazar differently because of his father's devotion to the national cause. In her own words, '[Lazar] Bojaxhiu was cast down by the state of Albania, the country for which his father had died.'[129]

Egan was careful, however, not to annoy the Albanian authorities when she accompanied Mother Teresa to the Albanian Embassy in Rome some time in the late 1960s. The visit was the nun's first and perhaps only direct attempt to contact the Albanian government while her mother and sister were still alive. Referring to her meeting with an embassy employee, Egan recalls:

> I explained that the woman who had come to see him was from an Albanian family. *Many years earlier, nearly forty years before, she had gone to India to become a Catholic nun.* In all that time she had not seen her mother and sister who were now living in Tirana. I told him how *she decided to serve the poor on the streets of Calcutta* and how many young women had joined her. *Her group was called the Missionaries of Charity.* While her name had been Agnes Gonxha Bojaxhiu, she was now known to everyone as Mother Teresa. *I pointed out that though she had become an Indian citizen, her origin was known and she had brought great honour to Albania.*
>
> *The Albanian's face lit up at my rather shameless appeal to nationalism. . . . I added '. . . I consider that she is one of the best-known Albanians outside of your country.'* (emphasis added)[130]

Aware that the Albanian official would not have been endeared to Mother Teresa for her religiosity at a time when Albania had already or was about to become officially an atheist country, Egan was keen to stress that Mother Teresa had decided to become a Catholic nun a long time ago, so long ago in fact that it was before the Albanian Communist Party had even been founded. Indeed, by the time Mother Teresa left her country in the late 1920s not many Albanians had heard of Communism or knew much about it. Egan is also careful not to draw too much attention to the religious aspect of Mother Teresa's work in India. The emphasis in her calculated speech is exclusively on the nun's efforts to serve the poor on the streets of Calcutta. In this context then, it is hardly a coincidence that the biographer refers to the Missionaries of Charity not as a religious order but simply as Mother Teresa's 'group'.

It is important to notice that Egan does not mention Lazar at all in her conversation with the embassy staff, and perhaps very wisely. The last thing that Egan wanted to remind the Albanian diplomat was that the nun was related to someone who, as she puts it, 'was on the "black-list" of the Albanian regime'.[131]

It is quite possible that Tirana's Communist rulers knew that Lazar, the fascist collaborator, and Mother Teresa, the devout Roman Catholic nun, were the children of the Albanian patriot Nikollë Bojaxhiu. Following the announcement of the Vatican's decision to beatify Mother Teresa in October 2003, several Albanian reporters and historians were eager to flag up every scrap of information they could get hold of to prove the saint's Albanian origin and especially her patriotic background. One such welcome evidence was the discovery of a document dated 1942 which is not directly related to the nun but to her sister Age. The document in question is an application Age made in 1942 for a post in the Ministry of Popular Culture. Half of the employees in important state institutions in Albania during the occupation were Italians; the other half were Albanians who were carefully vetted. Age was apparently recommended for the position, but those processing her application had made a note on her form asking her employer to keep an eye on her because she came from Albanian 'nationalist stock'.[132] Considering that by that time her brother Lazar had already enlisted in Mussolini's army in Italy, it is obvious that the note about Age's patriotic background was not related to him but to her father. The Italo-Albanian administration apparently knew about Nikollë's involvement in the Albanian nationalist movement and about his poisoning. Nikollë was known to have been on good terms with the Italian consulate in Skopje.

The fact that Mother Teresa was the daughter of a patriot may not have been common knowledge in Albania in the 1960s when the nun started to make some efforts to get her mother and sister out of Albania. On the other hand, for rulers like the Communists, who were obsessed with collecting and storing information about almost everyone, especially those individuals perceived as opponents or, even worse, enemies, it is quite possible that the authorities in Tirana knew about the patriotic background of the Bojaxhius. The fact that Nikollë had given his life for the national cause, however, would have hardly induced the Communists to forgive his son for what seems to have been quite a chequered past, or welcome to Tirana his daughter whose main, indeed only, allegiance was to the Vatican.

So far, no friendly biographer is known to have made any critical remarks about Lazar's dealings with the fascists. Kathryn Spink, for instance, makes only a brief and indirect comment about Lazar's predicament as an *émigré* when she refers to his and Mother Teresa's unsuccessful attempts to bring Drane and Age to Italy. In her words, '[e]xile that he was, there was a limit to what Lazar could do'.[133] Put more directly, Lazar could do absolutely nothing to bring about a reunion. He could not go to Albania to see his mother and sister for fear of arrest and possible execution. Nor could he take any direct step with the Albanian authorities, being on the list of their wanted men. The best way he could help his mother and sister was by keeping quiet and not contacting them directly.

While so far no evidence has been disclosed proving that the Albanian Communists had mistreated the two women, one could argue that they were apparently keeping Drane and Age 'hostage' in Albania, not because of Mother Teresa but because of Lazar. By the time Mother Teresa contacted the Albanian Embassy in Rome in the late 1960s, she was hardly the international religious and media icon she was to become a decade later. The Albanian government, it seems, saw Lazar's mother and sister in Tirana as their best hope of apprehending him. Anne Sebba insinuates that Mother Teresa herself had been continually refused a visa by the Albanian government because of Lazar's connections.[134]

Based on the little evidence available regarding Lazar's involvement with the Italian army during the Second World War, it is hard to say if the severe sentence the Communists gave him was justifiable. His alleged fascist connection is certainly something Mother Teresa scholars should look more seriously into. For the time being, it could be said that he was perhaps more of an opportunist than a war criminal. Like King Zog, whom he was known to admire strongly, Lazar apparently was not wise enough to foresee the consequences of his decision to abandon his post when Mussolini attacked Albania. As if desertion was not bad enough, Lazar also appears to have collaborated openly with the fascist army in Italy.

This was hardly the first time in his life that Lazar had behaved rashly. When he arrived in Austria in 1923 to pursue his studies, for instance, he concluded that he had chosen the wrong school. He is known to have transferred shortly to a *lycée* which was frequented by other young Albanians.

If Lazar's collaboration with Mussolini's army in Italy was down to his recklessness, so far no evidence has been found which shows that he felt any remorse for his fascist past. It appears Lazar did not feel he had to apologize for his activities during the 1939–1943 period because he obviously did not believe he had committed any crime. That he saw himself as an 'innocent' officer in the fascist army is seen from his decision to approach the Allied forces shortly after Italy's capitulation. 'When the Americans liberated Italy,' he once remarked, 'I went to an American colonel and said, "I am a colonel of a surrendered army. I can work for you. I can drive a car." He made me his jeep driver and I earned 250,000 lire (about $350) a month.'[135] In view of Lazar's wayward behaviour, it is hardly surprising that Mother Teresa apparently never seems to have taken him very seriously. Even when he was in his sixties she would see him as someone who remained 'always a boy'.[136]

We do not know if the nun's 'immature' brother was employed by the Allied forces just as a 'jeep driver'. Nor is it known if he was in any way involved in activities against Albania after the Communists came to power in November 1944. What is known for certain, however, is that, to quote Nicholas Bethell:

> [e]ven as a defeated nation Italy retained her interest in Albania. Here in an area of traditional Italian influence, she resented the way in which the United States and Britain used her territory as a base for subversive operations, without seeking permission. Her intelligence service employed Albanian exiles, mostly Catholics from the Independenza party who had been trained in Italy between the wars and served Italy during the 1939–43 occupation.[137]

Considering that Lazar studied at the Military Academy in Turin before the Second World War broke out, it would not be surprising if, like other Albanian officers studying in Italy in the 1930s, he too was recruited by the Italian intelligence service. This would also explain why he chose to move to Italy when Mussolini's troops occupied Albania and, more importantly, perhaps, why he was recruited with such apparent ease by the invading army.

Thus far, no one writing on Mother Teresa has concentrated on Lazar's activity in Italy after the war. All that has been reported, in fact all we know about him during the post-war period, is that in the early 1960s he was starting life anew as the representative of a pharmaceutical firm in Palermo.[138] Lazar is not known to have praised Albania's Communist government for any of its achievements. On the contrary, from what is reported about him, he was very critical of them. Most of his criticism is about the religious persecution that reached its peak in the 1960s. Whether this was what Lazar resented most about the government of Tirana or whether this is what his sister's biographers prefer to mention in their books in order to emphasize the religiosity of Mother Teresa's family is difficult to say. What is known for certain, however, is that Lazar was far from a devout Catholic as a young man. By his own frank admission, 'I had little of religion after I left home'.[139] In 1928 he strongly advised Agnes not to become a nun.[140] He does not seem to have been taken by religion throughout the many years he spent in Italy as an *émigré*, something which his devout sister apparently was very much aware of.

In a letter dated 5 December 1975, Mother Teresa has this advice for Lazar: 'What you need is to go to church ... go to Christ.'[141] The tone of the letter, which Mother Teresa penned in Addis Ababa, is not necessarily like the religious advice that the nun was wont to include in her letters to relatives and friends. It appears that this particular letter is intended either as a response to a call for help she seems to have received from Lazar, or as a continuation of an unfinished debate between the two siblings on the significance of attending church. Mother Teresa's letter reveals that she is aware and concerned that her brother's life is far from complete, and that he is neither happy nor at ease with himself. Should he follow her advice, Mother Teresa reassures him, Christ will fill his spirit with joy, peace and love.

The famous nun's simple and direct preaching obviously impressed many people around the world but her brother was hardly one of them. It appears she failed to have any impact on him until the end of his life. 'I was the one to tell him he had cancer,' Mother Teresa wrote to a friend in 1981, 'and that he would be joining the family in Heaven – very simple answer he gave, "If you want to join the family you go – but I have no desire to do so now." '[142]

While it is possible that much of Lazar's aversion to the Albanian Communist government had sprung from his opposition to the suppression of religion, especially of Catholicism, it is also possible that his strong feelings against the political system in Albania were to a large extent motivated by his dislike for the Albanian leader Enver Hoxha. Lazar apparently knew Hoxha personally; they had met when they both studied in Austria. Lazar once remarked:

> When I was given a scholarship to study in Vienna and then at the Lycée, one of my colleagues was Enver Hoxha, now head of Albania. Russian representatives came to the Albanian students and picked out a few for special attention. Enver was one of them. He was taken to Moscow where he became a firm Communist.[143]

It is difficult to say how much of this is fact or fiction. Enver had quite a reputation for being very cruel to his friends from his school years in Albania and abroad who spoke against him. Considering that Lazar does not seem to have been very reticent in Italy about the Albanian Communists and their policies, it is quite possible that his words were reported to the Albanian authorities. The Albanian Embassy in Rome is known to have been 'very active' in gathering information about political immigrants in Italy,[144] and a high-profile Albanian officer like Lazar, who had enlisted in the fascist army while his fellow countrymen were fighting for the liberation of the country, is unlikely to have escaped the attention of the embassy staff.

Moreover, Lazar did not do himself any favours by being so outspoken about Hoxha. To make things worse, he apparently talked publicly about Hoxha's early association with the Russians in the mid- or perhaps late 1960s, a time which marked a nadir in the relationship between Albania and the Soviet Union. The last thing Hoxha apparently wanted to hear in those critical years for him and his government was the claim that he had been a tool in the hands of the Russian intelligence services even before the foundation of the Communist Party of Albania in 1941.

The emergence of Mother Teresa as an international religious icon of Albanian origin in the late 1960s and throughout the 1970s could not have happened at a worst time for Hoxha. By the time many political leaders around the world, the Vatican and the international media were hailing the nun as a living saint, thanks to Hoxha and to those who hid behind him, Albania was fast acquiring the infamous distinction of being the first country in the world ever to ban all religions. In simple terms, this meant that Hoxha's government declared God *persona non grata* in a country that had been one of the cradles of Christianity in Western Europe. This irrational decision damaged Albania's and Hoxha's international standing to an unprecedented degree. It is not very often that human folly, obsession and lust for absolute power result in such an extreme decision like the one taken by Hoxha to declare the country, as Mother Teresa once put it, 'legally atheist'.[145] By adopting this official stance towards religion, Hoxha, who was obviously craving distinction and aspiring towards immortality, certainly succeeded in achieving his aims, although for all the wrong reasons.

Enver Hoxha apparently saw the rise of Mother Teresa's international reputation as an epitome of charity and humanitarianism as a direct challenge to his self-esteem and belief that he was the most famous living Albanian in the twentieth century. The renowned Albanian writer Ismail Kadare, who apparently knew Hoxha well, has often 'psychoanalyzed' the Albanian leader, portraying him as an ambitious and spiteful man who was hell-bent on achieving international recognition as a leader as well as a writer. In his 1991 *Pesha e Kryqit* ('The Weight of the Cross'),[146] Kadare implies that Hoxha was envious of him for his growing literary fame in the West, especially in France. Kadare also insinuates that Hoxha was keen to keep him down so that his fame as a writer would not eclipse Hoxha's own standing as a man of letters in Albania and abroad.

We should perhaps be cautious about Kadare's claim that Hoxha intended to achieve recognition as a writer. It could be argued that Kadare's fierce public criticism of Hoxha from the early 1990s onwards is somehow motivated by a guilty conscience and an effort to redeem and exonerate himself for having been one of Hoxha's confidantes, as well as for having helped him, although unwittingly and perhaps not wholeheartedly, to build the myth about him as Albania's saviour in the 1960s and the 1970s.

One wonders if Kadare would have been able to write the novel *Dimri i Madh* ('The Great Winter') (1977) if Hoxha had not granted him unprecedented access to privileged information regarding the events that took place behind the scenes when Albanian–Soviet relations reached rock bottom.

Kadare also obviously suffers because, unlike some writers and intellectuals from former Communist countries in Eastern Europe, he apparently lacked the courage to take a stand against Hoxha and his policies, and did not go into exile for as long as Hoxha was alive. The fact that Kadare was unable to defy the Albanian Communist government openly during Hoxha's lifetime is an indication of the tight grip the regime and its leader obviously had on this hugely talented writer who naturally craves and deserves more international recognition.

But while Hoxha apparently succeeded in keeping Kadare on a leash until his death in 1985, one would assume that Mother Teresa was completely beyond his reach. Not quite. Considering how reticent Mother Teresa was about the brutality with which the Communist government of Tirana treated several religious figures of various faiths, one could conclude that even this often outspoken nun was affected by Hoxha's ability to censor his opponents. Hoxha obviously had no power over Mother Teresa directly, but he could certainly silence her because of what he knew about her brother, whose dealings with fascism appear to have been more than just a harmless and passing flirtation. Had Mother Teresa condemned Hoxha's regime in public when she became world famous, her ruthless compatriot would not have hesitated for a moment in making public the fact that the living saint's brother had been an active high-ranking fascist officer. Such a public revelation, no matter how true or false, would have seriously dented Mother Teresa's reputation. Understandably, this was a public scandal that Mother Teresa was eager to avoid.

The nun was not worried only about her own reputation, however. As far as she was concerned, her image and identity were inseparable from the image and the identity of the Roman Catholic Church. Mother Teresa would do absolutely anything to avoid causing any trouble to the Holy See. A revelation about her brother's fascist past would raise once again the issue of some unsavoury historical truths about the Vatican itself, especially its attitude towards Hitler and Mussolini. It is a well-known fact that the Vatican started flirting with Hitler in 1919. In that year the Holy See gave Hitler money through Archbishop Eugenio Pacelli, Cardinal Secretary of State under Pope Pius XI, who later became Pope Pius XII. In 1933, Hitler had quite a lot to be grateful to the Vatican for: its influence led President Paul von Hindenburg to appoint Hitler German Chancellor; while a few years later the Vatican apparently facilitated Germany's occupation of Austria, Czechoslovakia, Poland and Belgium. The Vatican was also aware of Hitler's persecution of the Jews, but never denounced it publicly.

Closer to home, the Vatican was apparently on even better terms with Mussolini, giving its blessing to the fascist dictatorship in 1922. Mussolini expressed his gratitude by recompensing the accommodating Holy See for the loss of the Papal States in 1870. The love affair between the Vatican and Mussolini was ratified by the signing in 1929 of the Lateran Pacts, which marked the official recognition of the Vatican as an independent state and the restoration of the civil sovereignty of the Pope as a monarch. In 1936, both the Vatican and Mussolini sided with General Franco during the Spanish Civil War.

Prior to and during the Second World War, the Vatican is known to have offered its support to fascist parties and regimes in several European countries, such as Spain, Poland, Croatia and Slovakia. In 1939 the Vatican did not denounce Mussolini's aggression against Albania, nor did it condemn Italy's occupation of Greece the following year.

The Vatican's collaboration with Hitler and Mussolini did not stop many Catholic priests opposing Nazism and fascism across Europe. Numerous bishops in several Catholic countries expressed dismay and annoyance at the Vatican's contentious policy and raised their voice against atrocities perpetuated by the Italians and the Germans. Many bishops urged the Vatican, although without success, to condemn barbarous acts committed by the Nazis, especially in a Catholic country like Poland. Several nuncios and other high-ranking priests were known to have intervened personally in countries such as Slovakia, Hungary and Romania to help the Jews.

In spite of such praiseworthy acts of courage by many Catholic bishops, the Vatican's relationship with fascism and Nazism continues to be a contentious issue in the modern history of the Roman Catholic Church. The Vatican remains very touchy about its affinity with Mussolini and Hitler, and would prefer not to be reminded of it. The news that the brother of a living Catholic saint had allegedly been a fascist spy and an active member of Mussolini's army as early as 1939 would have caused embarrassment to the Vatican. Likewise, such revelations would have undermined further the standing of the Roman Catholic Church in Albania, some of whose high-ranking priests had already been accused and punished by the Communists for having allegedly collaborated with the fascists and the Nazis.

Lazar's involvement with the fascists would have given another excuse to Mother Teresa's opponents in Albania and abroad to accuse her of having a shady past. Thanks to Lazar's irresponsible escapades before, during and after the war, those who resented the nun would have been keen to argue that her own activities were part of a 'family tradition' of siding with and defending the wrong kinds of regimes, and of enjoying the company of and privileges granted by dictators and criminals. Neither a pious friend like Muggeridge, as he turned out to be following the second encounter with Mother Teresa in India in 1969, nor the very efficient Vatican spin doctors would have been able to dry-clean the nun's public image after revelations about her brother's murky past.

Any public accusation of treason on the part of the Communist government of Tirana against Lazar would have certainly made him mention a significant detail about his family, about which Mother Teresa apparently was equally eager to keep quiet. Lazar *did* refer to it in public, but his words never received the kind of attention he might have wished for, and were somehow played down by most of the colleagues and admirers of Mother Teresa who wrote books on her during her lifetime.

Mother Teresa, who did nothing to alleviate the sufferings either of her fellow Albanian Christians or Muslims during the religious repression exerted by the Hoxha regime, and her brother Lazar, who apparently collaborated with the Italian fascists before and after the occupation of Albania, were the children of an Albanian patriot. As we have already seen, Nikollë Bojaxhiu was thoroughly committed to the national cause. A successful businessman and a kind-hearted person who always donated generously to the church, invested in several projects that benefited the citizens of Skopje and helped out the poor and the old, he also gave financial support to many Albanian patriots. As David Porter notes:

> [h]e [Nikollë] often entertained his patriot friends. He loved to sit late into the night in their company, exchanging dreams of the bright future of Albania or arguing politics with tenacity and enormous enthusiasm – sometimes in one of the four foreign languages which he had learned in the course of his business. The house in Skopje often rang with songs of war and rebellion, and numerous photographs and other mementoes around the house were a constant reminder of 'The Cause'.[147]

Lazar and Mother Teresa were used as children to seeing distinguished guests in their home. Mother Teresa never mentioned her father's patriotism, however. None of her colleagues and friendly biographers has recorded any remark made by her about her father's devotion to Albania. Unlike his sister, Lazar would always draw the attention of her biographers to Nikollë's attachment to Albania. Lazar remembered especially how happy his father was when Albania became an independent country for the first time after five centuries of Turkish occupation:

> In November 1912 Albania achieved its independence and Kole [Nikollë] hosted a gathering in his home to mark the long-desired occasion. It was a celebrated assembly. [Bajram] Curri was there, the famous fighter against the Turks who had controlled Albania for centuries, and others such as Hasan Prishtina and Sabri Qytezi who

were also revered among patriots. All night long the patriots talked, and sang songs of victory to the traditional accompaniment of a mandoline.

Agnes's brother Lazar, then four years old, watched solemnly as matchboxes heaped in the centre of the room were set alight. The memory of the victory flames leaping to the ceiling stayed with him until his death.[148]

The joy was short-lived for Nikollë, his patriot friends and the whole Albanian nation, however. The festivities were hardly over when the news broke out that the Western powers had decided to dismember the Albanian nation. Were it not for the personal intervention of the American president Woodrow Wilson, Albania could well have become what the German Chancellor Bismarck had arrogantly called in the late nineteenth century 'merely a geographic expression'. In carving up Albanian territories in the wake of the collapse of the Turkish Empire, Europe started the twentieth century with a crime against itself. The consequences of this historical injustice and miscalculation were to haunt Europe throughout the twentieth century, and the war in Kosova in 1999 was a long-overdue attempt to set right the mess caused primarily as a result of imperial European diplomacy, intrigues and selfish interests.

Faced with the prospect of inheriting a fragmented nation, many Albanian patriots raised their voice in protest, but to no avail. By now, Nikollë Bojaxhiu appears to have concluded that he should no longer merely offer financial support or play host to his celebrated patriot friends. He felt he had to be more directly involved in the national cause. His involvement must have been very high profile since within a few years it cost him his life.

As part of his efforts to reunite the Albanian lands, Nikollë travelled to Belgrade in 1919 to attend an important meeting. No one seems to know where exactly in Belgrade the meeting took place or who attended. What is known is that Nikollë returned home several days later driven in a carriage by the Italian consul. He was desperately ill and died shortly afterwards. Some of Mother Teresa's biographers mention that her father could have died from poisoning but are reluctant to accept this as the cause of death. Anne Sebba, for instance, wrongly concludes that:

[p]oisoning as a method of eradicating a political enemy is almost unknown in Balkan history, because the emphasis placed on honour usually demands use of a gun or a knife. Death by poison was not only considered unmanly but it was also unnecessary as almost everyone at that time carried a weapon.[149]

Like many past and present Western writers, Sebba apparently tends to see the Balkans mainly through exotic glasses. Nikollë's death was not a tribal affair or a vendetta, where the author of the crime had to bother about the issue of honour, but a calculated political execution. Whoever killed Nikollë was obviously eager to remain anonymous. Moreover, poisoning *has* been one of the ways of getting rid of political enemies and patriotic and nationalist figures in the Balkans. So, for instance, around the same time that Mother Teresa's father was killed, another Albanian patriot lost his life in much the same mysterious circumstances. Ismail Qemali, who proclaimed Albania an independent state on 28 November 1912, died from poisoning in Perugia, Italy, by a gruesome coincidence also in 1919.

When the subject was raised as to how his father met his death and who was behind it, Lazar never minced his words. In an interview, which appeared in the Italian magazine *La Gente* in December 1979 and January 1980, he had no doubt as to who was behind Nikollë's murder:

> The suffering of our family started when the Yugoslavs and Albanians were fighting for Kosova and the other provinces of Albania in which was the City of Skopje. Our father ... was very active in politics and the Albanian National question. He tried very hard to obtain the national rights of Albanians, with all his heart he tried to keep the Albanian territories in Yugoslavia together with Albania. When Yugoslavia took over the territories the family was persecuted and my father was poisoned.[150]

In an attempt to realize their ambition of creating 'Greater Serbia', ultra-nationalist Serbs enlisted in infamous terrorist organizations such as *Narodna Odbrana* ('National Defence'), the Black Hand and the White Hand. They eliminated or threatened to eliminate several Albanian patriots like Mother Teresa's father who stood in their way. The same fate awaited those Macedonian Slavs whose allegiance was not to Serbia but to their own nation. According to Mihail Ognjanov, several Macedonian Slav patriots were intimidated, terrorized and even killed by members of such semi-secret Serbian societies, which were set up in the first two decades of the twentieth century and which enjoyed both the blessing and the financial support of Crown Prince Alexander and of the Serbian government.[151]

Unlike her brother, Mother Teresa herself never made any public statement about her father's mysterious death. Asked by Lush Gjergji if she knew anything about those who were responsible for Nikollë's poisoning when she was nine years old, Mother Teresa replied: 'There were rumours implicating the Serbs, but nothing has been confirmed.'[152]

It is difficult to say why exactly Mother Teresa kept quiet in public about the murder of her father who, as we will see in chapter five, was certainly the most important person in her life. Mother Teresa was obviously different from her outspoken brother in many ways. For a deeply spiritual human being like her, who preached forgiveness to millions of people throughout her life, making accusations without hard evidence was hardly an option. Would Mother Teresa have ever raised the issue of the murder of her father in public even if she had indisputable facts incriminating the Serbs? Most certainly not.

Had Mother Teresa ever mentioned in public that her father was killed by the Serbs, the Albanians would have felt even more vindicated in evoking her as a national heroine. She was aware of the myth of patriotism her fellow Albanians in Tirana, Prishtina and Tetova were fabricating about her, especially in the wake of her first visit to Albania in 1989.

Mother Teresa chose to keep quiet about her father's murder not simply because she did not want to be used by the Albanians. The main reason the nun never mentioned publicly her father's involvement in the national cause and his eventual murder was because she wanted to avoid any confrontation with the Serbs. Had she alluded even slightly in public that the Serbs were implicated in Nikollë's poisoning, this would have certainly incurred the wrath of Serbian propaganda. The Serbs would have rushed to paint her as a destructive force in the Balkans, as an Albanian *agent provocateur* in the service of the Western powers intent on destabilizing the former Yugoslavia, and more importantly, on weakening the Republic of Serbia by encouraging separatism and irredentism in the provinces of Kosova and Vojvodina, which the Serbs have been trying frenetically to colonize for a couple of centuries.

Ultranationalist Serbs and the Serbian Orthodox Church would have been keen to present a devout nun like Mother Teresa as a Judas figure in the service of her fellow Albanians. The implications of this accusation would have harmed considerably Mother Teresa's standing as an international religious and humanitarian icon. More importantly, such an attack on her personality would have ignited yet another row between the Catholic Church and its ancient rival the Eastern Orthodox Church. The Serbs have not forgotten the Vatican's silence during the Second World War when the Croatian fascist leader Ante Pavelić and his followers allegedly exterminated some 400,000 of their countrymen. They would have interpreted any allegation by the Albanian Roman Catholic nun about her father's assassination by the Serbian ultranationalists as an expression of her patriotism, as an 'intervention' in Serbia's 'internal' affairs, as a 'plot' hatched in and endorsed by the Holy See, and as yet further 'proof' of the Vatican's traditional 'hostility' towards the Serbian nation.

All things considered, it is obvious that Mother Teresa was extremely careful in what she decided to do and avoid doing in life. She was certainly not prepared to cause trouble and embarrassment to the Vatican for anyone, no matter how dear, not even in honour of her slain father, whom she would remember with so much fondness to the end of her life, and certainly for no national cause. Mother Teresa was determined not to allow anyone to undermine her lifetime devotion as a Catholic missionary. If she had to be a public figure of any sort, if she had to champion any cause, if she had to trigger any controversy, as we shall see in the next chapter, she knew for whose sake she would do such things, and gladly so.

The way to see by faith is to shut the eye of reason.

Benjamin Franklin

Religion is the impotence of the human mind to deal with occurrences it cannot understand.

Karl Marx

Religion is an illusion and it derives its strength from the fact that it falls in with our instinctual desires.

Sigmund Freud

5 Jesus the divine superstar

i. Early initiation into celebrity culture

Mother Teresa's devotion to the poor is not the only reason she was treated so sympathetically by most reporters. The nun handled the media and her fame so well and for so long also because she had been initiated into celebrity culture very early in her life, certainly before she was spotted by the Indian press in the early 1950s. In the vast literature about her this important formative aspect of her life has been completely ignored. This chapter highlights the impact her celebrity father had on Mother Teresa and her family. Of particular interest in this part of the book is the attempt to establish a connection between the death of Mother Teresa's father and her inclination to replace him with a heavenly father figure. The chapter offers an in-depth analysis of the stages Mother Teresa's attachment to Jesus went through from the age of nine onwards.

Mother Teresa the global celebrity was the daughter of a local celebrity. According to accounts provided by several people who knew her father Nikollë Bojaxhiu well, it is obvious that he was an exceptionally charismatic figure: a successful businessman who owned a construction as well as a wholesale food company, the only Catholic member of the Skopje City Council, a philanthropist, a patriot, a polyglot (in addition to his native Albanian, he spoke Serbo-Croat, Turkish, Italian and French), a natural story-teller, an artist, a patron of the arts, an enthusiastic traveller and, above all, a devoted husband and a doting father. He was adored by his family, relatives, friends, employees and the local clergy. He was venerated by the rich and the poor, Albanians and other ethnic groups, fellow Catholics and followers of other faiths.

Nikollë Bojaxhiu was the pride of Skopje. He sponsored the building of the town's first theatre. His company took part in the construction of the railway connecting Skopje with Kosova, an important project which he also partially funded. He was good-looking, brash, eloquent, a daredevil and a steadfast friend. You had status in Skopje if you were a friend or were seen in the company of Nikollë Bojaxhiu. He was a success story and he knew it.[1] Mother Teresa and her brother Lazar would always keep in mind what he told them repeatedly when they were small: 'Never forget whose children you are!'[2]

Nikollë's successful business and his esteemed status meant that every member of his family was familiar with some of the benefits and constraints that come with being in the public eye. Although not to the same extent as nowadays, it is obvious that celebrity culture was in place and did have an impact on those concerned even in a small Balkan metropolis like Skopje at the beginning of the twentieth century. Nikollë's fame meant that his wife Drane and their three children were also in the spotlight. They were all expected to behave in public in accordance with the family's status. Local fame brought them responsibilities as well as recognition. This was an experience which Mother Teresa would find very useful later in life when she herself became a public figure.

Nikollë's success, however, was short-lived; he died suddenly and in mysterious circumstances in 1919 at the age of forty-five.[3] His death was a dreadful blow not only to his immediate family but also to other relatives and many friends. The whole town was in mourning for Nikollë. Large crowds and representatives of all religions came to pay their final respects to the man who had touched the lives of so many people from all walks of life. On the day of the funeral every jeweller's shop in the town was closed as a mark of respect. All school children were given commemorative handkerchiefs. According to a local tradition, the numbers of handkerchiefs given away on such occasions is an indication of the dead person's wealth and of his family's social status. Nikollë's grand funeral was remembered for a long time in Skopje.

ii. Jesus the surrogate father

Mother Teresa once said, '[f]aith is a gift from God, and he gives it to whomever he chooses'.[4] This subjective interpretation is maintained by all her friendly biographers, especially the Catholics, who are eager to emphasize that, in her case, as in the case of any devout follower, faith is something we cannot and perhaps should not rationalize.

Some of the most profound thinkers of the nineteenth and twentieth century, such as Feuerbach, Marx, Nietzsche, Durkheim, Weber and Freud, approached religion as a socially generated phenomenon which has shaped much of human relations and perceptions of the world. Their efforts to rationalize the 'irrational' laid the foundations of the sociology of religion. In spite of some praiseworthy efforts in the latter half of the twentieth century by renowned scholars like Charles Y. Glock, Robert N. Bellah, Peter L. Berger, Rodney Stark and Robert Wuthnow to emulate the work of the founding fathers, the debate about religion and its role in society has not maintained the same excellence as in the days of Marx and Weber.

It is worth noting that the 'rational' approach to religion has not diminished our apparently pathological drive to have faith in something otherworldly. Millions of followers of different creeds prefer to look at the issue of faith much in the same way as Mother Teresa did. In spite of their long and rich tradition, the rationalists have been unable to demystify faith. On the contrary, for many people, the rational approach has only deepened further the mystery that is religion. Mother Teresa obviously spoke for followers of all religions in saying that, when it comes to faith, '[e]ither you have it, or you don't'.[5]

As someone who stands between the rationalists and the spiritualists, in this part of the book I will attempt to demonstrate that the two approaches need not be completely antagonistic, and that the mystery of faith can be explained rationally just as there are things about faith that are perhaps beyond our perceptive abilities. Concentrating on the death of Mother Teresa's father, I hope to offer some explanations about the time and circumstances in which the nun's extraordinary attachment to Jesus began and the impact this had on her for the rest of her life. I am fully aware of the sensitive nature of my approach, which explains why I feel it is important to emphasize that it is not my intention to trivialize something that was of such vital importance to Mother Teresa, and that remains so to millions of Christians and followers of other faiths.

Many biographers of Mother Teresa mention briefly in their works something about Nikollë's death. They often emphasize what a huge loss this was for the Bojaxhiu family and the community at large. It is difficult to find any Mother Teresa expert, however, who has ever attempted to explore the short- and long-term impact of this tragic event on Mother Teresa herself. No 'complete' biography so far contains even a passing reference to how the sudden loss of her father might have affected little Agnes. I have also been unable to find any book claiming that this tragic event had no effect whatsoever on her. Nikollë's death remains one of the most intriguing events in Mother Teresa's early life that has still to attract the attention of scholars interested in her and in the sociology of religion.

Agnes was nine years old when Nikollë passed away and, like everyone else in the family, was devastated. She could never forget him throughout her life. Shortly before she died, her biographer and friend Lush Gjergji asked her specifically if she remembered her father. To which an emotional Mother Teresa had replied: 'Like it was yesterday.'[6]

The unexpected loss of such a charismatic parent proved to be quite a traumatic event for all the Bojaxhiu children, but especially for Agnes, who was an exceptionally sensitive and introverted child. Like her two elder siblings, she adored her popular and caring father. Unlike them, though, she was apparently unable to make him fully aware of how much he meant to her. Nikollë loved all his three children dearly and yet he was more attached to his eldest daughter Age who 'had a special place in his affection'.[7] When he returned from trips abroad he enchanted the children with marvellous stories but, as his son Lazar would put it many years later, Nikollë would talk 'mainly with Age'.[8] While Agnes had the look of her mother, her elder sister took more after her father. Age meant so much to Nikollë that he would often call her 'my right hand'.[9]

We know almost nothing about Agnes's reaction to the news of her father's sudden illness and death in the eventful autumn of 1919. As mentioned earlier, Agnes does not figure in most accounts provided in numerous biographies of the moment when her father was taken ill and eventually died. She is mentioned only twice in this context. The first reference is found in Eileen Egan's 1986 biography *Such a Vision of the Street: Mother Teresa – The Spirit and the Work*. Even in this instance, the reader is left to infer how Agnes must have felt when her world suddenly fell apart. Sensing perhaps that her husband's life was slipping away, Drane:

> sent the young Agnes Gonxha to the nearby parish for the priest, but he was not there. The young girl must have thought that the priest could be leaving or coming back from a trip; in any case, she directed her steps to the Skopje Railway Station. A priest she did not know was on the platform. She approached him and told him about her desperately ill father. The priest rushed with her to her home. After administering the rites of the dying to Nikola, he went back to the station. The family never saw him again.[10]

The same incident is mentioned briefly also in Anne Sebba's 1997 biography *Mother Teresa: Beyond the Image*:

> Drana sent Agnes to fetch the parish priest, but when she could not find him she went for some reason to the Skopje railway station, where she found another priest unknown to the family. She persuaded him to come home, where he administered the last rites to Nikola.[11]

Neither Egan nor Sebba explains the source of this particular anecdote. Egan, who died in 2000, does not refer to the incident in her other books on Mother Teresa. We will probably never know for certain how Egan herself came to know about Agnes's brief encounter. It is possible that she might have heard it from the nun herself. Egan was one of Mother Teresa's most trusted biographers and the two women's friendship spanned over thirty years.

Eight years after the publication of her 1997 biography, Sebba does not remember where she found this particular anecdote. In her words, 'I suppose it was used in other accounts.'[12] Considering that the incident was mentioned for the first time in Egan's 1986 biography and that Sebba refers to this particular work quite often in her 1997 book on Mother Teresa, it seems likely that Sebba learned about the meeting between Agnes and the unidentified clergyman from Egan's work. Like Egan, Sebba does not attach any specific significance to this incident in her biography.

That her father's death had a huge impact on Agnes is also clear from the 1997 film *Mother Teresa: In the Name of God's Poor*, directed by Kevin Connor. The script-writers of this biopic are Dominique Lapierre and Jan Hartman. Lapierre had known Mother Teresa well since the early 1980s when he was writing his novel *The City of Joy*. He worked closely with the nun, especially when he was researching and writing the script for *In the Name of God's Poor*. In this film, Mother Teresa's character is played with gusto by Geraldine Chaplin. Of particular interest in the film is the scene in a boarding school where Sister Teresa tries to calm a little girl called Mary who cannot sleep apparently because she had witnessed the violence that had engulfed Calcutta in August 1946. This is what the nun had to say to the upset child:

> Mary, Mary, Hey!
> When I was nine years old, my father died. In my own country, Albania, where I was born, there was a lot of political strife. For many years I couldn't understand what happened, why my father didn't come home. And I used to recite a poem to myself, over and over:
>
> > His red heart beats with love,
> > For child, wife and country
> > And then bursts into bloom
> > Like crimson rose,
> > Dropped on crumpled shirt.
>
> This poem is about believing in love, Mary, even when everything you see around you is hatred and destruction.
> To bed. Mary, tomorrow I think you have a poem to write, just like I did, when I was nine years old and when my father died. Good night girls. God bless you.

We should not perhaps read too much into this particular scene or indeed into the film as a whole. After all, although this work is based on real events and had the initial blessing and co-operation of Mother Teresa, it is still a work of 'fiction' and as such cannot be treated as a reliable biographical source.

Given the close collaboration between the script-writers, especially Lapierre, and Mother Teresa, however, it would be unwise to ignore completely some of the biographical details recorded in the film, especially Sister Teresa's account of how she felt when she suddenly lost her father. The anguish, which is conveyed so convincingly in this moving scene, was probably what Mother Teresa herself experienced when Nikollë returned home in a dreadful state from the political meeting in Belgrade, when she was asked by her mother to go and find the local vicar and when she approached at the Skopje railway station the unknown priest asking him to follow her home to her dying father. This kind of anguish had apparently remained with Agnes for many years after her father's funeral as she struggled to make sense of what to her must have been both incomprehensible and utterly cruel.

The anecdote about Agnes's encounter with the unidentified vicar that appears in Egan's and Sebba's biographies and Mother Teresa's account of her turmoil as a child in the wake of her father's death included in Hartman's and Lapierre's script indicate that, after all, the nun did occasionally open her heart about some very personal and sad moments from her early years to her trusted friends who wrote books and made films and documentaries about her. Given her reluctance to have any intimate details from her early life recorded in any of her biographical works, however, it is safe to say that she always made such confessions in good faith, with the understanding that they would remain undisclosed.

None of Mother Teresa's friendly biographers broke her trust when she was alive and most of them have proved equally faithful confidantes after her death. All personal details that did not meet with Mother Teresa's approval were and are still being duly left out. As for the few 'personal' incidents that have trickled into a couple of biographical works, like the anecdote about her encounter with the mysterious vicar at the Skopje railway station, they are obviously deemed harmless by the biographers who have mentioned them. It could also be argued that a few revealing details eventually made it to the print more by accident (they were perhaps left by mistake in the final stages of editing) than by choice.

This can hardly be said about the scene in Connor's film, though. It is interesting that Sister Teresa's little story about her father does not appear in two earlier drafts of the script.[13] The nun's words were most probably added in the final stages, perhaps only in the final version of the script. The script-writers, of course, had to continuously edit the text as they learned more biographical details about and from Mother Teresa. On the other hand, the absence in early drafts of the nun's words about her state of mind when her father passed away could also indicate that perhaps the writers decided to include them only in the last version fearing that she would not approve of such a personal and painful story. It is also worth finding out if this was the only last-minute change to the script. Perhaps not, which might explain why, in spite of Mother Teresa's close involvement throughout the stages when the script was being written, in the end the co-operation between her and the production team turned sour. Some of the implications of this fallout will be addressed in the last chapter.

Unless those biographers of Mother Teresa who knew her well decide to write openly about certain aspects of her private life, something which seems unlikely in the foreseeable future, we have no choice but to make do with the little morsels of information we have about the nun's early life to try to get to know the elusive Agnes Gonxhe Bojaxhiu. Incidents like her meeting with the unidentified priest in 1919 (mentioned briefly in a couple of biographies) and the account of how she had felt when her father passed away (included in Connor's film) are like the tips of an iceberg which with further research would certainly reveal more interesting facts about Mother Teresa's early life and, more importantly, about the genesis and nature of her devotion to Jesus. It is in this context that such bits of information are particularly important.

Agnes's encounter with the priest in 1919 and her recollection in 1946 of the dismay and pain she had felt when her father died seem to complement each other. They are the closest authentic information yet through which we can build a picture of what exactly happened to Mother Teresa when her happy childhood turned unexpectedly into a nightmare. So far no Mother Teresa biographer or researcher interested in her has ever asked any of the following questions about these two intriguing incidents: What exactly did Agnes tell the unknown priest about her dying father? What did the priest say to the little stranger to comfort her at the train station and on the way home? Was Agnes present when the priest administered the last rites to her dying father? Did Agnes try to talk to anyone else in those days about the loss of such a dear and special father? Did she ever receive counselling from any household member, relative, family friend or teacher? Did anyone have the time and the right skills to comfort such a highly intelligent, sensitive and traumatized child? We do not know the answers to these questions and perhaps never will.

Most biographers of Mother Teresa, certainly all the admiring Catholics who have written about her, postulate that she came from a very religious family. Their faith has always been important to the Albanian Catholics in Skopje and it certainly was important to the Bojaxhius. It would be wrong, however, to see Agnes, her parents and her siblings as strict Catholic devotees. 'Mother Teresa,' notes David Porter, 'grew up with an artistic background. The whole family was musical. Singing, playing instruments and entertaining guests with impromptu concerts were everyday pleasures.'[14] Nikollë himself is known to have been a member of a local musical group which called itself 'The Voice of the Mountains'. As we have already seen in this chapter, the Sister Teresa character in Connor's 1997 biopic also does not mention anything about her father being a religious person let alone a strict adherent of the Catholic faith. All that the nun remembers about her loving father was that '[h]is red heart beats with love,/for child, wife and country'.

Nikollë's sudden death affected everyone in the Bojaxhiu family, especially his wife who was devastated. Drane's grief came as no surprise to her children. They all knew how close their parents had been. Mother Teresa would always remember with fondness her mother's love and veneration for her husband. Drane and Nikollë had apparently never exchanged angry words with each other, certainly not in the presence of the children. According to Mother Teresa and her brother Lazar, their parents made a perfect couple. Everyone who has written about this period of Mother Teresa's life notes that Drane could not come to terms with her loss for quite some time. So much so that in the wake of Nikollë's death it fell to Age to take care of the house and of her two younger siblings until her mother pulled herself together.

Agnes too proved very helpful to Drane during that time but in another way. The best help she could give to her inconsolable mother was to accompany her to the church, where they prayed ceaselessly together. The local church served them as a much needed refuge to grieve in silence for the man they had loved dearly.

According to Lazar, when his father was alive, the dominating activity was politics; after his death, the family was nourished by its faith.[15] Lazar also maintained that from 1919 onwards, religion became very important particularly for Drane and his two sisters, something which, in his view, was clear also by their frequent visits to the local church. He was so impressed by their religious devotion that, in his words, '[a]t times I had the feeling that my mother and sisters lived in the church'.[16]

We do not know if during this time Agnes prayed and felt sorry more for herself than for her mother. Nor do we know the extent to which her grief-stricken mother was aware of Agnes's pain. What is obvious, however, is that Drane's and Agnes's relationship took on a completely new meaning during their frequent visits to the parish church from 1919 onwards. Agnes had always been close to her mother but Nikollë's death brought them closer to each other than ever before. Theirs was a new form of propinquity that needed no articulation, a perfect understanding that required no affirmation, a communication of souls that connected with each other simply by being in proximity. Had they not understood and bonded with one another to such a level, it would be impossible to account for the speed with which Drane apparently came to terms in 1928 with Agnes's unexpected decision to become a nun.

The news that Agnes had decided to go to India as a missionary came as a shock to her elder sister and especially to her brother. In 1928, following his graduation from the Military Academy in Albania, Lazar had been offered a post in King Zog's army. Worried about his younger sister, he wrote to her urgently asking her to change her mind. Assuming that she had no idea what she was letting herself in for, he felt that it was his duty as a worldly brother to warn her that, by becoming a nun, she was sacrificing herself for the rest of her life. If she went ahead with her plan, he told her without mincing his words, she was actually burying herself alive in the middle of nowhere.[17] Age's and Lazar's far from enthusiastic reception of their sister's decision to become a nun contradicts seriously the long-held view that Mother Teresa came from a strictly religious family.

The announcement that Agnes had decided to become a nun also took by surprise many of her friends and relatives.[18] Those who knew her well were far from supportive at the beginning and some of them even tried to convince her to think twice before going ahead with her decision. They tried to persuade her that she had so much to look forward to if she stayed in Skopje. In an attempt to make her change her mind, her child-hood friend and relative, the well-known Kosova Albanian composer Lorenc Antoni, reminded her that she had a talent for writing and tried to convince her that she should consider this as a serious career oppor-tunity.[19] Others were eager to point out that if she did not believe she could be a writer she could certainly have a successful career as a teacher or even as a musician. And, of course, there were those who reminded her that she could get married and have children.[20]

Agnes may indeed have considered devoting herself to God from the age of twelve. As for becoming a nun, however, she seems to have come to this decision most probably in 1928, which is the year when she announced it for the first time to her family, relatives and friends. If Mother Teresa indeed had taken the decision to become a missionary before 1928, she must have had some very strong reasons for keeping this ambition secret. For a mature and sensible daughter and sister like her, she was aware that such a life-changing decision would affect not only her personally but also her family members, especially her mother and sister. Equally important is the fact that she was very much aware of the novelty of her ambition in the entire Albanian Catholic community in Skopje. Prior to Agnes's decision to become a nun in 1928, no other Albanian girl in Skopje had taken the same path; there was simply no tradition of Albanian girls becoming nuns.[21] What makes Agnes's decision even more unique is that not only did she want to serve God as a nun but she was also determined to realize her ambition in a foreign and very distant corner of the world.

It is widely believed that Drane was the only person who was on Mother Teresa's side from the moment she announced her decision to become a nun. While it is true that Agnes left Skopje in 1928 with her mother's blessing, Drane did not consent to her daughter's decision readily. The 'strictly religious' mother, as Drane is often described by many biographers, did not really jump for joy when Agnes broke the news to her. David Porter admits that Drane's initial response was 'cau-tious' and 'somehow discouraging', but he hastens to explain that, in his view, this 'was not because she disapproved of Agnes's desire to become a nun, but because she wanted to be absolutely sure that the vocation was a genuine one and given by God'.[22] The fact of the mater is that Drane did disapprove of Agnes's decision and not necessarily only because of the 'considered reason' provided by Porter. Referring to this life-changing moment some fifty years later, Mother Teresa would recall how at the beginning her mother was in fact against her decision.[23]

While Agnes did eventually win Drane over, we do not know much about what actually happened in their house, the discussions they had and how tense the situation was when they were debating such an important issue. Considering how reticent Mother Teresa always was about her early life, we will perhaps never learn anything substantial about what certainly was a very difficult stage in her relationship with her mother. The nun obviously did tell some of her trusted biographers about how Drane reacted to her decision in 1928 but they have hardly elaborated on this in their works. Perhaps Mother Teresa chose not to tell them too much. Perhaps she advised them not to make her words public. Referring to this life-changing moment in Agnes's life, this is what Eileen Egan notes in the opening chapter of her 1986 biography:

> Mother Teresa told me that her mother went to her room and closed the door. She stayed there for twenty-four hours. Undoubtedly she prayed, and she might have wept uncontrollably. Mother Teresa never knew. When she came out, her personal feelings were under control. She was able to help and strengthen Agnes Gonxha in taking the steps to part from her.[24]

The fact that she stayed in her room on her own for so long is a clear indication that Drane hardly expected to hear what Agnes told her. Six years earlier Agnes had told Drane that she felt that God was calling her. This was the first sign that Agnes was perhaps thinking of becoming a nun. At that time, however, the mother does not seem to have taken her daughter's words seriously. It was only in 1928 that Drane realized for the first time how far Agnes's religious devotion had gone. In the solitude of her room Drane also became aware of the role she herself had played unwittingly in Agnes's attachment to religion. Did Drane blame herself for having failed to notice the extent to which her grief over her husband's death and her attempt to find consolation in church had affected her youngest daughter? Was Drane bitter with remorse for having behaved so selfishly when she should have paid more attention to the emotional and spiritual welfare of her children, especially of the impressionable and highly sensitive Agnes? We simply don't know. What is obvious, however, is that Drane realized promptly that by 1928 things had gone too far for her to try to change Agnes's mind. Under such circumstances, Drane behaved as any responsible and sensible parent would; she saw no point in standing in her daughter's way.

That Drane was perfectly aware why Agnes had chosen to become a nun and what she expected to achieve as a missionary is obvious also from the words she used when she gave Agnes her consent: 'Put your hand in His – in His hand – and walk all the way with Him.'[25] Drane's words on such a solemn occasion are reported slightly differently in the many books about Mother Teresa. All versions, however, have something significant in common. They all mention the emphasis Drane put on the figure of Jesus. The mother was prepared to give Agnes her blessing to become a nun provided she would 'strive to live only all for God and for Jesus Christ'.[26] Drane apparently wanted reassurances from her daughter that she would 'belong only to God and Jesus'.[27]

In the months and years immediately after Nikollë's death, both Drane and Agnes appear to have found in religion an anchor in the midst of despair, a way out that enabled them at first not so much to come to terms with the irreplaceable loss but to retain their sanity. Theirs, and especially Agnes's extraordinary faith in God, is a classic example of religion being not so much 'the sigh of the oppressed, the heart of a heartless world, and the soul of a soulless condition',[28] as Marx puts it in his 'Introduction to A Contribution to the Critique of Hegel's Philosophy of Right', than the sigh of the depressed. For people to put their faith in God, to depend on religion, they do not necessarily have to be victims of economic exploitation. Social divisions and social injustice are neither the main nor the only reasons why religion was 'invented' in the first place, nor why so many people choose to have, follow and adhere to a faith.

If taken out of context, Marx's other characterization of religion as 'the opium of the people' reads like a sweeping statement. This particular phrase has been misquoted since 1844 when he used it for the first time by those who appropriate Marx wholesale as well as by those who reject him outright. Religion did work as a drug in Agnes's case although not entirely in a Marxist sense. Agnes apparently found the religious 'opium' very useful and, perhaps irreplaceably so, but not as a means through which she could come to terms with and accept social injustice as a member of a repressed ethnic community (Albanian), equally repressed religious minority (Catholic) or as a child with no financial security (in the wake of Nikollë's death, the Bojaxhius lost the family business). When she was nine years old Agnes was far too young to understand anything about political or religious persecution, and she never experienced poverty either when her father died nor at any time prior to her departure from Skopje in 1928. Agnes found the opium called religion very useful to protect herself from, what Shakespeare calls in *Hamlet*, 'the slings and arrows of outrageous fortune'. One such piece of 'outrageous fortune' befell Agnes at a very tender age and one can only wonder if she would have been able to cope without her faith in God when her father died in 1919.

Freud's contribution to the debate about the function and significance of religion in our lives is especially relevant in this context. In his 1927 work *The Future of an Illusion*, Freud defines religious ideas as:

> illusions, fulfilments of the oldest, strongest and most urgent wishes of mankind. The secret of their strength lies in the strength of those wishes. As we already know, the terrifying impression of helplessness in childhood aroused the need for protection – for protection through love – which was provided by the father; and the recognition that

this helplessness lasts throughout life made it necessary to cling to the existence of the father, this time a more powerful one.[29]

In the same work Freud argues that we humans need an all-powerful father to protect ourselves 'against the dangers of nature and Fate', and against the injuries that threaten us 'from human society itself',[30] as well as to look at death not as 'extinction' or 'a return to inorganic lifelessness, but as the beginning of a new kind of existence which lies on the path of development to something higher'.[31]

Children in particular find the concept of death very difficult to comprehend. At the same time they are more easily inclined than adults to accept as 'rational' religious interpretations that death is not the end of life as such but the start of a new mode of existence. This was what the mysterious priest apparently told Agnes at the Skopje train station in 1919 and what she heard him say to her dying father at home. It is quite possible that Agnes did not understand what exactly the priest was saying but his words as well as the advice she received from other priests and believers that she met at home and in church during the days when she, her family and the city of Skopje were in mourning and thereafter were crucial in fostering an 'illusionary' belief which, to adopt Freud's reasoning, was strongly motivated by a wish-fulfilment.

Unlike Marx, Freud argues that religion has clearly performed great services for individuals as well as for human civilization. According to Freud, religion is both the universal obsessional neurosis of humanity and an effective means of saving people from neuroses. Our neuroses, however, are not necessarily triggered only by socio-economic-political deprivation, as Marx often argued. Nor are neuroses the only or the main outcome of sexual frustrations experienced in childhood, as Freud constantly maintained. Freud's conclusion that religion as the universal obsessional neurosis of humanity, like the obsessional neurosis of children, arose out of the Oedipus complex, out of the relation of the father,[32] is not applicable in Agnes's case. Agnes and her mother were already close to each other when Nikollë was alive and they became even closer when he died. No matter how much she loved her father, Agnes would always love her mother dearly. As far as Mother Teresa was concerned, Drane was a saintly mother. Agnes never suffered from the Electra complex. She and her two siblings never saw Drane as someone who stood between them and their father. There was never any jealousy of this nature between the Bojaxhiu children and their parents.

By the time Agnes experienced her neurosis in 1919, religion was surely the main, if not the only, factor which made it possible for her to come round, to cope, to find some sense in her father's death. For Agnes this was an initiation that would have an impact on her for the rest of her life. Mother Teresa's strong faith in God was not bestowed upon her for mysterious reasons at the age of twelve, as most of her friendly biographers maintain. The nun acquired her extraordinary faith at least three years earlier. At that time Agnes was too young to rationalize about religion. The illusionary belief of 'wish-fulfilment' was apparently so strong in her that it stayed with her for the rest of her life. It would be difficult to determine whether as an adult Mother Teresa was more unable than unwilling to approach faith rationally. As far as she was concerned, talking about how she acquired faith, how anyone acquires faith, made no sense. She was reluctant to discuss the time, the place and the circumstances when she became attached to religion as this would require evoking and talking about a very painful memory. Mother Teresa chose to avoid talking about her father not only for the political reasons mentioned in chapter four but also because she never fully came to terms with his death. The only thing that kept her going and busy, and made living worthwhile was her strong faith in God, which she acquired shortly after and as a direct result of the greatest loss she ever experienced in her entire life.

In Mother Teresa's case, faith did not necessarily mean only devotion to a set of religious teachings or a religious doctrine as such. As far as she was concerned, faith meant first and foremost absolute devotion to the figure of Jesus. During her intense grieving that started in the autumn of 1919, and which most likely lasted for many years, religion had an irreplaceable therapeutic impact on both Agnes and her mother. Such a strong attachment to religion was made possible mainly because their saviour was not abstract but a very personal and personified God. From 1919 onwards, Drane and Agnes would establish a sacred bond not so much with religion as such but with the figure of Jesus. The Son of God apparently helped the grieving pair like no one and nothing else at a time when they had nowhere else to turn for comfort and when they were struggling so hard to make sense of their irreplaceable loss. Jesus had literally saved the traumatized wife and child. No wonder their bond with and affection for him would remain sacred for the rest of their lives.

At the age of nine Agnes was apparently desperate to seek a replacement for her dead father, whom she had obviously idolized. If not the most epiphanic event of her early years, the momentous encounter with the mysterious vicar at the Skopje train station in 1919 was certainly the beginning of a new stage in Agnes's relationship with God through the mediation of priests. The frequent and long visits to the parish chapel she made with her mother from 1919 brought her even closer to the men of the cloth.

Priests became influential figures in Agnes's life at the age of nine not only because she started spending so much time in church with her mother. Around the same time Agnes started her elementary education. For Catholic children of Agnes's age, going to school in those days meant having lessons in the hall of the local Sacred Heart Church. As a child and as a teenager Agnes was constantly in contact with priests not only by choice but also because of circumstances beyond her control. She grew up looking upon priests as family friends, teachers, educators and important members of the community. No wonder she treated priests with the utmost respect. They apparently made such a strong impact on her that she would respect them in the same way not only during the years she lived in Skopje but also throughout the long time she spent in India. Nothing would undermine her veneration for priests; she retained the highest regard for them and sought their advice constantly even when she became world famous.[33]

To Agnes, priests were not some men in religious uniform but representatives of Jesus Christ himself. Her encounter with the anonymous, almost phantom-like, priest at the Skopje train station in 1919 had convinced her that priests exist to perform a sacred mission: to bring Jesus to people, especially vulnerable people like her and her mother, in their hour of need. This explains why Agnes never judged any priest during her early years or at any time during her life. As a little girl, she would take issue with anyone who, in her view, did not show enough respect for priests, even if they happened to be disciplinarians. In 1921, for instance, when she was eleven years old, a new 'strict' priest arrived at her parish church. The Bojaxhiu children were rather apprehensive of the newly appointed Father Gaspër Zadrima, partly because his two predecessors had been family friends and partly because this new Albanian priest carried a thick walking stick during church services apparently to ensure that the young parishioners behaved themselves. This tactic obviously did not endear the priest to the children.

Agnes was the only child who saw nothing wrong with the new priest's tactic. She could not understand what the fuss was about, and one day she even challenged her 'irreverent' brother:

> 'I have the feeling that you are not very keen on Father Zadrima.'
> 'How do you expect me to like him,' retorted Lazar, 'when he is always swinging that enormous stick?'
> 'Even so,' Agnes replied thoughtfully, 'it is your duty to love him and give him respect. He is Christ's priest.'[34]

Agnes's enormous respect for priests makes more sense if we take into consideration how much they helped her relate to Jesus from 1919. It was mainly as a direct result of their influence that Jesus started replacing her biological father and would gradually become a much more significant paternal figure. Jesus was different from Nikollë because he was immortal and as such would never leave her. This explains why Mother Teresa did not seek 'consolation in human things', and would advise her nuns to follow her example.[35] From the moment her biological father passed away she would rely only on Jesus.[36] A father like Jesus meant that never again would Agnes experience the dreadful sense of loss, anguish, abandonment and torment she had gone through in the wake of her father's death. Gradually but steadily Jesus became everything for Agnes. He was the embodiment of life, hope and eternity. Above all, he was the epitome of love. She found in the figure of Jesus the eternal reliability and constancy no one else, certainly no mortal, could give her. It was this assurance that made sacrifices such as leaving her family in 1928 and not having children of her own worthwhile.[37]

Unless we understand what Jesus apparently did for Agnes Gonxhe Bojaxhiu in 1919 we will not be able to understand why Mother Teresa was so totally devoted to him for the rest of her life. Jesus obviously performed a significant role in Mother Teresa's life, much as some celebrities play a crucial part in the lives of their devoted admirers. This is not to say that Agnes's attachment to Jesus was synonymous with the adoration people often display today for their chosen stars. One could argue, however, that unconditional religious attachment and worship have some features in common with the obsessive devotion some fans display towards their celebrities from the world of music, film or sport.

The authors of the article 'Personality and Coping: A Context for Examining Celebrity Worship and Mental Health', which appeared in the *British Journal of Psychology* in 2004, draw attention to the growing evidence suggesting that celebrity worship may be of interest also to psychologists.[38] Psychologists hold that the celebrity worship phenomenon occurs more in adolescents or young adults than older persons.[39] Agnes's extraordinary attachment to the 'celebrity' Jesus at the age of nine, however, shows that celebrity worship apparently affects also children not normally included in the adolescent age group. Some psychologists attempting to see celebrity worship in the context of religious devotion have concluded that the phenomenon shares a negative association with some aspects of religiosity.[40] Drawing attention to the lack of empirical examination of the relationship between attitudes towards celebrities and religious orientation, the authors of the 2002 article 'Thou Shalt Worship No Other Gods – Unless They Are Celebrities: The Relationship Between Celebrity Worship and Religious Orientation' argue that such comparisons are worth investigating:

> if only to begin to understand some of the psychological processes that underlie celebrity worship. Such a study may help us to understand whether celebrity worship serves the same psychological needs or functions as does religious worship.[41]

Agnes's closeness to Jesus reveals that religious attachment and worship serve similar psychological needs and functions as celebrity worship and that their implications are not necessarily negative. Furthermore, Agnes's case proves that the psychological condition which is now known as the 'celebrity worship syndrome',[42] was not necessarily invented by the media in the first place, as is often presumed. Rather than blaming the media, it would be better to see this allegedly 'corruptive' force not as the orig-inator of our obsession with stars but as a catalyst, a handy facilitator of something fundamentally human. Our attachment to stars did not begin when we invented the means for mass dissemination of information about the great and the good. The earliest traces of the 'celebrity worship syndrome' are found in humans' efforts to establish some contact with and express devotion to deities both in the mythological past and during the age of revealed religions. In the eyes of devoted spiritual beholders, gods are venerated but never judged. They had this elevated status not only because of what and who they apparently were but also, and perhaps more importantly, because of what they could supposedly do to benefit their worshippers. This is as true now as it was then. Referring to the significant function some film actors obviously perform for some indi-viduals and certain generations, John Belton argues that:

> [t]he star answers a particular need that the public either consciously or unconsciously has at a particular time for a particular figure of identification. In other words, the star functions as a sociocultural barometer of sorts, giving expression to and providing symbolic solu-tions for specific fears, desires, anxieties, and/or dreams that haunt popular consciousness.[43]

Like film stars, prophets and seers also offer their disciples and followers a much-needed chance to identify themselves with a religious message and a religious cause that give expression to their fears as much as provide them with a way forward. Religious stars are savers and savers are not questioned by their devotees. Mother Teresa, whose preferred motto was '[i]f I judge, I cannot love', displayed a similar unconditional devotion to Jesus throughout her religious life. Her saviour had been there for her when she needed him most. He had told her through the unidentified priest that she came across in 1919 that her biological father had not died, he had simply gone to meet God. Nothing would have consoled the grieving child more than this 'rational' explanation when she found herself in a completely irrational situation. 'Where there is mystery,' Mother Teresa used to say, 'there must be faith.'[44] Jesus, she apparently believed, had made the mysterious very plain to her. He had performed a miracle for Agnes. He had given her hope when she was in despair. This was absolutely essential for her in finding some meaning in life and in death, and seeing them both as necessary stages leading to an eternal existence the mysteries of which are known only to the Heavenly Father. That Agnes found Jesus's 'intervention' therapeutic when she was nine years old is obvious from the following quote from the New Testament (Matthew 25: 34–6), which Mother Teresa used to refer to very often:

Come, you that are blessed by my Father, inherit the kingdom prepared for you from the foundation of the world; for I was hungry and you gave me food, I was thirsty and you gave me something to drink, I was a stranger and you welcomed me, I was naked and you gave me clothing, I was sick and you took care of me, I was in prison and you visited me.[45]

This is how Agnes had felt in her hour of need as an orphan: she had been spiritually hungry, thirsty, a stranger, naked and in prison. It was precisely at this time, when she felt so low, that her spiritual journey began in earnest. This was the moment when she was lost and saved at the same time. No wonder she was convinced that 'faith in Christ is the best thing to have in the world,[46] and why, to her, Jesus was 'everything',[47] and the only one she could rely on.[48] She did not need anyone to tell her what Jesus can do for vulnerable people like her. She had witnessed for herself his miraculous powers. That is why Jesus was her divine superstar, why, to quote her, 'I take Our Lord at his words',[49] why she was prepared to do anything for Jesus, and why she apparently was unable to comprehend the possibility of parting company with Jesus from 1919 onwards.

iii. Career choices

Although against her will, there was a time when even a child like Agnes who was immersed in God, did stay away from Jesus. This separation happened shortly after she became attached to her Saviour in 1919. Having completed her elementary education at the local Sacred Heart Church, she had no choice but to continue her secondary education in Skopje at a state-run school. As a rule, biographers do not pay much attention to the impact this move had on her. The only thing most of them are keen to record about this stage in Agnes's life is that at the age of twelve she had her 'first call' from God. To many subjectivist supporters of the nun, this was a supernatural experience which shows that she was chosen by God when she was twelve. Mother Teresa herself, however, never saw the 'first call' as a paranormal experience. Many years later she would tell her trusted biographer Kathryn Spink that by the age of twelve she had felt herself called to the religious life. This had obviously been 'an intensely personal experience on which she would not elaborate, other than to say that it did not take the form of any supernatural or prophetic apparition'.[50] In Mother Teresa's own words, what she had experienced at twelve was 'a private matter. It was not a vision. I've never had a vision.'[51]

Leaving the elementary church school to start her secular education in the town's secondary school was a rather traumatic experience for Agnes because she apparently thought that she was 'abandoning' Jesus. Having not forgotten what Jesus had done for her when she lost her father in

1919, by the age of twelve she was obviously experiencing pangs of guilt for, what in her eyes, was tantamount to turning her back on her adopted spiritual father. Mother Teresa would always refer to the 1922–1928 period as a very difficult time in her life. It took her six years of thinking, praying and soul-searching to finally decide whether she would continue to be away from Jesus, as she apparently felt she was as a pupil at the state-run secondary school, or return to her saviour much in the same way as during the years of her elementary education.

The dilemmas Agnes was faced with from 1912 onwards prior to her departure from Skopje in 1928 are quite normal for anyone making career choices. In Agnes's case her choice was apparently between a secular and religious career. A secular career was certainly tempting. Everyone in her family as well as her relatives and friends encouraged her to choose a secular profession, reminding her of the rewards and benefits. Considering how long it took Agnes before she eventually announced her final career decision to anyone, and especially the time she spent praying at her beloved shrine of the Madonna of Letnice prior to the announcement, it is obvious that she thought long and hard before deciding to abandon for good any plans of having a 'normal' career. By 1928 Agnes was a mature young woman who, contrary to her brother's hasty judgement, knew quite well what she was letting herself in for by deciding to choose an unconventional career.

Lazar and other people who loved and cared about Agnes apparently did not know that she was very clear about the career she would follow. While the idea of becoming a nun crystallized in her mind only in 1928, Agnes had in a sense known much earlier, if not since 1919 at least from 1922 onwards, that for her life to make any sense, for her to feel complete, she had to devote herself to Jesus. She was aware that a career of this nature would mean separating herself, probably forever, from the people she loved most. Her family and friends warned her that this was a price not worth paying. To Agnes, however, this painful separation was like being reborn, the threshold to a completely new and the only true and meaningful existence. She did not expect everyone to understand this. As far as she was concerned, serving Jesus was not an option; it was an obligation. Nothing else mattered, neither her life, nor her family, not even her mother, whom she knew she would perhaps never see again.

Sympathetic biographers of Mother Teresa usually take it for granted that she decided to become a nun simply because she was a devout Christian, which is perfectly true, except that most of them often fail to explain what exactly the figure of Christ meant to her from 1919 and why. Less enthusiastic supporters of the nun speculate that she decided to become a missionary because life would have been very grim for her in Skopje. According to Anne Sebba, for instance, Agnes had no choice but to emigrate because although she had many friends, she was shy with boys, implying that she perhaps was not fit to have a long normal relationship with someone of the opposite sex.[52] Agnes knew several boys during her childhood and adolescence and was on good terms with many of them. She is not known to have had any intimate relationship with any boy in Skopje, however.[53] So far, we have no evidence to suggest that she was courted by any young man or that she herself made any advance to anyone and was turned down. Agnes obviously did not choose to leave Skopje and become a nun because of unrequited love. Her heart was never broken by any man, and we do not know if her departure in 1928 broke the heart of anyone who was attracted to her. A strikingly good-looking young woman like her must have certainly had her admirers. Who they were and how they reacted to Agnes's decision, however, is likely to remain one of the mysteries about her life in Skopje.

Some biographers have argued that Agnes's shyness as a child and as a young woman, indeed her decision to rule out marriage altogether, had something to do with the fact that she was born with a club foot. Naturally, Agnes was upset about the defect in her foot. It is also possible that she may have seen this as something that would prejudice any young man asking for her hand in marriage. The fact that she suffered from the club foot, however, does not seem to have been common knowledge to many people in Skopje. More importantly, a strong-willed young woman like Agnes, who obviously had such a high opinion of her intellectual and spiritual ability, was certainly capable of coming to terms with such a minor physical disability.

Anne Sebba is one of the few biographers of Mother Teresa to date who has tried to explain Agnes's decision to leave Albania in 1928 in the context of difficulties she might have encountered in Skopje as a result of her ethnicity and religion:

> She [Agnes] loved teaching but as a member of a double minority [Albanian and Catholic] was she not bound to suffer discrimination in this career, with virtually no schools for the Albanian minority in Yugoslavia? After 1918, the situation for Albanians in Kosova and Skopje began to deteriorate as the Yugoslav government tried to colonise the area with Serbs and exerted pressure on the native Albanian population either to emigrate or be assimilated. Albanians were denied the right to use the Albanian language for official matters, all schooling was conducted in Serbo-Croat and Albanian surnames had to be altered to include a Serbian suffix such [sic] – vić or -vć. Under new laws on the Colonisation of the Southern Regions, advantages for Serb settlers included gifts of up to 50 hectares of land, the right of free transport up to the place of settlement, free use of state or communal forests and exemption from any taxation for three years. As Serb persecution intensified, the memories of Serb atrocities committed during her childhood could not be easily erased.[54]

Agnes Gonxhe Bojaxhiu was certainly aware of the Serbs' inhuman treatment of her fellow ethnic Albanians by the time she was thinking about her vocation. After all, her own father had been poisoned by the colonizing Serbs a decade earlier. In spite of the heavy personal loss she had suffered, Agnes is never known to have shown any interest in politics or the Albanian national cause throughout the years she lived in Skopje. She was never a member of any Albanian patriotic group or movement. While it is true that the Serbs often prosecuted Catholic Albanians on religious grounds, Agnes is not known to have attempted to condemn publicly the repression of the Catholic community in Skopje by the Belgrade government. Throughout her early years, she kept herself aloof from her country's political and religious problems. While her brother always retained a keen interest in politics and Albanian nationalism, his views apparently had no impact on his apolitical younger sister. Interpretations that Agnes left her country because she could not endure the brutal treatment of her fellow Albanians (both Christians and Muslims) by the colonizing Serbs or because she was unable to come to their assistance at such a critical moment are certainly worth considering, but unless evidence is found to back them up they remain pure speculations. Mother Teresa never was and never became an Albanian patriot in a conventional sense. Ascribing her the mantle of Albanian patriotism would be wrong and irresponsible.

Likewise, there is no evidence to prove that Mother Teresa left Albania in 1928 because she was unhappy with and unable to do anything about the social problems that Albanian society was facing at that time. Like most Westerners writing about Albania and the Albanian society of the first half of the twentieth century, Sebba cannot resist the temptation to explain Agnes's decision to leave her country in the light of some 'exotic' and 'barbaric' Albanian and Balkan traditions. Without any biographical evidence to substantiate her claim, Sebba postulates that '[a]nother reason compelling the clear-sighted teenager to leave was her despair over blood feuds, which continued unabated'.[55]

Agnes's decision to become a missionary and leave Skopje in 1928 was the natural outcome of her increasingly obsessive attachment to the figure of Jesus, an attachment that had began in earnest in 1919 and intensified further in the following years. Agnes was confident that her sacrifice was worthwhile as long as she was serving her divine celebrity. It is interesting to note that the row between the teenager and her brother Lazar prior to her departure from Skopje had all the signs of a fall-out between two young people who are eager to defend their own chosen celebrity. Like Agnes, by that time Lazar had also attached himself to a celebrity figure. Following his graduation from the Military Academy of Albania in 1928, he had joined the army of Ahmed Zog, who had only recently crowned himself King of Albania. Resenting Lazar's patronizing tone in the letter he sent her in an attempt to try to dissuade her from becoming a nun, Agnes wrote him a snappy reply which the Second Lieutenant of the Royal Albanian Army had not expected and certainly never forgot: 'You think you are important because you are an officer serving a king of two million subjects. But I am serving the King of the whole world! Which of us do you think is in the better place?'[56]

That Agnes Bojaxhiu decided to become a missionary only to serve Jesus can also be supported by the name she chose for herself shortly before leaving Ireland for India in 1928: Sister Mary Teresa of the Child Jesus. Several biographers have given different interpretations regarding the choice of her religious name. It is possible that Agnes decided to call herself Sister Teresa because of several famous nuns, one of whom could have been Teresa of Jesus, also known as Thérèse de Jésus Jornet e Ibars. This Teresa, who lived from 1843 to 1897, was the founder of the Little Sisters of the Poor, also known as the Little Sisters of the Abandoned Aged. She was beatified in 1958 and canonized in 1974.

Some writers and biographers argue that Agnes took her religious name from Marie Françoise Thérèse Martin, a French Carmelite nun who died from tuberculosis in 1897, at the age of twenty-four. This nun's religious name was Teresa of the Infant Jesus and of the Holy Face. Sister Thérèse was adored by Catholics for doing 'ordinary things with extraordinary love'. She was canonized with the title St Thérèse of Lisieux in 1927. Agnes was obviously aware of the French nun's standing, if not in Skopje, at least during her short stay in Dublin in 1928. The canonization of St Thérèse of Lisieux was bound to attract the attention of the Catholic world, especially of novices and nuns, if only because of the decision of Pope Pius XI to waive the fifty-year waiting period required at that time before the initiation of a cause for canonization.

It has also been suggested that Agnes's religious name was related to St Teresa of Ávila, another Carmelite nun, who lived in Spain in the sixteenth century. Those who hold this view apparently put too much emphasis on the Spanish spelling of Mother Teresa's name. Mother Teresa herself was often asked about this issue and she was always eager to set the record straight. 'Not the big St Teresa of Avila,' she was at pains to emphasize, 'but the little one.'[57] The story goes that Mother Teresa chose to spell the name of St Thérèse of Lisieux as *Teresa* to avoid confusion with Sister M. Thérèse Breen, another novice in Loreto.

In spite of Mother Teresa's efforts to clarify the issue of her name, it is possible that she was influenced and inspired by several famous nuns named Teresa, especially St Thérèse of Lisieux and St Teresa of Ávila. By the time she was thinking of choosing a religious name, Agnes was obviously trying to find among well-known nuns something of a kindred spirit.

By her own admission, Mother Teresa was particularly impressed by the life and spirituality of St Thérèse of Lisieux. There were many reasons why the Albanian missionary developed a keen interest in the French Carmelite nun. By a strange coincidence, St Thérèse of Lisieux was also known as the 'Little Flower'. As has already been mentioned, Agnes's own middle name 'Gonxhe' is the Albanian for 'rose bud' or 'little flower'. Incidentally, the name of Mother Teresa's mother, Drane, is the short form for 'rose', which suggests that Gonxhe's name was not perhaps given to her by accident. More importantly, the French nun acquired a special significance for Mother Teresa because she reminded her of Drane's spirituality. Like St Thérèse of Lisieux, Drane used to do small things (such as helping out neighbours, old people and orphans) with love. She was the first person to teach this important lesson to her little daughter Agnes. Like her own mother Drane and her patron saint St Thérèse of Lisieux, Mother Teresa would emphasize throughout her long service as a missionary the significance of doing things with love. The two women obviously served as two sources of inspiration for Agnes because of their extraordinary attachment to Jesus, an attachment which, in her case, mattered more than anything else from 1919 onwards.

iv. Jesus the heavenly spouse

No matter which of the Teresas mentioned earlier exerted the strongest impact on Agnes up until 1928, what is clear is that she shared with them and with many other famous nuns a kind of religious devotion which was Christo-centric in nature. By the time Agnes Gonxhe Bojaxhiu assumed the name of Sister Teresa, her attachment to Christ was undergoing a significant transformation. For Sister Teresa, Jesus the Heavenly Father would gradually become Jesus the Heavenly Spouse. It is possible that the change in question took place when Agnes went through puberty. As emphasized earlier, there is no evidence to suggest any sexual orientation in Agnes's attachment to her biological father when he was alive. Her early attachment to Jesus in the wake of her father's death was that of a grief-stricken daughter who was desperate to replace the person who had been so dear to her.

It appears Agnes's sexual attraction to Father Jesus developed further towards the end of her adolescence. Such sexual attachment became apparent especially after she left Skopje in 1928. This was also the period when she started to articulate her devotion to Christ in sexual terms. This significant change in Sister Teresa's relationship with Jesus, it appears, was hugely accelerated when Agnes came into direct contact in Dublin with a long-established tradition according to which nuns would normally see their attachment to Jesus in the context of a marriage, both spiritual and sexual. In the case of nuns and novices, the distinction between Jesus the spiritual father figure and Jesus the husband has never been very clear.

While it is difficult to say for certain when exactly Agnes began to see Jesus more as a husband than a father, one could argue that in her case the metamorphosis began mainly as a result of the reading she did in the last couple of years before her departure from Skopje and especially during the weeks she spent in Dublin. For a nun like Agnes, who had been such an avid reader throughout her early years, it was only natural that her passion for reading would only grow by the time she chose the career of a nun. Sister Teresa, as her superiors in Calcutta would soon see for them- selves, was an intelligent, inquisitive and independent-minded woman who was always eager to search for and find answers to her many inquiries, especially to questions that had to do with her relationship with Jesus.

It would be interesting to find out what exactly Agnes Gonxhe Bojaxhiu read in Skopje following her puberty, during the months she spent in Dublin in 1928, and throughout the seventeen years she spent in Calcutta as a teacher. Considering that the information about Mother Teresa's reading is sketchy, we can only draw conclusions on the basis of the occa- sional references Mother Teresa herself made to certain authors and particularly certain religious figures that apparently influenced her most.

We do not know if by 1928 the nuns at the Dublin convent where Agnes spent several weeks had a copy of St Thérèse of Lisieux's spiritual autobiography *The Story of a Soul*, which first came out in 1899. Considering how highly Mother Teresa thought of the Little Flower – so highly in fact that she chose 'Teresa' as her religious name – one could say that the Albanian novice was very familiar with the life-story and influence of this Catholic saint. What seemed to have impressed Agnes most about Thérèse of Lisieux was the saint's devotion to Jesus, and what Jesus had apparently done for her, something the French nun makes abun- dantly clear from the start of her autobiography.

It appears Mother Teresa became very fond of Thérèse of Lisieux also because of some parallels she apparently saw in their lives. Like the French saint, Agnes had experienced a very happy childhood. For both of them, however, such early happiness was very short-lived. Like Thérèse of Lisieux, who lost her mother at the age of four, Agnes came to know what it meant to lose a parent at a very tender age. Also like Thérèse, Agnes had thought very early of devoting herself to God. By a strange coincidence, the French and the Albanian young girls had seen Asia as the place where they could serve Jesus best; Thérèse had wanted to travel as a missionary to French Indochina and Agnes to India. In contrast to Agnes, though, poor health meant that Thérèse would never be able to achieve her ambition. All she could do to help spread the Gospel in these distant lands was to encourage the missionaries who worked there and pray for their success. Agnes, on the other hand, spent all her adult life as an active missionary.

As a missionary, Mother Teresa obviously had more in common with another famous religious namesake mentioned earlier, St Teresa of Ávila: a devout and single-minded woman who was always eager to set up new convents and foundations. What makes the Albanian Mother Teresa and the Spanish St Teresa of Ávila similar religious figures is that they were both very vocal about their attachment to Jesus.

This does not mean that this attachment was in any way weaker in the case of St Thérèse of Lisieux. In her spiritual autobiography, the French nun makes it very clear that she saw herself as 'the Little Flower gathered by Jesus'[58] and refers to him as 'my love'. She uses the word 'love', however, primarily in a spiritual sense. St Teresa of Ávila also used the word 'love' when referring to her attachment to Jesus, and most of the time in a spiritual sense. In some cases, though, it seems to have a more down-to-earth meaning. This particular mystic saint is seen at times as having also developed something of a physical attachment to Jesus. The Spanish nun professed to have had visions of Christ, which she interpreted as enjoyable experiences of a 'mystical marriage'. Her visions inspired the renowned seventeenth-century Italian master Giovanni Lorenzo Bernini to produce the sculptural masterpiece 'The Ecstasy of St Teresa of Ávila', which is the centrepiece in the Cornaro Chapel at the Church of St Maria della Vittoria in Rome. Lorenzo based the statue on the experiences related by the mystic nun in her autobiography:

> It pleased the Lord that I should sometimes see the following vision. I would see beside me, on my left hand, an angel in bodily form – a type of vision which I am not in the habit of seeing, except very rarely.... It pleased the Lord that I should see this angel in the following way. He was not tall, but short, and very beautiful, his face so aflame that he appeared to be one of the highest types of angel who seem to be all afire.... In his hands I saw a long golden spear and at the end of the iron tip I seemed to see a point of fire. With this he seemed to pierce my heart several times so that it penetrated to my entrails. When he drew it out, I thought he was drawing them out with it and he left me completely afire with a great love for God. The pain was so sharp that it made me utter several moans; and so excessive was the sweetness caused me by this intense pain that one can never wish to lose it, nor will one's soul be content with anything less than God. It is not bodily pain, but spiritual, *though the body has a share in it – indeed, a great share.* So sweet are the colloquies of love which pass between the soul and God that if anyone thinks I am lying I beseech God, in His goodness, to give him the same experience. (emphasis added)[59]

St Teresa's mystical experiences are also explored in Nigel Wingrove's 1989 short film *Visions of Ecstasy.* In this nineteen-minute video the nun is seen caressing and kissing Jesus, and a woman, personifying her psyche, touches her erotically. Seeing the film as 'an object of overt sexual passion' to which Jesus responds, the British Board of Film Classification held that 'the wounded body of the crucified Christ is presented solely as the focus of, and at certain moments a participant in, the erotic desire of St Teresa, with no attempt to explore the meaning of imagery beyond engaging the viewer in an erotic experience'. The BBFC eventually refused the video a classification certificate because, in their view, Christians 'would reasonably look upon it as being contemptuous of the divinity of Christ'.[60]

St Teresa of Ávila herself would incur the wrath of some church figures whenever she spoke openly of her 'relationship' with Jesus. Her candid confessions about the 'divine favours' she apparently received from Jesus were criticized sharply by several members of the clergy. Her religious censors found her claims embarrassing and interpreted them as being the work of the devil. She was attacked for expressing openly what was and still is common knowledge: for some nuns, their devotion to Christ takes the form of a love affair which is essentially spiritual but does not exclude some degree of sensuality. As James Hall notes in his review of Germaine Greer's *The Boy*:

> there is plenty of evidence of women engaging erotically with Christ
> – far more evidence, in fact, than of their ogling the images discussed
> by Greer. You only have to look at Bernini's 'The Ecstasy of St Teresa'
> to gauge the erotic possibilities of having visions of Christ. Nuns were
> known to lie under lifesize wooden effigies of the nude Christ, and
> to 'suckle' wooden dolls of the Christ child.[61]

Mother Teresa was not known to have made any 'embarrassing' confessions similar to those of St Teresa of Ávila about any encounter of an erotic nature with Jesus. One could argue that the Albanian nun was rather embarrassed by the Spanish nun's outspokenness about this sensitive issue. This is probably the main reason why at times she tried to distance herself from the Spanish nun in spite of the fact that they both obviously had so much in common in terms of spirituality and their practical minds. The fact that Mother Teresa, to quote Kathryn Spink, 'was at pains to emphasize' that her religious name had nothing to do with St Teresa of Ávila indicates further that she was eager to avoid any controversy with regard to her public image.[62]

In spite of such conscious efforts to distance herself from the Spanish Carmelite nun, over the years Mother Teresa too came to profess her own affection for Jesus in terms often not very dissimilar to those of St Teresa of Ávila. Mother Teresa would often remark that she was married to Jesus and that she found him a 'demanding' spouse.[63] An American teacher visiting the Home for the Dying in Kalighat once asked Mother Teresa if she would say something to him and his colleagues that they could keep as a 'memento' of the visit and that would also be useful to them in the future. Mother Teresa's advice was: 'Smile at one another. Smile at your wives.' Upon hearing her words, one of the teachers remarked: 'Mother, it is obvious that you are not married!' To which the nun replied: 'Yes I am. Sometimes it is very difficult for me to smile at Jesus because he asks too much of me.'[64] She always maintained that Jesus was 'the one to whom I belong: body, soul, mind, heart'.[65] Whenever she received guests at the headquarters of her order, the Missionaries of Charity, in Calcutta, she would tell them: 'Let us first greet the Master of the house.'[66] She would behave in exactly the same way whether she played hostess to ordinary people or to her 'fellow' Indian or foreign dignitaries.[67]

Mother Teresa, the dutiful and obedient bride of Jesus, would always encourage her fellow nuns to see themselves as Christ's spouses. The sisters, notes Lucinda Vardey, 'are called to enter into this relationship for the rest of their adult lives, to love Jesus with their whole hearts'.[68] Mother Teresa saw this relationship as being similar to the love of a wife for her husband. In her own words, '[w]e are all women who have the ability to make use of this love. We should not be ashamed of loving Jesus with our emotions.'[69] Her constant advice to her sisters was: 'You are the brides of Christ. He deserves all your love. None of you must love Jesus less than a wife loves her husband.'[70] She would stress the same thing even among her fellow Albanians in Kosova, where she was aware that such references to Christ would certainly raise eyebrows. Addressing a group of nuns in Binçë on 28 June 1980, she made it abundantly clear that '[w]e are Christ's fiancées and we must be clear that he is really our fiancé. That's why we are so much attached to him and why nothing could separate us from him.'[71]

Mother Teresa's attachment to Christ may have been indeed 'bizarre' or 'controversial', as some of her statements seem to indicate. As far as she was concerned, however, there was nothing bizarre or controversial in how she felt about Jesus. She was so immersed in him that she was prepared to face any challenge to serve him fully. She had sacrificed herself to please no person, no institution, no government and no particular country. She had forsaken herself in order to exist through and in Jesus. Those who stood in her way would soon learn that they were picking a fight with the wrong person. The woman who had left her family, who had chosen not to have a family and children of her own, was prepared to take on anyone who was foolish enough to believe that they could 'discipline' her. Some of her opponents learned in no time how wrong they were to find fault with her original devotion to Christ and her own understanding of missionary work. Those who were wise avoided quarrelling with her. And they were right. As will be seen in the next chapter, to serve her Jesus, the little nun was brave and strong enough to challenge absolutely anyone.

The desire for fame is the last infirmity cast off even by the wise.

Cornelius Tacitus

Genius is said to be self-conscious.

Charlotte Brontë

I'm sick of being the undiscovered genius,
I want fame NOW not when I'm dead.

Stephen Patrick Morrissey

6 From church rebel to church asset

i. Mother Teresa's first encounter with a church rebel

This chapter concentrates on Mother Teresa's expectations about the nature of her work in Calcutta before arriving in India in January 1929, her initial disappointment and growing frustration with her superiors at Loreto, and the support she received from the Roman Catholic establishment in Calcutta, Delhi and the Vatican by the time she began to challenge the long-established missionary tradition from the mid-1940s onwards. Particular attention is paid to efforts made by Mother Teresa and some of her friends and biographers to cover some of the details about the tension between Mother Teresa and some Loreto superiors before she finally left the Loreto order in 1948 to set up her congregation two years later.

When Agnes Gonxhe Bojaxhiu expressed her wish to become a nun she was in no doubt that she wanted to serve Jesus by going to India. It is debatable how much Agnes knew about this distant country when she lived in Skopje or even during the weeks she spent in Ireland in the later part of 1928. Anne Sebba suggests that:

> [b]y this time, Agnes had assiduously studied as much as she could about the history of the missionary movement in India, especially in its most recent, expansive phase. She would have known that attempts to Christianise the country had been made repeatedly for almost 400 years.[1]

In the second half of the second millennium India attracted the attention of several world powers such as Portugal, Spain and England. Their initial interest in India, however, was not triggered by their intention to 'Christianize' such a vast country; nor did they maintain their presence there for centuries mainly for evangelical purposes. The European powers went to and stayed put in India for as long as they could primarily because they were interested in the country's wealth. The scramble for India was hardly a religiously motivated venture. The Europeans employed religion to justify their exploitation of India very much as they had earlier used the crusades to justify their imperial and plundering wars in the Middle East, an approach adopted by some Western powers to this day although in a more sophisticated manner.

While Agnes was interested in India for the sake of its connection with Christianity, such a connection had begun not in the sixteenth century but almost nineteen hundred years earlier. The aspiring nun had obviously created an exotic picture of India partly from the stories about distant places she had heard as a little girl from her father, who was a well-travelled man and a gifted story-teller, and partly, and more importantly perhaps, from the letters of Croatian and Slovenian missionaries she used to read in her teens in the Zagreb magazine *Katoličke misije* ('Catholic Missions'). An avid reader like Gonxhe, who was immersed in the Bible as well as in secular literature from an early age, was endowed with a vivid imagination which enabled her to start writing on matters religious and secular from a very young age. Her first religious publications, for instance, were two articles on the significance of prayers and litanies, which appeared in the Skopje periodical *Blagovjest* ('Good Tidings'). Her talent for writing, especially on spiritual issues, is also evident in the letters she sent from India to *Katoličke misije* as soon as she arrived in Calcutta in January 1929. The magazine published several accounts of her impressions of India in the following years.

Although Mother Teresa maintained that Skopje was special to her, by the time she was thinking seriously about her vocation in the mid-1920s, the town must have gradually started to shrink in her eyes. The ambitious young woman obviously had no plans to spend all her life in such a dear but nevertheless small place. Gonxhe was eager to see for herself the world she had read so much about since she was a little girl. She was hardly interested in travelling abroad as a tourist, however. A spiritual creature like her, who was born and grew up in such an ancient Christian town as Skopje, was bound to take a keen interest in other lands, especially if they were related to Christianity. One such place was India, where Christianity is believed to have been introduced by Apostle Thomas in the first century AD.

India's ancient Biblical connection was not a detail that could have escaped the attention of the devout and impressionable Agnes. In expressing her wish to go to India, Agnes must have felt that she was not going to a strange place but to her 'land of dreams'[2] that had apparently welcomed Christianity as early as her native Albania, although not to the same extent. In religious terms, Sister Teresa's arrival in Calcutta at the start of 1929 was something of a homecoming.

Before setting off on her long voyage to Calcutta, Agnes had to travel first to Zagreb, Paris, London and Dublin where she stayed for about six weeks at Loreto Abbey at Rathfarnham.[3] To this day, this Irish convent houses the order of the Sisters of Loreto, which is a branch of the Institute of the Blessed Virgin Mary (IBVM).

That Mother Teresa spent some time at the Dublin convent is mentioned in almost every book about her. On the whole, biographers are keen to include in their publications, although in most cases not at length and at times only in passing, something about the history of this institution and the circumstances that led to its involvement in missionary work in India. As for the impact the place had on Agnes, this remains a topic that has yet to attract the attention of scholars. Like the reticence in Mother Teresa scholarship about her first eighteen years in Skopje, the six weeks Agnes, now Sister Teresa, spent in Ireland in 1928, constitute yet another important, though comparatively much shorter stage in her early life that needs explaining in more detail.

Coincidences seem to play a crucial role in the lives of many famous people. They certainly played an important part in Mother Teresa's case, both at the time when she was an anonymous nun and later when she became world famous. One such early influential coincidence is related to the Dublin convent.

Agnes probably did not know much about the history of the Loreto order prior to her arrival in Dublin, and it is not clear how much she learned about this place during the time she stayed there. Those who met Sister Teresa at the institution in 1928 remember that she spent most of her time reading.

So far, it has been taken for granted that Sister Teresa's main preoccupation at the Irish convent was to study English. Sister Teresa was certainly interested in progressing with the new language. After all, English would be her official medium of communication in India. Inheriting her father's gift for languages, the assiduous nun apparently picked up English very quickly.

Although studying English was one of her priorities, it would be unwise to assume that the inquisitive young nun did not occupy herself doing other things throughout the novitiating period at Loreto Abbey. For a sensitive and ambitious woman like her, it was only natural that she would try to learn something about the institution's connection with India and, more importantly, about its founder, Frances Teresa Ball. It could be argued that this Teresa, whose preferred advice to her sisters prior to their departure to overseas convents was 'Go and set the world on fire with the love of God', served as an early role model to the young Balkan nun. The life and work of this Irish nun perhaps had something to do with Agnes's decision in Dublin to choose for herself the name of Teresa.

During her stay in Ireland, Agnes must have also been curious to learn something about Mary Ward, the controversial English Catholic nun who founded the Institute of the Blessed Virgin Mary in 1609. It is quite possible that no one told Agnes in Dublin about the uneasy relationship between Mary Ward and the Catholic Church during her lifetime and long after her death. On the other hand, it is unlikely that no one at the Abbey said a word to the young Albanian nun about Ward's charitable work and especially about the girls' schools she set up abroad. In spite of the Vatican's reluctance to acknowledge Mary Ward's achievement, the troublesome nun had always been venerated like a saint by the sisters of her Institute, even when the Catholic establishment resented her bitterly.

Mary Ward was born into an affluent family in York, England, in 1585. When she decided to be a nun she went to Saint Omer, Northern France, where she joined a community of Poor Clares. Ward apparently had her reservations about the sisters' austere and secluded lives, which perhaps explains why at the age of twenty-four she returned to England confident that she wanted to do 'some other thing' as a nun. Having secured the support of several nuns, she travelled with them abroad setting up schools for girls, a move which was bound to upset the Church authorities. The Vatican refused to acknowledge her Institute, which is hardly surprising considering her unorthodox views. Ward upset the male-run Catholic Church by requesting that nuns should not be enclosed around the clock, that they should be governed by a mother superior instead of a male figurehead and that there should be flexibility in the hours of prayers so that sisters would have enough time both to pray and to serve the needy.

Ward paid heavily for her 'rebellious' demands; in 1630, she even found herself a prisoner in a Munich convent. Her order was always viewed with suspicion by the Church hierarchy; so much so that Pope Urban VIII compared it to 'a weed in a cornfield' that had to be uprooted. By the time of her death, the Vatican was as hostile as ever towards her and her order. Some seventy years later, Pope Benedict XIII finally validated her institution. In 1713, Ward's order was allowed to take the name of the Institute of the Blessed Virgin Mary provided that no one mentioned her as a founder. It appears that the Catholic Church has not always been the most forgiving of spiritual institutions towards its rebels within, whose restlessness and non-compliance have in the long run often proved more beneficial to the Holy See than the blind service of its docile devotees.

Throughout the eighteenth century, while Ward's order kept on expanding in Europe, some of the 'Jesuitesses', as her sisters were styled by Ward's opponents at the time her first congregation was suppressed in 1630, were often ignorant of their founder. The only place where Ward's memory was kept alive was her native York, where she returned towards the end of her life. Ward died in Heworth, near York, in 1645. In 1814, Ward's centre in York received an Irish novice, Frances Teresa Ball, who was so impressed by what she heard about Ward's visionary work and sufferings that she founded the Irish branch of the Institute in 1821. In the years that followed, the branch became known as Loreto Abbey.

Frances Teresa Ball christened the convent after Loreto, a shrine in Italy to which Mary Ward was particularly devoted.

During the nineteenth century, the Irish Loreto community set up branches in Australia, Africa and Asia. In 1841 they established a centre in India. The following year they set up Loreto House in Calcutta, where they started teaching girls from well-to-do families. Since then the schools established by the Loreto order in Calcutta have been offering very good educational opportunities for girls from mainly privileged backgrounds.

Even if Agnes was not told much about Mary Ward herself during the weeks she spent in Dublin, she is known to have been introduced to the history of the Institute. Considering how much the Irish branch of the IBVM owed to Ward, one could argue that Mother Teresa was also 'introduced' to Ward, an introduction which, in view of the English nun's standing with the Roman Catholic Church, could have been heavily censored.

Had Sister Teresa visited Loreto Abbey a couple of decades earlier, she would have probably not been told anything at all about Ward. As luck would have it, Sister Teresa arrived at the convent at a time when Mary Ward was well on the way to being rehabilitated by the Catholic Church. Ward's vindication had started in earnest mainly thanks to the keen interest Mother Catherine Chambers took in her in 1909 and the two-volume biography she produced several years later. This renewed and persistent interest in Ward's life eventually had an impact on the Church's attitude towards the memory of the rebellious nun. So much so that in 1953 the Vatican even referred to Ward as 'this incomparable woman whom England gave to the Church'.[4]

Sister Teresa's life shares some striking resemblances with that of Mary Ward. Both came from affluent backgrounds. They were also members of minority religious communities, which to some extent influenced their decision to go abroad; Ward's move to France at the age of twenty-four was triggered partly by the persecution of Catholics in England, whereas in Sister Teresa's case, her persecution was of an ethno-religious nature. The two nuns developed a growing sense of disquiet about the way the convents were run: in Ward's case, the community of Poor Clares in France, and, in the case of Sister Teresa, the Loreto order in Calcutta. Even at the beginning of their religious vocation, Mary Ward and Sister Teresa were missionaries with a vision of a new future. The difference between them was that Mary Ward lived at a time when the Vatican could silence female rebels. As for Sister Teresa, her rebellion took place when the Church was eager not only to avoid open dissent within its ranks but had also started to tolerate rebels who, with the right coaching, could be turned into great assets.

Mary Ward and Sister Teresa were church rebels also because of their attitudes towards education. This does not mean that both nuns shared the same views on this issue. On the contrary, if Ward upset the Church partly because she wanted to educate girls, Sister Teresa would annoy some of her Loreto superiors in Calcutta because she took issue with the rather 'excessive' attention they paid to the education of girls. This is not to say that Sister Teresa was against educating children or that she resented girls' education in particular. Her performance and dedication throughout the seventeen years she worked as a teacher in Calcutta reveal clearly that the Albanian nun was a gifted teacher and that she loved teaching Indian girls. According to some of her pupils and colleagues, she made classes very interesting and her subject 'come alive'.[5]

No matter how much she enjoyed teaching and loved children, Sister Teresa did not leave her family and native country to pursue a teaching career in India. Had she wanted to be a teacher, she could have just as well stayed in Skopje. Anne Sebba's theory that Sister Teresa was bound to have suffered discrimination as a teacher in Skopje, especially in view of the fact that that there were virtually no schools for the Albanian minority in Yugoslavia, is worth bearing in mind when assessing the reasons for Agnes's departure from her native city in 1928.[6] On the other hand, we should not perhaps place too much emphasis on Sebba's argument. If Agnes was indeed eager to teach Albanian children, she could have moved with her brother to Albania much in the same way as her sister and mother did in the 1930s.

No matter how much Agnes enjoyed teaching, her heart was not in the profession. While her notion of religious service included teaching, she did not see herself primarily as a teacher. As far as she was concerned, her move to India was inspired by one motive only. She went to Calcutta to serve Jesus not by being a teacher but by serving the poor.

ii. Education versus charity

Christian missionaries have traditionally viewed education as one of the most practical and useful means of spreading their faith. In the case of India, missionaries started paying particular attention to education especially in the nineteenth century. Catholic missionaries began to set up schools and colleges across India at that time for two main reasons: firstly, to convert Indians through the educational opportunities they provided for them and, secondly, to compete with other Christian missionaries with whom they were often involved in bitter disputes about protecting and expanding their areas of influence in different parts of India.

In spite of its old roots dating back to the time of St Thomas and the constant presence, efforts and sacrifices of many dedicated missionaries from the beginning of the sixteenth century, by the nineteenth century Christianity was still considered a 'foreign' religion in India. Preaching and living among the Indians of different strata and walks of life never bore the results some idealistic missionaries had expected. Indians did not hasten to convert to Christianity not only because of Indian society's and especially the higher Indian castes' mistrust and dislike of anything 'foreign'[7] but, perhaps more importantly, also because by the time Christian missionaries set foot in India in the sixteenth century, the Indians already had a well-established and sophisticated civilization of their own. In contrast to other parts of the world, where Christianity could make headway more easily because of the indigenous peoples' lack of 'sophisticated' creeds that could successfully compete with and resist the European invaders' religion,[8] Indians did not feel like hailing Christianity as a much-awaited faith. Hinduism and other 'indigenous' Indian religions were too deeply ingrained in the minds and hearts of Indians to be easily replaced by the 'arrogant' white man's religion. In this respect, India was no exception in Asia. China and Japan proved equally difficult terrains for Christian missionaries.

The increased presence of Protestant missionaries in India in the eighteenth century made the Roman Catholic missionaries reconsider their old-fashioned and often unproductive tactics for winning souls in this part of the world. The Protestants, especially the Anglicans, started paying particular attention to translating the Bible into local vernaculars, thus offering a chance to many Indians to see the Christian scriptures as something that did not necessarily 'belong' only to the European invaders.[9] Preaching to the Indians in their own mother tongues meant that Protestant priests secured for themselves a bigger and friendlier audience than their Catholic rivals. The Protestant model of preaching through teaching was soon followed by Catholics. Protestant and Catholic missionary orders started setting up schools in earnest across India in the hope that their students would sooner or later convert to their preferred brand of Christianity.

Many Indian Christians from the sixteenth century onwards came from the lower castes. Having found themselves for centuries on the margins of a caste-ridden society, they made the best of the opportunities offered by the European colonizers to improve their social status. One way of doing this was by sending their children to missionary schools. As Stephen Neill puts it in his book *Builders of the Indian Church: Present Problems in the Light of the Past*, '[t]he Church in India has always been a great educational power. . . . Every mission has its network of village elementary schools.'[10] The missionaries, however, did not go to India with the main purpose of converting the lower-caste groups:

> It is part of the mythology of missions that the missionaries turned naturally to the poor and degraded, among whom they would find less resistance to their message, and neglected the higher castes, but history shows that the exact opposite was the case. Almost every mission started with the attempt to reach the higher castes; when movements started among the poor, they were viewed with anxiety

and a measure of embarrassment by the missionaries, who saw that their whole cause might be prejudiced by the influx of masses of ignorant and despised people.[11]

In this sense the setting up of schools to educate the children of the 'ignorant and despised people' was an attempt to raise the cultural level and hopefully the social status of the future generations of Christians. Missionary schools would continue to offer places to children from lower castes throughout the eighteenth and nineteenth centuries. On the whole, however, the students that enrolled in the missionary-run educational institutions came mainly from Christian families, a large number of which were now far from poor, or from well-to-do families that followed other religions and had no intention of converting to Christianity. Non-Christian students would soon outnumber their Christian colleagues in the schools run by missionaries across India in the nineteenth century.

On the whole, missionary schools were welcomed by Indian society for the services they provided. The situation started to change, however, in the latter part of the nineteenth century, mainly as a result of the movement for the 'purification' of Hinduism. The leaders of the movement resented both Christianity and the West, and they called for the reconversion of those Indian Christians who had 'betrayed' Hinduism and India. The Indians grew more suspicious of missionaries and their schools, especially when the independence movement gained momentum towards the end of the nineteenth century and in the early decades of the twentieth century.

One of the vulnerable points of missionary schools in India has been the source of their funding. Traditionally, their money has always come from the West. This means that, to this day, in the eyes of the Indian nationalists, like churches operating in India, missionary schools, as a rule, are funded by and serve the interests of foreign powers. Education, which had made Christianity a rather friendly religion and ensured the conversion of the majority of Indian Christians, was well on the way to becoming a liability to the Church in the late nineteenth and early twentieth centuries.[12]

As a rule, missionary schools run by priests and nuns are located inside convents. This means that the teaching personnel, especially sisters, are isolated from the world outside their compounds most of their time. This is something Agnes Bojaxhiu obviously did not know in Skopje. The missionaries' letters she had read back home in *Katoličke misije* did not reveal much about the missionaries' daily routine in India. Sister Teresa became aware of the nuns' excessive confinement only when she arrived in India in 1929 and especially when she returned to Calcutta after completing her novitiate in Darjeeling in 1931.

In Calcutta Sister Teresa was assigned to the Loreto convent in the Entally district. At Entally, she and other nuns taught at the two schools inside the compound. Like every Loreto nun, Sister Teresa had limited contact with the ordinary people of Calcutta, especially during her first four years at Entally. The Entally convent was and still is next to slums but, like her fellow nuns, Sister Teresa could not leave the compound. For several years at Entally, Sister Teresa's 'contact' with the neighbouring slums and slum-dwellers would be through the stories she heard from her students who kept her informed of the poverty in Calcutta. During her 'isolation years', Sister Teresa also received information about the world outside the convent walls from the Indian nuns and students who belonged to the Sodality of the Blessed Virgin, an association similar to the one she had joined in Skopje. The members of the Entally Sodality did charity work in a local hospital and visited regularly the poor in the slums surrounding the convent. At Entally, Sister Teresa was head of an epis-copal community of Indian nuns known as the Daughters of St Anne. The nuns, who taught Bengali at the convent, regularly offered help to poor people living in the neighbouring slums.

Sister Teresa would always encourage and congratulate her Indian nuns and students at Entally for their charity work but, being a Loreto nun, she was prohibited from joining them outside the compound. 'Because of the rules of enclosure in pre-Vatican II times the Sisters did not go out of the convent enclosure freely.'[13]

The inability to join the members of the sodality and the Daughters of St Anne in their missionary work in the hospitals and slums of Calcutta made Sister Teresa feel increasingly uneasy. But she was not prepared to put up forever with Loreto's strict confinement rules, which obviously had nothing to do with the order's founder Mary Ward, who three hundred years earlier had taken issue with similar restrictions imposed by the Roman Catholic Church on the nuns in Europe. Like Ward, Sister Teresa decided to do something about such rigidity that kept missionaries strictly apart from the indigenous people they were supposed to be helping in the first place. A letter written by Sister Teresa, probably in 1935, reveals that around that time she finally found a way out of the cloister. In her own words, apart from teaching at the Entally school, 'I have taken on another task; the school of St Teresa, which is also in Calcutta.'[14]

It is not known how Sister Teresa managed to convince her superiors at Entally to allow her to leave the convent daily for several hours so that she could take on another teaching post, and more importantly, in a school that was not run by her religious order. What is known is that teaching outside the Entally compound, which she had rarely left since her assignment there four years earlier, was an opportunity that would have a lasting impact on her. Sister Teresa and another Loreto nun trav-elled daily to St Teresa's primary school in Moulali probably by 'ghora gharry' (a horse-drawn vehicle),[15] taxi tram,[16] and at times on foot. This meant that, unlike most of the Loreto nuns, Sister Teresa had an oppor-tunity to see and meet in person some of the numerous people of Calcutta and have first-hand experience of the poverty which until then she had glimpsed only from the windows of the convent. 'This was the time when she saw the dead bodies on the streets during the Bengal Famine of 1942 and the civil unrest of 1945–46.'[17]

By Mother Teresa's own admission, shortly after she started teaching at St Teresa's school, she also began to teach 'in another school where there are about 200 children, but it is not so much like a school as a stable! And then again I teach in another place, in a kind of courtyard'.[18] In the late 1930s Sister Teresa had yet another opportunity to meet the people of Calcutta, especially the poor. In her own words:

> [e]ach Sunday I visit the poor in the slums of Calcutta. I cannot be of material assistance to them, for I have nothing; but I go to make them happy. Last time, at least twenty children were anxiously awaiting their 'Ma'. When they saw me they ran up, all hopping along on one leg. In that building, twenty families live; each family has a single room, two metres long and a metre-and-a-half wide. The doors are so narrow I can scarcely squeeze through them, the ceilings so low it is impossible to stand erect. And these poor people have to pay four rupees for those hovels; if they do not pay promptly they are thrown out on to the street. I am no longer surprised that my pupils love their schools so much, nor that so many are ill with tuberculosis.[19]

The conversations Sister Teresa had with her students at St Mary's, her involvement with the Sodality and the sisters of St Anne, and especially her opportunity to teach outside the Entally compound enabled her to learn more about the wretched living conditions of the poor of Calcutta than any other Loreto sister. Such contacts with the outside world, however, were restricted, and the permission from Loreto for 'outings' could be withdrawn at any time. According to information released from Loreto House, it was during those years and especially as a result of what she had witnessed in the streets of Calcutta in the early 1940s, that she 'longed to do something' about the poor but '[t]he Rule of Enclosure restricted her'.[20]

The relative freedom she enjoyed as a nun from 1935 also enabled Sister Teresa to come more into contact with the ever-changing Indian society. Sister Teresa was a keen observer and an astute reader of events that were soon to have a huge impact not only on the future of the Indian nation but also, and more importantly as far as she was concerned, on the fate of Christianity in India. It was hardly surprising that Sister Teresa, who taught geography and history for almost two decades, showed a keen interest in what was going on in her adopted country. The nun was obviously educating herself as much as her pupils throughout the 1930s and the 1940s.

The seventeen years Sister Teresa spent as a teacher at Entally and the teaching she did outside the convent from 1935 onwards constitute one of the most formative stages in her life that has yet to attract the attention of biographers, who concentrate almost exclusively on her charity work from 1948 onwards. Studying the events that led to Sister Teresa's decision to break with the Loreto order would shed more light on her farsightedness and on what she had to go through to achieve her target.

By the mid-1940s, Sister Teresa was gradually drawing her own conclusions as to what was expected of the Roman Catholic Church and the missionaries in India. In the new India that was emerging, anything foreign and alien could be seen as undesirable and even be at risk. The days when Westerners could rule India as they pleased were soon coming to an end. Sister Teresa was not concerned about the extent to which the interests of the Western colonial powers would suffer in India. What concerned her first and foremost was that the animosity between the West and India, the departure of the British and the looming partition of the country could have drastic consequences for Christianity in this part of the world. Sister Teresa was not interested in politics. When it came to protecting the interests of the Church, however, she could obviously be quite political.

This 'political' Sister Teresa made her debut in the mid-1940s when she discussed with some fellow nuns and superiors at the Loreto order a few of her misgivings, fears and concerns about what was going on in India and what, in her view, missionaries should do to promote Christianity. It is difficult to say if Sister Teresa expected her views to be received sympathetically from the first at Loreto. What is known for certain is that she was not prepared to remain for much longer a member of the Loreto order when she realized that some of her superiors did not share her vision. India was changing fast and Sister Teresa saw herself as having a role to play in the process.

iii. The European who was not European enough

Sister Teresa was an obedient nun, but it appears she did not understand obedience if it meant keeping quiet when she felt that something was wrong and apparently no one was prepared to do anything about it. She was in a better position than most other Loreto nuns in Calcutta to have an opinion and make a judgement on what was going on in India throughout the 1930s and the 1940s and on how local and national events could affect the future of the Loreto order and, more importantly, of Christianity in India. Sister Teresa was intelligent, inquisitive, educated and, by the mid-1940s, she had been in contact with the outside world more than any other Loreto nun. All the same, Sister Teresa apparently had a 'weak point' which made her position in the order rather vulnerable. Unlike most of her fellow European sisters, she was at times perceived as and made to feel an 'outsider'. The celebrity Mother Teresa was and still remains a much loved and admired figure throughout Christendom, at least officially, but in the days of her anonymity at Loreto she was not necessarily an equal among the European nuns. As will be seen throughout this section, some of her fellow nuns and pupils did not consider the Albanian missionary to be European enough.

At the time Sister Teresa joined the order of the sisters of Loreto she was the only Albanian nun in India. In the first part of the twentieth century it appears not many people in Europe and other parts of the world knew much about the Albanian nation. As far as her native country and culture were concerned, Sister Teresa was something of a mystery to those she lived and worked with in India.

The Ottoman occupation of Albania which began in the fifteenth century and lasted for almost five hundred years meant that the Albanians were almost completely cut off from the West for longer than any other nation in the Balkans. While Western powers started exploring and conquering most of the world from the fifteenth century onwards, Albania was always a place they remained largely unaware of. Having been for so long a Turkish colony, no wonder people in the West presume to this day that all Albanians must be Muslims. Turkey was instrumental in bringing Islam to the Albanians but a large number of them kept their old Christian faith.

Like the history of Islam from the middle of the eighth century to the middle of the thirteenth century, a period which is known as Islam's golden age,[21] the history of Christianity in the latter part of the second millennium is inseparable from that of colonialism. It is hardly surprising that several Western powers embarking on their colonial and neo-colonial ventures have also claimed the status of the leading missionary country: Portugal and Spain in the sixteenth century, France in the seventeenth century, England in the eighteenth and the nineteenth centuries and finally the United States in the twentieth and twenty-first centuries.

The embarrassing proximity between the Church and the colonial powers was bound to affect the advent of Christianity in the European colonies. It certainly affected its progress in India. The Europeans' superiority complex did not allow them to share 'their' religion with the peoples they were supposed to win over to Christianity. As the 'superior' colonizers' faith, Christianity was traditionally perceived by local people as an ideological and spiritual means of justifying and endorsing the exploitation of 'inferior' and 'heathen' races by the 'superior' and 'civilized' Europeans. Some European missionaries were often as arrogant towards the indigenous people as their compatriots holding administrative, military and diplomatic posts. This arrogance and low opinion of the colonized people also explain the reluctance of the Church, especially of the Roman Catholic Church, to ordain Indian priests, appoint Indian bishops and, more importantly, establish an Indian Catholic Church. In his study *A History of Christian Missions*, Stephen Neill often emphasizes how 'extraordinarily slow' Western missionaries were 'to recognize and trust the gift of indigenous Christians. Even when ordained to the ministry, they were still regarded as no more than assistants to the missionary'.[22]

Although she came from one of the earliest European nations to have embraced Christianity during the apostolic age, Sister Teresa was not always an equal among the European nuns. She must have often sympathized with the Hindu girls studying at Loreto schools in Calcutta who were made aware on several occasions that they were not entitled to some of the 'privileges' that Indian Christian students used to take for granted. The discrimination against Indian Hindu girls apparently continued at some of the schools run by the Loreto order well after Mother Teresa left Entally in 1948.[23]

That Mother Teresa was perceived as an 'outsider' from the moment she arrived in India is seen perhaps also from the training programme she underwent during the two years of her novitiate in Darjeeling, where she was required to study the local Hindi and Bengali languages. The reason the Albanian nun was expected to pay particular attention to the Bengali language was because by the time her novitiate was over, unlike other Loreto European nuns, she was not going to stay at Loreto House, the headquarters of the Sisters of Loreto, where English was the only medium of communication. When her novitiate came to an end, Sister Teresa was assigned to Loreto Entally, a convent which, unlike Loreto House, was and still is in a very deprived area of Calcutta. Sister Teresa never stayed at Loreto House throughout the time she was a Loreto nun.[24]

The Loreto order ran several schools in Calcutta in the early 1930s. One such educational institution was Loreto College, which is part of Loreto House. During British rule Loreto House admitted only a limited number of Indian students. In those days, Loreto College was a preferred place for girls from Asian royal families who were taught, as Aroup Chatterjee puts it, by 'proper European people with proper accents – it is unthinkable that MT [Mother Teresa] would be allowed there'.[25]

When Sister Teresa arrived at Entally, the convent had two schools: St Joseph's was for wealthy Bengali girls from Christian, Hindu, Parsee and Anglo-Indian backgrounds. The other school, known as St Mary's, admitted girls from middle-class and poor backgrounds, including many orphans, who did not pay fees.[26] In contrast to the fee-paying Entally and Loreto College students, who were taught in English, the girls at St Mary's were taught in Bengali. Sister Teresa was, of course, assigned to teach at St Mary's, which was 'one of the least exclusive of the six Loreto schools in Calcutta',[27] and where most of the teachers were Indian women.

It appears that Sister Teresa was made aware that she was not a 'proper' European not only by some of her fellow nuns but also by some of the Loreto students. In her article 'The Saint Mother Teresa', which appeared in *Time* magazine on 14 June 1999, the Bengali-born academic and writer Bharati Mukherjee, herself a former Loreto College student, recalls that she and her school friends 'weren't quite sure what an Albanian was except that she wasn't as fully European as our Irish nuns'. Mukherjee also notes that '[d]uring the British raj, Loreto House had admitted very few Indians. By the time I became a student there [in the summer of 1951], the majority of students were Hindu Bengalis, the daughters of Calcutta's elite families.' In contrast to Mukherjee, Sister Moira IBVM, Archivist of the Loreto Provincialate in Calcutta, maintains that:

> [a]t the time of Mother Teresa most of the children in Loreto House were from the professional middle classes, many of them Christians. It is the same now but there are more children from the lower economic group as well.[28]

In the same article Mukherjee remarks that in the early 1950s 'the majority of teachers' at Loreto College 'continued to be Irish-born nuns'. Considering that Mukherjee began her studies only three years after Mother Teresa had left the order and that the nun never taught at Loreto College prior to her departure from the Entally convent in 1948, one could conclude that, had she remained a member of the Loreto congregation, she still would not have been offered a teaching post at Loreto College. This educational institution, which had been fundamentally elitist during the British Raj, obviously remained an equally elitist school even when India became independent.

Being made aware throughout the 1931–1948 period that she apparently was not European enough was certainly one of the factors that alienated Sister Teresa from the Loreto order. It would be naïve, however, to think that this was the only reason she finally decided to part company with an institution that she undoubtedly loved. In her own words, '[i]t was much harder to leave Loreto than to leave my family and my country to enter religious life'.[29]

One should understand Mother Teresa's fondness for Loreto and her sadness at leaving it not only in terms of her attachment to a place where she had lived for seventeen years. For Mother Teresa, the Loreto Entally convent was more than just her accommodation, and the Loreto order more than simply a religious congregation. When she said that 'Loreto meant everything to me',[30] she was also referring to what she had expected from the order. Mother Teresa the idealist apparently had anticipated that the Loreto sisters would be more dedicated to the service of the poor in India and not so involved with the education of wealthy girls. Referring to the clash between the nun's expectations and the reality she encountered in Calcutta, Georges Gorrée and Jean Barbier note in their 1974 book *For the Love of God: Mother Teresa of Calcutta* that '[s]omething troubled her' throughout her time at Loreto Entally:

> At first it was only minor, but each year it grew, challenging the comfort and order of the classrooms where she had been endowing

with culture and the norms of a good education the docile daughters of the rich.

It was the voice of poverty ringing in her ears from beyond the cloister; hands were stretching out in their thousands from the street, asking something completely different of her; the groans of the destitute, dying in squalor on the pavements of this nightmare city, were chilling her heart.[31]

Mother Teresa seems to have always resented the attention missionaries paid to the education of wealthy fee-paying children in India. In his book *We Do It for Jesus*, which appeared in 1977, Edward Le Joly includes an interesting exchange between Mother Teresa and another nun about what missionaries in India should and should not consider as priorities:

> 'At a meeting in Bangalore,' recalled Mother Teresa, 'a Sister attacked me for distributing food freely to the poor. She said that I spoiled the poor by my acts of charity. I answered her: "*If I spoil the poor, you and the other Sisters spoil the rich in your select schools.* And Almighty God is the first to spoil us. Does He not give freely to all of us? Then why should I not imitate my God and give freely to the poor what I have received freely." They [the nun and her company] had nothing to answer.' (emphasis added)[32]

Mother Teresa was obviously a strong-minded woman. She would not tolerate criticism from those who did not share her enthusiasm for her projects and especially from anyone who stood in her way. Mother Teresa's 'assertive' attitude became more apparent during the 1946–1948 period, when her relationship with some of her superiors at the Loreto order appears to have deteriorated further.

iv. The diary of frustration

Mother Teresa was not a revolutionary when it came to addressing fundamental and sensitive social and political questions regarding exploitation, colonization, distribution of wealth or caste. All the same, the Albanian nun was very much a revolutionary figure when it came to taking on some of her Loreto superiors so that she could implement her own vision of missionary work.

The 1946–1948 period is probably one of the most interesting and most dramatic stages in Mother Teresa's life in India. This was the time when she displayed to friend and foe alike what she really was made of, what she stood for, and the great lengths she was prepared to go to in order to realize her lifetime ambition, for which she had sacrificed so much in 1928 by leaving behind her mother, siblings and country.

Mother Teresa appears to have had a tense time at Loreto from 1946 to 1948. Unfortunately, we do not know much about these pivotal years because her friendly biographers are apparently not interested in exposing awkward tensions within the Catholic Church to wider scrutiny. Her opponents, on the other hand, are simply not interested in studying and highlighting this important stage when she emerged as a courageous and a far-sighted missionary who was genuinely concerned about the poor in Calcutta. As for Mother Teresa herself, she was obviously not interested in setting the record straight once she achieved what she wanted. The Albanian nun never spoke in public about the tensions between her and the leaders of Loreto because she apparently believed that her version of events could damage her beloved Loreto order as well as the standing of the Catholic establishment in Calcutta and beyond. Mother Teresa was first and foremost a very devout and loyal Roman Catholic nun. If she could find it in her heart never to blame the Serbs in public for poisoning her father, who was without doubt the most important and the dearest person in her entire life, she could certainly forgive her superiors at Loreto for giving her a hard time between 1946 and 1948.

The official policy of the Missionaries of Charity order these days is not to comment on the acrimony between their founder and the Loreto order; their staple reply about any 'controversial' questions about the way Mother Teresa was treated at Loreto and especially on her far-from-friendly departure from the Entally convent in 1948 is: 'We do not know.'[33] There is no attempt, however, on the part of the Missionaries of Charity to deny that there was a rift between Loreto and Mother Teresa when she was a Loreto nun.

As a rule, the last three years Mother Teresa spent at Entally – 1946, 1947 and 1948 – are mentioned by biographers mainly to highlight the significance of the so-called 'second call' that she apparently received from God on 10 September 1946 and the concerns some of the authorities at the Loreto order and the Catholic establishment in Calcutta expressed for her safety if she went ahead with her decision to work on her own in the slums of Calcutta. There is no doubt that Mother Teresa's proposal to live among the slum-dwellers worried her superiors at Loreto and beyond. What Mother Teresa wanted to do was quite risky, almost an adventure, which could have easily had very grave consequences for her safety and the reputation of the Loreto order and of Catholicism in Calcutta. Throughout the late 1940s, India and Calcutta were engulfed by communal and religious violence. The lives of many people were wrecked simply for being in the wrong place at the wrong time. Many Indians in those days believed that there was no room for Westerners in independent India. As for Western missionaries, they were viewed with suspicion and even hatred by a large number of Indians and some of their leaders. In the eyes of the majority of Indians, European priests and nuns had always been handy tools of the departing white masters, and they had no reason to linger behind now that India was about to throw off the yoke of colonialism. Although Rabindranath Tagore, himself a missionary school student, did not approve of his countrymen's cry 'for rejection of West',[34] one can easily see in his Nobel Prize acceptance speech in December 1913 that he too took issue with the kind of education the Indians were served under colonialism. In his words:

> [w]e lost our confidence in our own civilization for over a century, when we came into contact with the Western races with their material superiority over the Eastern Humanity and Eastern culture, and in the educational establishments no provision was made for our own culture. And for over a century our students have been brought up in utter ignorance of the worth of their own civilization of the past. Thus we did not only lose touch of the great which lay hidden in our own inheritance, but also the great honour of giving what we have and not merely begging from others, not merely borrowing culture and living like eternal schoolboys.[35]

Mother Teresa, of course, had other reasons for taking issue during the 1940s with the missionary education system in India. Some of these reasons become clear if we study her relationship with some of her superiors during the last three years at Entally. Several biographers are keen to emphasize that once she broke the news to her spiritual superiors of her intention to leave the order, they offered her all the support she needed. This is an erroneous perception which, to some extent, seems to have been initiated and sustained by Mother Teresa herself. Father Edward Le Joly asked Mother Teresa many years after her departure from Loreto if she had any difficulties with her superiors before she left, and she reportedly replied: 'None whatever, they were most understanding and cooperative.'[36] Of course, there were nuns at the Entally convent and perhaps even at Loreto House, who would have liked to support Mother Teresa, or who perhaps assured her in private that they sympathized with her. Such endorsement, however, is not known to have been voiced publicly. Declaring open support for a rebel like Sister Teresa was not something the Loreto nuns were capable of. The Loreto superiors would not tolerate any open display of solidarity with such a troublesome nun who had caused them difficulties and embarrassment. When Sister Teresa finally left the Loreto order in August 1948, a notice, which was put up on a blackboard, made it clear what was expected of all the nuns: 'Do not criticize. Do not praise. Pray.'[37]

It is difficult to say when exactly Sister Teresa's relationship with her superiors at Loreto suffered its first serious crack. Considering the fact that she took on another teaching post outside the Entally convent as early as 1935, one could assume that her superiors had plenty of evidence from the start that the Albanian nun was not there simply to follow orders. If Mother Teresa was indeed someone who, to quote Michael Gomes, one of her early Indian Catholic supporters, 'makes rules and then she breaks rules', she obviously was displaying such 'strength'[38] from the start of her missionary career.

The Loreto order in Calcutta had never before seen a nun like Sister Teresa who could be obedient and argumentative, quiet and restless, docile and stubborn. Those who express dismay at her reluctance to allow anyone to intervene in the running of her Missionary of Charity order from 1950 would be less surprised if they were familiar with the nun's uneasy relationship with some Loreto superiors and the efficiency with which she performed administrative duties.

Sister Teresa was a leader and she would display her leadership skills as Headmistress of St Teresa's school and especially when she replaced the Mauritius-born Mother du Cénacle as head of St Mary's in 1941.[39] Throughout her years as headmistress, Sister Teresa provided her superiors with plenty of evidence that she had authority, charisma and courage, and that she could be a team player but also firm when necessary. Sister Teresa had one final chance to show her leadership skills towards the end of her stay at Entally, by which time she appeared to have become *persona non grata* at Loreto. For reasons that will be discussed shortly, Sister Teresa was sent to the Loreto convent at Asansol towards the end of 1946. During the months of her absence from Entally a crisis developed at St Mary's school. The political events in India had made the relationship between pupils and nuns rather tense; the two parties obviously did not agree on many issues. Upon her return to the school, Sister Teresa called a meeting and succeeded in calming down the situation.[40]

It appears that Sister Teresa's relationship with some Loreto superiors deteriorated especially after she returned to Entally from her retreat in October 1946. She told some nuns about the 'call from God' she claimed to have received on the train a month earlier on her way to Darjeeling,[41] and even 'lost no time in seeking the support of her superiors'.[42] Sister Teresa obviously did not expect everyone at Loreto to understand and approve of her 'strange ideas'. After all, she was aware that in expressing her wish to leave the convent to help the poorest of the poor in the slums of Calcutta she was asking for something that was unheard of in the history of the order since the first Loreto sisters had arrived in India a century earlier. All the same, it appears nothing could have prepared her for the storm her words caused at Loreto. Some sisters were understandably 'astonished';[43] others had 'mixed feelings'.[44] As for some of her superiors, they made their position abundantly clear from the first. 'Not all the nuns and priest thought her wise,' notes Charlotte Gray in her 1990 book on Mother Teresa. 'One said, long after, "We thought she was cracked!" '[45] It appears several people used to call Sister Teresa 'a mad woman' in those days.[46]

That some Loreto officials were from the first hostile to Sister Teresa's intention to start her own congregation is also obvious from the way her 'issue' was presented to the head of the Calcutta archdiocese, Archbishop Ferdinand Périer. In his retirement, Archbishop Périer recalled how '[o]ne day, as I was making the visit of Entally Convent, someone told me that a young nun of the community had some *queer ideas*' (emphasis added).[47] Archbishop Périer's words were initially published in 1977. Interestingly enough, in another rendering of Archbishop Périer's account of how he first came to know of Mother Teresa's ambition, published in 1986, the word 'queer' is replaced with 'unusual'.[48] Mother Teresa literature is full of examples of writers taking liberties with the way they edit and paraphrase at will words attributed to the nun or her friends and colleagues. The apparently innocent and harmless modification in this case is further proof of the ongoing tendency to tone down any suggestions that Sister Teresa and her superiors were at loggerheads from 1946 to 1948.

In spite of the efforts of many biographers to erase any trace of animosity in Sister Teresa's relationship with Loreto, some of her religious superiors, it appears, did give the Albanian nun a hard time, especially from 1946 to 1948. When the dispute was still unfolding, some superiors apparently did not even care if the acrimony was noticed by outsiders. Sister Teresa's 'hidden drama',[49] to borrow a phrase from Eileen Egan, was often played out in the open. The story had gripped the nuns and to some extent divided the Loreto community in Calcutta not only during the time Sister Teresa was a member but also for years after her departure. So much so that the Loreto sisters would continue to debate about 'the nun who got away' for years after 1948. And not only the Loreto sisters. Several generations of students enrolling at Loreto schools from 1948 would show an interest in Sister Teresa's story. The Loreto students were apparently informed of what went on between Sister Teresa and her superiors by some of the nuns. One such Indian student who learned of Sister Teresa's far-from-friendly send-off from Loreto was Bharati Mukherjee, who joined Loreto College in 1951, three years after the rebel nun had left the cloister. According to Mukherjee, she and her friends 'thought her [Mother Teresa] a freak. Probably we'd picked up on unvoiced opinions of our Loreto nuns'.[50] If the rich girls of Loreto College were so informed of the rift between Sister Teresa and Loreto, one could easily imagine how well informed were the pupils studying at the two schools in the Entally compound.

That Sister Teresa was treated harshly by some nuns at Loreto during her last three years as a member of the order is clear also from an incident which took place immediately after she expressed her wish to work outside the Entally compound in October 1946, an issue which will be addressed shortly. Even during those difficult years, however, Sister Teresa was never without friends. She enjoyed especially the support of two

Belgian priests: Father Julien Henry, pastor of St Teresa's Church near the Entally convent and spiritual director of the Entally sodality of the Blessed Virgin, and Father Celeste Van Exem, who was chosen by Sister Teresa as her spiritual father and director in 1944.

What drew Mother Teresa towards Father Henry was his work with the Bengali community. Taking heart from his example, she would constantly encourage members of the Entally Sodality of Mary to continue to visit patients in hospitals and the poor in the slums surrounding the Entally convent. Father Henry was apparently aware of Sister Teresa's growing frustration over the years with Loreto's strict regulations that prevented nuns from helping poor people living in *bustees* (slums). Having worked closely together from 1941 to 1947, Father Henry knew only too well that, like him, Sister Teresa believed that '[p]rayer without action is no prayer at all'; they both 'want[ed] to work for the poorest of the poor'.[51]

Kathryn Spink holds that Father Henry did not know that Sister Teresa wanted to leave Loreto until a few days before her departure from Entally in August 1948.[52] Spink seems to overlook several important issues: firstly, that Sister Teresa and Father Henry had been good friends for years; secondly, that Archbishop Périer is known to have asked for Father Henry's advice regarding Sister Teresa's request to leave the cloister; and, thirdly, and perhaps more importantly, that even by 1946, the rift between Sister Teresa and her superiors had become too public not to be noticed by someone like Father Henry who was constantly in contact with the Entally convent. Contrary to Spink, Anne Sebba claims that Sister Teresa told Father Henry that she had heard 'the voice of God' while she was travelling to Darjeeling by train, and that he had 'interrogated' her about the incident.[53] The rift between Sister Teresa and her superiors obviously was not something that could have escaped the attention of a close friend like Father Henry.

As for Father Van Exem, Sister Teresa is known to have informed him in detail about her 'call within a call' as soon as she returned to Entally in October. In Father Van Exem's words, Sister Teresa handed him some slips of paper in which she expressed very clearly that:

> [s]he was to leave Loreto but she was to keep her vows. She was to start a new congregation. That congregation would work for the poorest of the poor in the slums in a spirit of poverty and cheerfulness. There would be a special vow of charity for the poor. There would be no institutions, hospitals or big dispensaries. The work was to be among the abandoned, those with nobody, the very poorest.[54]

Such clear 'demands' were not the result of an isolated spiritual incident on the train on the way to her retreat. Rather, the 'inspiration day', as 10 September is now known and celebrated annually by the order of the

Missionaries of Charity, and her request to leave Loreto marked a turning point in her long quest to make herself useful to the poor. The inspiration day was also the climax of the anguish she had been experiencing constantly, perhaps as early as 1935 when she apparently took issue with the confinement of the nuns for the first time. Some of her superiors' unsympathetic responses towards her 'encounter' with God on 10 September 1946 was bound to disappoint Sister Teresa and she was not very happy when some of them even tried to make fun of this important spiritual experience.

That some superiors were not sympathetic to Sister Teresa and even tried to ridicule her is obvious also from a few scenes in Kevin Connor's 1997 film *Mother Teresa: In the Name of God's Poor*. As mentioned in chapter five, this is a feature film and as such its story should not be seen as a replica of what happened in real life. Given Mother Teresa's close collaboration with the two script-writers for several years, however, we should not perhaps ignore completely the film's biographical value.

It is widely known that Mother Teresa's partnership with the authors of the biopic, especially the two script-writers, was not always amicable. The nun approved the project three times, only to retract permission in each case. Her behaviour was hardly a whim; obviously, something went wrong, so wrong in fact that some frictions and differences were apparently never resolved. We do not know as yet if such disagreements were between Mother Teresa and the production team or between the film-makers and the Roman Catholic Church. This film is the closest biographical account of the events that led to Sister Teresa's breaking with Loreto and eventually setting up her religious order in the late 1940s. Some personal details and frictions recorded in the film, although handled sensitively, were obviously deemed far too revealing and perhaps damaging for the Church either by Mother Teresa or by those who in the last years of her life spoke on her behalf. In the end, it was Mother Teresa herself who allegedly refused to endorse the film. The order of the Missionaries of Charity has yet to give its seal of approval to this biopic which has been praised for its accuracy by several friends of Mother Teresa, including two Roman Catholic Archbishops who knew her very well.[55]

In one of the 'controversial' scenes of the film, Archbishop Périer, a Loreto Mother Superior and Father Van Exem discuss how to handle Sister Teresa's request to leave the cloister. The discussion is said to have taken place at the Archbishop's Residence some time in the autumn of 1946:

Archbishop Périer: I've heard of nuns suffering delusions as a result of heatstroke but this takes the cake.

Father Van Exem: We've all been affected by the troubles, and it could be that Sister Teresa is struggling to affirm her faith, but she believes God has called her to follow him into the slum.

Archbishop Périer: Well?

Mother Superior: I believe that Sister Teresa is sincere; she just hasn't considered the implications.

Archbishop Périer: Which are?

Mother Superior: It will upset the entire convent if a nun of Sister Teresa's experience gives up everything and leaves.

Father Van Exem: She wants to apply for exclaustration, Mother Superior. This would allow her to remain in the Loreto order and live by her vows. All she is asking for is permission to work outside the walls.

Mother Superior: That's the other problem. The Loreto order has always been cloistered, and now a nun comes along and says she heard the voice of God, in a tunnel!

Father Van Exem: But she makes a compelling argument. She says that in the face of every suffering man, woman and child in India we can find the face of Jesus Christ. She calls it 'God's distress in disguise'.

Mother Superior: Heaven forbid, one of the children hears that the headmistress is hearing voices and seeing visions.

Archbishop Périer: I think it's clear that this matter should remain strictly confidential.

Father Van Exem: Of course, but what are we to tell Sister Teresa?

Archbishop Périer: Tell her nothing.

Father Van Exem: Your Grace!

Archbishop Périer: This isn't the first time a nun has asked for permission to leave the cloister. Last time I advised the applicant to wait a year. Twelve months later she sat in that chair thanking me for not taking her request seriously.

Father Van Exem: Sister Teresa, Your Grace, she's never not serious.

Archbishop Périer: Tell her to write me a letter in a year's time. Until then this matter is closed.

The frustration experienced by the Mother Superior character in this scene does not seem to have been much different from how some of Sister Teresa's superiors must have felt at that time. It is most likely that following a similar discussion with and advice from Archbishop Périer, the Loreto Provincial Superior expected Sister Teresa to forget about leaving the cloister and not to talk about it to anyone. Sister Teresa, of course, did not follow such advice. To make things worse, she continued to discuss her plans with Father Van Exem.

Sister Teresa's frequent conversations with Father Van Exem, notes Kathryn Spink, 'did not altogether escape her superiors' notice'.[56] They were obviously far from happy with the disobedient nun. Father Van Exem would remark later that they could only guess that 'something was going on – they did not know quite what'.[57] Under these circumstances, someone at Loreto House took a rather rash decision, which indicates not only how badly some superiors had taken Sister Teresa's 'challenge' to their authority but also what they were prepared to do to get rid of her. When no one expected it, certainly not Sister Teresa and Father Van Exem, the 'nuisance' nun was removed to the Loreto convent at Asansol, some 130 miles from Calcutta.

Sympathetic biographers prefer not to dwell on Sister Teresa's unexpected removal from Entally towards the end of 1946. If they refer to the incident at all, they either play down its significance or mention how useful Sister Teresa was to others at Asansol. There are even cases when her transfer is interpreted as an act of kindness on the part of her superiors. Edward Le Joly and David Porter, for instance, argue that soon after Sister Teresa was informed of Archbishop Périer's decision that she would have to wait a year before she could raise with him the same issue, she was sent to Asansol 'for reasons of health'.[58]

The removal must have struck Sister Teresa as too harsh a punishment, but this was not the first time her superiors had tried to teach her a lesson. A few months earlier, she had received the first 'clear warning' that she was not very popular when she was suddenly replaced as 'superior' (spiritual guide) by her predecessor Mother du Cénacle. According to Kathryn Spink, the demotion was the result of the divisions in opinions among the local ecclesiastical hierarchy about her 'competence' as a superior.[59] The controversial Sister Teresa was obviously not considered to be the right spiritual mentor for three or four Loreto nuns and of the Daughters of St Anne.

The only figure of authority that apparently Sister Teresa could depend on during those difficult times was Mother du Cénacle. Father Henry told biographer Desmond Doig in the early 1970s that Mother du Cénacle was 'a great protector of Mother Teresa',[60] but he did not elaborate on why the Albanian nun needed protection and from whom. No matter how willing Mother du Cénacle was to protect Sister Teresa, it is not clear if this Mauritian nun had any influence outside St Mary's school. Sister Teresa's main opponents, it seems, were not at St Teresa's and perhaps not even at the Entally convent, but at Loreto House. The Loreto Provincialate in Calcutta nowadays is adamant that '[t]here is no evidence of ill-feeling' between Sister Teresa and Loreto when she left the order.[61] To prove this, Sister Moira, Archivist at Loreto House, draws attention to the fact that '[i]n 1950 when the official inauguration of the Congregation of Missionaries of Charity took place in Creek Row the Loreto Provincial, Mother Francis Xavier Stapleton, specially delegated Mother du Cénacle to be the Loreto representative at the ceremony'.[62] Sister Moira also points out that, although Sister Teresa lived at the Entally convent and taught at St Mary's, she 'belonged to the Loreto community in the main house [Loreto House]'.[63] Considering how close Mother du Cénacle had always been to Sister Teresa and that she was neither European nor one of the superiors from the 'main house', one could conclude that the inauguration of Mother Teresa's order in 1950 was attended by none of her European-born superiors at Loreto House, which was and remains to this day the headquarters of the Loreto community in Calcutta.

That Mother du Cénacle was unable to protect Sister Teresa from some superiors is also clear from her failure to prevent her sudden transfer to the Loreto convent in Asansol. The removal indicated that Sister Teresa's relationship with Loreto House had reached a point where any reconciliation was almost impossible.

Some superiors were obviously so angry with and eager to banish Sister Teresa that they apparently did not even deign, or perhaps did not dare, to inform Archbishop Périer of their plan to remove her from Entally. While Sister Teresa was not in a position to challenge the transfer, Archbishop Périer obviously did not take lightly what seems to have been a snub to his authority. He asked for Sister Teresa to be returned without delay to Entally where she had to stay until her case was finally decided.

It was during these tumultuous times, when Sister Teresa's relationship with superiors had reached breaking point, that Father Van Exem is believed to have advised her on two important issues: not to talk to anyone at Loreto about her intention to leave the convent,[64] and to start keeping a diary. The advice proved invaluable to Sister Teresa.

Following her spiritual father's first piece of advice, Sister Teresa no longer updated her Loreto superiors in Calcutta on her efforts to leave the order. It appears that she did not inform them even when, in January 1948, she wrote to the Superior General, Mother Gertrude M. Kennedy, Mother General of the Loreto Order in Ireland, asking for her permission to apply to Rome for an indult of secularization (turning from a vowed nun into a laywoman), as Archbishop Périer had insisted, and not for an indult of exclaustration (living by her vows while working in the slums), which was what Sister Teresa would have wanted. Mother Gertrude's reply, dated 2 February, was an endorsement of Father Van Exem's advice to Sister Teresa not to discuss her case with her Loreto superiors after her return from Asansol. Mother Gertrude, who was obviously informed well in advance by the superiors in Calcutta of the 'troubles' caused by Sister Teresa, decided not to side with them on this sensitive issue. 'Since this is manifestly the will of God,' Mother Gertrude wrote to Sister Teresa:

> I give you permission to write to the Congregation in Rome and to apply for the indult. Do not speak to the Provincial. Do not speak to your superiors. Speak to nobody. I did not speak to my own counsellors. My consent is sufficient. However, do not ask for the indult of secularization, ask for the indult of exclaustration.[65]

Sister Teresa was delighted with Mother Gertrude's response but did not follow her advice entirely. Prior to writing to Rome, she showed her letter to Archbishop Périer, who again insisted that she should apply for an indult of secularization not exclaustration. Sister Teresa had no option but to follow the Archbishop's advice. On the other hand, following Father Van Exem's and Mother Gertrude's advice, she did not inform her Loreto superiors in Calcutta of her application to Rome, which was sent off in March 1948. That Sister Teresa's superiors knew nothing of her letter to the Holy See is confirmed by the following information released by the Loreto Provincialate in Calcutta:

> In the summer of 1948, the Provincial Superior, Mother Dorothy Maher, was away in Ireland at a meeting. Mother Columba Ormiston was left in charge of the Congregation in India. It seems that during this time the permission from the Vatican for Mother Teresa to start a new congregation was sent to Calcutta. *Mother Columba and her assistants had not known about Mother Teresa's application for this permission and there was uncertainty about how to proceed.* (emphasis added)[66]

Sister Teresa would also find very useful Father Van Exem's advice to keep a diary. Considering that Sister Teresa had been interested in writing since an early age and, more importantly, that she had been writing and publishing regularly since her arrival in India in 1929, it is possible that by the time she received her spiritual director's advice to keep a record of events she had already started keeping a journal. Father Pierre Fallon, who led the retreat in Darjeeling in September 1946, had seen Sister Teresa at intervals busying herself with writing. The 'slips of paper' she handed over to Father Van Exem on October 1946 were very much like entries from a diary she had been keeping on her own perhaps even before she began her September retreat.

Even if Sister Teresa did not get the idea to keep a diary from Father Van Exem in 1946, she certainly learned from him how important it was that she wrote down everything that was going on in her life at Loreto at that time. Father Van Exem was not only a good friend of Sister Teresa but also a very experienced and efficient official. He apparently envisaged that things could, as they eventually did, get rather nasty between his Albanian spiritual charge and some of her Loreto superiors.

Mother Teresa duly followed Father Van Exem's advice to keep a record of events as they enfolded from October 1946 onwards. A Loreto nun who knew Sister Teresa since 1947 would recall in 1985 that the Albanian nun used to write regularly in her diary.[67] The diary Sister Teresa kept in 1946 is obviously one of the most important documents she wrote at Loreto. This work is significant not only because of what she recorded about herself and some of her superiors. By 1946 Mother Teresa saw herself as being at one with the Indian nation and, in this sense, the diary represents an attempt to put on paper some of her thoughts about what was going on in India at that time. This was a work where the personal and the public were closely entwined.

It was only natural that a reflective person like Sister Teresa would resort to writing at such a crucial moment both in her life and in the history of India. As mentioned earlier, Sister Teresa had always been interested in writing. The poems she wrote as a child, as a young woman prior to leaving Skopje at eighteen and as a Loreto nun in Calcutta,[68] and more importantly the letters she submitted regularly to the magazine *Katoličke misije* from January 1929, in which she described the beauty of the places she had visited on her way to and across India and the poverty that hit her almost everywhere in her adopted country, indicate clearly that in a sense Sister Teresa had always been and remained a writer at heart. Her letters from India are fine samples of travel-writing which deserve to be published in their own right for their lyricism, astute observations and the authentic atmosphere they record. In such works, Sister Teresa emerges as a sophisticated writer who could paint with words some impressive landscapes. In her early correspondence as a missionary, Sister Teresa showed that, unlike many past and present Western tourist-writers, she was not interested in the exotic but in reality, especially in the harsh and cruel reality faced daily by 'human debris' in India. Sister Teresa's early letters from Calcutta were never contrived. They were spontaneous yet beautifully composed. It is in such letters that we perhaps see Sister Teresa at her best as a writer. The letters show that she did not suffer from any inhibition when she wrote them; she recorded and commented on reality without having to worry, as she would often do from the early 1950s onwards, that her words could undermine her image, the image of her order and that of Catholicism in India and beyond.

Mother Teresa's poetry, her early correspondence and the diary she kept in the late 1940s seriously challenge the long-held view of even some of her closest biographer-friends that, intellectually speaking, she was simply an 'ordinary' woman. This derogatory approach to her persona has its genesis in Muggeridge's 1971 book *Something Beautiful for God*, in which he makes it abundantly clear what he thought of the intellect of this 'living saint'. Muggeridge found Mother Teresa 'not particularly clever, or particularly gifted in the arts of persuasion',[69] which, to him, was hardly surprising in view of her 'humble' origin:

> [Mother Teresa] comes of peasant stock. This is apparent in her appearance and bearing and way of looking at things. Without the special grace vouchsafed her, she might have been a rather hard, and even grasping, person. God has turned these qualities to his own ends.[70]

In his 1977 biography *We Do It for Jesus*, Edward Le Joly remarks that Mother Teresa 'comes from peasant stock and from a community of hill people'.[71] Following Muggeridge's and Le Joly's example, other biographers have hastened to highlight Mother Teresa's 'rustic' background, appearance and even 'lack of wit' and, at times, make some remarks that today could be construed as betraying a prevailing superiority complex towards the 'uncivilized' and 'uncouth' human stock that Mother Teresa came from. Eileen Egan, for instance, is more specific about what, in her view, made Mother Teresa's physical appearance 'strange' in 1955:

> Her hands and feet were large for a woman little over five feet tall. Her eyes were brown with tawny lights, and her skin, after an uninterrupted stay of twenty-six years in India, was ochred by the sun. She could have been a woman from the Punjab or Kashmir. Actually, she had originated in a tiny country in southeastern Europe, little known and long isolated from the rest of the continent.[72]

Kathryn Spink, another close friend of Mother Teresa, is impressed by yet another physical 'peculiarity' of the nun, her 'strong-jawed face', which she finds 'earthy not ethereal'. To add weight to her observation, Spink argues that:

> [f]or people repelled by pale piety there was a toughness and vitality about it. If the quality which redeemed the wrinkles of time and weather was frequently referred to as 'luminosity', it could, extraordinarily, equally well be described as merriment. It was a face which spoke, as she did, of a sense of the mystery of God very much in the world.[73]

Some of the remarks about Mother Teresa's 'rusticity', 'less-than-appealing looks' and 'unprepossessing appearance' are made by writers who worked closely with and knew her intimately for years and yet never found time to visit her birthplace, where they could have easily noticed, one would hope, how surprisingly normal her fellow Albanians as well as their Balkan neighbours are, at least as far as appearances go. Some of Mother Teresa's biographers, including Catholics, obviously have still to learn that to be religious, a Christian, a Roman Catholic and above all an Albanian follower of Christ one does not necessarily have to comply with the now outdated, stereotypical biblical image of tribes and shepherds in the wilderness. Mother Teresa did not come from 'peasant stock'. Nor was she 'very ordinary in many ways'[74] and 'uneducated', as her Indian biographer Navin Chawla portrays her. Contrary to Chawla's conclusion that Mother Teresa never 'had the time to read much, other than the scriptures',[75] the Albanian nun was quite an educated woman. She was familiar from an early age not only with the best that was written in Albanian[76] but also with Italian and Russian literature. At her church in Skopje she had the opportunity to listen regularly to talks by parish priests on world literary classics, drama, poetry, medicine, science and even on how to conduct an orchestra.[77] Her local church library, which she visited regularly, had several books by Dante and Dostoevsky.[78] More importantly, like some other biographers, Chawla seems to forget that for seventeen years this 'uneducated' nun taught at St Mary's school at Entally not religious studies but history and geography.

If some of Mother Teresa's 'informed' biographers could have such a low opinion of her intellect even by the time she had apparently made quite an impact on millions of people around the world with her work and message, one could easily imagine, and perhaps be inclined not to judge too harshly, some of her Loreto superiors in the 1940s, who possibly did not know much about the world outside the walls of their convents. It appears that Sister Teresa failed to win some of them over not because she was not 'particularly gifted in the arts of persuasion', but perhaps because her courage, original ideas, power of argument and, more importantly perhaps, her 'impertinence' as an 'outsider' European came as a shock to them.

Mother Teresa would continue to shock to the end of her life some 'superior' Westerners who were unable to comprehend how someone like her, originating from the 'primitive' and 'uncivilized' Balkans, could have the 'temerity' to raise her voice to get what she wanted not only in India but also in Europe. Referring to an uncorroborated incident, which apparently took place in London when Mother Teresa allegedly refused to pay for the food she bought for her nuns at the value of £500, this is how Walter Wüllenweber condemns the 'uncivilized' nun in his article 'Mother Teresa: Where are her Millions?', which appeared first in Germany in *Stern* magazine on 10 September 1998:

> When she was told she'd have to pay at the till, the diminutive seemingly harmless nun showed her *Balkan temper* and shouted, 'This is for the work of God!' She raged so loud and so long that eventually a businessman waiting in the queue paid up on her behalf. (emphasis added)[79]

Wüllenweber, who does not give any information about the exact location where or the time when the alleged 'extortion' took place, has obviously read too much into Muggeridge's observation mentioned earlier that, '[w]ithout the special grace vouchsafed her', Mother Teresa 'might have been a rather hard, and even grasping, person'. One can only imagine how much the German people would be insulted, and rightly so, if a journalist commenting on a scandal involving a German citizen outside Germany saw it as epitomizing what is wrong with or typical of not only all Germans but also all West Europeans.

Stern ran Wüllenweber's article on the first anniversary of Mother Teresa's death. Had the piece appeared in her lifetime, the nun would not have been surprised by Wüllenweber's remark about her 'Balkan temper'. Mother Teresa had been used to such cultural reminders from as early as the mid-1940s when her relationship with some Loreto superiors went from bad to worse. As Bharati Mukherjee notes in her *Time* article 'The Saint Mother Teresa', the views of some Loreto nuns about Mother Teresa's 'freakishness' and 'non-Europeanness' were noticed also by some of the rich Indian girls studying at Loreto College.[80]

By the time she became a public figure, as a rule, Mother Teresa was unwilling to take issue with personal derogatory remarks made not only by her opponents but also by some of her trusted biographers. As long as her friends publicized her work, which to Mother Teresa meant publicizing Jesus, she was prepared to tolerate some insults thrown at her, her family, the Albanian nation and the Balkans. If Mother Teresa ever expressed disquiet about the way she and her background were portrayed, it was only in private. 'When I asked Mother Teresa if her people had been mountain people,' Eileen Egan notes in her 1986 biography, 'she answered, "No, they were not. As far as we can know, they were city people. They say that we were peasants, but that is not true." '[81] 'They', of course, were people like Malcolm Muggeridge and Edward Le Joly, who had done so much to publicize Mother Teresa's work and the Missionaries of Charity order that she was willing to go along with some of their incorrect conclusions and even derogatory remarks about her personally and her background.

What did Mother Teresa do if someone at Loreto made disparaging remarks about her or her roots during the 1940s? We do not know, and perhaps we never will. The diary she kept during those years obviously helped her to calm herself and thus avoid any open confrontation. Mother Teresa never stopped loving Loreto and she would prove this by insisting when she became famous on concealing whatever happened between her and her superiors from 1946 to 1948. Protecting the Loreto order was one of the reasons why, perhaps in the late 1960s, Mother Teresa finally destroyed the diary and the correspondence she kept in the late 1940s and early 1950s.

Some fragments from Mother Teresa's diary have survived partly because those, like Father Van Exem, who had a chance to read it, could remember many years after its disappearance what she had intimated in it. Father Van Exem's and other people's references to some entries have been recorded in several biographies. Mother Teresa would also occasionally mention to some of her biographers what she had scribbled in her diary. She was, of course, cautious not to refer to any controversial entry.

Most biographers who 'quote' from the diary, of course, have never seen it. All the same, some of them are keen to give the impression that they are very well informed about what was written in it. In his 1996 biography, for instance, Navin Chawla refers frequently to this document which, of course, vanished before he first came across Mother Teresa. This is especially the case in chapter four, entitled 'Motijhil'.[82]

Like many other Christian and non-Christian biographers referring to the diary, Chawla does not refer to any controversial entry regarding the tense relationship between Mother Teresa and her superiors in the 1940s, partly because he never saw the diary and partly because it was highly unlikely that a devout Roman Catholic like Mother Teresa would reveal her difficulties at Loreto to a Hindu writer. Mother Teresa remained loyal to Loreto long after the order had made her an 'outcaste'.

The destruction of the diary is a loss to Mother Teresa scholarship. Had the diary survived, we would have been made privy to a fascinating stage in the life of this twentieth-century public figure and media icon. The diary would have disclosed information about some of the hurdles she had to overcome before she left Loreto and about the people who put them in her way.

That some superiors disliked Sister Teresa and were eager to stop her from leaving the order is also clear from their attempts to censor her writing. This tendency became more obvious by the time she was sent to the Loreto convent at Asansol. Her superiors were especially eager to censor Sister Teresa's letters to Father Van Exem. As Kathryn Spink explains, by the time Sister Teresa's Loreto saga had reached such a dramatic point:

> any correspondence written by a nun would have to be left unsealed, possibly read by her superior and only then sealed prior to dispatch. Father Van Exem protested that this obligatory procedure would put an end to all secrecy and render Mother Teresa's life within Loreto impossible, but his objections were instantly quashed. Mother Teresa was entitled to write to her bishop and he to her in a sealed envelope. Father Van Exem and his spiritual charge would therefore correspond in this way via the Archbishop. Archbishop Périer himself would act as intermediary and postboy.[83]

Spink notes that throughout the five to six months Mother Teresa was away she wrote to Father Van Exem not only about 'matters of conscience' but also about her life in Asansol. Spink also emphasizes that at Asansol the banished nun was having a great time, especially because '[s]he was ... put in charge of the convent garden, and she wrote with sensitivity of the beauty of the flowers she tended, in letters almost all of which would subsequently be destroyed'.[84] In view of the fact that Spink does not refer to anything controversial in Sister Teresa's letters to her spiritual director during those months, it appears that the Archbishop of Calcutta agreed to act as a 'postboy' so that Sister Teresa's letters about gardening would go uncensored.

Sister Teresa's diary and her Asansol letters were obviously about far more important issues than her trusted biographers would care to mention. If such documents were indeed so 'harmless', Mother Teresa's friends have still to explain why she was so keen to destroy them. Asked by Father Le Joly some time in the early or mid-1970s if she still had the diary, Mother Teresa shrugged her shoulders saying: 'No, I think I threw it away.'[85] Considering that the diary in question had always been in her possession, Mother Teresa could afford to be very matter-of-fact about it. After all, she had managed to destroy it without having to struggle to obtain it in the first place, unlike the letters she had sent to Father Van Exem during the months she stayed at the Asansol convent. Mother Teresa was obviously so desperate to retrieve and destroy this correspondence that she pursued the issue for many years. Father Van Exem refused to give in to her persistent requests, saying that the correspondence did not belong only to her; the letters were the property of the congregation. When she saw that she would not be able to convince him to hand over the correspondence, Mother Teresa asked for the help of Archbishop Périer. The Archbishop told her that she could have the documents destroyed provided that she wrote the history of the Missionaries of Charity. Mother Teresa was obviously not prepared to comply with this request and so the Archbishop could be of no further assistance to her on this matter.

By the time Archbishop Périer retired in 1960, the issue of Mother Teresa's letters remained unresolved. His three successors, Archbishop Vivian Dyer, Cardinal Lawrence Picachy and Archbishop Albert D'Souza were also unable to convince Mother Teresa that she should no longer insist on the destruction of the correspondence. They also failed to convince her that she should record the history of her order. In the end, seeing that Mother Teresa had no intention of giving up, Father Van Exem gave in and sent her two boxes of documents. According to Spink, the issue of the disposal of this documentation was the only one over which Mother Teresa and Father Van Exem had ever quarrelled.[86] Later Father Van Exem would remark that although he asked her to spare the important papers that belonged to her congregation, he was not confident that she had kept much. It is not known if Mother Teresa kept anything at all from that correspondence.

There are several possible reasons why Mother Teresa was so adamant that she had to destroy these letters, especially when she was becoming a public figure in India and internationally. Perhaps she wanted to preserve the myth that she set up the order of the Missionaries of Charity entirely on her own, whereas several biographers, including some of her close friends, have hinted that she received support from many priests, as well as from the Loreto order. According to Navin Chawla, the Loreto sisters 'were bound by church law to provide for her needs, and they certainly did so',[87] whereas Kathryn Spink holds that when she finally left Loreto in 1948, she took with her only the ticket for Patna and five rupees, although the Loreto nuns 'would readily have provided her with more' if she had asked them.[88]

Mother Teresa's supporters offer many reasons for her determination to get rid of the documents. Edward Le Joly, for instance, believes that Mother Teresa's discarding of important documents such as her diary was '[t]he right thing to do' because the work in question, which he claims to have seen perhaps in the early 1950s, contained 'no special secrets, no revelations, just small notes on the persons she had met or on some particular happening'.[89] David Porter, on the other hand, holds that, had 'her diaries' survived, they would have certainly made 'an illuminating record of many acts of charity and personal sacrifice, which is probably why Mother Teresa considered it unnecessary to preserve them'.[90] The interesting thing about Porter's statement is not why, in his view, Mother Teresa decided not to preserve such early personal records but that he uses the word 'diary' in plural. Mother Teresa is known to have kept more than just one diary, or to put it another way, it appears that she expressed interest in keeping a diary at several times from the mid-1940s until the early 1950s. Her 'diaries' obviously included the notes she kept before, during and immediately after her retreat in 1946, the diary she started keeping following the advice of Father Van Exem when her relationship with her Loreto superiors started to deteriorate from October 1946, the letters she sent to Father Van Exem from Asansol and, finally, the diary she started keeping following Archbishop Périer's advice when she left the Loreto order in the summer of 1948. What ties all these autobiographical documents together is their common fate: Mother Teresa apparently destroyed them all.

Reflecting on the motives that could have led Mother Teresa to destroy her personal writings, especially the diary she kept in the first couple of years immediately after leaving Loreto, Anne Sebba argues that:

> [h]er action could merely reflect an understandable desire for privacy once she realised that millions of people would be interested in reading such a diary but seems also to indicate a concern for shaping the image perhaps not anticipated in traditional concepts of sainthood, where the ego is expected not to intrude.[91]

In spite of the 'saintly' qualities that Mother Teresa had or her image-makers ascribe to her, she was very much an 'ordinary' human being with her own share of doubts, ambitions, frustrations and, at times, 'weaknesses' not usually associated with saints. Mother Teresa's personal and spontaneous writings would have given us a chance to see the charitable nun in all her human regalia, something which perhaps would not always have been very flattering. Whether or not such intimate information would have made her appear less 'saintly' when she was alive or after her death is a matter for debate. What is almost certain is that such intimate confessions would have made her appear more of a down-to-earth person. They could also have embarrassed several individuals and institutions dealing with her in the late 1940s and early 1950s. Mother Teresa, obviously, chose not to embarrass anyone for all the above-mentioned reasons and, as Father Gaston Roberge puts it, because she 'would not build herself up by pulling others down. She was too genuinely charitable for that, and, moreover, she did not need to pull anyone down'.[92] Mother Teresa, it appears, destroyed the documents not so much to protect herself, any particular person or the Loreto order as such, but the image of Christianity and of the Roman Catholic Church.

v. The symbolism of 16 August 1946

Mother Teresa was essentially a spiritual but also a down-to-earth woman and an astute reader of the events that were unfolding in India in the 1940s. Her decision to leave Loreto could well have been inspired by God, as she herself obviously believed. Such inspiration, however, was grounded in the tense political, religious and nationalistic fervour that had been brewing for decades in India. Of particular importance in her case was her knowledge of the civil unrest of 1945–1956 and especially her witnessing of the violence that broke out in Calcutta on 16 August 1946, an event also known as the Day of the Great Killing. Earlier that day, the Muslim League had called a mass meeting in Calcutta's main park, the *Maidan*. As the meeting was over, communal clashes erupted and what was planned by the Muslim League as 'Direct Action Day' turned into one of the bloodiest events in India prior to its independence.

As a result of the clashes, St Mary's school received no food supplies for its three hundred girls. As headmistress, Sister Teresa had to find a solution, and rather than risk the lives of her colleagues, she decided to leave the compound to try to secure some food. This is Mother Teresa's own account of that dreadful day:

> I saw the bodies on the streets, stabbed, beaten, lying there in strange positions in their dried blood. We had been behind our safe walls. We knew that there had been rioting. People had been jumping over our walls, first a Hindu, then a Muslim. You see, our compound was between Moti Jihl, which was mainly Muslim then, and Tengra, with the potteries and tanneries. That was Hindu. We took in each one and helped him to escape safely. When I went out on the street – only then I saw the death that was following them.[93]

According to Eileen Egan, whenever Mother Teresa referred later to the Day of the Great Killing and its aftermath 'her face clouded over with indescribable sadness'.[94] This was the moment when Mother Teresa apparently felt more than ever before as a missionary that she had been sheltered for far too long from the poor people of India. The massacre she witnessed on 16 August 1946 did not turn her suddenly into the charitable missionary she soon became. The apocalyptic scene, however, seems to have served as a catalyst. Her faith in Jesus was not challenged by the hatred, death and destruction she saw on that day; what was seriously challenged was whether she had been living her life all these years at Loreto according to the promise she had made to her mother Drane in 1928 that she was going to India to serve Jesus by helping the poor. Mother Teresa had already received what David Porter calls 'a timely reminder'[95] from her mother about this after she had informed her in 1937 that 'I am a teacher, and I love the work. I am also Head of the whole school, and everybody wishes me well here.'[96] Rather than congratulating her 'successful' daughter, Drane replied:

> Dear child, do not forget that you went out to India for the sake of the poor. Do you remember our File? She was covered in sores, but what made her suffer much more was the knowledge that she was alone in the world. We did what we could for her. But the worst thing was not the sores, it was the fact that she had been forgotten by her family.[97]

The August massacre was the best and the cruellest reminder Mother Teresa received as a Loreto nun, and she was obviously not prepared to wait for another chance to sort out once and for all why she had gone to India in the first place. She may well have heard a 'call' from God on the train to Darjeeling less than a month later but that call was certainly the outcome of the shock she received on 16 August.

That Mother Teresa's decision to leave Loreto had something to do with the impact events in India had on her, and especially with what she witnessed on 16 August 1946, has been strongly denied at times by some of her friends and biographers. Father Van Exem, for instance, holds that:

> Mother [Teresa] had met poverty well before 1946. This was especially so in 1942 and 1943, when the Great Bengali Famine stalked the land. People were starving, people were lying on the road. The girls in Entally were poor girls. But the Call had not come at that time, so Mother never thought of leaving the Convent. She knew the poverty of Calcutta and its people and she wanted to work for them, but she thought only of working through the Convent, as a Loreto nun. That was the ideal.
>
> Some accounts have tried to make a connection between her life behind convent walls and the poverty and communal killings in Calcutta in those days, but these accounts are completely wrong, only a hypothesis. This was not the inspiration for her vocation. The

inspiration came from Heaven. She was very sure from the beginning, and I must say that I was very sure as well.[98]

While it is true that Sister Teresa had seen poverty in Calcutta well before 1946, her encounters with the poor had been limited. From 1935 when she first started teaching outside the Entally convent at St Teresa's school she certainly had more chances than most other Loreto nuns to study more closely the wretched life a large number of Indians lived in those days. Such erratic and brief contacts with grim reality, however, did not necessarily mean that she was fully aware of the extent of poverty in Calcutta. As late as 1948, she apparently had no idea what her deprived neighbourhood was even called. Shortly after she left Loreto, Sister Teresa asked Father Henry at St Teresa's church about the location of Motijhil. To which, her friend, unable to hide his surprise, replied: 'You ought to know it very well. It is the slum on the far side of the convent in which you taught.'[99]

That 16 August 1946 apparently made a lasting impact on Mother Teresa might also be seen by the fact that she decided to leave Loreto exactly two years after the massacre: on 16 August 1948.[100] A coincidence? Probably. On the other hand, we should perhaps remember that Mother Teresa had a habit of paying attention to coincidences. Why Mother Teresa chose to leave the Entally convent on the anniversary of the Day of the Great Killing will perhaps always remain a mystery. God apparently chose to 'talk' to Mother Teresa at moments of intense personal loss, as was the case when her father died suddenly in 1919, or collective tragedies, such as the communal violence that erupted on 16 August 1946. Mother Teresa is known to have said that it was not the Day of the Great Killing that had made her think of leaving the convent; she apparently believed that the impulse had come less than a month after the massacre of 16 August 1946.[101] On the other hand, she is not on record as having denied that she left the convent on 16 August 1948 or that this date had no symbolism attached to it.

In an attempt perhaps to downplay the impact the Day of the Great Killing had on Sister Teresa, some biographers do not record 16 August 1948 as the date of her departure from the Entally convent. Malcolm Muggeridge, for instance, claims that Mother Teresa left Loreto on 8 August,[102] which is the day when the news that she had been granted the indult of exclaustration was made public.[103] Eileen Egan clearly implies that the massacre of 1946 had some importance to Sister Teresa. In her words:

August 16, 1948 was two years to the day after the Day of the Great Killing had bathed the streets of Calcutta in blood. In ten days, Sister Teresa would be thirty-eight years of age. She could hardly have dreamed that her life was to become so inextricably woven with the agonies of Calcutta that the very name of the city would become affixed to her own name.[104]

Egan does not say explicitly that Mother Teresa left Loreto on 16 August but she clearly believes this to be the case.[105] As for Desmond Doig, he records 18 August as the departure day,[106] a detail he claims to have learnt from Father Henry's diary.[107] Referring to the same diary, some biographers note that Father Henry recorded that Sister Teresa left Loreto not on 18 August, as Doig claims, but on the sixteenth.[108] Doig included in his biography the facsimile of the entry of Father Henry's diary in which he made the note about Sister Teresa's departure from Loreto. Interestingly enough, the entry records 'sixteenth of August 1948' very clearly as the day when Sister Teresa 'is leaving St Mary's Entally for Patna'.[109] An unfortunate discrepancy? Perhaps.

The interesting thing about Muggeridge and Doig, who do not record 16 August as the day when Sister Teresa parted company with Loreto, Egan who obviously believes that that was the day but does not make it explicit, Porter and Spink, who have no doubt about 16 August being the departure day, and Sebba, who prefers not to refer to any specific date, is that they are all keen to emphasize not so much when exactly Mother Teresa finally left the Loreto order but that she went to the Medical Mission Sisters in Patna for some basic medical training. It appears some friendly biographers are keen to tone down and in some cases even deny completely that there were some hard feelings between Sister Teresa and Loreto when she left the order on 16 August 1948. According to information obtained from the Loreto Provincialate in Calcutta, in the summer of 1948 Mother Columba Ormiston, who at that time was in charge of the Congregation in India, and her assistants 'provided generously for her [Sister Teresa] and as required by Canon Law. She was sent for a training with the Medical Missionary Sisters at Patna. . . . Mother Teresa left Loreto in December 1948.'[110]

Sister Teresa's going to Patna had nothing to do with Loreto. According to Eileen Egan, Sister Teresa wrote to the Medical Mission Sisters working at the Holy Family Hospital following Father Van Exem's advice and after she had secured the agreement of Archbishop Périer.[111]

By the time Sister Teresa returned from Patna to Calcutta in December 1948, paying a visit to Loreto was hardly one of her priorities. She had said her goodbyes to Loreto on 16 August 1948.

vi. The rest is history . . . almost

How did Mother Teresa become so famous in the last three decades of her missionary work? The answer to this question is never simple. The media and the Vatican certainly played a crucial role in turning her into an archetypal 'charity worker' and a 'living saint'. Thanks to the constant interest the world media and the Holy See showed in her work and image, Mother Teresa became one of the most influential personalities of the twentieth century.

No matter when, how and to what extent certain individuals, institutions, countries and governments supported her, Mother Teresa was essentially a self-made woman. While the media, for instance, certainly played a crucial role in making her famous worldwide, they did not 'create' her. Mother Teresa was *there* and the media simply cannot fail to recognize people like her.

While it is true that Mother Teresa co-operated with the media from the start of her congregation, she hated publicity *per se*. The attention she paid to the media has often been misinterpreted not only by her opponents but also by some of her supporters. The Indian reporter and one of her early biographers, Desmond Doig, for instance, recalled in the mid-1970s that he was advised by a Catholic official and fellow reporter in the late 1940s to be careful with Sister Teresa because 'she's seeking publicity. The Church is rather concerned.'[112] Sister Teresa, obviously, did pay attention to the media even before the official inauguration of her order of the Missionaries of Charity in 1950, but not because she was publicity hungry. As she explained to some biographers, she used publicity 'for the love of Jesus'.[113]

Quite often Mother Teresa found it difficult to reconcile what Anne Sebba calls 'the greedy demands of a rapacious press',[114] and there were cases when she felt that some reporters were biased towards her. No matter how intrusive and unreliable she found the media at times, Mother Teresa never ceased using every medium of mass communication. She obviously saw journalists as having a very important role in promoting her efforts to help the people living in the slums of Calcutta. In her own words, '[t]he press makes people aware of the poor, and that is worth any sacrifice on my part'.[115]

On the fortieth anniversary of 'Inter Mirifica', the Second Vatican Council's Decree on the Media of Social Communications which was promulgated by Pope Paul VI on 4 December 1963, Pope John Paul II drew attention to the need to animate the media 'with a humane and Christian spirit'.[116] Mother Teresa had been using the media very efficiently to this end from the early 1950s. The 'un-intellectual' Albanian nun, who believed that even journalists can do the work of God, had employed the media efficiently to promote Christianity almost fifteen years before the issuing of the conciliar decree on social communications. She understood from the beginning of her congregation the important role the media could play not only in promoting her work but also as a modern means of keeping Christianity alive in India after independence. Obviously, Mother Teresa was well ahead of the strategists at the Vatican in understanding the potential of the media.

It appears that the Vatican first became aware of Mother Teresa's work in Calcutta through the media. Had it not been for the attention that the Catholic media in India and the United States paid to her throughout the 1950s and in the early 1960s, the Holy See would have perhaps never noticed the Albanian nun trotting along in the slums of Calcutta.

Some scholars writing on celebrities nowadays tend to put too much emphasis at times on 'agencies' that apparently make famous people who they are. As a result of this tendency, successful individuals are often perceived and depicted as playing a negligible role on their road to fame and fortune. This attitude seems to prevail in Ellis Cashmore's book *Beckham*. Cashmore sees the football celebrity David Beckham largely as an easily controlled marionette in the hands of his wife Victoria, his clubs Manchester United and Real Madrid, sportswear sponsors such as Nike and Adidas and his PR team, to mention but a few.

While all these 'agencies' are important, the bottom line is that no one has ever achieved success without being utterly committed to their career. There would have been no Beckham phenomenon if David Beckham himself were not both talented and hungry for fame and fortune. No one becomes great without single-mindedness and ambition, and this applies to successful people from any walk of life, including religious celebrities, of whom Mother Teresa is perhaps one of the best examples.

Agnes Gonxhe Bojaxhiu's efforts to do something with her life began in earnest in 1928 when she left her family and country, and reached another turning point thirty years later. There were perhaps other Loreto nuns in Calcutta in the 1940s who were unhappy with the excessive isolation from the world outside the walls of their convents. It was only Sister Teresa, however, who managed to break free. Not many Loreto nuns would have dared to take on their strict disciplinarian superiors, argue their case passionately with several priests including the Archbishop of Calcutta, write to the Mother General of Loreto at Rathfarnham in Dublin and even send a letter to the Pope to ask to be allowed to leave the convent to work in the slums of Calcutta. Sister Teresa did all this and more. She was so determined to realize her ambition that in the end she was prepared, although reluctantly, to leave the convent as a laywoman.

The significance of what Sister Teresa wanted to do in the late 1940s was not understood at once by the Vatican. In fact, the Holy See did not know much about Sister Teresa for at least ten years after she had set up the Missionaries of Charity order in 1950. There are reasons to believe that even the indult of exclaustration she received in 1948 had nothing to do with the Vatican. For reasons that are not entirely clear to this day, Sister Teresa's letter to the Pontiff never went beyond Delhi, in spite of Mother Teresa's claim to Muggeridge in 1969 that 'I wrote to the Holy Father, Pope Pius XII, and by return post I got the answer on the 12th of April. He said that I could go out and be an unenclosed nun'.[117] Mother

Teresa learned in 1970 that the Apostolic Nuncio in Delhi rather than the Vatican had granted her the indult of exclaustration (and not of secularization, as Archbishop Périer had insisted). Moreover, Sister Teresa received the good news not on 12 April, when the letter was dated, but in July 1948. It is not clear whether the letter was posted in Delhi much later than when it was dated, whether it was delivered late by the Indian postal service or whether Archbishop Périer took some time before deciding to inform Sister Teresa of its contents.

Eileen Egan believes that, had Sister Teresa's request for secularization reached the Vatican, it is quite possible that they would have granted it. This would have meant the end of Sister Teresa's religious life, in which case we would have never heard of her. To Egan, someone's decision at the Delhi nunciature to change 'secularization' to 'exclaustration' was a providential intervention and a sort of prevenient grace.[118]

It is not clear why the Catholic authorities in Delhi never sent off Sister Teresa's letter to Rome or why they decided to allow her to leave the cloister as a nun. The covering letter that Archbishop Périer enclosed in Sister Teresa's letter to the Pope could well have made an impression on his colleagues in Delhi, who as Anne Sebba remarks, 'recognised the desperate need for anyone who was prepared to offer themselves with any social or humanitarian aid'.[119]

It could also be that the leaders of the Roman Catholic establishment in Delhi recognized the benefits Sister Teresa's initiative could have not only for the Catholic Church but also for Christianity at large when the future of this religion in India seemed bleak. By 1948, not only the colonized people but also the younger Churches worldwide, to quote Stephen Neill, 'had come to think of "mission" almost exclusively in terms of Western aggression and financial domination, and of the missionary as the representative of alien and undesired control'.[120]

In view of Neill's assessment of the standing of missionary work in the late 1940s, it is obvious that Sister Teresa apparently did not choose the best time to set up her own missionary congregation in India. As will be seen shortly, however, Sister Teresa was fully aware of the precarious situation she was in and was very clear from the first about the way she would proceed.

The Vatican, or more precisely the Sacred Congregation for the Propagation of Faith, recognized the Missionaries of Charity as a new congregation for the diocese of Calcutta on 7 October 1950, a move which was initiated and supported by Archbishop Périer, who had raised the issue with his superiors during his visit to Rome in April that year. The Vatican's endorsement, however, does not mean that its officials were able to predict how this new order would fare in India.

Mother Teresa's first direct contact with the Vatican took place in 1960 when she went to Rome after she had completed her visit to the United States. This was the first time she had been outside India since her arrival there in 1929. Mother Teresa stopped in Rome to ask that her congregation be placed under the Holy See. This would allow the Missionaries of Charity to expand outside India.

Even by 1960, Mother Teresa was still not very well known at the Holy See. She managed, however, to attract the attention of some senior Vatican officials when, at the end of the Mass in the Sistine Chapel, she stepped forward to kiss the ring of Pope John XXIII. The following day Mother Teresa got what she wanted from Gregory Cardinal Agagianian and Archbishop Pietro Sigismondi, but not until she had answered their numerous questions. Her conversation with them reveals that they did not know much about her work and congregation.

From 1960 onwards the Vatican's interest in Mother Teresa's work and order would increase significantly. This intensified interest can be best explained in the context of an important event in the history of the Roman Catholic Church, the Second Vatican Ecumenical Council, which opened under Pope John XXIII in 1962 and closed under Pope Paul VI in 1965. The Council called 'all the faithful of Christ of whatever rank or status ... to the fullness of the Christian life and to the perfection of charity'.[121] By 1965 Mother Teresa had been working hard for almost two decades to attain such 'fullness of the Christian life' and 'perfection of charity', and had already started to attract the attention of the world media for her exemplary piety and charitable work in India.

The attention the Vatican paid to Mother Teresa from the early 1960s has often been resented by many people inside the Church. This 'preferential' treatment, they argue, overshadows the dedication and sacrifices of numerous missionaries in India since the fourteenth century as well as during Mother Teresa's lifetime. That Mother Teresa's special treatment by the Vatican is not necessarily approved of by everyone in Christendom is also obvious from the fact that many scholars who have written extensively and authoritatively on Christian missions do not pay any attention to Mother Teresa. So, for instance, the nun and her Missionaries of Charity order are not mentioned even in passing in the 1986 revised second edition of Stephen Neill's acclaimed study *A History of Christian Mission*.

One could argue that by the time the Vatican apparently 'singled out' Mother Teresa in 1960, much of what she had been doing in India since 1948 when she left the Loreto order had already been done by other missionaries in India and elsewhere in the world.[122] Mother Teresa did not attract the attention of the Holy See simply because she was a female missionary; many women had served the Catholic Church as nuns from as early as the eighth century, if not earlier. Nor was the order of the Missionaries of Charity the first religious congregation set up by a woman operating outside Europe. The nineteenth century in particular saw the formation of many new sisterhoods devoted to missionary work. Anne-Marie Javouhey (1779–1851), for instance, is widely believed to have given a new impetus to African missions when, in 1805, she set up the

Congregation of the Sisters of St Joseph of Cluny. Twelve years later her sisters were sent to Réunion, an island in the Indian Ocean, and in 1919 to Senegal.

Mother Teresa also did not attract the attention of the Vatican because she was so close in many ways to the people of Calcutta. Several centuries before she arrived in India, Christian missionaries had achieved good results in their efforts to connect with indigenous people by learning their vernaculars, as some Catholic missionaries had done in Latin America in the sixteenth century, and as some Protestant missionaries started doing in India at the beginning of the eighteenth century.

Sister Teresa was not breaking new ground as a missionary either by dressing like a poor Indian woman in 1948. In the fourteenth century, Franciscan missionaries in Mongolia used to dress like the local people. In the seventeenth century, Roberto Nobili (1577–1656) turned himself into an Indian in the way he dressed and what he chose to eat. In the later part of the nineteenth century, James Hudson Taylor would dress like a Chinese. Even if Sister Teresa had not heard of these missionaries by the time she was preparing to leave Loreto, she was certainly aware of the example set by Gandhi, who sought to connect with poor people by dressing and living like them.

To identify fully with India, Sister Teresa became an Indian citizen shortly after leaving Loreto. Her naturalization, however, was not without precedent in the history of missions. Although not necessarily for the same reasons, several missionaries in the first part of the twentieth century took the citizenship of the countries in which they served.

Nor was Mother Teresa unique for the respect she showed towards the local culture in Calcutta. Over the centuries, numerous Catholic, Protestant and Orthodox missionaries alike have shown respect for local cultures, traditions and creeds. This sensible attitude perhaps has its roots in the late sixth century when the missionaries arriving in England showed respect and understanding for the customs and traditions of the indigenous population. A millennium later, one of the most revered Roman Catholic missionaries, Francis Xavier (1506–52), realized how important it was to respect the cultural heritage of non-Christians when he visited Japan. Shortly afterwards, another famous Catholic missionary, Matthew Ricci (1552–1610), showed enormous respect for the ancient Chinese civilization and culture. Following the example set by Xavier and Ricci, the Jesuits also behaved very tactfully and were flexible regarding local traditions in China and India throughout the seventeenth and the eighteenth centuries.

The Vatican did not decide to acknowledge Mother Teresa's order in 1950 and pay particular attention to her work from 1960 because of her long service in India. The history of Christianity, of any church, is full of examples of devoted missionaries who have spent most of their lives serving Christ across the world. Christian Friedrich Schwartz (1726–98), Robert

Moffat (1795–1883) and Timothy Richard (1845–1919) served for almost fifty years each in India, South Africa and China respectively.

Mother Teresa was hardly the first missionary to prove that Christianity can bring people of different faiths together and, more importantly perhaps in the context of India, to preach that no religion should be used to initiate or justify communal conflict. In this respect, Mother Teresa was following in the footsteps of Francis of Assisi (c. 1181–1226) and Thomas Aquinas (1225–1274), who in the thirteenth century had the courage to raise their voice against the crusades. Likewise, Mother Teresa was hardly the first missionary to preach that we humans have one God although we give him different names. In the seventeenth century Roberto Nobili preached at great personal risk that 'the true God is not the God of one race but the God of all'.[123]

What made Mother Teresa special to Vatican strategists in the early 1960s is that by then the Albanian nun was doing everything that other missionaries before her had done or were doing and much more. Mother Teresa had asked permission to set up an order in the late 1940s without requiring any financial support from her spiritual fathers in Calcutta, Delhi and the Holy See. As such, from the start her order was not, nor was it likely to become, a financial burden to the Church. On the contrary, in the years that followed, Mother Teresa allegedly even accumulated huge sums of money, which, critics like Christopher Hitchens and Aroup Chatterjee allege, she handed over to the Vatican.

Even if such allegations were true, this is not why the Vatican apparently singled out Mother Teresa in the early 1960s for 'preferential treatment'. The Holy See paid special attention to Mother Teresa because of the unique service she could offer to Christianity at a critical stage in the history of India. 'Christian missions will render true service to India,' Mahatma Gandhi once remarked, 'if they can confine their activities to humanitarian service without the ulterior motive of converting India or at least her unsophisticated villagers to Christianity.'[124] Mother Teresa, it appears, absorbed Gandhi's message like few other missionaries in India. By 'secularizing' missionary work, Mother Teresa presented Christianity as a faith that could still play a role and have a future in the new India.

As a European, Mother Teresa was obviously aware that, in spite of her devotion to the poor, she would always be considered a foreigner in India. She also seems to have realized the extent to which Catholicism had suffered in India as a result of what Stephen Neill calls, 'its extreme foreignness'.[125] To make Christianity a friendlier religion to the Indians, from the first Mother Teresa encouraged Indian girls to join her order. This meant that, from its inception, the Missionaries of Charity was never strictly speaking a European congregation. While the Vatican had been dragging its feet for centuries over the creation of indigenous churches outside Europe,[126] Mother Teresa had the far-sightedness to set up on her own an 'indigenous' Roman Catholic order in a predominantly Hindu country. Her life and congregation make for one of the most original and successful examples of inculturation and enculturation in the twentieth century. Missiology has yet to acknowledge Mother Teresa's vision as a modern missionary in a post- and neo-colonial world.

Mother Teresa was important to the Church in the early 1960s also because of the media interest her spirituality and humanitarian work had already started to generate in India and other countries. Several scholars such as Elisabeth Schüssler Fiorenza, Elizabeth A. Johnson and Kathleen Jones have drawn attention over the last three decades to the need to acknowledge the significant role women have played throughout the history of Christianity.[127] This was a sensitive issue which the Vatican was set to address during and after the Second Council. In Richard P. McBrien's words, '[o]ne of the most significant postconciliar developments has been that of feminist spirituality'.[128] A decade before the Vatican Council opened, Mother Teresa had already been hailed as a 'living saint' by journalists and politicians alike not only in India but also in the West.

In the early 1960s the Vatican realized that someone like Mother Teresa could not and should not be ignored. The Albanian nun was far too important to the Church and not necessarily only in an Indian context. Mother Teresa could serve the Holy See more if she was allowed to expand outside India. This explains why in 1965 the Vatican issued the *Decretum Laudis* (Decree of Praise), a decision which meant that her order became a Society of Pontifical Right. As a rule, to quote Stephen Neill, 'it takes a long time for anything to happen in the Christian world'.[129] Mother Teresa, however, had shown from the start of her missionary life that she would not follow rules that she did not approve of. The usually 'conservative' Vatican too, it appears, is prepared to break some rules when it is deemed convenient. This is obvious especially from the speed with which Pope Paul VI gave his endorsement to the Missionaries of Charity order in 1965. The move was apparently so unusual that it even took Mother Teresa by surprise, who by then was already a seasoned rule-breaker. In her own words:

> [t]his has been the biggest miracle of all because as a rule congregations are not raised to the pontifical order so fast. It takes most of them many years, thirty, forty years sometimes, before they become a pontifical. This shows the great love and appreciation the Holy Father has for our work and for the congregation.[130]

The Vatican's endorsement meant that Mother Teresa had permission to expand her brand of charity and inculturation in areas of the world where, as a rule, there have never been enough indigenous missionaries and priests. One such region was South America and one such country was Venezuela.

On 26 July 1965 Mother Teresa opened her first home in Concorte, the diocese of Barquisimeto, Venezuela.

It appears that, as was the case when she was given the indult of exclaustration in 1948, the Delhi nunciature played a crucial role in paving the way for Mother Teresa to create her first home overseas in 1965. The difference was that this time Mother Teresa was not the person who made the application; the idea came from the Papal Nuncio in New Delhi.

Mother Teresa obviously wasted no time in going to Venezuela, a move which marked a whole new chapter in her life and work and in the history of the Missionaries of Charity. From 1965, Mother Teresa became a convenient envoy for the Vatican. Her engagements on behalf of the Holy See meant that she was increasingly distracted from her original purpose of serving the poor of Calcutta. This does not mean that Mother Teresa stopped helping the needy in India or that she did not offer support to the poor in Venezuela and other countries where her congregation expanded. What is significant in the post-1965 stage of the history of Missionaries of Charity is that it soon turned into a religious multi-national with Mother Teresa apparently at the helm, but with the Vatican fully in charge of the congregation's strategy of expansion. The year 1965 signalled the beginning of the end of Mother Teresa as a 'saint of the gutters' and the emergence of an international religious figure who would prove increasingly helpful to the Vatican in revitalizing Catholicism in South America and other undeveloped parts of the world and, more importantly perhaps, in undermining Communism in Eastern Europe.

It would be naïve to think that Mother Teresa did not know that she was being used. She was too clever not to notice who was interested in her work and for what reasons. One of the most spiritual public figures of the twentieth century was obviously endowed with a very practical mind. Mother Teresa clearly had no qualms about being used as long as she believed that what she did for others, including the Vatican, meant that she was serving Jesus.

Mother Teresa served both the cause of Jesus, as she understood it, and the politics of the Vatican with exemplary devotion. This is the reason why the Holy See paid enormous attention to her from the early 1960s, and why Pope John Paul II sped up her canonization. Mother Teresa's carefully crafted public image came to epitomize both the spirituality of the Roman Catholic Church and its charitable disposition.

Those who were actively involved in promoting Mother Teresa's image from the mid-1960s onwards gradually developed an obsession for statistics. Most biographies of Mother Teresa abound in figures about the homes she apparently opened in India and across the globe and the people she, her sisters, brothers and co-workers taught, gave shelter to or cured. The statistics were important in building up the profile of Mother Teresa, but they should not be viewed uncritically. As Stephen Neill repeatedly remarks in *A History of Christian Missions*, as a rule, Christian figures are 'greatly exaggerated'.[131] It is possible that some of the statistics about the spread and achievements of Mother Teresa's multi-national charitable corporation the Missionaries of Charity have also been considerably inflated.

In the eyes of the Vatican and of her admirers, however, Mother Teresa's true worth does not depend only on the figures reported about the activity of her congregation. Mother Teresa's critics often draw the wrong conclusions about the 'worth' of Mother Teresa's work because they take the statistics literally. If quantified, Mother Teresa's work is insignificant. As she often put it, '[w]e ourselves feel that what we are doing is just a drop in the ocean'.[132] A United States Senator once asked Mother Teresa: 'Don't you get discouraged when you can see the magnitude of the poverty and realize how little you can really do?' To which the nun replied: 'God has not called me to be successful. God has asked me to be faithful.'[133] Mother Teresa obviously believed that the real value of her work was symbolic.

The Vatican has continuously emphasized the symbolism of Mother Teresa's work since her death in 1997. In his first Encyclical Letter of 25 December 2005, Pope Benedict XVI presented charity as being the most representative feature of Christianity, and Catholicism in particular. The Pontiff referred three times to Mother Teresa in this document, ranking her alongside Francis of Assisi and Ignatius of Loyola as one of the 'lasting models of social charity for all people of good will'.[134]

Agnes Gonxhe Bojaxhiu remained true to her vocation, although there will always be those who question the means she chose to achieve her end. Whatever her opponents say now or in the future, no one can accuse the Albanian nun of not having courage, determination and far-sightedness. She was a rare individual who served her divine celebrity with absolute integrity. The issue is where this little woman's divine inspiration and integrity came from. It is equally important to explore further our fascination with devout seers such as her, whose names are carved for ever in our collective memory.

Conclusion

Like any public figure of her calibre, Mother Teresa was an intricate human being. Famous individuals like her are interesting and yet difficult to fathom. They are multi-faceted partly because they are unique creatures and partly because they are products of various influences and traditions. This book is an attempt to show the extent to which the Albanian-born nun Agnes Gonxhe Bojaxhiu reflected, brought together and influenced people, cities, countries, regions, cultures, religions, ideologies and civilizations in the West, Asia and throughout the world.

The complexity of the Mother Teresa phenomenon meant that I was confronted from the start of the project with several daunting epistemological, ontological and methodological challenges. An ardent supporter of Mother Teresa, who was sceptical of and even hostile towards this book, warned me accordingly that I should not go ahead with it because I lacked the analytical tools to conduct a study of this nature which was beyond the scope of my academic discipline.

To research Mother Teresa I had to employ tools I had not used before as a researcher, and more importantly to trespass into fields of knowledge that I have no formal education in. The writer, literary critic and journalist in me had to quarrel and make peace with the sociologist, theologian, historian, anthropologist, psychologist, cultural studies expert and the political and media analyst whenever they tried to establish their supremacy over each other. My challenge was to let them be and keep them on the team. Without their collaboration this book would have never been finished.

Although I was aware from the start of the multi-disciplinary nature of the study, it was never my intention to write a book only for 'specialist' readers. While my main purpose was to study both Mother Teresa and our fascination with and objections to her in the context of the sociology of fame, media, religion and nationalism, it is hoped that readers who have no background or particular interest in these disciplines do not find themselves in *terra incognita*. Celebrity discourse is and should be multi-disciplinary, which is further proof of the complex nature and importance of celebrity culture as well as of its impact on so many people from all walks of life.

My purpose was to write a book that would allow scholars and general readers alike, no matter how much or how little they know about Mother Teresa, how highly or lowly they think of her, how much they approve or disapprove of her intentions, work and legacy, or how committed, hostile or indifferent they are to Catholicism, Christianity, any other religion or to the issue of faith in general, to get to know for themselves how complicated and simple a person the woman behind the nun was. I also intended to introduce readers not exclusively to the missionary called Mother Teresa or to the woman originally named Agnes Gonxhe Bojaxhiu. I wanted to unveil the extent to which the nun and the woman were both in harmony and at odds with each other.

The lives of celebrity-heroes are interesting not because of what we know about them but because of what they are keen to keep undisclosed. The example of Mother Teresa illustrates that public figures are among the most private of people. They guard fanatically any personal information they believe should never become public.

Public figures are public property and so are their private lives. Our interest in well-known people is to a large extent of a voyeuristic nature. We are not keen to know our heroes inside out, however, only to satiate our curiosity about their lives. We are attracted to them and their biographical details because of the huge impact such individuals have on us. We study them in the hope of finding in their personal lives not only the secret of their success but also some answers to our problems. In this context, it is justifiable and advisable to study their lives thoroughly. No matter how trivial, insignificant or irrelevant some of their biographical details may look or are, they are still worth studying meticulously. The hero is always in the details.

People like Mother Teresa are brilliant examples of how personal tragedies and family tensions turn some individuals into outstanding personalities who are keen to and eventually succeed in life against all odds. Thomas Carlyle believed that we should clean the 'dirt' from great men before placing them on their proper pedestals. The 'dirt' Carlyle refers to does not have to be seen always as 'filthy' and 'defamatory', however. Such 'dirt' is often the private, personal and intimate information about heroes that they as well as those who invest in their public image deem unacceptable for public consumption. In Mother Teresa's case, her 'dirt' is the 'raw material', the trials and tribulations she had to go through and as a direct result of which she became one of the best-known humanitarian, religious and media icons of the twentieth century. Without such 'dirt', celebrities like Mother Teresa would look odd on their pedestals, especially in our information-infatuated age.

Cleaning the 'dirt' from heroes was convenient and possible during Carlyle's nineteenth century, but not so in our times. Our media virtually feeds on such 'dirt' (read information). Celebrities are the fuel on which the news industry runs and their personal lives the soil that is dug around the clock for fresh supplies.

This is not to say that this study is an attempt to uncover some new controversial details about Mother Teresa's life, especially during the 1910–1965 period, *per se*. Nor can one equate the new information unearthed and recorded in this work with the 'dirt' the media constantly dishes out on celebrities. It is hoped that the hitherto unknown biographical details about Mother Teresa that are made public in this book for the first time, and the information about the strenuous attempts she made throughout her life in the limelight to keep them out of her biographies, will help us to understand her better and perhaps sympathize more with her and her work.

Mother Teresa spent her entire life in the service of Jesus. Pursuing her religious vocation in a predominantly Hindu country meant that she had to be careful that her devotion to Christ was not construed as threatening to Hindus and people of other faiths in India and other countries where she succeeded in establishing houses for her sisters and brothers. Mother Teresa served Jesus by serving the poorest of the poor. It could be argued that the poor in her case served as a convenient justification and cover for her religious activity. On the other hand, her concern for the poor and especially her insistence that she was allegedly not interested in politics were some of the main factors that endeared her to religious and secular people throughout the world. Mother Teresa belongs to that group of public figures that is acceptable to many people, especially by those in power, because she was and more importantly was perceived as someone who could be outspoken and controversial and yet meant and did no harm to anyone. The Roman Catholic nun is a good example of how a rebel, an outsider and a revolutionary ends ups joining the establishment while keeping all the time the mantle of the servant of the poor.

The media played a crucial part in publicizing Mother Teresa as a charity worker who was always eager to help the poor and yet never posed any threat to the rich. This all-inclusive quality set her apart from other humanitarian icons. The media would not have been able to promote Mother Teresa in this light so successfully for so long if she herself had not played an equally crucial, although largely unpublicized, role in the process.

Celebrities like Mother Teresa are brands and like every valuable brand they are not manufactured overnight. They need a large and dedicated team that invest in and is determined to develop, protect and polish them constantly. Mother Teresa the Roman Catholic nun, who apparently devoted her life to the poorest of the poor in Calcutta and to the needy and the abandoned throughout the world, was and remains a highly appealing brand. This explains why the Vatican gave her and her congregation preferential treatment especially from the mid-1960s, and is equally determined to keep her memory alive. Mother Teresa's work among the poor and her spirituality are and will remain for some time to come one of the Vatican's most marketable charity and spiritual brands in an age when, like any other religion, Roman Catholicism is striving hard to play a more active and influential role in the lives of the faithful and to make new converts.

Although influential personalities like Mother Teresa are 'products' of the media and other powers that 'discover', promote and keep them constantly in the public eye, it would be wrong to assume that such figures exist only because of the media and such other external forces. No media outlet or support could turn Agnes Gonxhe Bojaxhiu into the committed nun she became in 1928. For highly motivated individuals like Mother Teresa, the media and other sponsors and supporters are important but they do not determine who they are. Mother Teresa viewed the media and anyone that took an interest in her work as useful tools that enabled her to accomplish better and to a larger scale her lifetime and unconditional devotion to Jesus.

This book is intended to challenge some of the long-held erroneous views about Mother Teresa's 'unsophisticated' nature, 'lack' of wit and 'inability' to articulate herself. Those who still underestimate Mother Teresa's role in creating, sustaining and protecting her public image should perhaps remember that there are few other people who have survived in public life for so long and without getting hurt. Mother Teresa obviously has many things in common with those highly motivated and successful individuals who serve no one but their own egos. As for the beneficiaries of their work, they are like hitchhikers who end up paying for the ride, some without even knowing they have been charged.

In the case of Mother Teresa, she helped the poor and served the Vatican not so much to serve her ego, although self-interest was certainly not far away. Mother Teresa was one of the first religious personalities in a twentieth century dominated by celebrity culture to understand that support from and endorsement by influential religious, media, political, and government people and institutions was of paramount importance in accomplishing on a grand scale what she had initially hoped to achieve only in one of the slums of Calcutta.

Mother Teresa's expertise in handling the media grew as her image was beamed around the world. Did she realize that fame could derail her from her original purpose and that she was being used by those who control the publicity industry? I would be surprised if she did not realize rather early in her life that people often help each other for selfish purposes. She herself apparently had such a purpose when she became a nun. If this makes a saintly figure like her a sinner, then it would be difficult to find someone who is sin-free.

We humans remain as mysterious and unpredictable as ever even in a day and age when we have obviously made impressive progress in our search for self-knowledge. I only hope this book will be a modest contribution to this ongoing quest. And if in the course of my own quest as a spiritual-rationalist I have unintentionally insulted anyone, I hope my sin will be forgiven. If saints can sin, then one should not find it too difficult to forgive an ordinary mortal like me with no claim to sanctity alive or dead.

I also hope that Mother Teresa, who could forgive everyone, has forgiven me for writing about those aspects of her life she obviously wanted to remain unpublicized when she was alive and perhaps forever. I have the distinct feeling, however, that she would not have bothered about this book even if it came out when she was alive. This would have been hardly surprising; after all, this self-made woman always thought and acted otherly. For someone obsessively devoted to a religious superstar like Jesus, she could have even seen this 'controversial' book as 'something beautiful for God'.

While we dilly-dally over uncertainties, Mother Teresa had no doubt that she had found her rock in early childhood. This book is a tribute to her otherworldly imagination and self-integrity and a sincere though imperfect attempt to tap into their source.

Notes

Introduction

1 For more information on Germaine Greer's criticism of Mother Teresa see her article 'Greer Versus A Saint', *The Melbourne Age*, 6 October 1990.

1 Mother Teresa and celebrity culture

1 T. Carlyle, *On Heroes, Hero-Worship and the Heroic in History*, C. Niemeyer (ed.), Lincoln and London: University of Nebraska Press, 1966, p. 29.

2 D. J. Boorstin, *The Image: A Guide to Pseudo-Events in America*, New York: Vintage Books, 1992, p. 57.

3 Quoted in E. Egan, *Such a Vision of the Street: Mother Teresa – The Spirit and the Work*, Complete and Unabridged, New York and London: Doubleday, 1986, p. 407.

4 D. Doig, *Mother Teresa: Her People and Her Work*, London: Collins, 1978, p. 48.

5 See L. Gjergji, *Nëna e Dashurisë*, Prishtinë: Akademia e Shkencave dhe e Arteve e Kosovës, 2000, p. 64.

6 E. Johnson, *Mother Teresa*, London and Sydney: Franklin Watts, 2003, p. 38.

7 K. Spink, *Mother Teresa: An Authorized Biography*, London: Fount, 1998, p. 22.

8 M. Teresa, *In My Own Words*, José Louis González-Balado (ed.), London: Hodder & Stoughton, 1997, p. 87.

9 For more information on Mother Teresa's poor health throughout the 1910–1928 period see D. Porter, *Mother Teresa: The Early Years*, Oxford and New York: ISIS Large Print, 1986, pp. 12, 24; L. Gjergji, *Dashuria Tërheqëse: Nëna jonë Tereze*, 2nd edn, Ferizaj, Kosova: Drita; Zagreb, Croatia: Kršćanska Sadašnjost, 1990, pp. 11, 15; Spink, op. cit., p. 9; A. Sebba, *Mother Teresa: Beyond the Image*, London: Orion, 1997, p. 17; Gjergji, 2000, op. cit., pp. 47, 54, 70; and Johnson, op. cit., p. 6.

10 Porter, op. cit., p. 24.

11 Spink, op. cit., p. 22.

12 1 Corinthians 12: 1–31, in *The Holy Bible, containing the Old and New Testaments with the Apocryphal/Deuterocanonical Books*, New Revised Standard Version, New York and Oxford: Oxford University Press, 1989, pp. 182–3.

13 Gjergji, 1990, op. cit., pp. 21, 22; Gjergji, 2000, op. cit., pp. 47, 58, 63.

14 Gjergji, 1990, op. cit., pp. 20, 43; Gjergji, 2000, op. cit., p. 63.

15 Porter, op. cit., pp. 35–8, 40–1.

16 For more information on the importance Mother Teresa and her admirers attached to coincidences see Egan, op. cit., pp. 362–3; E. Egan and K. Egan (eds), *Living the Word: A New Adventure in Prayer Involving Scripture, Mother Teresa, and You*, London: Collins, 1990, pp. 64–5; and N. Chawla, *Mother Teresa*, London: Vega, 2002, p. 182.

17 During his visits to Mother House, the Headquarters of the Missionaries of Charity, in Calcutta in the summer of 2005, the author was given by a sister two kinds of 'relics': a couple of laminated pictures of Mother Teresa containing a tiny piece of cloth taken from her sari and some medallions featuring her image. Prior to handing the medallions to the author, the sister put them on Mother Teresa's grave for 'blessing'.

18 Since September 2003 the author has received a large number of e-mails, letters and phone calls from numerous Catholic and non-Catholic admirers of Mother Teresa professing the huge impact she had apparently made on them when they first met her. They explain Mother Teresa's charismatic appeal to them with her profound faith which enabled her to help people in a way that others could not.

19 Author's interviews with several individuals who met Mother Teresa in the 1990s. The interviewees, who do not wish to be identified, were contacted from July 2003 to August 2005.

20 M. Muggeridge, *Something Beautiful for God: Mother Teresa of Calcutta*, London: Collins, 1971, p. 41.

21 Quoted in C. Hitchens, *The Missionary Position: Mother Teresa in Theory and Practice*, London and New York: Verso, 1995, pp. 26–7.

22 Muggeridge, op. cit., p. 45.

23 Ibid., pp. 41, 44.

24 Boorstin, op. cit., p. 8.

25 Hitchens, op. cit., p. 27.

26 Egan, 1986, op. cit., p. 359.

27 Spink, op. cit., p. 159.

28 Chawla, op. cit., p. 161. That this incident actually happened was confirmed to the author of this book by Father Gaston Roberge SJ, a friend of Mother Teresa, who had asked her specifically about it. Mother Teresa also told Father Roberge that the police officer in question eventually became her friend. Gaston Roberge (2005) 'The Incident' and 'Dominique Lapierre'. E-mails (22 May 2005).

29 Author's conversation with the psychiatrist Dr Ashish Kumar Basu in Calcutta on 29 June 2005. Dr Basu did voluntary work for Mother Teresa's religious order in Calcutta in the 1960s and 1970s.

30 P. K. Varma, '*The Argumentative Indian*, by Amartya Sen, *The Independent*, 12 August 2005.

31 K. Spink, *For the Brotherhood of Man under the Fatherhood of God: Mother Teresa of Calcutta, her Missionaries of Charity and her Co-Workers*, Surrey, UK: Colour Library International, 1981, p. 227.

32 C. Rojek, *Celebrity*, London: Reaktion Books, 2001, p. 33.

33 See Hitchens, op. cit., pp. 43–8. Shortly after Mother Teresa's death, Susan Shields published parts of her manuscript in her article 'Mother Teresa's House of Illusions', which appeared in *Free Inquiry*, 1998, Vol. 18, No. 1. Shields's account is probably one of the most damaging attacks on Mother Teresa to have come from an insider of the order of the Missionaries of Charity.

34 J. Eberts, R. Joffé and M. Medoff, *City of Joy: The Illustrated Story of the Film*, New York: Newmarket Press, 1992, p. 20.

35 For more information on the alleged role played by Mother Teresa in 'tarnishing' the image of Calcutta in the West see S. K. Datta-Ray, 'Halo Goodbye', *Telegraph*, 1 February 1997, and 'Saviour of the Needy Driven by Self-interest', *Australian*, 11 September 1997; K. Dutta, 'Saint of the Gutters with Friends in High Places', *Times Higher Education Supplement*, 16 May 2003; D. Shah, 'Mother Teresa's Hidden Mission in India: Conversion to Christianity', 2003. Online. Available HTTP: <http://www.indiastar.com/DhiruShah.htm> (accessed 16 August 2004); and R. Srinivasan, 'The Saint Business', 17 October 2003. Online. Available HTTP: <http://in.rediff.com/news/2003/oct/17rajeev.htm> (accessed 17 April 2005).

36 See G. Alpion, 'Oh! Not Calcutta', *Guardian*, 6 September 2003.

37 The author has written at length on the issue of biased representation of the 'other' in English literature and in the British media in 'Images of Albania and Albanians in English Literature: from Edith Durham to J. K. Rowling', *BESA Journal*, Vol. 6, No. 2, Spring 2002, pp. 30–4; and 'Western Media and the European "Other": Images of Albania in the British Press in the New Millennium', *Albanian Journal of Politics*, Vol. I, Issue 1, September 2005, pp. 7–27. For more information on how the 'other' from different parts of the world is stereotyped and pigeonholed in the West see L. Wolff, *Inventing Eastern Europe: The Map of Civilization on the Mind of the Enlightenment*, Stanford, California: Stanford University Press, 1994; M. Todorova, *Imagining the Balkans*, New York and Oxford: Oxford University Press, 1997; V. Goldsworthy, *Inventing Ruritania: The Imperialism of the Imagination*, New Haven and London: Yale University Press, 1998; and R. S. Hillman (ed.), *Understanding Contemporary Latin America*, Boulder: Lynne Rienner Publishers, 2001.

38 Shah, op. cit.

39 A. Chatterjee (2005) 'Navin Chawla'. E-mail (26 January 2005).

40 S. K. Datta-Ray, 1 February 1997, op. cit.

41 Ibid.

42 This is based on information supplied by a film-maker in India.

43 See A. Lalaj, 'Shqipëria, asnjëherë faktor i rëndësishëm', *Korrieri*, 29 June 2004.

44 A. Chatterjee, *Mother Teresa: The Final Verdict*, Kolkata, India: Meteor Books, 2003, p. 61.

45 J. Belton, *American Cinema/American Culture*, 2nd edn, Boston: McGraw-Hill, 2005, p. 98.

46 C. Gledhill, 'Introduction', in C. Gledhill (ed.), *Stardom: Industry of Desire*, London and New York: Routledge, 2003, (pp. xiii–xx), p. xiv.

47 R. deCardova, 'The Emergence of the Star System in America', in C. Gledhill (ed.), *Stardom: Industry of Desire*, London and New York: Routledge, 2003, pp. 17–29. See especially pp. 26–8.

48 Rojek, op. cit., p. 11.

49 See C. Gray, *Mother Teresa: The Nun whose 'Mission of Love' has Helped Millions of the World's Poorest People*, Herts, UK: Exley, 1990, p. 51.

50 Ibid., p. 49.

51 Ibid., p. 51.

52 Ibid.

2 The Balkans appropriation of Mother Teresa

1 See A. Ramaj, 'Nëna Terezë – Bojaxhinjtë dhe prejardhja e tyre', 15 November 2003. Online. Available HTTP: <http://www.stublla.com/Shqip/fjalalir/Zef

Ahmeti/Shkrimet001/November/Nenaterezeramaj41.htm> (accessed 17 November 2003).

2　For claims that Mother Teresa spoke little or no Albanian at all see I. Fisher, 'Vying for a Piece of Mother Teresa's Past', *International Herald Tribune*, 7 August 2003; J. Mironski, 'The Mother is Still Agnes in Macedonia', 3 September 1998. Online. Available HTTP: <http://www.indianexpress.com/ie/daily/19980904/24750084.html> (accessed 27 February 2004); and J. Mironski, 'Macedonians, Albanians Squabble over Teresa's Legacy', 15 October 2003. Online. Available HTTP: <http://quickstart.clari.net/qs_se/webnews/wed/ad/Qindia_vatican-pope.Rm5s_DOF.html> (accessed 27 February 2004).

3　E. Egan, *Such a Vision of the Street: Mother Teresa – The Spirit and the Work*, Complete and Unabridged, New York and London: Doubleday, 1986, pp. 174–5.

4　The phrase *Sou de Schipteru* seems to come from a neo-Latin language, although the experts contacted by the author are not able to determine which one. While *Sue de* clearly means 'I am from/of', *Schipteru* appears to be a corruption of the Albanian words *Shqiptar* (Albanian) or *Shqipëri* (Albania). The author has also been advised that the correct spelling of *Sou* is *Sue*.

5　Egan, op. cit., 408.

6　K. Spink, *Mother Teresa: An Authorised Biography*, London: Fount, 1998, p. 96.

7　Ibid.

8　Dr Lush Gjergji is an Albanian Catholic priest, academic and journalist from Kosova. He was probably one of Mother Teresa's closest friends in the Balkans and certainly her main contact among the Albanians. Father Gjergji told the author in Binçë, Kosova, on 30 October 2003 that he had met Mother Teresa more than 50 times, something which he also reiterated in his letter to the author of 10 November 2003.

9　Interview with Father Lush Gjergji, Binçë, Kosova, 30 October 2003; Father Gjergji's letter to the author of 10 November 2003.

10　For samples of letters Mother Teresa wrote in Albanian see L. Gjergji, *Dashuria Tërheqëse: Nëna jonë Tereze*, 2nd edn, Ferizaj, Kosova: Drita; Zagreb, Croatia: Kršćanska Sadašnjost, 1990, pp. 108, 109, 110–11, 121, 146–7, 207, 245–6, 299–300; and L. Gjergji, *Nëna e Dashurisë*, Prishtinë: Akademia e Shkencave dhe e Arteve e Kosovës, 2000, p. 92.

11　S. Schwartz, 'Mother Teresa's Family Tree', *The Weekly Standard*, 27 October 2003, Vol. 9, Issue 7.

12　See Gjergji, 2000, op. cit., p. 43.

13　Some of the Catholic saints and martyrs called Agnes are: St Agnes, a twelve- or thirteen-year-old Roman girl martyred in the second half of the third century; St Agnes of Poitiers, who headed the Holy Cross convent in Poitiers, France, until she died in 586; St Agnes of Assisi (1197–1253), canonized in 1753; St Agnes of Bohemia (1205–1282), canonized in 1989; St Agnes De, a Vietnamese Christian martyr, canonized in 1988; and Bl. Agnes Tsao-Kouy, a Chinese martyr, beatified in 1900.

14　See Gjergji, 1990, op. cit., p. 10.

15　Ramaj, op. cit.

16　See A. Plasari, 'Bojaxhitë e Nënë Terezës', *Shekulli*, 29 September 2003.

17　Ramaj, op. cit.

18　See Fisher, op. cit.; Mironski, 1998, op. cit.; and Plasari, op. cit.

19 See Ramaj, op. cit.; Xh. Ukshini, 'Debati, origjina e Nënë Terezës është shqiptare', *Shekulli*, 11 October 2003; and P. Xhufi, 'Kujt t'ia japim Nënë Terezën', *Shekulli*, 14 October 2003.

20 For more information about the communication between the Albanian intellectuals and politicians and the Mayor of Rome Walter Veltroni in the summer of 2003 see E. Spaho, 'Nënë Tereza "maqedonase" refuzohet nga Roma', *Shekulli*, 18 July 2003.

21 Clement XI was born on 23 July 1649, elected pope on 23 November 1700 and died on 19 March 1721. The other pontiffs believed to be of Albanian origin are: Saint Pius I (the exact dates of his birth, death and pontificate are not known, but it is believed he was pope from 140 to 154); Saint Eleutherius (date of birth is unknown, became pope about 174 and died in 189); Saint Caius (not much is known about him apart from the dates of his pontificate: 17 December 283 to 22 April 296); John IV (exact date of birth unknown, died on 12 October 642, by which time he had been pope for almost three years); and Clement XII, whose original name was Lorenzo Corsini (born on 7 April 1652, died on 6 February 1740, his pontificate lasting for two decades).

22 The three French authors maintain that Napoleon came from the Albanian community in Corsica. Albania's defeat by the Turks in the latter part of the fifteenth century caused a huge exodus of the Albanian population towards the West. Napoleon's ancestors are thought to have moved from Albania to Mani in Southern Greece before emigrating to Corsica. The remarks of the above-mentioned French authors about Napoleon's Albanian origin have not escaped the attention of the Albanians, who are understandably interested in exploring further the genealogy of such a prominent European figure. For more information on Napoleon Bonaparte's Albanian origin see M. Kokalari, 'A ishte Napoleoni i rrënjëve arbëreshe', *Ekskluzive*, II, No. 22, February 2002, pp. 73–4.

23 The following is a list of famous people who were born in Albania or were of Albanian descent: Master Sinan, the architect who built the Selimiye Mosque between 1568 and 1575; Mehmet Isa, a seventeenth-century architect, who acted as the chief builder of the Taj Mahal; Karl von Ghega (1802–1860), the architect of the world's first mountainous railway in Semmering, Austria; Francesco Crispi (1818–1901), the charismatic Italian politician who served twice as prime minister; and Aleksandër Moisiu (1879–1935), also known as Alexander Moissi, a brilliant stage and film actor praised highly by the director Max Reinhardt.

24 For more information on the positive impact of Mohammad Ali's reforms on Egypt see G. Alpion, 'Foreigner Complex', (pp. 1–21) pp. 15–16; 'An Interview with Mohammad Ali's Ghost', (pp. 22–32) pp. 27–32; 'A Parade of Porters', (pp. 33–41) p. 33; 'Egyptian Coffee Shops', (pp. 42–55) p. 44; 'The Bride of *Hapi*', (pp. 56–65) pp. 62–4, in G. Alpion, *Foreigner Complex: Essays and Fiction About Egypt*, Birmingham, UK: The University of Birmingham CPS, 2002.

25 For more information on Alexander's Illyrian origin and connections with Illyria, see W. W. Tarn, *Alexander the Great: Narrative*, Vol. I, Cambridge: Cambridge University Press, 1979, pp. 1, 3, 6.

26 For more information on Skanderbeg's importance to Western Europe and Catholicism see S. K. Varvarica, 'Edhe një ide në figurë rreth Skënderbeut', *Korrieri*, 20 March 2005.

27 More than half a dozen places in Greece lay claim to be the birthplace of Homer. The two contenders with the strongest claims, however, are the city

of Smyrna (Izmir in Turkey) and the Island of Chios. As for Skanderbeg's *pátria*, only recently have Albanian historians agreed that his family originally came from Dibra, a region in the North-East of Albania proper. Other regions in Albania claiming to be the places where Skanderbeg's family originated from are Mat, Kukës, Mirditë and Krujë.

28 Y. Lili, 'Parlamentarët e Shkupit: Skënderbeu është maqedonas', *Shekulli*, 22 September 2004.

29 For more information on the row between the Macedonian Slav and Albanian politicians regarding Eleonora Petrova-Mitevska's remarks about Skanderbeg being Macedonian (read 'Macedonian Slav') see V. Memedaliu, 'Deputetja Petrova pohon se Skënderbeu ka qenë maqedonas', 20 September 2004. Online. Available HTTP: <http://www.agimi.com/modules.php?name=News&file=print&sid=7> (accessed 16 January 2005); and Y. Lili, 'Xhelili: Maqedonasit janë mësuar të përvetësojnë figurat shqiptare', *Shekulli*, 22 September 2004.

30 'Maqedoni, zyrtarisht: Shqiptarët përbëjnë mbi 25% të popullsisë', *Korrieri*, 2 December 2003. The Albanians living in Macedonia claim the figure is higher, perhaps above 30 per cent.

31 Gjergji, 1990, op. cit., pp. 10, 14.

32 See Gjergji, 2000, op. cit., p. 46.

33 For more information on the Albanian origin of Mother Teresa's parents see Gjergji, 1990, op. cit., pp. 10, 14; and Gjergji, 2000, op. cit., p. 46.

34 Egan, op. cit., p. 413.

35 See Mironski, 1998, op. cit; I. Fisher, 'Saintly Spirit Remembered, in a Truly Balkan Way', *New York Times*, 6 August 2003; Fisher, 7 August 2003, op. cit; N. Wood, 'Nations Row over Mother Teresa', 10 August 2003. Online. Available HTTP: <http://news.bbc.co.uk/1/hi/world/europe/3139003. stm> (accessed 27 February 2004); A. Ilievska, 'Notes from Skopje: Post-Mortem Politics', 13 August 2003. Online. Available HTTP: <http://www. tol.cz/look/TOLnew/tolprint.tpl?IdLanguage=1&IdPublication=4&NrIssue= 49&NrSection=17&NrArticle=10408&ST1=body&ST_T1=letter&ST_AS1= 1&ST_max=1> (accessed 18 March 2006); AFP, 'Mother Teresa Statue Stirs Spirits in Macedonia, Albania', 27 August 2003. Online. Available HTTP: <http://www.balkanpeace.org/hed/archive/aug03/hed5966.shtml> (accessed 29 August 2005); Mironski, 15 October 2003, op. cit; A. Freeman, 'Mother Teresa's Origins Spark Squabble', *Globe and Mail*, 17 October 2003.

36 D. Porter, *Mother Teresa: The Early Years*, Oxford and New York: ISIS Large Print, 1986, p. 93.

37 Ibid.

38 Romans 15: 19, in *The Holy Bible, containing the Old and New Testaments with Apocryphal/Deuterocanonical Books*, New Revised Standard Version, New York and Oxford: Oxford University Press, 1989, p. 171.

39 G. Alpion, 'Foreigner Complex', in G. Alpion, *Foreigner Complex: Essays and Fiction About Egypt*, Birmingham, UK: The University of Birmingham CPS, 2002 (pp. 1–21) p. 2.

40 D. Kirka, 'Nations Fight over Mother Teresa's Ancestry', 14 October 2003. Online. Available HTTP: <http://www.therunningzone.com/CNEWS/Weird News/2003/10/14/225887-ap.html> (accessed 24 February 2004).

41 V. Čubrilović, 'The Expulsion of the Albanians: Memorandum Presented in Belgrade on 7 March 1937', in R. Elsie (ed.), *Kosovo: In the Heart of the Powder Keg*, Boulder, CO: East European Monographs, 1997 (pp. 400–24) p. 402.

42 Ibid., p. 406.

43 Ibid., p. 409.

44 Ibid., p. 416.

45 Ibid., p. 413.

46 Ibid., p. 405.

47 Ibid.

48 See I. Andrić, 'Draft on Albania', in R. Elsie op. cit., pp. 435–48.

49 V. Čubrilović, 'The Minority Problem in the New Yugoslavia: Memorandum of 3 November 1944', in R. Elsie op. cit. (pp. 449–64), p. 449.

50 Ibid., p. 454.

51 Ibid., p. 457.

52 See ibid., p. 450.

53 See ibid., p. 456.

54 Ibid.

55 The 'stigma' attached to Serbia as 'the jailer of the other Yugoslav nations' was deeply resented by the Serbs and especially Serbian academics. See 'Serbian Academy of Arts and Sciences Memorandum', September 1986. Online. Available HTTP: <http://www.ess.uwe.ac.uk/Kosovo/Kosovo-Background17.htm> (accessed 20 February 2005).

56 I. Banac, *The National Question in Yugoslavia: Origins, History, Politics*, Ithaca, New York: Cornell University Press, 1994, p. 293.

57 Kaplan Resuli-Burovich 'The Albanian Racism Towards Its Neighbours Is Based on Historical Falsifications', Interview with Vitomir Dolinski, *Vest*, 25 February 2003, Trans. Z. Apostolovski. Online. Available HTTP: <http://www.unitedmacedonians.org/macedonia/kaplan_english.html> (accessed 20 February 2005).

58 Čubrilović, 1937, op. cit., p. 419.

59 Ibid., p. 418.

60 Ibid.

61 See Resuli-Burovich, op. cit.

62 Čubrilović, 1937, op. cit., p. 410.

63 For more information on the Battle of Kosova see chapter four 'The Battle and the Myth', in N. Malcolm's *Kosovo: A Short History*, London: Papermac, 1998, pp. 58–80.

64 For more information about atrocities alleged to have been committed by the Serbian army against Albanian Catholics in Kosova, Macedonia and Albania proper at the turn of the twentieth century see L. Freundlich, *Albania's Golgotha*, Trans. S. S. Juka, New York: Juka Publishing Co. Inc., 1998. Online. Available HTTP: <http://www.alb-net.com/juka1.htm> (accessed 30 July 2003). The Serbian army also allegedly massacred some Albanian Catholics on the eve of the Kosova War in 1999 (see S. Schwartz, 'Behind the Balkan Curtain: Religious Communities Carry on Gjon's Mission', *San Francisco Faith*, May 2000).

65 Malcolm, op. cit., p. xxviii. For more information on the Serbs' and other Balkan Slavs' efforts to mobilize and manipulate religion for ideological purposes and as a cover for what the US diplomat George Kennan calls their 'aggressive nationalism', see *The Other Balkan Wars. A 1913 Carnegie Endowment Inquiry in Retrospect with a New Introduction and Reflections on the Present Conflict by George F. Kennan*, Washington, D.C.: Carnegie Endowment for International Peace, 1993; and Edith Durham, *Twenty Years of Balkan Tangle*, London: George Allen & Unwin, 1920.

66 See S. Shameti, 'Një Mjekër për Maqedoninë', *Revista Klan*, 7 August 2005.
67 For more information on the discrimination against and the police abuse of the Albanians in Macedonia see E. Mete, 'What Does the Future Hold for the Albanians in FYROM?', 27 February 2002. Online. Available HTTP: <http://www.aacl.com/AlbFutMacE.htm> (accessed 22 February 2005).
68 M. Price, 'Milosevic Says Trial Will Fuel Terrorism', *Birmingham Post*, 31 October 2001.
69 For more information on arguments and counter-arguments regarding police abuse of the Albanians in Macedonia and the 'involvement' of Albania, the Kosova Liberation Army (KLA) and the National Liberation Army (NLA) with international Islamic terrorists see D. Williams, 'Evidence of a Macedonian Execution: Scene in Ethnic Albanian House in Skopje Belies Police Account of Killing', *Washington Post*, 8 August 2001; C. Deliso, 'Barbarism and the Erasure of Culture', 24 August 2001. Online. Available HTTP: <http://www.antiwar.com/orig/deliso2.html> (accessed 22 February 2005); T. Domi and J. Kovac, 'Balkan Anxieties over American Tragedy', *BCR*, No. 280, 14 September 2001; M. Glenny, 'Macedonian Attitudes "Polarising"', 23 September 2001. Online. Available HTTP: <http://news.bbc.co.uk/1/hi/programmes/from_our_own_correspondent/1559270.stm> (accessed 22 February 2005); U. Pascali, 'U.S. Protects Al-Qaeda Terrorists in Kosovo', *Executive Intelligence Review*, Vol. 28, No. 42, 2 November 2001; C. Deliso, 'Macedonia Capitulates', 20 November 2001. Online. Available HTTP: <http://www.unitedmacedonians.org/newspaper/nd01/antiwar.htm> (accessed 20 February 2005); U. Pascali, 'Macedonia's "Truth" Strategy Connects U.S. Ambassador to KLA Terrorists', Vol. 28, No. 45, 23 November 2001; S. Taylor, 'Bin Laden's Balkan Connection', December 2001. Online. Available HTTP: <http://www.espritdecorps.ca/new_page_209.htm> (accessed 22 February 2005); M. Seraphinoff, 'A Macedonian Golgotha: In the Dark of 9–11 and 12–21–01'. Online. Available HTTP: <http://www.united macedonians.org/newspaper/nd01/golgothalite.doc> (accessed 20 February 2005); H. Ivanovski, 'NLA Directly Linked With Bin Laden's Terrorists', Trans. A. Ilievska. Online. Available HTTP: <http://www.realitymacedonia.org.mk/web/news_page.asp?nid=417> (accessed 20 February 2005); and 'The NLA: Human Rights Fighters or Terrorists?' Online. Available HTTP: <http://www.macedonia.org/crisis/story2.html#top> (accessed 22 February 2005).
70 A. Sebba, *Mother Teresa: Beyond the Image*, London: Orion, 1997, pp. 234–5.
71 E. Johnson, *Mother Teresa*, London and Sydney: Franklin Watts, 2003, p. 98.
72 The author received this information in writing from a source who was closely involved in the preparation of Mother Teresa's first visit to Albania in 1989 and who does not wish to be identified.
73 R. Orizio, *Talk of the Devil: Encounters with Seven Dictators*, Trans. A. Bardoni, London: Vintage, 2004, p. 103.
74 Ibid., p. 102.
75 Ibid., p. 103.
76 Sebba, op. cit., p. 234.
77 Ibid., p. 235.
78 Gjergji, 1990, op. cit., p. 209.
79 Author's interview with Father Lush Gjergji, op. cit.
80 See Sebba, op. cit., p. 257.
81 A. Chatterjee, *Mother Teresa: The Final Verdict*, Kolkata, India: Meteor Books, 2003, p. 379.

82 Čubrilović, 1937, op. cit., p. 410.
83 M. Velo, 'Mauzoleu i Nënës Mbretëreshë', *Shekulli*, 2 August 2005.
84 'Festa e Nënë Terezës, administrata në punë', *Korrieri*, 20 October 2004.
85 'Moisiu, Nano, Berisha e Meidani, bashkë në Vatikan', *Korrieri*, 16 October 2003.
86 See 'Në Tiranë heshtje në ditën e Lumturimit', *Gazeta Shqiptare*, 20 October 2004; A. Meta, '19 tetori: "Dita e Lutjes së Përbashkët"', *Korrieri*, 21 October 2004.
87 E. Metaj, '6 Presidentë "zbulojnë" Nënë Terezën', *Korrieri*, 8 December 2004; A. Mile, 'Presidentët e Ballkanit përurojnë shtatoren e Nënë Terezës, *Shekulli*, 10 December 2004.
88 H. Nallbani, 'Shtatorja e Nënë Terezës, larg glorifikimit folklorik', *Shekulli*, 18 January 2005.
89 'Qilimi i lutjeve në Katedralen e Shën Palit', *Korrieri*, 12 October 2003; V. Zhiti, 'Institucioni i shenjtë i Nënë Terezës', *Korrieri*, 28 August 2005.
90 Interview with Father Lush Gjergji, op. cit.; Father Gjergji's letter to the author of 10 November 2003.
91 Father Lush Gjergji's letter to the author of 10 November 2003. Mother Teresa's prayers 'Për Shqipërinë Time'/'For my Albania', and 'Lutja e fundit – Dua të kthehem në Shqipëri'/'Last Prayer – I want to come back to Albania' are included in the anthology of poems *Nënë Tereza – Mërmërime Shenjtoreje*, Tirana: OMSCA-1, 2003, on pp. 129 and 131 respectively, and in *Mësomë të Dua/Teach me to Love*, Trans. A. Spahiu et al., Prishtina: Rozafa, 2003, on pp. 198–9 and 200–1.
92 P. Kola, *The Search for Greater Albania*, London: Hurst & Company, 2003, p. 383.
93 E. Koliqi, 'Një udhëtim i paharruar me Dr Dom Lush Gjergjin', 27 May 2003. Online. Available HTTP: <http://www.garni-eberherr.de/agimi/kulture/reportazh/Dom_Lush_Gjergji.htm> (accessed 6 August 2003).
94 'Letërkëmbim Nënë Tereza – Ramiz Alia', *Korrieri*, 15 October 2003.
95 For similar and other inaccurate recordings and interpretations in Albanian newspapers and on Albanian websites of Mother Teresa's letter to Ramiz Alia of 16 August 1989 see *Zëri i Ditës*, 17 October 2003; Ramaj, op. cit; and Sh. Sinani, '"Pashaporta" shqiptare e Nënë Terezës'. Online. Available HTTP: <http://www.albmuzika.com/nene_tereza.htm> (accessed 31 July 2005).
96 Egan, op. cit., p. 136.
97 K. Spink, *For the Brotherhood of Man under the Fatherhood of God: Mother Teresa of Calcutta, her Missionaries of Charity and her Co-Workers*, Surrey, UK: Colour Library International, 1981, pp. 202–7.
98 Sebba, op. cit., p. 257.
99 Fisher, 7 August 2003, op. cit.
100 Johnson, op. cit., p. 45. According to Dr Aroup Chatterjee's e-mail to the author of 4 September 2005, 'Ami Bharater' translates as 'I am of India' rather than 'I am Indian'.
101 'President Rugova: "Mother Teresa Is a Guardian Angel for Kosova and the Albanian Nation"', 8 September 1997. Online. Available HTTP: <http://www.hri.org/news/balkans/kosova/97-09-06.ksv.html> (accessed 6 August 2003).
102 For more information on Christopher Hitchens's vitriolic attacks on Mother Teresa see his following publications: 'The Ghoul of Calcutta', *Nation*, 13 April 1992; *The Missionary Position: Mother Teresa in Theory and Practice*, London and New York: Verso, 1995; Interview given to S. Capen,

Worldguide, 24 December 1995; 'Christopher Hitchens on Mother Teresa', Interview given to M. Cherry, *Free Inquiry*, Vol. 16, No. 4, Fall 1996; '"Mother Teresa", Letter to the Editors of the NYR in Response to "In Defense of Mother Teresa"', *New York Review of Books*, Vol. 43, No. 20, 19 December 1996; 'The Missionary Position: Mother Teresa's Crimes Against Humanity', Interview given to D. Postel, *LiP Magazine*, 15 September 1998; 'Why Mother Teresa Should Not Be a Saint', *Mirror*, 2 January 2003; 'Mommie Dearest: The pope beatifies Mother Teresa, a fanatic, a fundamentalist, and a fraud', *Slate*, 20 October 2003; and 'Less than Miraculous', *Free Inquiry*, Vol. 24, No. 2, February–March 2004.

103 See Hitchens's interview, *LiP Magazine*, 15 September 1998, op. cit.
104 See Hitchens's interview, *Free Inquiry*, Fall 1996, op. cit.
105 I. Katz, 'When Christopher Met Peter', *Guardian*, G2, 31 May 2005.
106 Hitchens, *Missionary Position*, p. 98.
107 Ibid., p. 85.
108 Ibid., p. 82.
109 Egan, op. cit., p. 10.
110 Hitchens, *Missionary Position*, p. 79.
111 Hitchens, 2 January 2003, *Mirror*, op. cit.
112 Hitchens, *Missionary Position*, p. 11.
113 Hitchens, 13 April 1992, *Nation*, op. cit.
114 For more information regarding allegations of the involvement of the Serbian Secret Police in the intoxication of Kosova Albanian children in March and April 1990, and on the former Yugoslav Army's production of chemical weapons see Z. Toth, 'Serbian Plants of Death', *Večernji List*, 28 November 1995; 'The Albanian Children, Victims of Serbian Death Factories', 29 November 1995, Online. Available HTTP: <http://www.hri.org/news/balkans/koscom/1995/95-12-04.koscom.html> (accessed 20 December 2003); H. Hyseni, *E Vërteta për Helmimet në Kosovë: 1987–1990*, Prishtinë: Redaksia e Botimeve e Partisë Shqiptare Demokristiane e Kosovës, 1996; and Malcolm, op. cit., p. 345. The author is grateful to the following Kosova Albanians – Sami Islami, Xhemail Peci and Xhevat Ukshini – who on 24 February 2004, 26 February 2004 and 20 November 2004 respectively shared with him their own memories of the incident. Sami Islami (2004) 'Kriza shëndetësore për fëmijët e Kosovës në 1990'. E-mail (26 February 2004).
115 Initially, the author received the information in writing from a source that does not wish to be identified. That Mother Teresa and her order declined the request of the Albanian Americans to distribute the medical supplies in Kosova in spring 1990 was confirmed to the author by Father Lush Gjergji during the interview in Binçë, Kosova, on 30 October 2003, and in Father Gjergji's letter to him of 10 November 2003.
116 Author's interview with Father Lush Gjergji, op. cit.; Father Gjergji's letter to the author of 10 November 2003.
117 See G. Gorrée and J. Barbier, *For the Love of God, Mother Teresa of Calcutta*, Trans. P. Speakman, Dublin: Veritas, 1974, pp. 71–2, 75; Egan, op. cit., p. 411.
118 See Gorrée and Barbier, op. cit., pp. 73, 75.
119 Egan, op. cit., p. 411.
120 Ibid., p. 457.
121 N. Chawla, *Mother Teresa*, London: Vega, 2002, p. 225.
122 Ibid., pp. 225–6.
123 Ibid., p. 226.
124 Spink, 1998, op. cit., p. 238.

125 Gjergji, 1990, op. cit., p. 289.
126 Ibid., p. 210.

3 The forgotten years

1 Some of the works about Mother Teresa that mention India in the title are: B. S. Murthy's *Mother Teresa and India* (1983), D. Lapierre's *The City of Joy: An Epic of Love, Heroism, and Hope in the India of Mother Teresa* (1985), and S. K. Majumdar's *Mahatma Gandhi, Mother Teresa, Swami Vivekananda and Some Important Events of India from 1941 to March 1995* (1996). For complete bibliographical details of these and other works on Mother Teresa mentioned in this chapter see the select bibliography at the end of the book.

2 The following is a modest list of books and films dedicated to the nun whose titles include both her name and that of Calcutta: *For the Love of God: Mother Teresa of Calcutta* (1974), *Teresa of Calcutta: A Pictorial Biography* (1980), *The Miracle of Love: Mother Teresa of Calcutta* (1981), *For the Brotherhood of Man under the Fatherhood of God: Mother Teresa of Calcutta, her Missionaries of Charity and her Co-Workers* (1981), *Teresa of Calcutta: Serving The Poorest of the Poor* (1984), *Mother Teresa of Calcutta: Her Call, Her Example, Her Life Story* (1994), *The Young Life of Mother Teresa of Calcutta* (1996), *Works of Love are Works of Peace: Mother Teresa of Calcutta and the Missionaries of Charity* (1996), *Blessed Teresa of Calcutta: Missionary of Charity* (2003) and *I Thirst: Thérèse of Lisieux and Mother Teresa of Calcutta* (2005).

3 Some of the works referring to the author-nun as 'Mother Teresa of Calcutta' are: *A Gift for God: Prayers and Meditations* (1979), *Life in the Spirit: Reflections, Meditations, Prayers* (1983), *Jesus, the Word to Be Spoken: Prayers and Meditations for Every Day of the Year* (1987), *My Life for the Poor* (1987), *He's Put The Whole World In Her Hands* (1993) and *A Fruitful Branch on the Vine, Jesus* (2000).

4 J. Joyce, *A Portrait of the Artist as a Young Man*, London: Penguin, 1996, p. 231.

5 Mother Teresa gave her unreserved support to President Ronald Reagan's campaign to put an end to abortion in the USA in the early 1980s. She also urged the relatives of thousands of people who lost their lives or were injured in Bhopal in 1984 to forgive the chemical-producing multinational Union Carbide, which is widely held responsible for the tragedy. In January 1992 Mother Teresa wrote to Judge Lance Ito at the Superior Court in Los Angeles imploring him to be lenient towards Charles Keating.

6 K. Spink, *Mother Teresa: An Authorized Biography*, London: Fount, 1998, p. xi.

7 Ibid., pp. vi–vii.

8 K. Matto, '"Mother" Teresa'. Online. Available HTTP: <http://www.scionofzion.com/teresa.htm> (accessed 29 July 2003).

9 D. Porter, *Mother Teresa: The Early Years*, Oxford and New York: ISIS Large Print, 1986, p. 3.

10 W. Jackman, *Mother Teresa*, East Sussex, UK: Wayland, 1993, p. 4.

11 C. Gray, *Mother Teresa: The Nun whose 'Mission of Love' Has Helped Millions of the World's Poorest People*, Herts, UK: Exley, 1990, p. 5.

12 R. Tames, *Mother Teresa*, London: Franklin Watts, 1989, p. 4.

13 Ibid., p. 6.

14 E. Johnson, *Mother Teresa*, London and Sydney: Franklin Watts, 2003, p. 9.

15 See M. Muggeridge, *Something Beautiful for God: Mother Teresa of Calcutta*, London: Collins, 1971, p. 154; G. Gorrée and J. Barbier, *For the Love of God: Mother Teresa of Calcutta*, Trans. P. Speakman, Dublin: Veritas, 1974, p. 10; D. Doig, *Mother Teresa: Her People and Her Work*, London: Collins, 1978, p. 173; K. Spink, *For the Brotherhood of Man under the Fatherhood of God: Mother Teresa of Calcutta, her Missionaries of Charity and her Co-Workers*, Surrey, UK: Colour Library Information, 1981, p. 16; and E. Egan and K. Egan (eds), *Living the Word: A New Adventure in Prayer Involving Scripture, Mother Teresa and You*, London: Collins, 1990, p. 4.

16 N. Chawla, *Mother Teresa*, London: Vega, 2002, p. 178.

17 Ibid., p. 1.

18 Tames, op. cit., p. 31.

19 Gray, op. cit., p. 60.

20 Jackman, op. cit., p. 29.

21 For similar leaps in 'chronological tables'/'important dates' sections see Muggeridge, op cit., p. 154; and Doig, op. cit., p. 173.

22 See Muggeridge, op. cit., pp. 16, 18.

23 Muggeridge, op. cit., p. 154.

24 Gorrée and Barbier, op. cit, p. 10.

25 Doig, op. cit., p. 173.

26 Spink, 1981, op. cit., p. 16.

27 L. Vardey, 'Introduction', in M. Teresa, *A Simple Path*, L. Vardey (ed.), London and Sydney: Rider, 1995, (pp. 13–34), pp. 17–18.

28 J. Cairns, 'How This Book Came About', in M. Teresa, *A Simple Path*, L. Vardey (ed.), London and Sydney: Rider, 1995, (pp. 7–12), p. 10.

29 Gorrée and Barbier, op. cit., p. 10.

30 Doig, op. cit., p. 173.

31 Spink, 1981, op. cit., p. 16.

32 Vardey, op. cit., pp. 17–18.

33 E. Egan, *Such a Vision of the Street: Mother Teresa – The Spirit and the Work*, Complete and Unabridged, New York: Doubleday, 1986, p. 7.

34 Porter, op. cit., p. 18.

35 See L. Gjergji, *Nëna e Dashurisë*. Prishtinë: Akademia e Shkencave dhe e Arteve e Kosovës, 2000, p. 58.

36 Ibid.

37 For more information on the generosity of Mother Teresa's parents towards the poor of Skopje see Porter, op. cit., pp. 7, 8; A. Sebba, *Mother Teresa: Beyond the Image*, London: Orion, 1997, pp. 12, 16, 18; Spink, 1998, op. cit., pp. 5, 6, 7; and Johnson, op. cit., pp. 6, 9.

38 Porter, op. cit., p. 8.

39 Ibid., pp. 7–8.

40 Ibid., p. 7.

41 For the Bojaxhius' attachment to music see Gjergji, op. cit., p. 63.

42 L. Gjergji, *Dashuria Tërheqëse: Nëna jonë Tereze*, 2nd edn, Ferizaj, Kosova: Drita; Zagreb, Croatia: Kršćanska Sadašnjost, 1990, p. 23.

43 See Gjergji, 1990, op. cit., pp. 22, 23; and Gjergji, 2000, op. cit., p. 63.

44 See Gjergji, 1990, op. cit., p. 29; and Gjergji, 2000, op. cit., pp. 58, 59.

45 See Gjergji, 1990, op. cit., p. 21; and Gjergji, 2000, op. cit., pp. 70–1.

46 Gorrée and Barbier, op. cit., p. 10.

47 Egan, op. cit., p. 5.

48 Ibid., pp. 29–30.

49 The author visited India from 25 June to 2 July 2005 and gave four lectures in Calcutta and Shantiniketan, three of which were on Mother Teresa. In the first talk on 28 June at 'Mother House', the Headquarters of Mother Teresa's order the Missionaries of Charity, he concentrated on Agnes Gonxhe Bojaxhiu's search for a 'father figure' in the wake of the death of her father. The two lectures at St Xavier's College, Calcutta, on 1 July were on how Mother Teresa became a media icon, and on the influence of her Albanian roots on her ministry among the poor.

50 The author's interview with Father Lush Gjergji in Binçë, Kosova, on 30 October 2003; Father Gjergji's letter to the author of 10 November 2003.

51 Father Lush Gjergji mentioned the issue of plagiarism during the interview with the author in Binçë, Kosova, on 30 October 2003, and in his letter to the author of 10 November 2003.

52 See Porter, op. cit., p. ix; Sebba, op. cit., p. 14; and Spink, 1998, op. cit., p. 3.

53 Author's interview with Father Lush Gjergji, Binçë, Kosova, 30 October 2003; Father Gjergji's letter to the author of 10 November 2003. When asked by the author if he is Mother Teresa's cousin, Father Gjergji replied 'No, I am not', adding that he suspects that some Western biographers pigeonhole him as her cousin 'because in my publications I refer to my aunt Mrika Gjergji who was a friend of Mother Teresa throughout her years in Skopje'. The author of this book has found no evidence to corroborate Father Gjergji's claim that he is seen as a relative of Mother Teresa because of his aunt's friendship with the nun.

54 See Sebba, op. cit., p. 14; and Porter, op. cit, p. ix.

55 C. Hitchens, *The Missionary Position: Mother Teresa in Theory and Practice*, London and New York: Verso, 1995, p. 12.

56 See Gjergji, 2000, op. cit., p. 11.

57 See Gjergji, 1990, op. cit., p. 9.

58 Gjergji, 2000, op. cit., p. 35.

59 In some cases certain details from the recollections and diaries of people who knew Mother Teresa during the 1910–1928 period included in the 1990 edition of Lush Gjergji's *Dashuria Tërheqëse: Nëna jonë Tereze*, which was first published in 1980, do not always fully match their versions in his 2000 book *Nëna e Dashurisë*. Compare Gjergji, 1990, op. cit., pp. 17, 29, with Gjergji, 2000, op. cit., pp. 50, 59 respectively. Like many other biographers of Mother Teresa, Gjergji also edits at times the nun's words in direct speech (see Gjergji, 1990, op. cit., p. 18; and Gjergji, 2000, op. cit., p. 51).

60 Feedback from the author's lecture 'Mother Teresa and the Western Media' at the University of Prishtina, Kosova, and from his television interviews on Mother Teresa on KTV and RTV21 on 30 October 2003.

61 Author's conversations with Albanian academics at the University of Prishtina, Kosova, on 29 and 30 October 2003, University of Tirana, Albania, on 19 and 20 November 2004, and Tetova State University, Macedonia, on 9 and 10 April 2006. See also G. Alpion, 'Media, Ethnicity and Patriotism – the Balkans "Unholy War" for the Appropriation of Mother Teresa', *Journal of Southern Europe and the Balkans*, Vol. 6, No. 3, December 2004 (227–43), pp. 234–5.

62 Porter, op. cit., p. ix.

63 Hitchens, op. cit., p. 79.

4 Mother Teresa's attitude towards her early years

1 E. Le Joly, *We Do It for Jesus: Mother Teresa and her Missionaries of Charity*, London: Darton, Longman and Todd, 1977, p. 12.
2 L. Gjergji, *Dashuria Tërheqëse: Nëna jonë Tereze*, 2nd edn, Ferizaj, Kosova: Drita; Zagreb, Croatia: Kršćanska Sadašnjost, 1990, p. 6.
3 Ibid.
4 Ibid.
5 See K. Spink, *Mother Teresa: An Authorized Biography*, London: Fount, 1998, p. vii.
6 A. Chatterjee, *Mother Teresa: The Final Verdict*, Kolkata, India: Meteor Books, 2003, p. 236.
7 For Kathryn Spink's gratitude to Mother Teresa see her 1998 biography, op. cit., p. vii.
8 N. Chawla, *Mother Teresa*, London: Vega, 2002, p. vii.
9 See Chawla, op. cit., p. xxi.
10 Ibid., p. 197.
11 Ibid., p. xxi.
12 Ibid., pp. 192–3.
13 See Chawla, op. cit., p. 192.
14 Chatterjee, op. cit., p. 31.
15 Chawla, op. cit., p. 192.
16 J. Cairns, 'How This Book Came About', in M. Teresa, *A Simple Path*, L. Vardey (ed.), London: Rider, 1995, (pp. 7–12), pp. 11–12.
17 See Cairns, op. cit., p. 10.
18 Gjergji, op. cit., p. 20.
19 K. Spink, *For the Brotherhood of Man under the Fatherhood of God: Mother Teresa of Calcutta, her Missionaries of Charity and her Co-Workers*, Surrey, UK: Colour Library International, 1981, p. 16.
20 Spink, 1998, op. cit, p. 3.
21 See Spink, 1981, op. cit., pp. 16–18; and Spink, 1998, op. cit., p. 3.
22 A. Sebba, *Mother Teresa: Beyond the Image*, London: Orion, 1997, p. xii.
23 Le Joly, op. cit., p. 6.
24 Sebba, op. cit., p. 13.
25 Spink, 1998, op. cit., p. 3.
26 See M. Muggeridge, *Something Beautiful for God: Mother Teresa of Calcutta*, London: Collins, 1971, p. 154; D. Doig, *Mother Teresa: Her People and Her Work*, London: Collins, 1978, p. 173; Gjergji, op. cit., p. 19; and Spink, 1981, op. cit., p. 16.
27 See L. Gjergji, *Nëna e Dashurisë*, Prishtinë: Akademia e Shkencave dhe e Arteve e Kosovës, 2000, p. 52.
28 Spink, 1998, op. cit., p. 3.
29 M. Teresa, *A Simple Path*, L. Vardey (ed.), London: Rider, 1995, p. 186.
30 Doig, op. cit., p. 51.
31 See Doig, op. cit., pp. 45, 173; and M. Teresa, op. cit., p. 183.
32 Doig, op. cit., p. 51.
33 This spelling of Mother Teresa's baptismal name is used by the Albanians in Macedonia and Kosova. In this dialect form the word appears in the early work of the Kosova-based Albanian author Lush Gjergji, such as *Dashuria Tërheqëse: Nëna jonë Tereze* (1990, p. 19). In his 2000 book *Nëna e Dashurisë* (p. 52), Gjergji uses the literary Albanian spelling 'Gonxhe' instead. See also R. Tames, *Mother Teresa*, London: Franklin Watts, 1989, p. 4.

34 Like 'Ganxhe', 'Gonxha' is another dialect form of 'Gonxhe', which is used by the Albanians in Macedonia and Kosova. 'Gonxha' is found in several books that have appeared in English since 1970. Considering that most of these works were written by Western and Indian friends of Mother Teresa, it is obvious that the nun was their main if not the only source of information about her baptismal name and its spelling in this particular form. By the time Mother Teresa left Skopje in 1928, the Albanians did not have an 'official' literary language. This became possible only in the 1970s, but as Father Lush Gjergji informed the author of this book when they met in Binçë, Kosova, on 30 October 2003, Mother Teresa was never confident enough to use literary Albanian either when she spoke or in writing. See also G. Gorrée and J. Barbier, *For the Love of God: Mother Teresa of Calcutta*, Trans. P. Speakman, Dublin: Veritas, 1974, p. 10; Doig, op. cit., pp. 45, 173; E. Egan, *Such a Vision of the Street: Mother Teresa – The Spirit and the Work*, Complete and Unabridged, New York: Doubleday, 1986, p. 8; C. Gray, *Mother Teresa: The Nun whose 'Mission of Love' Has Helped Millions of the World's Poorest People*, Herts, UK: Exley, 1990, p. 5; and M. Teresa, op. cit., p. 183.

35 Spink, 1981, op. cit., p. 16; W. Jackman, *Mother Teresa*, East Sussex, UK: Wayland, 1993, p. 29.

36 See Gjergji, 2000, op. cit., pp. 52, 54.

37 See Egan, op. cit., p. 8.

38 Spink, 1998, op. cit., p. 3.

39 Egan, op. cit., p. 7.

40 For more information regarding the professions ascribed to Mother Teresa's father see Spink, 1981, op. cit., p. 16; Egan, op. cit., p. 7; Gjergji, 1990, op. cit, p. 11; and Spink, 1998, op. cit., p. 4.

41 Author's interview with Father Lush Gjergji on 30 October 2003.

42 See Sebba, op. cit., p. 14.

43 Gjergji, 2000, op. cit., p. 43.

44 Sebba, op. cit., pp. 14–16.

45 Doig, op. cit., 51.

46 Author's conversations with friends of Mother Teresa and followers of the Catholic faith in Calcutta from 26 June to 1 July 2005.

47 D. Porter, *Mother Teresa: The Early Years*, Oxford and New York: ISIS Large Print, 1986, p. xi.

48 Spink, 1998, op. cit., p. 3.

49 Sebba, op. cit., p. xii.

50 Porter, op. cit., p. xi.

51 Sebba, op. cit., p. 13.

52 Spink, 1998, op. cit., p. xii.

53 Author's conversations with friends of Mother Teresa and followers of the Catholic faith in Calcutta from 26 June to 1 July 2005.

54 Spink, 1981, op. cit., p. 18.

55 Le Joly, op. cit., p. 180.

56 Ibid., p. 6.

57 Porter, op. cit., p. x.

58 Spink, 1998, op. cit., p. xii.

59 Chawla, op. cit, p. xxi.

60 Muggeridge, op. cit., pp. 83–4.

61 Ibid., p. 15.

62 Ibid.

63 Le Joly, op. cit., p. 13. Mother Teresa's words seem to have been inspired not by Colossians 1:11, as Le Joly maintains, but by Colossians 1:15–20. The author is grateful to Father Gaston Roberge for the information.

64 See Le Joly, op. cit., p. 180; and E. Egan and K. Egan (eds), *Living the Word: A New Adventure in Prayer Involving Scripture, Mother Teresa, and You*, London: Collins, 1990, p. 81.

65 Muggeridge, op. cit., p. 58.

66 For information on the formative impact his early years and especially his father had on Malcolm Muggeridge see chapter one 'Childhood', in R. Ingrams, *Muggeridge: The Biography*, London: HarperCollins, 1995.

67 Muggeridge, op. cit., p. 22.

68 F. S. Sellers, 'A Satirist in Search of Salvation', *Washington Post*, 3 March 1996.

69 Muggeridge, op. cit., p. 15.

70 Ibid., pp. 16–17.

71 Ibid., p. 16.

72 Ibid.

73 Ibid., pp. 16, 18.

74 Chatterjee, op. cit., p. 51.

75 Muggeridge, op. cit., p. 37.

76 Ibid., p. 31.

77 Ibid., p. 37.

78 Ibid., pp. 31–2.

79 Muggeridge, op. cit., p. 47.

80 See N. Bethell, *The Great Betrayal: The Untold Story of Kim Philby's Biggest Coup*, London: Hodder and Stoughton, 1984, p. 95.

81 Ingrams, op. cit., p. 200.

82 Chatterjee, op. cit., p. 52.

83 For Muggeridge's alleged abhorrence to liberalism see J. Bright-Holmes (ed.), *Like It Was: The Diaries of Malcolm Muggeridge*, London: Collins, 1981, pp. 422, 452.

84 For information on Muggeridge's alleged 'anti-Semitic' views see Chatterjee, op. cit., pp. 43, 44, 66.

85 Bethell, op, cit., p. 102.

86 For more information about Muggeridge's alleged involvement with the MI6 and the CIA see Chatterjee, op, cit., pp. 47, 48.

87 Ibid., p. 51.

88 Ibid., p. 48.

89 N. Chawla, 'Tribute: Remembering Mother Teresa', *Frontline*, Vol. 17, No. 19, September 2000, pp. 16–29.

90 K. Chaudhuri and P. Menon, 'For the Poorest of the Poor: People the World over Mourn the Death of Mother Teresa', *Frontline*, Vol. 14, No. 19, 20 September to 3 October 1997.

91 In the autumn of 2003, the Roman Catholic community in Calcutta expressed surprise and dismay at the West Bengali leftist government's lack of interest in the celebrations scheduled for the beatification of Mother Teresa. The official line of the Communist Party of India (Marxist), CPI(M), was that its leaders were not happy with the Vatican's claim that the tribal woman Monica Basra was cured of stomach cancer in 2002 thanks to Mother Teresa's miraculous intervention. Buddhadeb Bhattacharya, the current Chief Minister of Bengal, who replaced Mother Teresa's friend Jyoti Basu in 2000, was reported to have refused to receive the organizers of the beatification events. Rather

than their opposition to the Monica Basra affair, it is widely believed that the West Bengali leftist leaders decided to snub some beatification celebrations because, in their view, the Roman Catholic nun never addressed the main reasons for Calcutta's grinding poverty.

92 Sebba, op. cit., p. 102.
93 Gjergji, 1990, op. cit., p. 291.
94 Ibid., p. 289.
95 J. V. Schall SJ, 'Periodicals Review: "The *Albanian Catholic Bulletin* – A Remarkable Source of Information on Albania"', *Religion in Eastern Europe*, Vol. XIII, No. 2, April 1993, p. 47.
96 For more information on the stance of the Enver Hoxha government towards religions and clerics, especially Catholic priests, from the early 1940s until the 1980s see Egan, op. cit., pp. 182–3; Spink, 1998, op. cit., pp. 237–8; J. V. Schall, op. cit.; F. Hiorth, 'Albania: An Atheistic State?', *Religion in Eastern Europe*, Vol. X, No. 5, October 1990, pp. 14–21; E. Koliqi, 'Reverend Lazer Shantoja (1892–1945): A Brilliant Stylist of Albanian Literature', *Albanian Catholic Bulletin*, Vols. 7–8, 1986–87; Z. Shestani, 'Brother Gjon Pantalija SJ: An Albanian Christian Martyr', *Albanian Catholic Bulletin*, Vols 7–8, 1986–87; G. Silvestri, 'Fr. Gjon Fausti SJ: Strength in Serenity', *Albanian Catholic Bulletin*, Vols 7–8, 1986–87; P. Duka-Gjini, 'Designated to Die: The Martyrdom of Fr. Gjon Shllaku OFM', *Albanian Catholic Bulletin*, Vols 7–8, 1986–87; R. Llazari, 'At Gjon Shllaku – heroi i katolicizmit', *Koha Jone*. Online. Available HTTP: <http://www.shkoder.net/al/gj_shllaku.htm> (accessed 25 September 2005); Z. Simoni, 'Persekutimi i Kishës Katolike në Shqipni nga 1944–1990'. Online. Available HTTP: <http://www.forumishqiptar.com/showthread.php?=3856> (accessed 12 August 2005); and K. Kapinova, 'Kujtesë: Jo gjyq të dytë për At Anton Harapin! – I harruari i paharrueshëm: At Anton Harapi ofm, martir i fesë dhe i shqiptarizmës së kulluar'. Online. Available HTTP: <http://groups.yahoo.com/group/Albemigrant/message/68?viscount=100> (accessed 2 September 2005).
97 Hiorth, op. cit.
98 S. Bates, 'Church Backs PM's Right to Choose', *Guardian*, 9 July 2002.
99 Ibid.
100 Egan, op. cit., pp. 182–3. For more information on the alleged reasons for the execution of Stephan Kurti by the Communists see Simoni, op. cit. Simoni does not allude to any family connections between Kurti and Mother Teresa, nor that the nun was in anyway the reason for Kurti's persecution and execution in 1971.
101 That Mother Teresa's sister, Age, was in the employ of Radio Tirana during the Communist regime was confirmed to the author by one of her colleagues who does not wish to be identified. For more information on Age's employment history see Egan, op. cit., p. 174; Porter, op. cit., p. 50; Gjergji, 1990, op. cit., p. 18; Spink, 1998, op. cit., p. 19; and E. Johnson, *Mother Teresa*, London and Sydney: Franklin Watts, 2003, p. 11.
102 Gjergji, 1990, op. cit., p. 18.
103 For more information on the friendship between Marije Kraja and Mother Teresa's mother and sister see Sebba, op. cit., p. 16; and A. Peçi, 'Gjithë miqësia e ngushtë mes këngëtares dhe familjes së Nënë Terezës – Marije Kraja, një letër bekimi nga Nënë Tereza', *Korrieri*, 5 March 2005.
104 Gjergji, 2000, op. cit., p. 73.
105 Spink, 1998, op. cit., 96.
106 See Egan, op. cit., p. 154.
107 Spink, 1998, op. cit., p. 97.

108 Egan, op. cit., p. 153.
109 See Egan, op. cit, pp. 173–6.
110 See Gjergji, 1990, op. cit., p. 306.
111 Gjergji, 1990, op. cit., pp. 304–5.
112 Ibid., pp. 306–7.
113 Spink, 1998, op. cit., p. 97.
114 Porter, op. cit., pp. 80–1.
115 For more information on the alleged attempts of prominent people to reunite Mother Teresa with her mother and sister see Porter, op. cit., p. 87; and Gjergji, 1990, op. cit, p. 305.
116 See Porter, op. cit., p. 25. Eileen Egan (op. cit., p. 12) maintains that Lazar went to Austria not in 1923 but in 1924.
117 Porter, op. cit., p. 29.
118 Egan, op. cit., p. 17.
119 See Peçi, op. cit.
120 Gjergji, 2000, op. cit., p. 73.
121 Egan, op. cit., p. 182.
122 Gjergji, 1990, op. cit., p. 20.
123 See Spink, 1981, op. cit., pp. 16, 18; and Spink, 1989, op. cit., p. 3.
124 Sebba, op. cit., p. 76.
125 See Egan, op. cit., p. 183.
126 Egan, op. cit., p. 153.
127 Ibid., p. 183.
128 Ibid., p. 153.
129 Ibid., p. 183.
130 Ibid., p. 175.
131 Ibid., p. 173.
132 See Sh. Sinani, '"Pashaporta" shqiptare e Nënë Terezës'. Online. Available HTTP: <http://www.albmuzika.com/nene_tereza.htm> (accessed 31 July 2005); and 'Zbulohet letra në shqip e Nënë Terezës', *Tirana Observer*, 25 August 2005.
133 Spink, 1998, op. cit., p. 97.
134 See Sebba, op. cit., p. 76.
135 Egan, op. cit., p. 183.
136 See Egan, op. cit., p. 182.
137 Bethell, op. cit., p. 99.
138 See Egan, op. cit., p. 154.
139 Egan, op. cit., p. 182.
140 See Porter, op. cit., p. 29.
141 Gjergji, 1990, op. cit., p. 108.
142 Spink, 1998, op. cit., p. 185.
143 Egan, op. cit., p. 182.
144 See Bethell, op. cit., p. 98.
145 Spink, 1998, op. cit., p. 237.
146 I. Kadare, *Invitation à l'atelier de l'écrivain suivi de le poids de la croix*, Trans. J. Vrioni, Paris: Fayard, 1991.
147 Porter, op. cit., p. 4.
148 Ibid.
149 Sebba, op. cit., p. 13.
150 Ibid., p. 14. According to Anne Sebba, Lazar made the statement about the poisoning of his father by the Serbs in an interview in 1982. Lazar died in 1981.

151 For more information on the persecution of Macedonian Slav patriots by members of secret Serbian committees at the beginning of the twentieth century see M. Ognjanov, 'Ju tregoj Shqipërinë e Nolit dhe Mbretit Zog'. Online. Available HTTP: <http://www.panorama.com.al/20040123/faqe12/1.htm> (accessed 18 April 2005). The article, which was first published in the Albanian daily *Panorama*, includes excerpts from chapter 7 of Ognjanov's book *Maqedonia: Fat i Mbijetuar*.
152 Author's interview with Father Lush Gjergji on 30 October 2003. This is the first time Mother Teresa's words about the Serbs' alleged involvement in the poisoning of her father appear in print.

5 Jesus the divine superstar

1 For more information on Mother Teresa's celebrity father see L. Gjergji, *Dashuria Tërheqëse: Nëna jonë Tereze*, 2nd edn, Ferizaj, Kosova: Drita; Zagreb, Croatia: Kršćanska Sadašnjost, 1990, pp. 11–14; L. Gjergji, *Nëna e Dashurisë*, Prishtinë: Akademia e Shkencave dhe e Arteve e Kosovës, 2000, pp. 38–9, 41, 43–4; D. Porter, *Mother Teresa: The Early Years*, Oxford and New York: ISIS Large Print, 1986, pp. 4–9; E. Egan, *Such a Vision of the Street: Mother Teresa – The Spirit and the Work*, Complete and Unabridged, New York: Doubleday, 1986, pp. 7–8, 10; C. Gray, *Mother Teresa: The Nun whose 'Mission of Love' Has Helped Millions of the World's Poorest People*, Herts, UK: Exley, 1990, pp. 5, 7; A. Sebba, *Mother Teresa: Beyond the Image*, London: Orion, 1997, pp 10–13; and E. Johnson, *Mother Teresa*, London and Sydney: Franklin Watts, 2003, p. 6.
2 Porter, op. cit., p. 7. Nikollë's advice to his children to keep in mind that he was a well-respected member of the community is reported in slightly different versions also in Gjergji, 1990, op. cit., p. 12; Gjergji, 2000, op. cit., p. 39; and Egan, op. cit., p. 8.
3 According to Lush Gjergji (2000, op. cit., p. 43), Mother Teresa's father passed away in 1918. Eileen Egan (op. cit., p. 9), who was very close to the nun for over thirty years, holds that Nikollë died in 1919. In one of the early scenes of Kevin Connor's 1997 biopic *Mother Teresa: In The Name of God's Poor*, a film which was produced in close collaboration with Mother Teresa, reminiscencing about her father, the nun says that he died when she was nine years old. Mother Teresa was born on 26 September 1910.
4 M. Teresa, *In My Own Words*, J. L. González-Balado (ed.), London: Hodder & Stoughton, 1997, p. 101.
5 See D. Doig, *Mother Teresa: Her People and Her Work*, London: Collins, 1978, p. 162.
6 Author's interview with Father Lush Gjergji in Binçë, Kosova, on 30 October 2003.
7 Porter, op. cit., p. 7.
8 Gjergji, 1990, op. cit., p. 11.
9 Porter, op. cit., p. 10.
10 Egan, op. cit., p. 10. During his visit to Skopje on 9 April 2006, the author of this book noticed that the city's new train station is not very near the place where Mother Teresa's family home used to be. When Agnes came across the mysterious priest in 1919, the train station was a couple of hundred metres away from her house.
11 Sebba, op. cit., p. 13.
12 A. Sebba (2005) 'Mother Teresa'. E-mail (25 March 2005).

13 The author is grateful to Father Gaston Roberge SJ, for showing him in Calcutta in July 2005 two versions of the Lapierre–Hartman script that do not include the scene where Sister Teresa speaks to the distressed Indian girl about how she had felt when she lost her father at the age of nine. The quotations from Dominique Lapierre's and Jan Hartman's script of the film *Mother Teresa: In the Name of God's Poor* (dir. Kevin Connor, USA, 1997) that appear in this book and on pp. 161 and 205–6 are reproduced by kind permission of Dominique Lapierre.

14 Porter, op. cit., p. 23.

15 Ibid., p. 22.

16 Gjergji, 2000, op. cit., p. 64.

17 See Porter, op. cit., p. 29.

18 See Gjergji, 1990, op. cit., p. 32.

19 Ibid., p. 21.

20 See Gjergji, 1990, op. cit., pp. 21, 32.

21 Author's interview with Father Lush Gjergji in Binçë, Kosova, on 30 October 2003.

22 Porter, op. cit., p. 29.

23 See Gjergji, 1990, op. cit., p. 18; and Gjergji, 2000, op. cit., p. 51.

24 Egan, op. cit., p. 16.

25 Ibid.

26 Porter, op. cit., p. 29.

27 Gjergji, 2000, op. cit., p. 51.

28 K. Marx, 'Introduction to A Contribution to the Critique of Hegel's Philosophy of Right', *Deutsch-Französische Jahrbücher*, February 1844.

29 S. Freud, *The Future of an Illusion*, Trans. W. D. Robson-Scott, J. Strachey (ed.), London: The Hogarth Press, 1962, p. 26.

30 Ibid., p. 14.

31 Ibid., p. 15.

32 Ibid., p. 39.

33 Author's conversations with former Archbishop of Calcutta, Henry D'Souza, and Father Gaston Roberge SJ, in Calcutta and Shantaniketan, India, from 26 June to 1 July 2005.

34 Porter, op. cit., pp. 19–20.

35 See E. Le Joly, *We Do It for Jesus: Mother Teresa and her Missionaries of Charity*, London: Darton, Longman and Todd, 1977, p. 116.

36 See M. Teresa, op. cit., p. 35.

37 See E. Egan and K. Egan (eds), *Living the Word: A New Adventure in Prayer Involving Scripture, Mother Teresa, and You*, London: Collins, 1990, pp. 94–5.

38 See J. Maltby, et al., 'Personality and Coping: A Context for Examining Celebrity Worship and Mental Health', *British Journal of Psychology*, 95, 2004, (411–28), p. 411.

39 See R. W. Larsen, 'Secrets in the Bedroom: Adolescents' Private Use of Media', *Journal of Youth and Adolescence*, 24, 1995, 535–50; D. Giles, *Illusions of Immortality: A Psychology of Fame and Celebrity*, London: Macmillan, 2000; D. D. Ashe, and L. E. McCutcheon, 'Shyness, Loneliness, and Attitude Toward Celebrities', *Current Research in Social Psychology*, 6, 2001, 124–33; and Maltby, et al., 2004, op. cit.

40 See J. Maltby, et al., 'Thou Shalt Worship No Other Gods – Unless They Are Celebrities: The Relationship Between Celebrity Worship and Religious Orientation', *Personality and Individual Differences*, 32, 2002, 1157–72.

41 Maltby, et al., 2002, op. cit., p. 1158.

42 Dr John Maltby told the author of this study that, contrary to the general belief, he and his colleagues 'never used the term Celebrity Worship Syndrome, this was a media invention' attached to the acclaimed article 'Personality and Coping: A Context for Examining Celebrity Worship and Mental Health'. J. Maltby (2005) 'Celebrity Worship Paper'. E-mail (16 January 2005).

43 J. Belton, *American Cinema/American Culture*, 2nd edn, Boston: McGraw-Hill, 2005, p. 103.

44 Doig, op. cit., p. 162.

45 Matthew 25: 34–6, in *The Holy Bible, containing the Old and New Testaments with the Apocryphal/Deuterocanonical Books*, New Revised Standard Version, New York and Oxford: Oxford University Press, 1989, p. 29.

46 M. Teresa, op. cit., p. 101.

47 Ibid., p. 34.

48 Ibid., p. 35.

49 Le Joly, op. cit., p. 87.

50 K. Spink, *Mother Teresa: An Authorized Biography*, London: Fount, 1998, p. 8

51 Ibid.

52 Sebba, op. cit., p. 19.

53 Author's interview with Father Lush Gjergji, op. cit.

54 Sebba, op. cit., p. 19.

55 Ibid.

56 Porter, op. cit., p. 29.

57 Egan, op. cit., p. 21.

58 Saint Thérèse of Lisieux, *The Story of a Soul*, Trans. J. Beevers, New York: Doubleday, 1989, p. 21.

59 Saint Teresa of Ávila, *The Complete Works of Saint Teresa of Jesus*, Vol. I, Trans. E. A. Peers (ed.), London: Sheed & Ward, 1946, pp. 192–3. It is believed that St Teresa had this mystical experience initially some time between 1559 and 1562, and again between 1571 and 1574.

60 'Submission from the British Board of Film Classification'. Online. Available HTTP: <http://www.parliament.the-stationery-office.co.uk/pa/ld200203/ldselect/ldrelof/95/95w07.htm> (accessed 24 October 2005).

61 J. Hall, 'In Praise of Younger Men', *Sunday Times*, 19 October 2003, pp. 40–1.

62 See Spink, op. cit., p. 12.

63 See L. Vardey, 'Introduction', in M. Teresa, *A Simple Path*, L. Vardey (ed.), London and Sydney: Rider, 1995, (13–34), pp. 27–8.

64 M. Teresa, 1997, op. cit., p. 76.

65 Egan and Egan, op. cit., p. 99.

66 Le Joly, op. cit., pp. 12–13.

67 Ibid., p. 69.

68 Vardey, op. cit., p. 27.

69 Ibid., p. 28.

70 Le Joly, op cit., p. 116.

71 Gergji, 1990, op. cit., p. 266.

6 From church rebel to church asset

1 A. Sebba, *Mother Teresa: Beyond the Image*, London: Orion, 1997, p. 21.

2 D. Porter, *Mother Teresa: The Early Years*, Oxford and New York: ISIS Large Print, 1986, p. 35.

3 Mother Teresa's biographers are not unanimous about the exact length of time she stayed at Loreto Abbey in Dublin. Eileen Egan (*Such a Vision of the Street: Mother Teresa – The Spirit and the Work*, Complete and Unabridged, New York: Doubleday, 1986, p. 17), Charlotte Gray (*Mother Teresa: The Nun whose 'Mission of Love' Has Helped Millions of the World's Poorest People*, Herts, UK: Exley, 1990, p. 9) and Kathryn Spink (*Mother Teresa: An Authorized Biography*, London: Fount, 1998, p. 12) hold that she spent six weeks in the novitiate, whereas David Porter (op. cit., p. 34) and Anne Sebba (op. cit., p. 31) put it as 'several months'.

4 Sebba, op. cit., p. 31.

5 See N. Chawla, *Mother Teresa*, London: Vega, 2002, p. 13.

6 See Sebba, op. cit., p. 19.

7 For more information on the dislike and prejudices of the higher Indian castes towards foreigners, see S. Neill, *A History of Christian Missions*, 2nd edn, London, Penguin, 1990, p. 156.

8 For more information on 'inferior' gods, creeds and cultures that apparently failed to compete with and resist the European invaders' religion see K. S. Latourette, *A History of the Expansion of Christianity: The Great Century in the Americas, Austral-Asia, and Africa, A.D. 1800–A.D. 1914*, Vol. V, London: Eyre and Spottiswoode, 1943, pp. 222–3; and Neill, op. cit., pp. 353, 354.

9 For more information about the importance Protestant missions attached to the translation of the Scriptures into Indian languages see Neill, op. cit., p. 177.

10 S. Neill, *Builders of the Indian Church: Present Problems in the Light of the Past*, London: Edinburgh House Press, 1934, p. 118.

11 Neill, 1990, op. cit., p. 308.

12 For more information on the increasing suspicion with which missionaries and their Western-funded schools were regarded in India as well as in other European colonies in Asia in the latter part of the nineteenth century see Neill, 1990, op. cit., pp. 303–5, 385.

13 Sister Moira IBVM, archivist, Loreto Provincialate, Calcutta (2006) 'Reply to Questionnaire'. E-mail (attachment) (22 February 2006).

14 Porter, op. cit., p. 45.

15 Sister Moira IBVM, op. cit.

16 The Missionaries of Charity (2006) 'Questionnaire on M. Teresa'. E-mail attachment received from Father Gaston Roberge SJ, containing the information provided by one of the sisters at Mother House, Calcutta, as advised by Sister Nirmala MC (10 February 2006).

17 Sister Moira IBVM, op. cit.

18 Porter, op. cit., p. 47.

19 Ibid., p. 48.

20 Sister Moira IBVM, op. cit.

21 For more information on imperial Islam see I. Manji, *The Trouble with Islam Today: A Wake-Up Call for Honesty and Change*, Edinburgh and London: Mainstream Publishing, 2005, especially Chapter 3 'When Did We Stop Thinking?' pp. 61–84.

22 Neill, 1990, op. cit., p. 384.

23 A former Loreto student, who does not wish to be identified, told the author in Calcutta on 29 June 2005 that, although she and other Hindu girls had repeatedly asked the school authorities to be allowed to go to Mother Teresa's homes to help the poor, their wish was never granted. The Indian Christian girls, on the other hand, were never refused permission if they volunteered to work in charity centres run by Catholic nuns.

24 Sister Moira IBVM, op. cit.
25 Aroup Chatterjee (2005) 'Loreto'. E-mail (14 June 2005).
26 According to Sister Moira IBVM, (op. cit.) at their inception, both schools at the Entally convent were orphanages:

> When the Loreto sisters arrived in Calcutta at the end of December 1841 they immediately began working in the Bengal Female Orphanage in Moorghyhatta (attached to the Cathedral). This orphanage was later shifted to Entally and in 1844 children from the recently opened orphanage in Chandernagore also moved to Entally. Some of the orphans were Bengali speaking and in 1912 a separate Bengali medium orphanage was opened for them. This became known as St Mary's Orphanage while the English medium orphanage was, and still is, known as St Joseph's Orphanage. Besides orphans, St Mary's also had children of Bengali, working parents such as cooks, mainly from the Dhaka area. At the time of the great Bengal famine in the 1940s those families who were able, returned to Dhaka leaving the more destitute behind in Calcutta.

27 Sebba, op. cit., p. 35.
28 Sister Moira IBVM, op. cit.
29 Egan, op. cit., p. 35.
30 Ibid.
31 G. Gorrée and J. Barbier, *For the Love of God: Mother Teresa of Calcutta*, Trans. P. Speakman, Dublin: Veritas, 1974, pp. 10–11.
32 E. Le Joly, E., *We Do It for Jesus: Mother Teresa and her Missionaries of Charity*, London: Darton, Longman and Todd, 1977, p. 63.
33 The Missionaries of Charity, op. cit.
34 R. Tagore, 'The Noble Prize Acceptance Speech', in R. Tagore, *Gitanjali: Song Offerings*, Trans. R. Tagore, New Delhi: UBSPD, 2005 (pp. 291–300), p. 299.
35 Ibid., pp. 296–7.
36 Le Joly, op. cit., p. 21.
37 Spink, op. cit., p. 31.
38 See Gray, op. cit., p. 25.
39 Different biographers give different years for Sister Teresa's appointment as headmistress of St Mary's school. David Porter (op. cit., p. 51) holds that Sister Teresa took on the new post in 1937 or shortly afterwards, whereas Navin Chawla (op. cit., p. 14) implies that this took place in 1944. According to Sister Moira IBVM, Archivist of the Loreto Provincialate in Calcutta (22 February 2006, op. cit.), Sister Teresa took over from Mother du Cénacle as Principal in 1941. Biographers like Porter, who put the appointment date in the 1930s, apparently mix up Sister Teresa's position as headmistress of St Mary's with her other post as principal of St Teresa's primary school in Moulali, which she apparently took on not long after she had started teaching there in 1935.
40 See Porter, op. cit., p. 57.
41 See Le Joly, op. cit., p. 18; Porter, op. cit, p. 56.
42 Porter, op. cit., p. 56.
43 Ibid.
44 Le Joly, op. cit., p. 18.
45 Gray, op. cit., p. 20.
46 See D. Doig, *Mother Teresa: Her People and Her Work*, London: Collins, 1978, p. 53.
47 Le Joly, op. cit., p. 18.
48 See Porter, op. cit., p. 56.

49 Egan, op. cit., p. 30.
50 Bharati Mukherjee, 'The Saint Mother Teresa', *Time*, 14 June 1999.
51 Doig, op. cit., p. 48.
52 Spink, op. cit., p. 27.
53 Sebba, op. cit., p. 46.
54 Spink, op. cit., p. 23.
55 The author is grateful to Father Gaston Roberge SJ for showing him his unpublished paper 'Mother Teresa, Abortion and the Media'. In this work, Father Roberge pays due attention to the biographical value of Kevin Connor's 1997 film *Mother Teresa: In the Name of God's Poor*.
56 Spink, op. cit., p. 27.
57 Ibid.
58 See Le Joly, op. cit., p. 19; Porter, op. cit., p. 57.
59 See Spink, op. cit., pp. 21.
60 Doig, op. cit., p. 49.
61 Sister Moira IBVM, op. cit.
62 Ibid.
63 Ibid.
64 See Spink, op. cit., pp. 26–7.
65 Spink, op. cit., p. 29.
66 Sister Moira IBVM, op. cit.
67 L. Gjergji, *Nëna e Dashurisë*, Prishtinë: Akademia e Shkencave dhe e Arteve e Kosovës, 2000, p. 133.
68 The same Loreto nun who knew Sister Teresa from 1947 would also remark in 1985 that the Albanian nun wrote poems regularly at Loreto. See Gjergji, op. cit., p. 133.
69 M. Muggeridge, *Something Beautiful for God: Mother Teresa of Calcutta*, London: Collins, 1971, p. 22.
70 Ibid., p. 18.
71 Le Joly, op. cit., pp. 14–15.
72 Egan, op. cit., p. 2.
73 Spink, op. cit., p. xiii.
74 N. Chawla, op. cit., p. 194.
75 Ibid.
76 Gjergji, op. cit., 58.
77 Ibid, p. 59.
78 See L. Gjergji., *Dashuria Tërheqëse: Nëna jonë Tereze*, 2nd edn, Ferizaj, Kosova: Drita; Zagreb, Croatia: Kršćanska Sadašnjost, 1990, p. 22; and Gjergji, 2000, op. cit., p. 59.
79 W. Wüllenweber, 'Mother Teresa: Where are her Millions?', *Stern*, 10 September 1998. Online. Available HTTP: <http://www.geocities.com/willdirne/mo.html> (accessed 18 September 2003).
80 See Mukherjee, op. cit.
81 Egan, op. cit., p. 7.
82 See Chawla, op. cit., pp. 30–44.
83 Spink, op. cit., p. 27.
84 Ibid.
85 Le Joly, op. cit., p. 27.
86 Spink, op. cit., p. 35.
87 Chawla, op. cit., p. 28.
88 Spink, op. cit., p. 32.
89 Le Joly, op. cit., p. 27.
90 Porter, op. cit., p. 69.

91 Sebba, op. cit., p. 53.
92 In his e-mail to the author of 30 January 2006, Father Gaston Roberge SJ, holds that people belittle the contribution of Loreto to Mother Teresa.
93 Egan, op. cit., pp. 27–8.
94 Ibid., p. 28.
95 Porter, op. cit., p. 52.
96 Ibid., p. 51.
97 Ibid., p. 52.
98 Chawla, op. cit., p. 20.
99 Porter, op. cit., p. 63.
100 David Porter (op. cit., p. 61) and Kathryn Spink (op. cit., p. 31) are some of the biographers who hold that Mother Teresa left Loreto on 16 August 1948.
101 See Egan, op. cit., p. 28.
102 Muggeridge, op. cit., p. 155. Mother Teresa did not '[lay] aside the Loreto habit and [clothe] herself in the white sari on 8 August 1946', as Muggeridge wrongly believed. As Eileen Egan (op. cit., p. 36) confirms, 'Sister Teresa came to Fr. Van Exem in the sacristy of the convent chapel on August 8 or 9, most likely the eighth, the priest recalled' asking him to bless 'the typical sari of a poor Bengali woman' she had purchased at the bazaar.
103 See Spink, op. cit., p. 31.
104 Egan, op. cit., p. 36.
105 Ibid.
106 Doig, op. cit., p. 173.
107 See Doig, op. cit., p. 51.
108 See Porter, op. cit., p. 61; and Egan, op. cit., p. 36.
109 Doig, op. cit., p. 52.
110 Sister Moira IBVM, op. cit.
111 See Egan, op. cit., p. 36.
112 Doig, op. cit., p. 48.
113 Egan, op. cit., p. 423.
114 Sebba, op. cit., p. xiv.
115 Egan, op. cit., 1986, p. 423.
116 For more information on the attention the Vatican has been paying to the media from the early 1960s see Pope Paul VI, 'Decree on the Media of Social Communications: *Inter Mirifica*', 4 December 1963. Online. Available HTTP: <http://www.vatican.va/archive/hist_councils/ii_vatican_council/documents/vat-ii_decree_19631204_inter-mirifica_en.html> (accessed 26 February 2006); and Pope John Paul II, 'Apostolic Letter: The Rapid Development', 24 January 2005. Online. Available HTTP: <http://www.vatican.va/holy_father/john_paul_ii/apost_letters/documents/hf_jp-ii_apl_20050124_il-rapido-sviluppo_en.html> (accessed 26 February 2006).
117 Muggeridge, op. cit, p. 86.
118 See Egan, op. cit., p. 37.
119 Sebba, op. cit., p. 50.
120 Neill, 1990, op. cit., p. 411.
121 R. P. McBrien, *Lives of the Saints: From Mary and St. Francis of Assisi to John XXIII and Mother Teresa*, New York, NY: HarperSanFrancisco, 2003, p. 37.
122 For information on the work carried out by dedicated missionaries in India and throughout the world from the start of the sixteenth century see R. D. Paul, *The Cross Over India*, London: SCM Press Ltd., 1952; and Neill, 1990, op. cit.

123 Neill, 1990, op.cit., p. 158.
124 Paul, op. cit., p. 122.
125 See Neill, 1990, op. cit., p. 343.
126 For information on the reluctance of Roman Catholic and Protestant mission-
     aries to ordain indigenous priests and establish younger churches in India
     and other countries in Asia, Africa and Latin America see Neill, 1990,
     op. cit., pp. 150, 156, 177, 341, 343, 362, 462.
127 For information on the significant role of women in the history of the Church
     see E. S. Fiorenza, *In Memory of Her: A Feminist Theological Reconstruc-
     tion of Christian Origins*, New York: Crossroad, 1983; E. A. Johnson, *Friends
     of God and Prophets: A Feminist Theological Reading of the Communion
     of Saints*, New York: Continuum, 1998; and K. Jones, *Women Saints:
     Lives of Faith and Courage*, Maryknoll, NY: Orbis Books, 1999.
128 McBrien, op. cit., p. 39.
129 Neill, 1990, op. cit., p. 324.
130 Muggeridge, op. cit, p. 93.
131 See Neill, 1990, op. cit., pp. 159, 167, 450.
132 E. Egan and K. Egan (eds), *Living the Word: A New Adventure in Prayer
     Involving Scripture, Mother Teresa, and You*, London: Collins, 1990, p. 69.
133 Spink, op. cit., p. 245.
134 Pope Benedict XVI, 'Encyclical Letter: *Deus Caritas Est*', 25 December 2005.
     Online. Available HTTP: <http://www.zenit.org/english/visualizza.phtml?sid=
     83355> (accessed 27 January 2006).

Select bibliography

Adams, J., 'Forked Tongues', *Guardian*, 18 January 2003.

Allegri, R., *Teresa of the Poor: The Story of Her Life*, San Francisco: Ignatius Press, 1996.

Alpion, G., 'Images of Albania and Albanians in English Literature: from Edith Durham to J. K. Rowling', *BESA Journal*, Vol. 6, No. 2, Spring 2002, pp. 30–4.

—— *Foreigner Complex: Essays and Fiction About Egypt*, Birmingham, UK: The University of Birmingham CPS, 2002.

—— 'Foreigner Complex', in G. Alpion, *Foreigner Complex: Essays and Fiction About Egypt*, Birmingham, UK: The University of Birmingham CPS, 2002, pp. 1–21.

—— 'Oh! Not Calcutta', *Guardian*, 6 September 2003.

—— 'Media, Ethnicity and Patriotism – The Balkans "Unholy War" for the Appropriation of Mother Teresa', *Journal of Southern Europe and the Balkans*, Vol. 6, No. 3, December 2004, 227–43.

—— 'Western Media and the European "Other": Images of Albania in the British Press in the New Millennium', *Albanian Journal of Politics*, Vol. I, No. 1, September 2005: 7–27.

Andrić, I., 'Draft on Albania', in R. Elsie (ed.), *Kosovo: In the Heart of the Powder Keg*, Boulder, CO: East European Monographs, 1997, pp. 435–48.

Ashe, D. D., and L. E. McCutcheon, 'Shyness, Loneliness, and Attitude Toward Celebrities', *Current Research in Social Psychology*, 6, 2001, 124–33.

Augustine, Saint, *Confessions*, Trans. H. Chadwick, Oxford: Oxford University Press, 1998.

Banac, I., *The National Question in Yugoslavia: Origins, History, Politics*, Ithaca, New York: Cornell University Press, 1994.

Bates, S., 'Church Backs PM's Right to Choose', *Guardian*, 9 July 2002.

Béhar, P., *Vestiges d'empires: La Décomposition de l'Europe centrale et balkanique*, Paris: Éditions Desjonquères, 1999.

Belton, J., *American Cinema/American Culture*, 2nd edn, Boston: McGraw-Hill, 2005.

Benedict XVI, Pope, 'Encyclical Letter: *Deus Caritas Est*', 25 December 2005. Online. Available HTTP: <http://www.zenit.org/english/visualizza.phtml?sid=83355> (accessed 27 January 2006).

Bethell, N., *The Great Betrayal: The Untold Story of Kim Philby's Biggest Coup*, London: Hodder and Stoughton, 1984.

Boorstin, D. J., *The Image: A Guide to Pseudo-Events in America*, New York: Vintage Books, 1992.

Bright-Holmes, J. (ed.), *Like It Was: The Diaries of Malcolm Muggeridge*, London: Collins, 1981.

Brown, L., *The Indian Christians of St Thomas: An Account of the Ancient Syrian Church of Malabar*, Cambridge: Cambridge University Press, 1982.

Bunyan, J., *The Pilgrim's Progress*, London: J. M. Dent & Sons Ltd, 1957.

Cairns, J., 'How This Book Came About', in M. Teresa, *A Simple Path*, L. Vardey (ed.), London: Rider, 1995, pp. 7–12.

Carlyle, T., *On Heroes, Hero-Worship and the Heroic in History*, C. Niemeyer (ed.), Lincoln and London: University of Nebraska Press, 1966.

Carrera, E., *Teresa of Avila's Autobiography: Authority, Power and the Self in Mid-Sixteenth-Century Spain*, London: Legenda, 2005.

Cashmore, E., *Beckham*, 2nd edn, Cambridge: Polity Press, 2004.

Chatterjee, A., *Mother Teresa: The Final Verdict*, Kolkata, India: Meteor Books, 2003.

Chaudhuri, K., and P. Menon, 'For the Poorest of the Poor: People the World Over Mourn the Death of Mother Teresa', *Frontline*, Vol. 14, No. 19, 20 September to 3 October 1997.

Chawla, N., 'Tribute: Remembering Mother Teresa', *Frontline*, Vol. 17, No. 19, September 2000, pp. 16–29.

—— *Mother Teresa*, London: Vega, 2002.

Collopy, M., *Works of Love Are Works of Peace: Mother Teresa of Calcutta and the Missionaries of Charity: A Photographic Record*, San Francisco: Ignatius Press, 1996.

Conroy, S., *Mother Teresa's Lessons of Love and Secrets of Sanctity*, Huntington, IN: Our Sunday Visitor, 2003.

Constant, A., *In the Streets of Calcutta: The Story of Mother Teresa*, Norwich: Religious and Moral Education Press, 1980.

Čubrilović, V., 'The Expulsion of the Albanians: Memorandum Presented in Belgrade on 7 March 1937', in R. Elsie (ed.), *Kosovo: In the Heart of the Powder Keg*, Boulder, CO: East European Monographs, 1997, pp. 400–24.

—— 'The Minority Problem in the New Yugoslavia: Memorandum of 3 November 1944', in R. Elsie (ed.), *Kosovo: In the Heart of the Powder Keg*, Boulder, CO: East European Monographs, 1997, pp. 449–64.

Datta-Ray, S. K., 'Halo Goodbye', *Telegraph*, 1 February 1997.

—— 'Saviour of the Needy Driven by Self-interest', *Australian*, 11 September 1997.

Dawn, P., *Mother Teresa: Apostle of the Unwanted*, Melbourne: ACTS Publications, 1969.

deCardova, R., 'The Emergence of the Star System in America', in C. Gledhill (ed.), *Stardom: Industry of Desire*, London and New York: Routledge, 2003, pp. 17–29.

Dils, T. E., *Mother Teresa*, New York: Chelsea House Publishers, 2002.

Doig, D., *Mother Teresa: Her People and Her Work*, London: Collins, 1978.

Doraisawmy, S., *Christianity in India: Unique and Universal Mission*, Madras, India: The Christian Literature Society, 1986.

Duka-Gjini, P., 'Designated to Die: The Martyrdom of Fr. Gjon Shllaku, OFM', *Albanian Catholic Bulletin*, Vols. 7–8, 1986–87.

Durham, E., *Twenty Years of Balkan Tangle*, London: George Allen & Unwin, 1920.

—— *High Albania*, London: Virago, 1985.

Durkheim, E., *The Elementary Forms of the Religious Life*, Trans. J. W. Swain, London: George Allen & Unwin Ltd, 1976.

Dutta, K., 'Saint of the Gutters with Friends in High Places', *Times Higher Education Supplement*, 16 May 2003.

Eberts, J., R. Joffé and M. Medoff, *City of Joy: The Illustrated Story of the Film*, New York: Newmarket Press, 1992.

Egan, E., *Such a Vision of the Street: Mother Teresa – The Spirit and the Work*, Complete and Unabridged, New York: Doubleday, 1986.

—— *At Prayer with Mother Teresa*, Liguori, MO: Liguori Publications, 1999.

Egan, E., and K. Egan (eds), *Living the Word: A New Adventure in Prayer Involving Scripture, Mother Teresa, and You*, London: Collins, 1990.

Egan, E., and K. Egan (eds), *Suffering into Joy: What Mother Teresa Teaches About True Joy*, Ann Arbor, MI: Servant Publications, 1994.

Elsie, R. (ed.), *Kosovo: In the Heart of the Powder Keg*, Boulder, CO: East European Monographs, 1997.

Eysenck, H. J., 'The Structure of Social Attitudes', *British Journal of Social and Clinical Psychology*, 14, 1975, 323–31.

Fiorenza, E. S., *In Memory of Her: A Feminist Theological Reconstruction of Christian Origins*, New York: Crossroad, 1983.

Firth, C. B., *An Introduction to Indian Church History*, Madras, India: The Christian Literature Society, 1961.

Fisher, I., 'Saintly Spirit Remembered, in a Truly Balkan Way', *New York Times*, 6 August 2003.

—— 'Vying for a Piece of Mother Teresa's Past', *International Herald Tribune*, 7 August 2003.

Fisher, M. P., and R. Luyster, *An Encyclopedia of the World's Faiths: Living Religions*, London and New York: I. B. Tauris & Co., 1990.

Freeman, A., 'Mother Teresa's Origins Spark Squabble', *Globe and Mail*, 17 October 2003.

Freud, S., 'Obsessive Actions and Religious Practice', in J. Strachey (ed.), *The Standard Edition of the Complete Psychological Works of Sigmund Freud*, Vol. 9. London: The Hogarth Press & The Institute of Psychoanalysis, 1959, pp. 167–75.

—— *The Future of an Illusion*, Trans. W. D. Robson-Scott, J. Strachey (ed.), London: The Hogarth Press, 1962.

Freundlich, F., *Albania's Golgotha*, Trans. S. S. Juka, New York: Juka Publishing Co. Inc., 1998. Online. Available HTTP: <http://www.alb-net.com/juka1.htm> (accessed 30 July 2003).

Gauthier, J., *I Thirst: Thérèse of Lisieux and Mother Teresa of Calcutta*, Trans. A. Plettenberg-Serban, New York: Alba House, 2005.

Giles, D., *Illusions of Immortality: A Psychology of Fame and Celebrity*, London: Macmillan, 2000.

Gjergji, L., *Dashuria Tërheqëse: Nëna jonë Tereze*, 2nd edn, Ferizaj, Kosova: Drita; Zagreb, Croatia: Kršćanska Sadašnjost, 1990.

—— *Nëna e Dashurisë*, Prishtinë: Akademia e Shkencave dhe e Arteve e Kosovës, 2000.

Glavich, K., and B. Kiwak, *Blessed Teresa of Calcutta: Missionary of Charity*, Boston, MA: Pauline Books, 2003.

Gledhill, C., 'Introduction', in C. Gledhill (ed.), *Stardom: Industry of Desire*, London and New York: Routledge, 2003, pp. viii–xx.

Goldsworthy, V., *Inventing Ruritania: The Imperialism of the Imagination*, New Haven and London: Yale University Press, 1998.

González-Balado, J. L., *Mother Teresa: Her Life, Her Work, Her Message: 1910–1997: A Memoir*, Liguori, MO: Liguori Publications, 1997.

Gorrée, G., and J. Barbier, *For the Love of God: Mother Teresa of Calcutta*, Trans. P. Speakman, Dublin: Veritas, 1974.

Gray, C., *Mother Teresa: The Nun whose 'Mission of Love' Has Helped Millions of the World's Poorest People*, Herts, UK: Exley, 1990.

Hall, J., 'In Praise of Younger Men', *Sunday Times*, 19 October 2003, pp. 40–1.

Hillman, R. S. (ed.), *Understanding Contemporary Latin America*, Boulder: Lynne Rienner Publishers, 2001.

Hiorth, F., 'Albania: An Atheistic State?', *Religion in Eastern Europe*, Vol. X, No. 5, October 1990, pp. 14–21.

Hitchens, C., 'The Ghoul of Calcutta', *The Nation*, 13 April 1992.

—— *The Missionary Position: Mother Teresa in Theory and Practice*, London and New York: Verso, 1995.

—— Interview, Interviewer S. Capen, *Worldguide*, 24 December 1995.

—— Interview, 'Christopher Hitchens on Mother Teresa', Interviewer M. Cherry, *Free Inquiry*, Vol. 16, No. 4, Fall 1996.

—— '"Mother Teresa", Letter to the Editors of the NYR in response to "In Defense of Mother Teresa"', *New York Review of Books*, Vol. 43, No. 20, 19 December 1996.

—— Interview, 'The Missionary Position: Mother Teresa's Crimes Against Humanity', Interviewer D. Postel, *LiP Magazine*, 15 September 1998.

—— 'Why Mother Teresa Should Not Be a Saint', *Mirror*, 2 January 2003.

—— 'Mommie Dearest: The Pope Beatifies Mother Teresa, a Fanatic, a Fundamentalist, and a Fraud', *Slate*, 20 October 2003.

—— 'Less than Miraculous', *Free Inquiry*, Vol. 24, No. 2, February–March 2004.

Hyseni, H., *E Vërteta për Helmimet në Kosovë: 1987–1990*, Prishtinë: Redaksia e Botimeve e Partisë Shqiptare Demokristiane e Kosovës, 1996.

Igric, G., 'The Dark Side of Serbia', *Balkan Investigative Reporting Network* (BIRN), 15 March 2006. Online. Available HTTP: <http://www.birn.eu.com/insight_25_8_eng.php> (accessed 21 March 2006).

Ilievska, A., 'Notes from Skopje: Post-Mortem Politics', 13 August 2003. Online. Available HTTP: <http://www.tol.cz/look/TOLnew/tolprint.tpl?IdLanguage=1&IdPublication=4&NrIssue=49&NrSection=17&NrArticle=10408&ST1=body&ST_T1=letter&ST_AS1=1&ST_max=1> (accessed 18 March 2006).

Ingrams, R., *Muggeridge: The Biography*, London: HarperCollins, 1995.

Jackman, W., *Mother Teresa*, East Sussex, UK: Wayland, 1993.

Johnson, E., *Mother Teresa*, London and Sydney: Franklin Watts, 2003.

Johnson, E. A., *Friends of God and Prophets: A Feminist Theological Reading of the Communion of Saints*, New York: Continuum, 1998.

Jones, K., *Women Saints: Lives of Faith and Courage*, Maryknoll, NY: Orbis Books, 1999.

Joyce, J., *A Portrait of the Artist as a Young Man*, London: Penguin, 1996.

Kadare, I., *Invitation à l'atelier de l'écrivain suivi de le poids de la croix*, Trans. J. Vrioni, Paris: Fayard, 1991.

Kapinova, K., *Engjëll Vuajtje dhe Shprese*, Shkodër, Albania: Çamaj-Pipa & Volaj, 2002.

—— 'Kujtesë: Jo gjyq të dytë për At Anton Harapin! – I harruari i paharrueshëm: At Anton Harapi ofm, martir i fesë dhe i shqiptarizmës së kulluar'. Online. Available HTTP: <http://groups.yahoo.com/group/Albemigrant/message/68?viscount =100> (accessed 2 September 2005).

Katayanagi, H., *My Dear Children: Mother Teresa's Last Message*, Trans. H. Katayanagi, Mahwah, NJ: Paulist Press, 2001.

Katz, I., 'When Christopher Met Peter', *Guardian*, G2, 31 May 2005.

Kirka, D., 'Nations Fight over Mother Teresa's Ancestry', 14 October 2003. Online. Available HTTP: <http://www.therunningzone.com/CNEWS/WeirdNews/ 2003/10/14/225887-ap.html> (accessed 24 February 2004).

Kola, P., *The Search for Greater Albania*, London: Hurst & Company, 2003.

Koliqi, E., 'Reverend Lazer Shantoja (1892–1945): A Brilliant Stylist of Albanian Literature', *Albanian Catholic Bulletin*, Vols. 7–8, 1986–87.

Kumar, S., *Mother Teresa of Calcutta*, San Francisco, CA: Ignatius Press, 1998.

Lapierre, D., *The City of Joy: An Epic of Love, Heroism, and Hope in the India of Mother Teresa*, Trans. K. Spink, New York: Doubleday, 1985.

Larsen, R. W., 'Secrets in the Bedroom: Adolescents' Private Use of Media', *Journal of Youth and Adolescence*, 24, 1995, 535–50.

Latourette, K. S., *A History of the Expansion of Christianity: The Great Century in the Americas, Austral-Asia, and Africa, A.D. 1800–A.D. 1914*, Vol. V, London: Eyre and Spottiswoode, 1943.

Lazo, C. E., *Mother Teresa*, New York: Maxwell Macmillan International, 1993.

Le Joly, E., *We Do It for Jesus: Mother Teresa and her Missionaries of Charity*, London: Darton, Longman and Todd, 1977.

—— *Mother Teresa of Calcutta: A Biography*, San Francisco, CA: Harper & Row, 1985.

Leigh, V., *Mother Teresa*, New York: The Bookwright Press, 1986.

Lewis, C. A., and J. Maltby, 'Religious Attitude and Practice – The Relationship With Obsessionality', *Personality and Individual Differences*, 19, 1995, 105–8.

McBrien, R. P., *Lives of the Saints: From Mary and St. Francis of Assisi to John XXIII and Mother Teresa*, New York: HarperSanFrancisco, 2003.

McBrien, R. P., and H. W. Attridge (eds), *The HarperCollins Encyclopedia of Catholicism*, San Francisco: Harper, 1995.

Majumdar, S. K., *Mahatma Gandhi, Mother Teresa, Swami Vivekananda and Some Important Events of India from 1941 to March 1995*, Calcutta: Firma KLM, 1996.

Malcolm, N., *Kosovo: A Short History*, London: Papermac, 1998.

Maltby, J., 'Personality Dimension of Religious Orientation', *The Journal of Psychology*, 133, 1999, 631–9.

Maltby, J., et al., 'Thou Shalt Worship No Other Gods – Unless They Are Celebrities: The Relationship Between Celebrity Worship and Religious Orientation', *Personality and Individual Differences*, 32, 2002, 1157–72.

Maltby, J., et al., 'Personality and Coping: A Context for Examining Celebrity Worship and Mental Health', *British Journal of Psychology*, 95, 2004, 411–28.

Manji, I., *The Trouble with Islam Today: A Wake-Up Call for Honesty and Change*, Edinburgh and London: Mainstream Publishing, 2005.

Marx, K., 'Introduction to A Contribution to the Critique of Hegel's Philosophy of Right', *Deutsch-Französische Jahrbücher*, February 1844.

Matto, K., '"Mother" Teresa'. Online. Available HTTP: <http://www.scionofzion.com/teresa.htm> (accessed 29 July 2003).

Metcalf, B. D., and T. R. Metcalf, *A Concise History of India*, Cambridge: Cambridge University Press, 2003.

Mete, E., 'What Does the Future Hold for the Albanians in FYROM?', 27 February 2002. Online. Available HTTP: <http://www.aacl.com/AlbFutMacE.htm> (accessed 22 February 2005).

Milošević, S., *Les Années décisives*, Lausanne and Paris: L'Age d'Homme, 1990.

Mironski, J., 'The Mother is still Agnes in Macedonia', 3 September 1998. Online. Available HTTP: <http://www.indianexpress.com/ie/daily/19980904/24750084.html> (accessed 27 February 2004).

—— 'Macedonians, Albanians Squabble over Teresa's Legacy', 15 October 2003. Online. Available HTTP: <http://quickstart.clari.net/qs_se/webnews/wed/ad/Qindia_vatican-pope.Rm5s_DOF.html> (accessed 27 February 2004).

Mohan, C. J., *The Young Life of Mother Teresa of Calcutta*, Worcester, PA: Young Sparrow Press, 1996.

Morgan, N., *Mother Teresa: Saint of the Poor*, Orlando, FL: Raintree Steck-Vaughn Publishers, 1998.

Muggeridge, M., *Jesus Rediscovered*, Garden City, NY: Doubleday, 1969.

—— *Something Beautiful for God: Mother Teresa of Calcutta*, London: Collins, 1971.

—— *Jesus: The Man who Lives*, London: Collins, 1975.

—— *Christ and the Media*, London: Hodder and Stoughton, 1979.

—— *Confessions of a Twentieth-Century Pilgrim*, San Francisco: Harper & Row, 1988.

Mukherjee, B., 'The Saint Mother Teresa', *Time*, 14 June 1999.

Murthy, B. S., *Mother Teresa and India*, Long Beach, CA: Long Beach Publications, 1983.

Neill, S., *Builders of the Indian Church: Present Problems in the Light of the Past*, London: Edinburgh House Press, 1934.

—— *A History of Christian Missions*, 2nd edn, London: Penguin, 1990.

Ognjanov, M., 'Ju tregoj Shqipërinë e Nolit dhe Mbretit Zog'. Online. Available HTTP: <http://www.panorama.com.al/20040123/faqe12/1.htm> (accessed 18 April 2005).

Orizio, R., *Talk of the Devil: Encounters with Seven Dictators*, Trans. A. Bardoni, London: Vintage, 2004.

Pace, A. L. (ed.), *From Grief to Action: 'Caring' on the Spirits of Princess Diana and Mother Teresa*, Beaverton, OR: Baby Steps Press, 1998.

Paul, R. D., *The Cross Over India*, London: SCM Press Ltd, 1952.

Plasari, A., 'Bojaxhitë e Nënë Terezës', *Shekulli*, 29 September 2003.

Pope Benedict XVI, 'Encyclical Letter: *Deus Caritas Est*', 25 December 2005. Online. Available HTTP: <http://www.zenit.org/english/visualizza.phtml?sid=83355> (accessed 27 January 2006).

Pope John Paul II, 'Apostolic Letter: The Rapid Development', 24 January 2005. Online. Available HTTP: <http://www.vatican.va/holy_father/john_paul_ii/apost_letters/documents/hf_jp-ii_apl_20050124_il-rapido-sviluppo_en.html> (accessed 26 February 2006).

Pope Paul VI, 'Decree on the Media of Social Communications: *Inter Mirifica*', 4 December 1963. Online. Available HTTP: <http://www.vatican.va/archive/hist_councils/ii_vatican_council/documents/vat-ii_decree_19631204_inter-mirifica_en.html> (accessed 26 February 2006).

Porter, D., *Mother Teresa: The Early Years*, Oxford and New York: ISIS Large Print, 1986.

Price, M., 'Milosevic Says Trial Will Fuel Terrorism', *Birmingham Post*, 31 October 2001.

Rae, D., *Love Until It Hurts: The Work of Mother Teresa and of Her Missionaries of Charity*, San Francisco: HarperCollins, 1981.

Ramaj, A., 'Nëna Terezë – Bojaxhinjtë dhe prejardhja e tyre', 15 November 2003. Online. Available HTTP: <http://www.stublla.com/Shqip/fjalalir/ZefAhmeti/Shkrimet001/November/Nenaterezeramaj41.htm> (accessed 17 November 2003).

Resuli-Burovich, K., Interview, 'The Albanian Racism Towards Its Neighbours is Based on Historical Falsifications', Interviewer Vitomir Dolinski, *Vest*, 25 February 2003, Trans. Z. Apostolovski. Online. Available HTTP: <http://www.unitedmacedonians.org/macedonia/kaplan_english.html> (accessed 20 February 2005).

Richards, J., S. Wilson and L. Woodhead (eds), *Diana: The Making of a Media Saint*, London: I. B. Tauris & Co Ltd, 1999.

Roberge, G., *Cyberbani: Being a Human in the New Media Environment*, Anand, Gujarat, India: Gujarat Sahitya Prakash, 2005.

—— 'Mother Teresa, Abortion and the Media', unpublished paper, 2006.

Rojek, C., *Celebrity*, London: Reaktion Books, 2001.

Said, E. W., *Orientalism*, London: Penguin, 2003.

Schall, J. V., 'The *Albanian Catholic Bulletin* – A Remarkable Source of Information on Albania', *Religion in Eastern Europe*, Vol. XIII, No. 2, April 1993: 47.

Schwartz, S., 'Behind the Balkan Curtain: Religious Communities Carry on Gjon's Mission', *San Francisco Faith*, May 2000.

—— 'Mother Teresa's Family Tree', *Weekly Standard*, 27 October 2003, Vol. 9, No. 7.

Scopes, W., *Indian Opportunity*, London: Edinburgh House Press, 1961.

Sebba, A., *Mother Teresa*, London: Franklin Watts, 1982.

—— *Mother Teresa: Beyond the Image*, London: Orion, 1997.

Sellers, F. S., 'A Satirist in Search of Salvation', *Washington Post*, 3 March 1996.

Sen, A., *The Argumentative Indian: Writings on Indian History, Culture and Identity*, London: Penguin, 2005.

'Serbian Academy of Arts and Sciences Memorandum', September 1986. Online. Available HTTP: <http://www.ess.uwe.ac.uk/Kosovo/Kosovo-Background17.htm> (accessed 20 February 2005).

Serrou, R., *Teresa of Calcutta: A Pictorial Biography*, New York: McGraw-Hill, 1980.

Shah, D., 'Mother Teresa's Hidden Mission in India: Conversion to Christianity', 2003. Online. Available HTTP: <http://www.indiastar.com/DhiruShah.htm> (accessed 16 August 2004).

Shaw, S., *Mother Teresa of Calcutta: Her Call, Her Example, Her Life Story*, Ann Arbor, MI: Servant Publications, 1994.

Shestani, Z., 'Brother Gjon Pantalija SJ: An Albanian Christian Martyr', *Albanian Catholic Bulletin*, Vols. 7–8, 1986–87.

Shields, S., 'Mother Teresa's House of Illusions', *Free Inquiry*, 1998, Vol. 18, No. 1.

Silvestri, G., 'Fr. Gjon Fausti SJ: Strength in Serenity', *Albanian Catholic Bulletin*, Vols. 7–8, 1986–87.

Simoni, Z., 'Persekutimi i Kishës Katolike në Shqipni nga 1944–1990'. Online. Available HTTP: <http://www.forumishqiptar.com/showthread.php?=3856> (accessed 12 August 2005).

Slade, C., *St. Teresa of Avila: Author of a Heroic Life*, Berkeley: University of California Press, 1995.

Smiles, S., *Self-Help: With Illustrations of Character, Conduct, and Perseverance*, P. W. Sinnema (ed.), Oxford: Oxford University Press, 2002.

Smith, A., 'All in a Good Cause?' *Observer*, 27 January 2002.

Spaho, E., 'Nënë Tereza "maqedonase" refuzohet nga Roma', *Shekulli*, 18 July 2003.

Spink, K., *For the Brotherhood of Man under the Fatherhood of God: Mother Teresa of Calcutta, her Missionaries of Charity and her Co-Workers*, Surrey, UK: Colour Library International, 1981.

—— *The Miracle of Love: Mother Teresa of Calcutta*, San Francisco, CA: Harper & Row, 1981.

—— *Mother Teresa: An Authorized Biography*, London: Fount, 1998.

Srinivasan, R., 'The Saint Business', 17 October 2003. Online. Available HTTP: <http://in.rediff.com/news/2003/oct/17rajeev.htm> (accessed 17 April 2005).

Stone, E. M., *Mother Teresa: A Life of Love*, Mahwah, NJ: Paulist Press, 1999.

Tagore, R., *The Religion of Man*, Calcutta: Visva-Bharati Publishing Department, 2000.

—— 'The Noble Prize Acceptance Speech', in R. Tagore, *Gitanjali: Song Offerings*, Trans. R. Tagore, New Delhi: UBSPD, 2005, pp. 291–300.

—— *Gitanjali: Song Offerings*, Trans. R. Tagore, New Delhi: UBSPD, 2005.

Tames, R., *Mother Teresa*, London: Franklin Watts, 1989.

Tarn, W. W., *Alexander the Great: Narrative*, Vol. I, Cambridge: Cambridge University Press, 1979.

Teresa, M., *Life in the Spirit: Reflections, Meditations, Prayers*, K. Spink (ed.), New York: HarperCollins, 1983.

—— *A Mother Teresa Treasury*, San Francisco: Harper, 1985.

—— *Heart of Joy: The Transforming Power of Self-Giving*, J. L. González-Balado (ed.), Ann Arbor, MI: Servant Publications, 1987.

—— *Jesus, the Word to Be Spoken: Prayers and Meditations for Every Day of the Year*, New York: Walker and Company, 1987.

—— *Love, a Fruit Always in Season: Daily Meditations from the Words of Mother Teresa of Calcutta*, D. S. Hunt (ed.), San Francisco, CA: Ignatius Press, 1987.

—— *Meditations on the Way of the Cross* (With Brother Roger of Taizé), Cleveland, OH: Pilgrim Press, 1987.

—— *One Heart Full of Love*, J. L. González-Balado (ed.), Ann Arbor, MI: Servant Publications, 1988.

—— *Total Surrender*, A. Devananda (ed.), Ann Arbor, MI: Servant Publications, 1990.

—— *Loving Jesus*, J. L. Gonzáles-Balado (ed.), Ann Arbor, MI: Servant Publications, 1991.

—— *Quotations of Mother Teresa of Calcutta, India: He's Put The Whole World In Her Hands*, D. Paulos (ed.), San Francisco: Ignatius Press, 1993.

—— *The Best Gift Is Love: Meditations by Mother Teresa*, S. Lovett (ed.), Ann Arbor, MI: Servant Publications, 1993.

—— *A Life for God: The Mother Teresa Reader*, L. Neff (ed.), Ann Arbor, MI: Servant Publications, 1995.

—— *A Simple Path*, L. Vardey (ed.), London: Rider, 1995.

—— *My Life for the Poor*, J. L. Gonzáles-Balado and J. N. Playfoot (eds), New York: Ballantine Books, 1996.

—— *The Blessings of Love*, N. Sabbag (ed.), Cincinnati, OH: Saint Anthony Messenger Press & Franciscan Communications, 1996.

—— *The Joy in Loving: A Guide to Daily Living*, J. Chaliha and E. Le Joly (eds), New Delhi: Viking, 1996.

—— *In My Own Words*, J. L. González-Balado (ed.), London: Hodder & Stoughton, 1997.

—— *In the Heart of the World: Thoughts, Stories, & Prayers*, B. Benenate (ed.), Navato, CA: New World Library, 1997.

—— *No Greater Love*, B. Benenate and J. Durepos (eds), Navato, CA: New World Library, 1997.

—— *Everything Starts from Prayer: Mother Teresa's Meditations on Spiritual Life for People of All Faiths*, A. Stern and L. Dossey (eds), Ashland, OR: White Cloud Press,1998.

—— *Jesus, The Word to Be Spoken: Prayers and Meditations for Every Day of the Year*, A. D. Scolozzi (ed.), Ann Arbor, MI: Servant Publications, 1998.

—— *A Fruitful Branch on the Vine, Jesus*, Cincinnati, OH: St. Anthony Messenger Press and Franciscan Communications, 2000.

—— *Thirsting for God: A Yearbook of Prayers and Meditations*, A. D. Scolozzi (ed.), Ann Arbor, MI: Servant Publications, 2000.

—— *A Gift for God: Prayers and Meditations*, San Francisco: HarperCollins, 2003.

—— *Mësomë të Dua/Teach me to Love*, Trans. A. Spahiu et al., Prishtina: Rozafa, 2003.

—— *Nënë Tereza – Mërmërime Shenjtoreje/A Saint Mother*, Trans. V. Zhiti, Tirana: OMSCA-1, 2003.

Teresa of Ávila, Saint, *The Complete Works of Saint Teresa of Jesus*, Vol. I, Trans. E. A. Peers (ed.), London: Sheed & Ward, 1946.

The Holy Bible, containing the Old and New Testaments with the Apocryphal/ Deuterocanonical Books, New Revised Standard Version, New York and Oxford: Oxford University Press, 1989.

The Other Balkan Wars. A 1913 Carnegie Endowment Inquiry in Retrospect with a New Introduction and Reflections on the Present Conflict by George F. Kennan, Washington, D.C.: Carnegie Endowment for International Peace, 1993.

Thérèse of Lisieux, Saint, *The Story of a Soul*, Trans. J. Beevers, New York: Doubleday, 1989.

Thompson, E. P., *Writing by Candlelight*, London: Merlin Press, 1980.

Todorova, M., *Imagining the Balkans*, New York and Oxford: Oxford University Press, 1997.

Toth, Z., 'Serbian Plants of Death', *Večernji List*, 28 November 1995.

Vardey, L., 'Introduction', in M. Teresa, *A Simple Path*, L. Vardey (ed.), London and Sydney: Rider, 1995, pp. 13–34.

Varma, P. K., '*The Argumentative Indian*, by Amartya Sen', *Independent*, 12 August 2005.

Vazhakala, S., *Life with Mother Teresa: My Thirty-Year Friendship with the Mother of the Poor*, Cincinnati, OH: Servant Books, 2004.

Watson, D. J., *Teresa of Calcutta: Serving the Poorest of the Poor*, Fenton, MI: Mott Media, 1984.

Weber, M., *The Protestant Ethic and the Spirit of Capitalism*, Trans. T. Parsons, London and New York: Routledge Classics, 2004.

Wellman, S., *Mother Teresa: Missionary of Charity*, Uhrichsville, OH: Barbour Publishing, 1997.

Wolff, L., *Inventing Eastern Europe: The Map of Civilization on the Mind of the Enlightenment*, Stanford, CA: Stanford University Press, 1994.

Wordsworth, W., 'Ode: Intimations of Immortality from Recollections of Early Childhood', in D. Wright (ed.), *English Romantic Verse*, London: Penguin, 1986, pp. 133–9.

Wright, D. (ed.), *English Romantic Verse*, London: Penguin, 1986.

Wüllenweber, W., 'Mother Teresa: Where are her Millions?', *Stern*, 10 September 1998. Online. Available HTTP: <http://www.geocities.com/willdirne/mo.html> (accessed 18 September 2003).

Xhufi, P., 'Kujt t'ia japim Nënë Terezën', *Shekulli*, 14 October 2003.

Zambonini, F., *Teresa of Calcutta: A Pencil in God's Hand*, New York: Alba House, 1993.

Select filmography

Something Beautiful for God (dir. Peter Chafer, UK, 1969)
Mother Teresa and Her World (dir. Shigeki Chiba, Japan, 1983)
Mother Teresa (dirs Ann and Jeanette Petrie, USA, 1986)
Mother Teresa: A Life of Devotion (dir. Kevin Burns et al., USA, 1987)
City of Joy (dir. Roland Joffé, USA, 1992)
Hell's Angel (dir. Christopher Hitchens, Channel 4, UK, 1994)
Mother Teresa: In the Name of God's Poor (dir. Kevin Connor, USA, 1997)
Love Can Do Anything (dir. Saso Zajkov, Macedonia, 2002)
Mother Teresa of the Century (dir. Amar Kr Bhattacharya, India, 2001; shorter version 2003)
Mother Teresa: The Legacy (dirs Ann and Jeannette Petrie, USA, 2004)
The Fifth Word (dir. Cristobal Guierrero, Spain, 2004)
Mother Teresa of Calcutta (dir. Fabrizio Costa, Italy, 2005)
The Beatification of Mother Teresa (dir. Gautam Das, India, 2005)

Index